MOON

JOSHUA TREE & PALM SPRINGS

JENNA BLOUGH

Contents

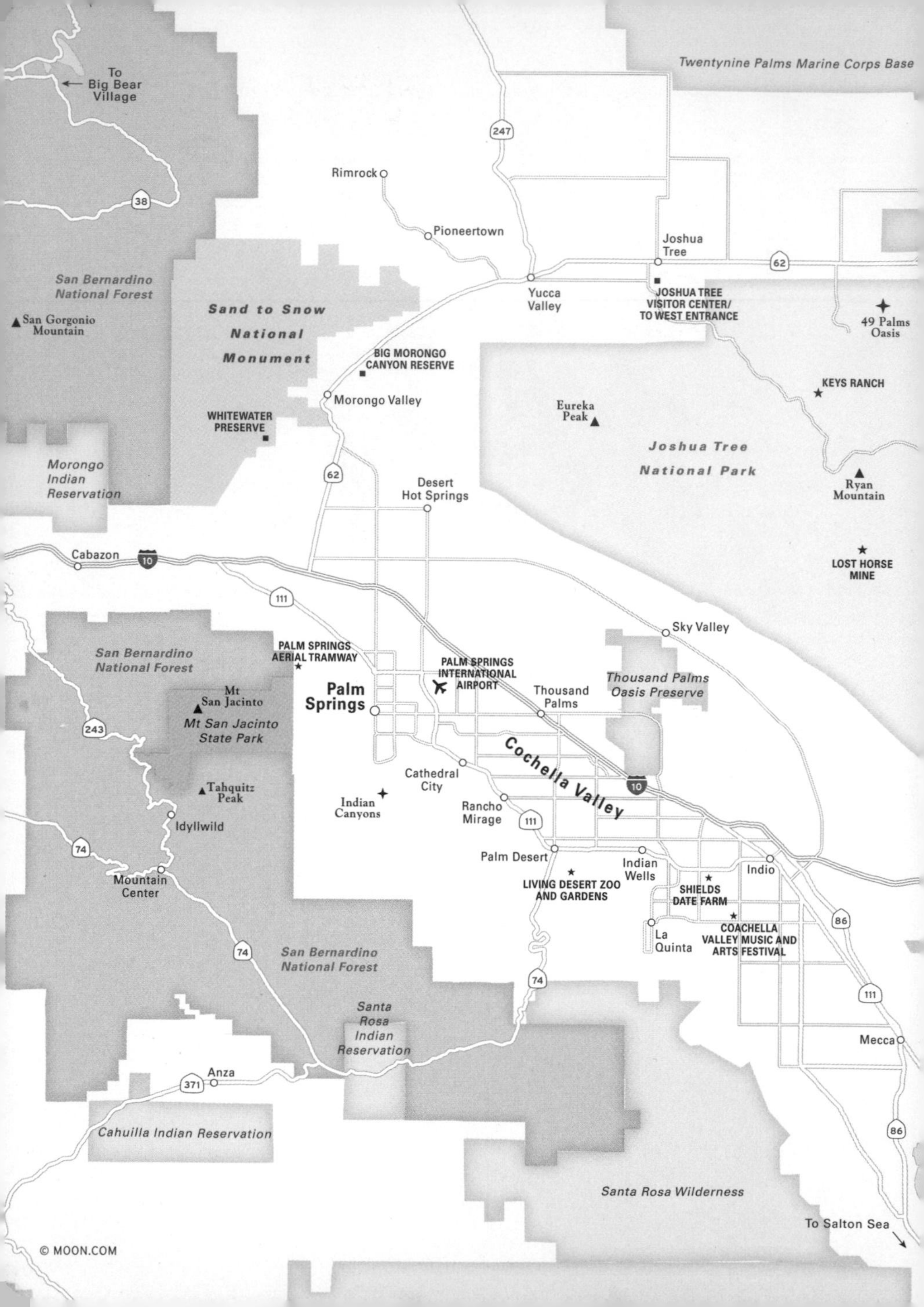

To Big Bear Village
Twentynine Palms Marine Corps Base
247
38
Rimrock
Pioneertown
Joshua Tree
62
Yucca Valley
JOSHUA TREE VISITOR CENTER/ TO WEST ENTRANCE
49 Palms Oasis
San Bernardino National Forest
San Gorgonio Mountain
Sand to Snow National Monument
BIG MORONGO CANYON RESERVE
Morongo Valley
WHITEWATER PRESERVE
KEYS RANCH
Eureka Peak
Joshua Tree National Park
Morongo Indian Reservation
Ryan Mountain
Desert Hot Springs
Cabazon
10
LOST HORSE MINE
111
Sky Valley
San Bernardino National Forest
PALM SPRINGS AERIAL TRAMWAY
PALM SPRINGS INTERNATIONAL AIRPORT
Thousand Palms Oasis Preserve
Mt San Jacinto
Palm Springs
Thousand Palms
243
Mt San Jacinto State Park
Cochella Valley
Cathedral City
Tahquitz Peak
Indian Canyons
Rancho Mirage
Idyllwild
74
Palm Desert
Indian Wells
Indio
Mountain Center
LIVING DESERT ZOO AND GARDENS
SHIELDS DATE FARM
COACHELLA VALLEY MUSIC AND ARTS FESTIVAL
86
La Quinta
San Bernardino National Forest
Santa Rosa Indian Reservation
Mecca
Anza
371
Cahuilla Indian Reservation
Santa Rosa Wilderness
To Salton Sea
© MOON.COM

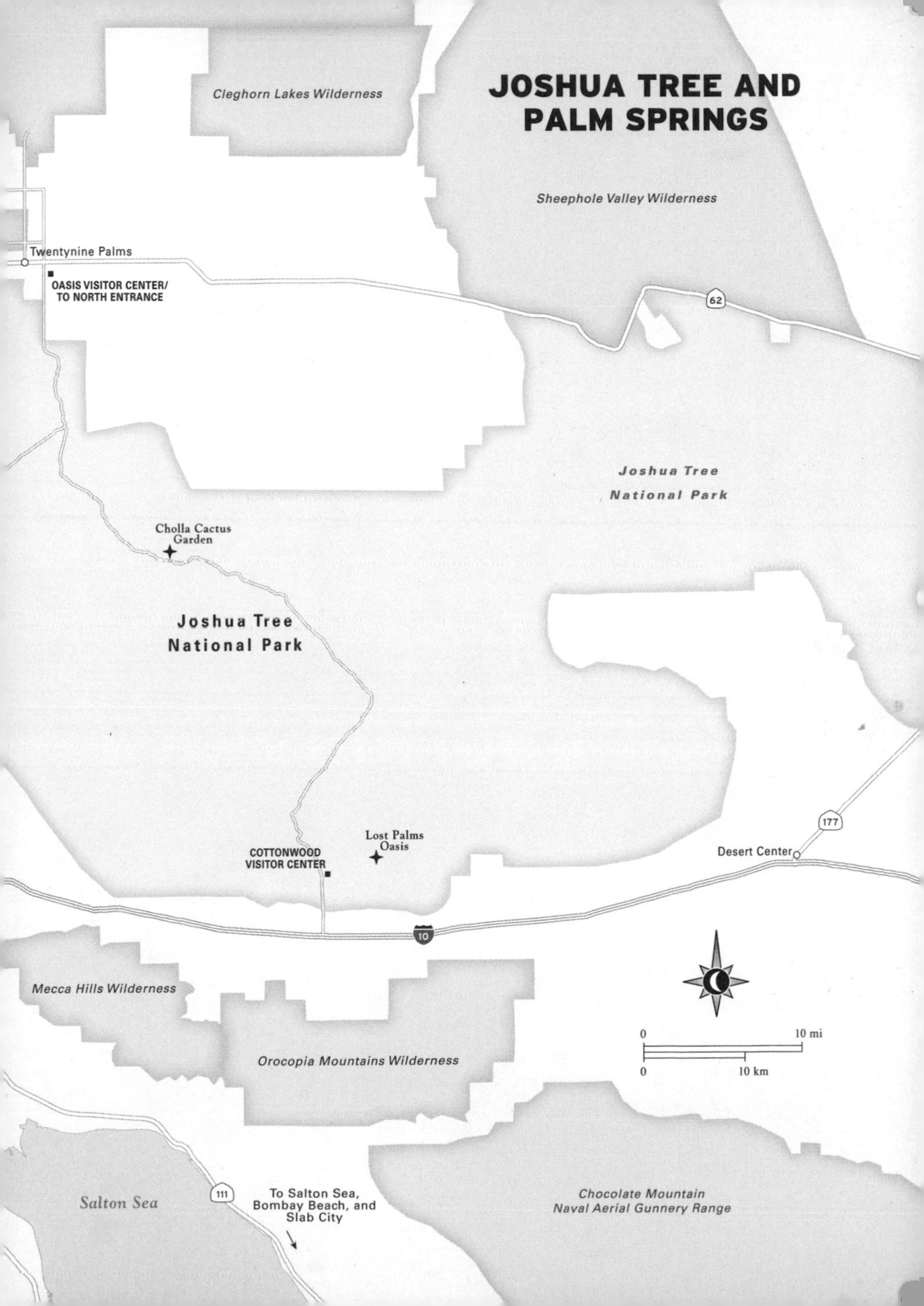
JOSHUA TREE AND PALM SPRINGS
Cleghorn Lakes Wilderness
Sheephole Valley Wilderness
Twentynine Palms
OASIS VISITOR CENTER/ TO NORTH ENTRANCE
62
Joshua Tree National Park
Cholla Cactus Garden
Joshua Tree National Park
Lost Palms Oasis
COTTONWOOD VISITOR CENTER
177
Desert Center
10
Mecca Hills Wilderness
Orocopia Mountains Wilderness
0
10 mi
0
10 km
Salton Sea
111
To Salton Sea, Bombay Beach, and Slab City
Chocolate Mountain Naval Aerial Gunnery Range

DISCOVER

Joshua Tree & Palm Springs

Despite being such near neighbors, the spiky swath of Joshua Tree National Park and the sleek urban chic of Palm Springs appear to have little in common. Their link is the California desert, where relentless sunshine and rocky landscapes evoke a sense of the unknown.

Joshua Tree is wild, eroded, and fantastical. Its surreal rock formations were cooked up through millions of years of erosion, sedimentation, and continental collisions to form hulking, toothy piles of granite. The namesake Joshua trees, with their jagged silhouettes, run rampant among the jumbled piles of boulders. This is the high desert—gorgeous in spring and fall, searing hot in summer, and cold enough in winter that snow sometimes dusts the agave.

The resort town of Palm Springs got its start in the 1920s, and its popularity escalated as a getaway for the Hollywood Rat Pack. Today, it's a stylish time capsule with impeccable mid-century architecture, luxury resorts, boutique hotels, and retro gems tucked away against the rocky foothills. In a landscape of drama and leisure, the gleaming blue of its plentiful swimming pools competes with the crystal-blue sky.

Joshua Tree was my first experience with the California desert, and I could

Clockwise from top left: rappelling in Joshua Tree; Palm Springs' Uptown Design District; giant saguaro cactus; rock arch in Joshua Tree; the 29 Palms Inn; Cottonwood Spring in Joshua Tree.

hardly believe something so magical existed—the right blend of rustic, funky, and chic. I went to Palm Springs that same summer and navigated my way to a classic mid-century boutique hotel, where all the guests in the pool knew each other and welcomed us with Bloody Marys.

It's these contrasts that shape Joshua Tree and Palm Springs: The confluence of nearly perpetual sun, well-watered canyons, and bubbling hot springs backdropped by snowcapped mountains and a scoured desert make any visit here unique.

Clockwise from top left: stunning views from Mastodon Mine; fan palm oasis on the McCallum Trail; Palm Springs Aerial Tram; cholla cactus in the Sonoran Desert.

6 TOP EXPERIENCES

1 **Take a Hike:** Hidden waterfalls, fan palm oases, stunning canyons, and twisted boulder piles are all begging to be explored on foot (page 26).

2 Go Pool Hopping: The Hollywood elite began flocking to Palm Springs in the 1920s for rest, relaxation, and near-perpetual sunshine. The tradition is still going strong today at stylish boutique resorts (page 23).

3 Go Window Shopping: The walkable and chic **Uptown Design District** offers vintage couture clothing, pristine mid-century antiques, and reproduction housewares and furnishings (page 49).

TRINA TURK
residential
Open!!

4 **Explore Mid-Century Modernism:** The laid-back desert lifestyle gave architects the creative freedom to experiment with modernist concepts, designing structures inspired by the clean lines of the desert (page 46).

5 **Climb a Rock:** Joshua Tree's signature rock formations make it a mecca for rock climbers, with more than 400 climbing formations and 8,000 recognized climbs (page 141).

^
^
^

6 **Hit the Road:** If it's too hot to hit the trails, soak up Joshua Tree's dramatic landscape on a scenic drive (page 115).

Planning Your Trip

Where to Go

Palm Springs

Palm Springs is a charmed escape. Filled with preserved **mid-century architecture,** nonstop **pool parties,** and lounges to release your inner **Rat Pack,** it was Hollywood's playground in the 1920s through the 1960s—and it still delivers retro pleasures in a modernist time capsule. Take a whirlwind flight up the **Palm Springs Aerial Tramway,** wander amid Picassos and Warhols at the **Palm Springs Art Museum,** or simply park yourself **poolside** and soak in the rays.

The Coachella Valley

Surrounding Palm Springs is the **Coachella Valley,** with day trips to **date farms, desert museums, hot and cold mineral pools,** and designer shopping. **Desert Hot Springs, Thousand Palms, Cathedral City, Rancho Mirage, Palm Desert, Indian Wells, La Quinta,** and **Indio** comprise the constellation of towns, but the region is perhaps best known for its popular outdoor music festival: the **Coachella Valley Music and Arts Festival.**

Idyllwild

Idyllwild is an **artsy, rustic mountain town** set one-mile high in the forests of the **San Jacinto Mountains.** In under an hour, you can **escape the desert heat** of the searing valley floor with a quick tram ride or a short drive to hike **cool mountain trails** or spend the night in a **picturesque cabin.**

The Coachella Valley Preserve alternates between stark and lush landscapes.

Palm Springs Loves a Party

Palm Springs knows how to throw a party. Palm Springs and the Coachella Valley have several signature events throughout the year from music festivals to modernism events. Plan your trip around these weekends or take note to avoid these times if you're looking for a low-key getaway.

Palm Springs' signature event **Modernism Week** celebrates mid-century modern architecture, design, and culture with tours, exhibits, and parties over a packed two weekends in February.

Each October Palm Springs hosts **Modernism Preview,** a mini-Modernism Week to kick off the resort season.

The **Palm Springs International Film Festival** draws thousands of visitors to screen more than 200 films over 12 days in January.

Downtown Palm Springs blocks off streets every November to host **Pride Weekend,** with music, entertainment, and host hotels, to celebrate diversity and foster pride in the LGBT community.

The **Coachella Valley Music and Arts Festival** draws iconic music headliners and hundreds of thousands of festival-goers to this three-day music festival over two weekends in April.

Stagecoach music festival brings hot names in country music to the Coachella Valley stage on the last weekend in April every year.

Palm Springs LGBT Pride banner

Joshua Tree National Park

Dusty desert roads, jagged **boulder piles,** and spiky **Joshua trees** draw droves of **hikers, rock climbers,** and day-trippers to this otherworldly geologic landscape. Tour the **historic mines** and **ranches** of desert dreamers, wander amid strange cacti and colorful **wildflowers,** and take in the views from **scenic peaks.**

The Hi-Desert

Peppered along the northern border of Joshua Tree National Park are the gateway towns of **Yucca Valley, Joshua Tree, Pioneertown, Landers, Twentynine Palms, and Wonder Valley.** All offer **unique accommodations** and alternatives to camping in the park, as well as **local saloons, live music,** and **epic desert art** worthy of exploration.

Know Before You Go

High Season (Oct.-Apr.)

October-April is the high season for both Palms Springs and Joshua Tree National Park, with spring being the busiest time of year. Advance reservations for hotels in Palm Springs and campsites in Joshua Tree are a good idea during big events like **Modernism Week** and the **Coachella Valley Music and Arts Festival.**

At only 479 feet above sea level, Palm Springs' low elevation means that temperatures are fairly mild in **winter.** The months of October through April are the most temperate, with temperatures ranging from the high 60s to the low 90s during the day.

Low Season (May-Sept.)

Summer is the low season, with **brutally hot temperatures** holding fast in the triple digits for much of **June, July, August,** and **September.** Some businesses in Palm Springs have **limited hours,** however the resort town remains a destination, compensating with pool parties and lower hotel rates. Joshua Tree National Park remains open, with average highs in the 100s and temperatures not dipping lower than the high 70s at night. Recreational activities are extremely limited and can even be dangerous.

The San Jacinto Mountains and the town of **Idyllwild** offer a cool retreat during these searing months.

Transportation

The **Palm Springs Airport** (PSP, 3400 E. Tahquitz Canyon Way, 760/318-3800, www.palmspringsca.gov) services the resort town and can save you the three- to four-hour drive from Los Angeles. The airport has fewer airline options, however, and prices may be higher than at larger airports. International travelers may want to fly into **Los Angeles International Airport** (LAX, 1 World Way, Los Angeles, 424/646-5252, www.lawa.org) and spend a few days in LA before renting a car for the drive east along I-10.

The only public transportation in Joshua Tree National Park is a new **shuttle** program. Further exploration of the Coachella Valley and Joshua Tree National Park will require **your own vehicle.**

Entrance Stations

Joshua Tree National Park (www.nps.gov/jotr) has three entrance stations open year-round. The entrance fee is **$30 per vehicle** ($25 per motorcycle, $15 for bike or on foot), which is good for seven days. The Annual Park Pass is $55, and season pass-holders are often offered a shorter line at entrance stations.

- **West Entrance** (Hwy. 62 and Park Blvd.) is accessed from the gateway town of Joshua Tree and sees the heaviest visitation.
- **North Entrance** (Hwy. 62 and Utah Trail) is located in the gateway town of Twentynine Palms and is a good alternative during the high season, when lines are long at the West Entrance.
- **South Entrance** (off I-10) accesses Cottonwood Spring and sees the fewest visitors.

Visitors Centers

The **Palm Springs Visitors Center** (2901 N. Palm Canyon Dr., 760/778-8414, www.visitpalmsprings.com, 9am-5pm daily) is housed in the 1965 Tramway Gas Station, near the entrance to the aerial tramway.

The **Joshua Tree Visitors Center** (6554 Park Blvd., 760/366-1855, 8am-5pm daily) is in the town of Joshua Tree on Park Boulevard before the park's West Entrance and offers a bookstore, restrooms, and a café.

The **Oasis Visitors Center** (74485 National Park Dr., 760/367-5500, 8:30am-5pm daily) is at the North Entrance in the town of Twentynine

Palms and offers a bookstore, drinking water, restrooms, and picnic tables.

Reservations

In **Palm Springs,** you'll want to book accommodations well in advance during spring events **(February-April).**

Camping reservations (877/444-6777, www.recreation.gov, $15-20) in Joshua Tree National Park are required at four campgrounds—**Black Rock, Indian Cove, Cottonwood,** and **Jumbo Rocks—October-May**; demand is especially high in spring. Campgrounds tend to fill all weekends October–May. If you're planning a weekend camping trip in the park during this time, make reservations ahead of time or have alternate overnight plans. First-come, first-served sites are available at Belle, Hidden Valley, Ryan, and White Tank but are limited and tend to fill fully by **Thursday afternoon**. During the summer months, all campgrounds are first come, first served and reservations are not needed. Some campgrounds may close. Only three campgrounds—Black Rock, Indian Cove, and Cottonwood—have **drinking water.**

Visiting the historic **Keys Ranch** in Joshua Tree is by **reservation only.** Book your tour at by calling 760/367-5522 at least one day in advance.

Tramway Gas Station is now the Palm Springs Visitors Center.

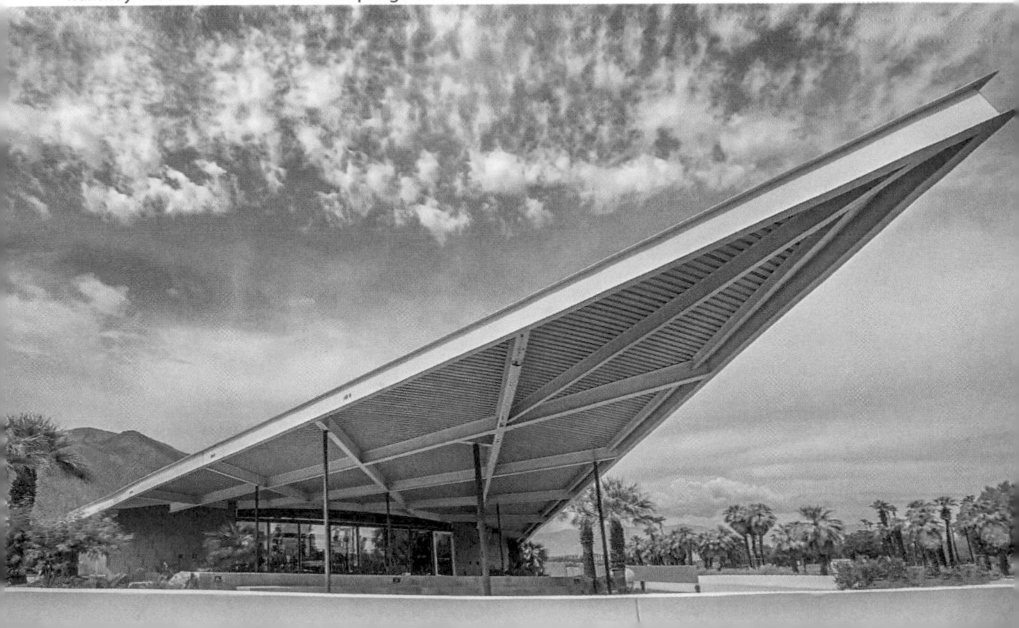

Best of Joshua Tree and Palm Springs

Day 1 Travel Day

Traffic into Palm Springs can be a beast, especially as you head into the weekend and especially coming from Los Angeles. Set yourself up for a full day of relaxing on Day 2 by making Day 1 a travel day. Your only goal is to check into your hotel of choice, whether it's the classic **Ingleside Inn,** stylish mid-mod **Monkey Tree Hotel,** or luxuriously exuberant **Parker Hotel.** Late night drink and eats can be hard to come by in Palm Springs, but they are available in a handful of spots including The Reef tiki bar and lounge, Truss & Twine cocktail lounge, and Shanghai Red's Bar & Grill.

Day 2 Palm Springs

Wake up and rejoice that you are in sunny Palm Springs, then get yourself to the sidewalk line at **Cheeky's** to wait for fresh Bloody Marys and brunch specials like Blondie's eggs Benedict, homemade cinnamon rolls, and a bacon flight.

Palm Springs and the Coachella Valley are surrounded by epic desert beauty. Nowhere is this more evident than during a hike through **Indian Canyons.** The **Lower Palm Canyon Trail** visits the world's largest fan palm oasis, while **Tahquitz Canyon** offers a short but scenic stroll to a rare desert waterfall, great for a post-brunch walk.

If you need something to tide you over until dinner, grab a gourmet sandwich or charcuterie and cheese snack at downtown's **On the Mark** to take poolside for the afternoon. While you're there, pick up some extra provisions for your day trip to Joshua Tree tomorrow.

Dinner is on the tropical patio at **The Tropicale,** with its throwback supper club feel

the Lost Palms Oasis near Cottonwood Springs

Day Trips from Palm Springs

Palm Springs can be a base camp for day trips to the Coachella Valley, Sand to Snow National Monument, San Jacinto Mountains State Park, and Joshua Tree National Park. Drives within an hour and a half of Palm Springs allow you to experience shaded desert oases, forested mountain peaks, outsider art installations, charming mountain towns and the famous cracked boulders of Joshua Tree National Park.

Visit the crystal-clear waters of the **Whitewater River,** remarkable for its rocky desert location in the Whitewater Preserve (25 min). Hiking trails, including a small section of the Pacific Crest Trail, offer river access and canyon views, while a wading pond is fun for families.

The **Thousand Palms Oasis Preserve** (30 min) highlights desert landscape along the San Andreas Fault, including shaded palm oases and eroded mud hills.

The mountain town of **Idyllwild** (1 hr 20 min) has a picturesque downtown with shops, restaurants, and local art for strolling in cooler summer temperatures or winter snow.

Accessed from the mountain town of Idyllwild, the **San Jacinto Mountains State Park** (1 hr 20 min) has forested hikes like the Ernie Maxwell Scenic Trail and Tahquitz Peak with long vistas to reward for the climbs.

The charming village of **Forest Falls** (1 hr) is nestled in a canyon on the edge of the San Gorgonio Wilderness, making it a scenic mountain drive with opportunities to picnic and hike.

the Whitewater River near Whitewater Preserve

Joshua Tree National Park (1 hr) can be explored as a day trip from Palm Springs, with scenic stops and hikes along Park Boulevard, Joshua Tree's main road, which winds through the iconic Joshua Tree forest and rock formations.

The low-lying **Salton Sea** (1.5 hrs.) provides surreal desert views and opportunities to see outsider art at Salvation Mountain and East Jesus.

and Pacific Rim menu, or opt for seafood on **Shanghai Red's** patio, offering live music on weekends.

Wind down the night at La Serena Villas's **Sugar High** roof-top open-air lounge surrounded by deep couches, a fire pit, and twinkle lights, or try **Bootlegger Tiki** for flocked wallpaper, deep booths, and layered rum drinks.

Day 3 Joshua Tree Day Trip

Today you will explore Joshua Tree. Pack a cooler with drinks, snacks, lunch, and water and head to the South Entrance at Cottonwood Spring (1 hr). Stop at the Cottonwood Visitor Center for maps and tips then check out scenic **Cottonwood Spring,** where you can take a short hike around the spring or a longer hike to the **Mastodon Mine** or **Lost Palms Oasis.** Continue north along Pinto Basin Road to soak in the stark landscape of the Sonoran Desert with a stop at the **Cholla Cactus Garden.**

At the intersection with Park Boulevard, take

a left to head west and watch as the landscape shifts into dramatic Mojave Desert with its signature spiky Joshua trees and otherworldly boulder piles. Enjoy a scenic drive along Park Boulevard into the popular **Hidden Valley** region of the park, stopping off to explore the short nature trails at **Barker Dam, Cap Rock,** and **Skull Rock.**

Your trip through the park will end at the West Entrance in the town of Joshua Tree, just in time for dinner with other hikers, rock climbers, and locals at the casual **Joshua Tree Saloon** with a menu that includes burgers, salads, sandwiches, and tacos. Sometimes the back patio is open; good for kids and dogs.

Or if you've made a reservation (reserve one of their seatings up to two weeks in advance), head up to **Pappy & Harriet's** restaurant and saloon, a former Wild West movie set in aptly named Pioneertown. Debrief your day, people-watch, and enjoy the funky surroundings while digging into the hearty Tex-Mex menu at this one-of-a-kind spot.

From either place, the drive back to Palm Springs is about 45 minutes.

Day 4 Palm Springs

Get back into the swing of Palm Springs by celebrating with brunch at **Pinocchio in the Desert,** where the bottomless mimosas draw a packed patio crowd.

After brunch head to the **Uptown Design District** for **vintage shopping.** Browse the wares at **The Shops at Thirteen Forty-Five,** where the stunning architecture matches the vintage clothing and accessories inside, then pick up some Bakelite adornments at **Dazzles.**

The afternoon is spent relaxing poolside, soaking up your last day in Palm Springs.

For dinner check out one of the Uptown Design District's buzziest spots. **Sandfish** offers Japanese sushi and seafood paired with an extensive whiskey list all set against a stylishly spare Scandinavian interior.

Day 5 Travel Day

Enjoy the last moments of your hotel's amenities while you pack. On the way out of town, enjoy a low-key lunch at **Tyler's Burgers** then grab a coffee for the road at **Ernest Coffee** in the Uptown Design District.

Retro Palm Springs Weekend

Palm Springs' treasure trove of mid-century architecture and reputation as a winter playground for the Hollywood Rat Pack-era elite make Palm Springs a stylish resort destination that's perfect for a weekend getaway. Whether you're lounging poolside at a mid-century resort, partying at a ladies' weekend, or relaxing at a couples' spa getaway, you can soak up Palm Springs' dazzling history and sunshine at this timeless haven.

Friday

Fly into Palm Springs Airport. Or if you're driving from LA, hop in the car Thursday night to avoid rush hour, and start the weekend early. Spend the afternoon visiting the **Palm Springs Art Museum** or riding the **Palm Springs Aerial Tramway** to the top, where you can take in the refreshing view of the valley below. You can't miss Tramway Road, marked by an iconic building with a cantilevered roofline designed by famed architect Albert Frey in 1965 as the Tramway Gas Station. It now serves as the visitor center. Back on the desert floor, check in to a chic mid-century hotel, such as the freshly restyled **Holiday House,** originally designed in 1951 by noted architect Herbert W. Burns, or the classic 1948 William F. Cody **Del Marcos Hotel** and enjoy some time poolside. For dinner, dine on steak frites at **Mr. Lyons,** a classic steakhouse from a bygone era. From the dining room, move to their backroom, **Seymour's,** for some of the best cocktails in town—bartenders have classic Hollywood movies on for ambience behind the bar. Alternately, opt for

Best Pool Scenes

For most people, a Palm Springs vacation means catching up on summer reading at the hotel pool. Of course there are other things to do—golfing, shopping, day tripping. But at the end of the day (probably sometime after lunch), you will likely be relaxing at your hotel of choice. Choose your hotel wisely: Some pools are known for their serene atmosphere, while others have a party vibe. Some are BYOB, while others have a full-service bar. Some skew young, while others...you get the picture. Here are some of the best pool-centric hotels to keep in mind when planning your trip.

Poolside chairs at **The Monkey Tree Hotel** allow you to zen out on the San Jacinto Mountains jutting above the low-angled rooflines of the 1960s Albert Frey-designed hotel. The central saltwater pool is one of four on the property, varying in size and temperature, while room snacks, happy hour sangria, and a fridge stocked with icy bevvies ensure you keep up your strength.

The central pool at the 1951 **Holiday House** is surrounded by citrus trees and the clean lines of the hotel designed by Herbert H. Burns, one of the heavy hitters of Palm Springs' mid-century modern style. An open-air lobby bar and restaurant adds margaritas, sandwiches, and more reasons not to leave the property.

The atomic-style **Orbit In** designed by Herb Burns, who introduced Palm Springs to the luxury, ultramodern motor court inn, offers nine poolside rooms, a hot tub, and a terrazzo bar for Orbitini hour, when guests gather to chat over fruity "Orbitinis," the house concoction.

Snag the Eames poolside suite complete with terrazzo floors and period furnishings at the **Del Marcos Hotel**, the stone-and-redwood post-WWII modern resort designed by William Cody. A central saltwater pool is surrounded by the hotel's 17 suites and offers a complimentary, low-key happy hour.

Relax around the heated pool at the **Ingleside Inn** on weekends for Acoustic Saturdays (3pm-6pm). Live music and a poolside cocktail bar are the perfect accompaniment to the swimming pool of this historic estate originally built in 1925 as a private home for the Birge family of the Pierce Arrow Motor Car Company.

Ingleside Inn pool

An impeccably restored 1950s retreat, the **Sparrows Lodge** features a high-end rustic-chic design with 20 poolside rooms and garden cottages around a central pool and hot tub. The Barn, the open-air onsite bar and restaurant, serves drinks, lunch, and communal dinners twice a week.

Two pools on 13 tropical, landscaped acres are at the center of **The Parker Palm Springs**, which began life in 1959 as California's first Holiday Inn. From roadside stop to resort destination, the property features a poolside bar, firepit, croquet lawn, and numerous tucked away spots to while away and embrace the day.

Best Spa Experiences

For the best spa experiences near Palm Springs, head north to the town of Desert Hot Springs, uniquely positioned over both hot and cold mineral aquifers. Homesteader, artist, and traveler Cabot Yerxa (of Cabot's Pueblo Museum) is credited with bringing the mineral springs to the attention of homesteaders and developers when he arrived in Desert Hot Springs in 1913. He discovered hot mineral water outside his door when he dug his first well. He dug another 600 yards away and discovered pure, cold aquifer water. Development began in the 1930s with the goal of making Desert Hot Springs a spa destination. Today, boutique mid-century hotels offer calming pools and spas, where you can take the waters.

- **Desert Hot Springs Spa Hotel** offers day passes to its 1940s mid-century resort, with eight mineral pools in a palm-studded courtyard.
- The Moroccan-themed **El Morocco Inn** offers a courtyard mineral pool, covered hot spa, sauna, and spa treatments for guests and nonguests.
- The **Miracle Springs Hotel & Spa** offers eight mineral pools for day use as well as an on-site salon and spa services.
- **The Spring Resort** features three mineral pools, including a central courtyard pool, as well as massages and body treatments to promote relaxation for guests and day use.
- The Italian-inspired **Tuscan Springs Hotel & Spa** offers two hot pools and a mineral spring-fed swimming pool maintained at various temperatures for swimming and soaking, as well as on-site spa services for guests and day use.
- The rustic, family-friendly **Sam's Family Spa Hot Water Resort** has a spring-fed swimming pool and hot pools in a parklike setting with camping.

tropical drinks at **The Reef** in the kitschy 1960s Polynesian Caliente Tropics hotel.

Saturday

After a breakfast at **King's Highway,** a former Denny's with Naugahyde booths and original terrazzo floors in the Ace Hotel, check out some of the area's stunning **mid-century architecture.** Pick up a driving tour map at the **Palm Springs Visitor Center,** itself housed in the Albert Frey-designed **Tramway Gas Station,** and discover the works of **Donald Wexler, William F. Cody, and Richard Neutra,** among others. For a sneak peek inside, sign up for a tour of **Elvis's Honeymoon Hideaway** or historic **Sunnylands,** which has hosted everyone from British royalty to Hollywood icons. Afternoon is spent relaxing poolside, of course.

Around dinnertime, enjoy a romantic dinner at Copley's, part of the former Cary Grant estate, then continue in the footsteps of the Rat Pack with retro-chic cocktails at **Melvyn's** iconic Palm Springs lounge.

Sunday

To wind down your weekend, head to Palm Springs mainstay **Spencer's** for upscale resort dining tucked away in the historic Palm Springs Tennis Club.

Work out the kinks of mind and body with a massage at one of nearby Desert Hot Springs' many **day spas** before packing your bags for the flight or long drive back to reality.

Joshua Tree Camping Trip

The landscape of Joshua Tree National Park is mesmerizing—from the spiky trees to the scoured desert and jumbled boulders begging to be climbed. A visit here typically means **camping,** with extra time spent exploring the funky sights of the surrounding desert towns. **Bring water** and **your own vehicle** and plan a two-night camping trip to visit this desert wonderland **October-May.**

Day 1

Arrive in the town of Joshua Tree and fortify after your drive with lunch at the nouveau diner **Crossroads Café** for a creative take on diner classics, including plenty of veggie options. The laid-back vibe and fresh plates ranging from grilled herbed polenta and eggs to buttermilk hotcakes will set you up for making camp and exploring in the park.

After lunch, continue on Highway 62 to the less crowded **North Entrance,** stopping at the **Oasis Visitors Center** to pick up maps before entering the park.

Check in to your reserved campsite at the centrally located **Jumbo Rocks Campground** and set up camp, enjoying your spot amid the iconic boulder-strewn scenery. You don't have to venture far from your campsite to find short, scenic hiking trails for the afternoon: **Skull Rock Loop** and **Split Rock Loop** allow you to immerse in the landscape while still getting you back in time for a relaxing camp dinner.

After staking your campsite, consider **evening stargazing events** through the **Sky's the Limit Observatory and Nature Center.**

Day 2

Enough of these easy nature trails! Today, it's time to get those lungs pumping with a more rigorous hike. For epic views, climb **Ryan Mountain** to its 5,457-foot summit. If you want to explore the park's mining ruins, opt instead for a steep climb to the **Lost Horse Mine.** And for those irresistible boulder piles, the **Willow Hole Trail** offers a scenic out-and-back ramble.

If it's too hot to hit the trail today, hit the road instead on a backcountry drive. The **Geology Tour Road** is accessible to all vehicles for the first 5 of its 18 miles through the park's unique geologic formations. The dirt roads crisscrossing the Queen Valley also cut through Joshua Tree forest with opportunities to explore the park's cultural history.

After your hike, enjoy a picnic lunch in the park at one of the numerous picnic areas, then enjoy a scenic drive along Park Boulevard into the popular **Hidden Valley** region of the park, making a detour to **Key's View** if you haven't had your fill. Continue north to end in the town of Joshua Tree.

Take a night off from campfire cooking to grab a burger with other hikers, rock climbers, and locals at the lively **Joshua Tree Saloon,** a 20-minute drive west from the Willow Hole Trailhead.

Day 3

Pack up camp and save yourself the dishes by enjoying a late breakfast at the **JT Country Kitchen.** Before you head out of town, browse the shops in Joshua Tree.

Best Hikes

The Palm Springs and Joshua Tree region is host to hidden waterfalls, fan palm oases, stunning canyons, and twisted boulder piles, all begging to be explored. The best season to hit the trail is **October-April;** in the hotter months, plan to start from the trailhead early to miss the heat of the day. Or if it's too hot, opt instead for the lofty and much cooler San Jacintos, just a short drive (or tram ride) away.

Indian Canyons

Andreas Canyon (page 58) is an easy—and popular—loop in scenic **Indian Canyons** near Palm Springs. The shaded trail follows a permanent creek for **2 miles round-trip** through stands of leafy fan palms.

Tahquitz Peak

This steep **8.6-mile round-trip** trail switchbacks through the manzanita, Jeffrey pine, and white fir forests of the **San Jacinto Wilderness** to reward with breathtaking views from the historic lookout tower at the top of **Tahquitz Peak** (page 101).

McCallum Grove

A **2-mile round-trip** stroll leads across open desert to a series of shaded pools hidden under an impressive cluster of fan palms in the **Thousand Palms Oasis Preserve** (page 88).

Ryan Mountain

This **3-mile round-trip** hike climbs more than 1,000 feet in elevation to panoramic **views** from the 5,457-foot wind-scoured vantage point atop **Ryan Mountain** (page 135).

Lost Horse Mine

This moderate out-and-back or loop hike scales **Lost Horse Mountain** (page 129) in about

views of the San Jacinto Wilderness

4-7.4 miles round-trip to visit one of the best-preserved **mining sites** in Joshua Tree National Park.

Willow Hole Trail

Admire the spiky **Joshua trees** and **boulder piles** on this **7-mile round-trip** flat track into the heart of the **Wonderland of Rocks** (page 130).

49 Palms Oasis

This easy-to-follow trail is only **3 miles round-trip** yet offers no hint to the secret oasis of **native fan palms** (page 138) that awaits.

Lost Palms Oasis

As the south entrance to Joshua Tree, this exposed trail wanders **7.5 miles round-trip** through **desert gardens** to the **Lost Palm Oasis** (page 140), a watering hole for bighorn sheep and other wildlife.

Red Dome

In **Whitewater Preserve** (page 171), a **4-mile out-and-back** scenic walk through a wide canyon ends at the **Whitewater River,** which maintains a surprising and brisk presence across the open desert floor for much of the year.

iconic cracked granite boulders in the Wonderland Wash

Palm Springs and the Coachella Valley

When considering its 300 days of annual sun,

well-watered canyons, and natural hot springs, it's hard to imagine what could make Palm Springs more charmed...

...until you see its impeccable mid-century architecture preserved like a time capsule. After the town's initial heyday for the Hollywood set from the 1920s through the 1960s, it was somehow left alone in its former glory. Lucky for us. Today, you can stay in a retro boutique hotel, lounge by a gleaming pool, shop the design district, and live like you're on permanent vacation in this timeless hot spot.

The western border to this desert oasis, the San Jacinto Mountains, offer a quick place to cool off from the valley heat. The charming mountain

Highlights

Look for ★ to find recommended sights, activities, dining, and lodging.

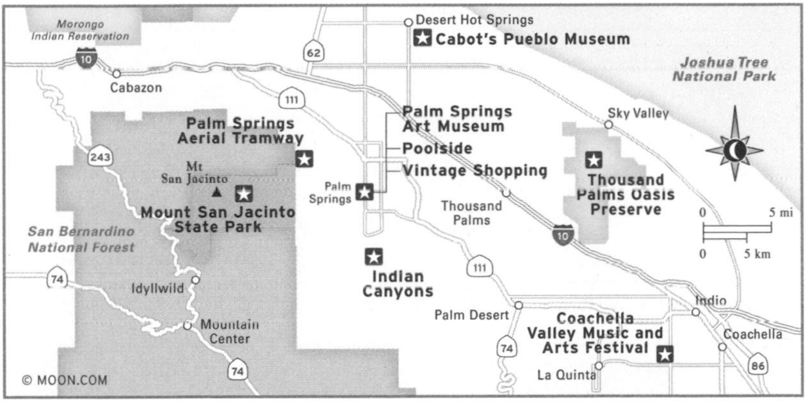

★ **Palm Springs Aerial Tramway:** This dizzying feat of engineering whisks you nearly 6,000 feet from the desert floor to the San Jacinto Mountains (page 30).

★ **Palm Springs Art Museum:** This highly acclaimed art museum houses contemporary and Western American art in its sleek, lofty space (page 34).

★ **Go Poolside:** Choose between lively party scenes and quiet oases—poolside is the place to be (page 40).

★ **Vintage Shopping:** The walkable and chic Uptown Design District offers vintage couture clothing, pristine mid-century antiques, and reproduction housewares and furnishings (page 49).

★ **Indian Canyons:** Hike through the world's largest fan palm oasis and explore miles of trails through sacred land, scenic streams, and dramatic canyons (page 55).

★ **Mount San Jacinto State Park:** Escape the heat of the desert at this 14,000-acre state park in the San Jacinto Mountains (page 59).

★ **Cabot's Pueblo Museum:** This Hopi-inspired pueblo is an artistic masterpiece (page 85).

★ **Coachella Valley Music and Arts Festival:** This annual music festival draws big names and huge numbers of people to the desert valley south of Palm Springs (page 86).

★ **Thousand Palms Oasis Preserve:** Short hiking trails lead to shaded fan palm oases set against the rocky landscape along the San Andreas Fault line (page 88).

town of Idyllwild provides a good jumping-off point for camping, hiking, and skiing.

The Coachella Valley sprawls eastward, stretching all the way to the barren Salton Sea and encompassing the mostly residential towns of Desert Hot Springs, Palm Desert, and Coachella. Today, it's best known as the home of the popular Coachella Valley Music and Arts Festival.

PLANNING YOUR TIME

Los Angeles residents have a special relationship with Palm Springs; being so close, it's easy for them to pop out here for a **weekend** or enjoy a couples' spa getaway.

October-May is high season in Palm Springs, with Christmas week, spring break, and big events like Modernism Week and the Coachella Valley Music and Arts Festival packing in the crowds (and raising the prices). Advanced hotel reservations during these peak times are always a good idea. In **summer**, tourism slows, and rates drop significantly.

Sights

Palm Springs may be on the small side, but the town sprawls widely across the valley floor. The North Palm Springs and Uptown Design District runs along North Palm Canyon Drive from East Vista Chino (north) to Alejo Road (south). The Central Palm Springs and Downtown neighborhood encompasses the blocks south of Alejo Road all the way to Ramon Road. A bit farther off the beaten path, Ramon Road forms the northern boundary of South Palm Springs, which stretches south to Indian Canyons and east past the "curve."

Palm Springs is a vibrant resort city that is continually reinventing itself. New businesses are constantly being added as old ones are refreshed and made contemporary. Call to confirm operating hours in advance of planning a trip.

UPTOWN DESIGN DISTRICT AND NORTH PALM SPRINGS

★ Palm Springs Aerial Tramway

One of the paradoxes of California's dramatic geography is that at times, stark desert and green alpine push up against each other as strange neighbors, separated only by a few thousand feet of rocky elevation. The **Palm Springs Aerial Tramway** (1 Tram Way, 760/325-1391, www.pstramway.com, every half hour, 10am-8pm Mon.-Fri., 8am-8pm Sat.-Sun., $25.95) allows you to marvel at just how startling this transition can be. The tramway consists of suspended cable cars that zip visitors from Valley Station on the desert floor (elevation 2,643 feet) to Mountain Station in the lofty San Jacinto Mountains (elevation 8,516 feet) over the course of a 2.5-mile, 10-minute ride traversing rugged Chino Canyon. As you dangle from the cable, the cars rotate, offering dizzying views of the rocky canyon below, salt-crusted desert, and pine-studded mountain peaks.

Frances Crocker, a young electrical engineer living in the heat-stoked town of Banning, dreamed up the project in 1935 as a way to get to the cooler temperatures that were within sight but out of reach. After a series of interruptions and political roadblocks, the project was finally completed in 1963.

When the sun is blazing in the desert, the tram provides swift relief as temperatures average about 40 degrees cooler at the

Previous: cactus landscape at the Living Desert Zoo and Gardens; Palm Springs Art Museum Architecture and Design Center; wooden bridge and palm trees at Thousand Palms Oasis Preserve.

Palm Springs and the Coachella Valley

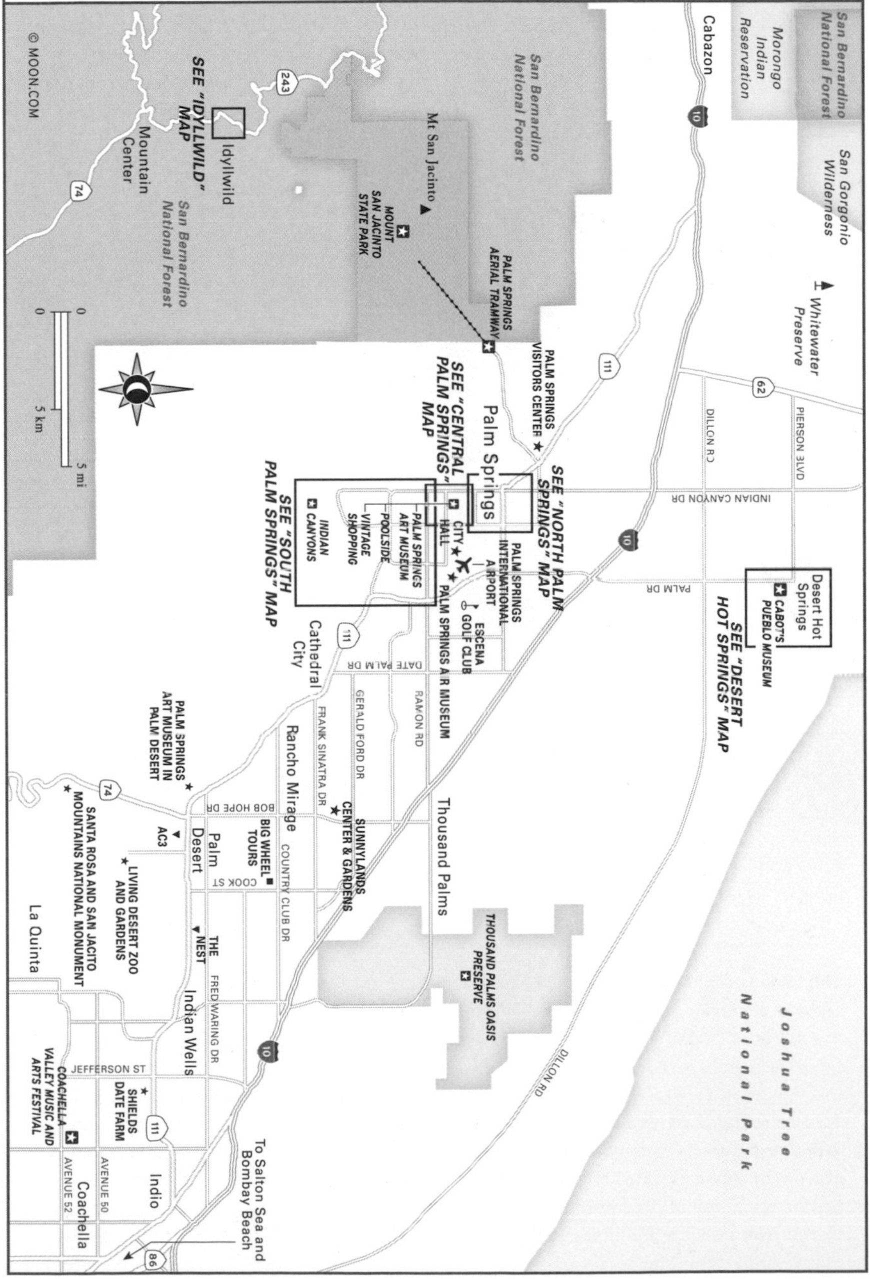

North Palm Springs

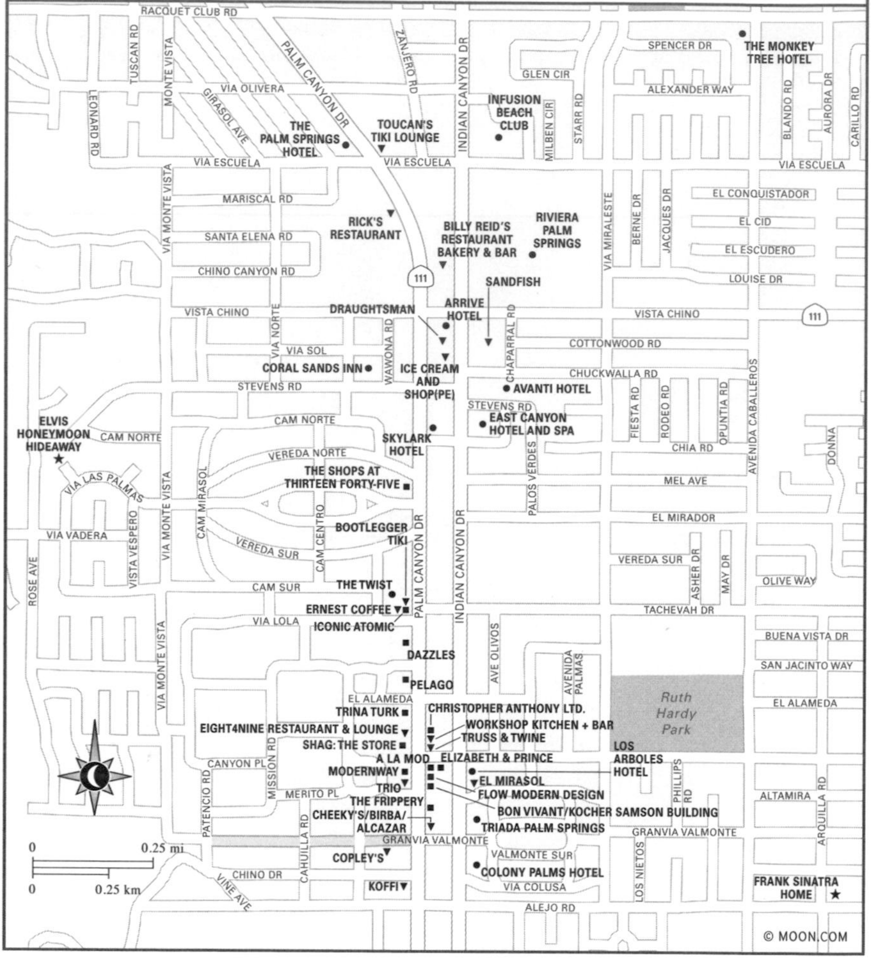

top. In summer, most visitors buy day passes and spend the day picnicking and hiking the San Jacintos, which offer a range of options from easy interpretive trails like the 1.5-mile Desert View Trail to the more difficult 11-mile round-trip trek to San Jacinto Peak. Wilderness permits are required for day hikes and can be obtained at the Long Valley Ranger Station at the top of the tramway. Mountain Station also provides a jumping-off point for many well-established backpacking routes.

The mountains are often crusted with snow in winter months, when visitors enjoy snowshoeing, cross-country skiing, snow camping, or just good, old-fashioned snow frolicking. A **Winter Adventure Center** (10am-4pm Mon. and Thurs.-Fri., 9am-4pm Sat.-Sun.) is open seasonally and rents snowshoe and ski equipment.

Mountain Station has year-round amenities, including restrooms, a gift shop, lockers, and the **Pines Café** (11am-8:30pm daily),

The Hollywood Rat Pack

In the 1930s, the arrival of Hollywood celebrities put Palm Springs on the map. By the 1950s and '60s, the scene was in full swing. Hollywood A-listers fled from Los Angeles to "winter" in Palm Springs, kicking off with a party at the now-gone Racquet Club, presided over by Frank Sinatra, Sammy Davis Jr., Bing Crosby, and Bob Hope.

Sinatra and Hope settled in Palm Springs permanently, while celebrities like Elvis Presley, Dean Martin, Dinah Shore, and Lucille Ball continued to winter here. Today, you can still experience the nostalgia of the Rat Pack era in a few of the old hangouts and homes.

- **Bob Hope Residence:** Hike the Araby Trail for views of the entertainment icon's former home, a massive, orbital glass-and-concrete structure designed by John Lautner.
- **Colony Palms Hotel:** In the late 1950s, this former underground casino, speakeasy, and brothel drew the glitterati (including Frank Sinatra, Zsa Zsa Gabor, Kirk Douglas, Howard Hughes, and Ronald Reagan), who reveled at its poolside supper club, featuring Las Vegas acts.
- **Copley's Restaurant:** Experience a piece of Cary Grant's former 1940s estate (the guest-house, to be specific), located in the historic Movie Colony neighborhood.
- **Elvis Honeymoon Hideaway:** Tour the site of Elvis and Priscilla Presley's May 1, 1967, honeymoon.
- **Frank Sinatra Home:** Designed by E. Stewart Williams, Sinatra's former Palm Springs estate set the standard for Hollywood glamour post-World War II.
- **Melvyn's:** At this time capsule where Frank Sinatra once held court, you're as likely to see longtime regulars swanning around in matching pantsuits as you are young hipsters yearning for a glimpse of the old days.
- The **Purple Room:** It's one of the last holdouts of the Rat Pack nightlife. The usual suspects—Frank Sinatra, Sammy Davis Jr., and Dean Martin—graced the place with their presence, and you can, too.
- **Riviera Palm Springs:** Back in the day, the Riviera hosted movie stars, entertainers, and presidents. It was featured in the 1963 film *Palm Springs Weekend,* about a group of college students on a spring weekend romp.
- **The Willows:** Throughout the 1930s, this glamorous mansion was the occasional home of superstar lawyer Samuel Untermyer, who entertained luminaries like Hollywood child star Shirley Temple and scientist Albert Einstein.

with cafeteria-style dining and snacks. The **Lookout Lounge** provides cocktails, while the **Peaks Restaurant** (760/325-4537) offers fine dining and spectacular views from its perch at the top of Mountain Station.

For guests with disabilities, the Valley Station has designated parking, and the tramcars are handicap-accessible. Mountain Station has accessible dining and a viewing platform.

Frank Sinatra Home

Located in the historic Movie Colony district, the original Palm Springs estate owned by **Frank Sinatra** (877/318-2090, www.sinatrahouse.com) was designed by E. Stewart Williams in 1947 as Sinatra's weekend house. It was Williams's first residential commission. Sinatra originally wanted a Georgian-style mansion with columns and a brick facade, but Williams was able to lure him into a more desert-appropriate modernist style. The 4,500-square-foot residence features four bedrooms, seven bathrooms, and a piano-shaped swimming pool. The house is now available for private vacation rental, private events, dinner parties, and tours.

Elvis Honeymoon Hideaway

Originally christened the House of Tomorrow for its iconic shape (three stories of four concentric circles), this estate was built by well-known Palm Springs developer Robert Alexander for his family. It was leased for Elvis and Priscilla Presley in 1966, and they retreated here for their honeymoon on May 1, 1967. The **Elvis Honeymoon Hideaway** (1350 Ladera Cir., 760/322-1192, www.elvishoneymoon.com, tours) offers daily tours (1pm and 3:30pm daily with advance reservation, $35 pp, walk-ins welcome space permitting).

Tours are geared toward Elvis Presley fans. Knowledgeable docents share a wealth of information about the home's architecture and Elvis's history. Tours include the home's interior, where visitors are allowed to touch all of the furniture—and even sit on the honeymoon bed.

CENTRAL PALM SPRINGS AND DOWNTOWN

★ Palm Springs Art Museum

With its three lofty floors kept at a cool 75 degrees, the sophisticated **Palm Springs Art Museum** (101 N. Museum Dr., 760/322-4800, www.psmuseum.org, 10am-5pm Sun-Tues., noon-8pm Thurs., 10am-5pm Fri.-Sat., $14, children and active duty military free) is a refreshing oasis of art. Spread across 28 galleries and two outdoor sculpture gardens, the museum showcases collections of international modern and contemporary painting and sculpture, architecture and design, Native American and Western art, photography, and glass. The midsize collection approaches those of metropolitan museums with works by such well-known artists as Marc Chagall, Ansel Adams, Roy Lichtenstein, Pablo Picasso, and Andy Warhol. The museum was originally established in 1938 as the Palm Springs Desert Museum, specializing in Native American artifacts and the natural history of the Coachella Valley. The current museum, designed by architect E. Stewart Williams in 1974, has expanded as a cultural center with an Architecture and Design Center and the Annenberg Theater. The museum also houses a café and a museum store. Admission is free every Thursday evening 4pm-8pm and the second Sunday of each month.

Frey House II

Up the road from the Palm Springs Art Museum, the 1963 **Frey House II** (686 Palisades Dr.) sits tucked on a hillside 220 feet above the desert floor. The tiny, rectangular glass box is the second home of famed architect Albert Frey, with an interior that comes in at less than 1,000 square feet—much of that being taken up by the giant boulder that the house was built around. Frey House II is owned and managed by the Palm Springs Art Museum Architecture and Design Center. Tours are offered through The Modern Tour as an add-on to their Insider's Tour ($250 per person), a two and a half hour tour featuring celebrity homes, famous residences, and the work of notable Palm Springs' architects, www.moderntour.com, 760/904-0904 or info@themoderntour.com).

Palm Springs Art Museum Architecture and Design Center

The **Palm Springs Art Museum Architecture and Design Center** (300 S. Palm Canyon Dr., 760/423-5260, www.psmuseum.org, 10am-5pm Sun.-Tues. and Fri.-Sat., and noon-8pm Thurs., $5 adults, children under 18 free) is the hub of the Palm Springs Art Museum's growing collection of architecture and design holdings, which includes drawings, photography, and models. The center is intended as a space for architects, scholars, and the general public. Free docent-guided **tours** of current exhibitions are available several times per week with a rotating schedule

In addition, the center offers **walking**

Central Palm Springs

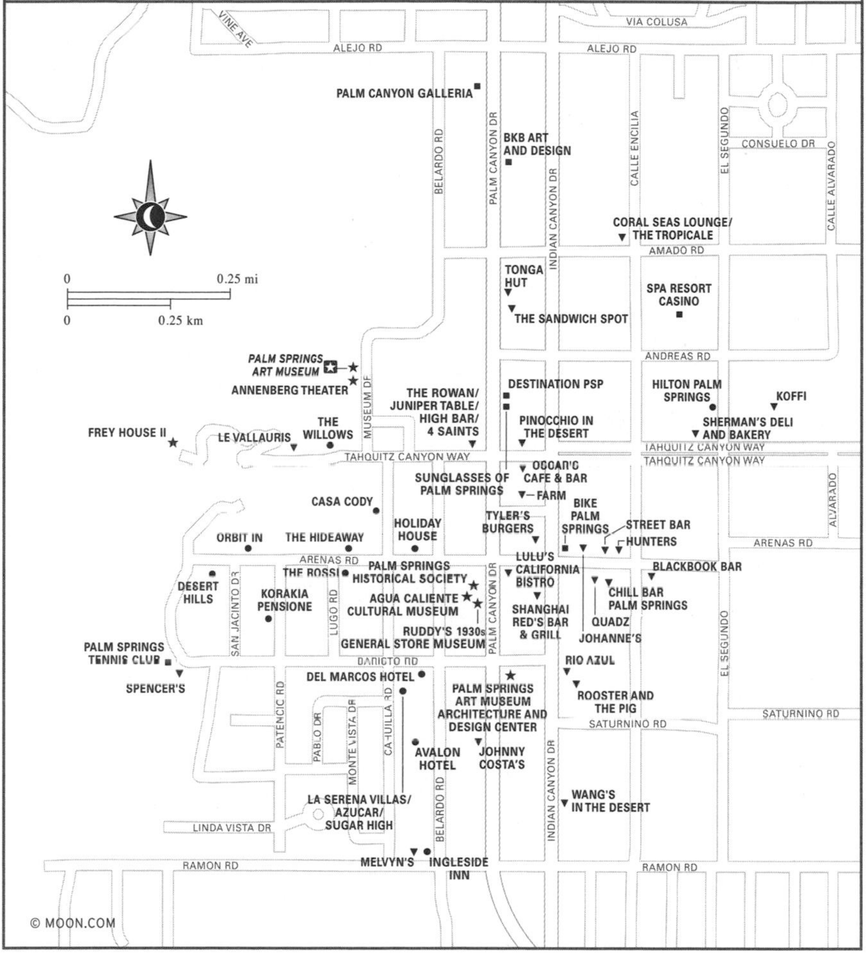

tours (www.psmuseum.org, $25 per person, reservations required; tickets are available online) in conjunction with Palm Springs Historical Society. The Historic City Center Tour highlights the Palm Springs architectural arc from the late 1800s to mid-century modern to the 21st century. The Midcentury Modern Icons of Fashion and Finance Tour points out some of Palm Springs' best examples of mid-century modern architecture in its historic banking and retail businesses. The tours are 75-90 minutes long and free admission to the center is included in the ticket price.

The best way to gain access to Frey II is with **The Modern Tour** (www.moderntour.com, 10am and 2pm by reservation, $250), the official tour provider for the Palm Springs Architecture and Design Center. The Modern Tour specializes in the Insider Tour of Palm Springs with access to residential interiors of celebrity homes, historic homes, and homes by noted architects. Visiting the Frey II is an add-on to one of their Insider Tours. To book a tour, visit The Modern Tour website and request a tour via a reservation request form with your available dates and the number of people in your party. Tours are extremely popular and require advance booking.

Village Green Heritage Center

The village green at the center of downtown is home to a collection of museums and cultural exhibits that allow visitors to explore different aspects of Palm Springs' history from on one block (219-221 S. Palm Canyon Drive). It is comprised of the Palm Springs Historical Society, McCallum Adobe, Cornelia White House, and Ruddy's General Store.

The **Palm Springs Historical Society** (PSHS, 221 S. Palm Canyon Dr., 760/323-8297, www.pshistoricalsociety.org, 10am-4pm Mon., 10am-4pm Wed.-Fri., 10am-5pm Sat. and Sun., summer hours vary) keeps the history of Palm Springs alive through exhibits and walking tours of Palm Springs' historic neighborhoods. It also runs the Palm Springs Historical Research Library at the Welwood Murray Memorial Library (760/656-7469, 9am-5pm Mon.-Fri. by appointment). The historical society is based in the two oldest remaining buildings in Palm Springs, both open to the public. The **McCallum Adobe** was built in 1884 as a home for Palm Springs' first pioneer family. It now houses varying exhibits focusing on Palm Springs history, architecture, and culture. In addition, the museum houses hundreds of photographs documenting Palm Springs' history dating from the 1880s to the 1980s. The **Cornelia White House** (built in 1893) is an example of a turn-of-the-last-century Palm Springs residence. The house was originally part of The Palm Springs Hotel, Palm Springs' first hotel, and is named for the pioneer Cornelia White, who later called the residence home. It closed for refurbishing in 2018 until further notice.

A wide range of docent-led **walking tours** (reserve at 760/323-8297 or www.pshistoricalsociety.org, $20) give visitors a chance to see Palm Springs' charming neighborhoods through the lens of architecture, celebrity, and pioneering efforts. Explore historic neighborhoods, including the Golden Era Hollywood Homes in Old Las Palmas, Rat Pack Playground Modernist Homes in Vista Las Palmas, or Stars and Starchitects in Deepwell. The tours run 1-2.5 hours and must be reserved ahead of time through the Palm Springs Historical Society or the Welwood Murray Memorial Library (100 S. Palm Canyon Dr.). The PSHS is also a local partner of **Modernism Week** and offers tours ($35) during the February event.

Stepping through the doors of **Ruddy's 1930s General Store Museum** (221 S. Palm Canyon Dr., 760/327-2156, www.palmsprings.com, 10am-4pm Thurs.-Sun., $0.95) is a nostalgic trip to a simpler time. The recreated general store is stocked with an extensive collection of unused packaged goods from the 1930s and 1940s. It is chock-full of more than 6,000 unused goods from hardware and clothing to groceries, medicines, and beauty aids.

Agua Caliente Cultural Museum

Native American ties to the Coachella Valley are strong. The ancestral lands of the Agua Caliente Band of Cahuilla Indians span the scenic water- and palm-filled Indian Canyons (open to visitors for hiking) at the base of the San Jacinto Mountains. A new **Agua Caliente Cultural Museum** (www.accmuseum.org) is in the works and slated to open in 2020 in downtown Palm Springs adjoining the village green at the corner of E. Tahquitz Canyon Way and S. Indian Canyon Drive. The center's design is inspired by traditional pottery, basket weaving, and desert landscapes. Intended to celebrate history, culture, and modern times, the center will feature a museum, plaza, gardens, and an oasis trail. The center will also feature a spa and

1: Palm Springs Visitors Center **2:** the Palm Springs Art Museum **3:** Moorten Botanical Gardens **4:** views of the Coachella Valley from the Palm Springs Aerial Tramway

1

2
PALM
SPRINGS
ART
MUSEUM

3
MOORTEN
BOTANICAL GARDEN
VISITORS WELCOME

4

bathhouse fed by the ancient hot mineral springs for which the tribe is named.

Palm Springs Air Museum

The fact that most of the aircraft are still flyable at the **Palm Springs Air Museum** (745 N. Gene Autry Trail, 760/778-6262, www.palmspringsairmuseum.org, 10am-5pm daily, $17.50) makes their larger-than-life exhibits even more impressive. This living history aviation museum features 40 flyable static aircraft from World War II, the Korean War, and the Vietnam War as well as permanent and temporary exhibits and artwork across three climate-controlled hangars and outside tarmac. Docents give added depth to the experience since many are veterans. A small **café** (10am-4pm daily Nov.-May; 10am-4pm Tues.-Sun. June-Oct.) and gift shop are on-site.

SOUTH PALM SPRINGS

Moorten Botanical Garden

Moorten Botanical Garden (1701 S. Palm Canyon Dr., 760/327-6555, www.moortenbotanicalgarden.com, 10am-4pm Thurs.-Tues., 10am-4pm Fri.-Sun. in summer) has been introducing visitors to the wonders of cacti and other desert plants since 1938. Chester "Cactus Slim" Moorten and his wife, Patricia, established the landmark on their own one-acre property, and the gardens have remained in the family, operated today by their son, Clark Moorten. You'll glimpse the Moorten's Mediterranean-style home, "Cactus Castle," as you wander the sinewy pathways.

The private desert garden was established just two years after Joshua Tree National Park became a National Monument, when appreciation for desert life was less widespread. Seeing the homespun sign for Moorten Botanical Gardens, it's easy to imagine motoring along a dusty road in a different era to stop for this curious roadside attraction. The minimal entrance fee allows you to wander the wide trails among the jagged lattice formed by the more than 3,000 varieties of plants that make up this natural habitat. It's a peaceful place despite the spiky shapes and the rattling screech of desert insects that have made the habitat their home. The hushed green of the place quickly transports visitors from the street to a microcosm of desert trees, cacti, and plants from around the world. Hand-painted rocks provide labels for the myriad fuzzy, spiky, leafy, jaunty, and snaky plants. A small nursery offers desert plants and pottery for sale. It's a feel-good place—educational, relaxing, and filled with nature—and it offers a novel break from the dining, shopping, and pool lounging that make up much of the Palm Springs experience. The hotel pool will feel that much more refreshing when you return.

Sunnylands

In its history as private residence and high-level retreat center, Sunnylands has seen a host of distinguished guests, including U.S. presidents, British royalty, and Hollywood icons. The historic modernist estate now known as **Sunnylands Center and Gardens** (37977 Bob Hope Dr., Rancho Mirage, www.sunnylands.org, 8:30am-4pm Wed.-Sun., gardens free, house $48) was designed for media tycoon Walter Annenberg and his wife, Leonore, in the mid-1960s by Los Angeles-based architect A. Quincy Jones. The architect's signature style is apparent in the statement roof (a pink pyramid), overhangs to shield the sun, and glass walls for brightness.

Outside, nine acres of sustainable landscape design transcend politics to create a serene setting designed to change with the seasons. When drought-mandated water restrictions put an end to the era of the estate's traditional green lawns, landscape architect James Burnett created a canvas of native and drought-resistant plants, with inspiration from the Annenbergs' large collection of Impressionist and Post-Impressionist art (including Cézannes and Van Goghs). Garden paths wander through arid species and more than 53,000 individual plants. The center

South Palm Springs

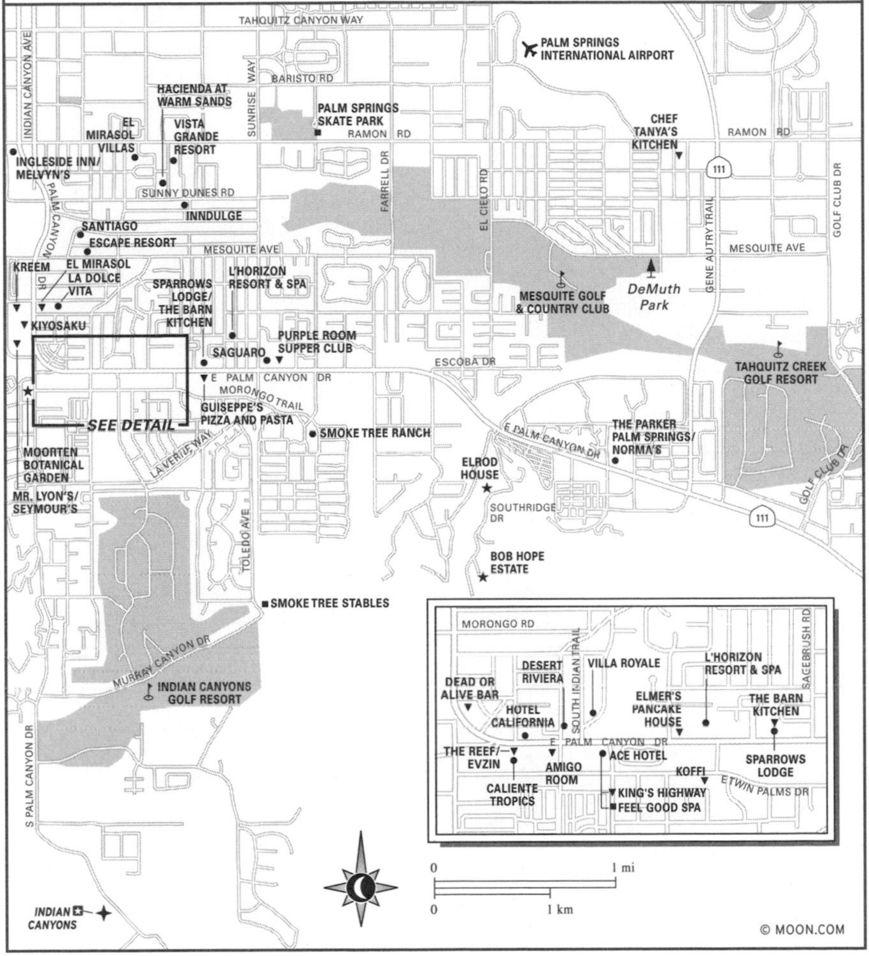

and gardens are open to the public with no reservation.

Tours of the historic house are available by online reservation only. The 90-minute guided house tour takes guests to key areas of the home and features information about the estate's history and architecture and interior design. Tickets must be purchased two weeks in advance. They are released in blocks on the first and 15th of each month at 9am PST for the following two-week block. They often sell out, so getting them the morning of release is advisable. No children under 10 years old are allowed. Wheelchairs can be accommodated with advance notice.

The Sunnylands Center and Gardens offers a gift shop and café on-site. The **café** (8:30am-4:00pm Thurs.-Sun.) serves a variety of light breakfast and lunch items, including pastries, salads, wraps, coffee, and tea.

Entertainment and Events

★ POOLSIDE

I have yet to hear of a hotel in Palm Springs that does not have a pool. If it exists, no one goes there. Chances are you'll never need to leave the confines of your hotel to put in the poolside lounge time that may very well form the backbone of your vacation. Choose your hotel wisely: Some pools are known for their serene relaxation, while others have a party vibe. Some are BYOB, while others have a full-service bar. Some skew young, while others... you get the picture.

The pool scene in Palm Springs tends to be relaxed compared to, say, Las Vegas. But a handful of hotels book deejays and sling poolside cocktails with events that are open to both hotel guests and the public. Check individual hotel websites for event information. The pool party season runs **March-September.**

If you do want some Vegas with your Palm Springs, **The Riviera** (1600 N. Indian Canyon Dr., 760/327-8311, www.rivierapalmsprings.com) has a Summer Splash Pool Party series every Friday, Saturday, and Sunday during the summer, featuring guest deejays and live music. The Soleil Pool & Bar is the official party pool, while the Chiki pool, away from the center of the resort, has a quieter atmosphere with food and drink service on weekends. Pool passes are $10 Monday-Thursday and $15 Friday-Sunday for non-guests. Cabana rentals are available.

The chic, uptown **ARRIVE** hotel (1551 N. Palm Canyon Dr, 760/507-1640, www.arrivehotels.com) offers a scene-y pool hang with drinks and food by on-site Wexler's Deli. Cabana rentals are available if you really want to step it up. The hotel prides itself on being open to the neighborhood and typically allows non-guests and neighborhood folks. During special events or when the pool is extra crowded, it may be limited to hotel guests only.

The **Kimpton Rowan** claims the only rooftop pool in the desert. From seven stories up you will have the stunning mountain views visitors demand from their poolside loungers as well as panoramic views of Palm Springs. The open-air High Bar, aptly named, serves snacks and craft cocktails. Day passes are available for $30 on weekdays (Monday-Friday). The pool is closed to the public on weekends.

With the reinstatement of a tiki bar on the premises, the **Caliente Tropics** (411 E. Palm Canyon Drive, 760/327-1391 www.calientetropics.com) hotel regained its purpose in the world. Quirky Polynesian architecture, affordable motel rooms, a child-allowed policy, and a free-for-all vibe mean that the Caliente Tropics has always had a pool scene. However, The Reef brings some purpose to the mayhem. Tiki snacks and libations are available poolside at The Reef. Day passes to the pool are $20 at the front desk.

The stylish, sprawling **Ace Hotel & Swim Club** (701 E. Palm Canyon Dr., 760/325-9900, www.acehotel.com/palmsprings) is home to some of the biggest weekend pool parties in town, with poolside drink service, outdoor bar, and deejays. The enthusiastic crowds are carefree and cool (some might say "too cool for school").

The **Amigo Bar** is open to the public, so you can enter through the lobby and enjoy the bar's poolside offerings. Non-hotel guests can pay for a **Swim Club Membership** ($350 per year) or a **Day-Use pass** ($30). The yearly Swim Club Membership gets you a lot for that price, including daily pool and hot tub access (7am-2pm), admittance to pool parties and events, the use of the hotel spa and gym, and discounts on spa services and the restaurant. Day passes will gain you a full day's entrance to the pool or pool event. Blackout dates apply.

The trendy **Saguaro** (1800 E Palm Canyon Dr., 760/323-1711, www.thesaguaro.com) has a lively pool scene. An outdoor pool with two hot tubs, lounge seating, and an outdoor bar offers a great place to relax and party against the Technicolor hotel backdrop. The hotel also hosts pool parties during Coachella weekend (Apr.) and Splash House (June and Aug.), with international deejays and high-profile art, music, and fashion influencers catering to a young, dance-loving crowd. The hotel pool is open to anyone, which means it can get crazy.

NIGHTLIFE

Despite being a resort and party destination, Palm Springs has only a moderate number of bars. They range from well-styled watering holes to Rat Pack-era piano lounges to gay dance clubs. Depending on the type of scene you're looking for, you might want to get creative and check out some of Palm Springs' restaurants, which also have a festive cocktail scene.

Bars and Cocktails

UPTOWN DESIGN DISTRICT AND NORTH PALM SPRINGS

Bootlegger Tiki (1101 N. Palm Canyon Dr., 760/318-4154, www.bootleggertiki.com, 4pm-2am daily) took on the legacy of tiki bar royalty when it opened on the site of the original Don the Beachcomber, Palm Springs (established 1953). Velvet paintings, flocked wallpaper, red lighting, and guarded secret recipes impress with dramatic style, and the layered drinks earn their place in tiki history. Grab a friend and grab a booth. Pro tip: If you're not up for a heavily laced rum drink, the gin-based Tom Collins is sprucey and refreshing.

Trio (707 N. Palm Canyon Dr., 760/864-8746, www.triopalmsprings.com, 11am-10pm Mon.-Thurs., 11am-11pm Fri., 10am-11pm Sat., 10am-10pm Sun.) in the Uptown Design District is a sleekly styled destination for celebrations (bachelorette parties love this place). Its side bar can be lively.

Eight4Nine Restaurant and Lounge (849 N. Palm Canyon Dr., 760/325-8490, www.eight4nine.com, 11am-10pm Mon.-Thurs., 11am-11pm Fri., 9am-11pm Sat., 9am-10pm Sun.) offers a crisp white decor for its restaurant and lounge set in the building that was home to the Palm Springs Post Office in 1954. Its swanky lounge with backlit onyx bar is a fun place to linger over cocktails. The lounge stays open all day, offering a bar menu every day from 11am to close.

CENTRAL PALM SPRINGS AND DOWNTOWN

The industrial-chic **Truss & Twine** (800 N. Palm Canyon Drive, 760/459-3451, https://trussandtwine.com, 4pm-12:30am Sun.-Thurs., 4pm-1:30am Fri.-Sat.) offers a cocktail program cleverly divided by era alongside inspired small plates. Try a classic Old-Fashioned from the golden age or go crazy and order up a Surfer on Acid from the Dark Ages. Small plates range from ricotta toast to Wagyu beef tartare and are meant to accompany your drinks, making this more upscale watering hole and less restaurant.

The aptly named **High Bar** (100 W. Tahquitz Canyon Way, 760/904-5015) is located poolside on the rooftop of downtown's chic Kimpton Rowan seven-story hotel. The bar offers an open, luxe setting with mountain views, fresh cocktails and California Mediterranean-inspired salads and snacks. The bar is open for hotel guests 10am-10pm daily. It opens to the public at 4pm. A happy hour 7pm-9pm Sunday-Thursday makes a great spot to watch the sunset.

Lulu's California Bistro (200 S. Palm Canyon Dr., 760/327-5858, www.lulupalmsprings.com, 8am-10pm Sun.-Thurs., 8am-midnight Fri.-Sat.), right on the main downtown strip, has a central bar located in its bright open-design space with good views of Palm Canyon Drive.

The retro-tropical **Tropicale Restaurant** features the swanky, neon-lit **Coral Seas Lounge** (330 E. Amado Rd., 760/866-1952, www.thetropicale.com, 4pm-10pm Sun.-Thurs., 4pm-11pm Fri.-Sat., 11am-3pm Sat.-Sun.) as well as an oasis-like patio bar.

The tiki gem that is the **Tonga Hut** (254 N Palm Canyon Dr, 760/322-4449, www.tongahut.com, 2pm-midnight Sun.,

5pm-midnight Tues.-Thurs., 5pm-2am Fri.-Sat.) is tucked away on the second floor on the main strip of downtown. You'll be fully transported to tiki times as you step through the doorway to excessively garnished drinks, loungey atomic-era seating, low-lit lamps, tiki gods, and hand-carved island art. A full menu offers a pupu platter, pork sliders, pineapple fried rice, and other retro-inspired dishes.

Wang's in the Desert (424 S. Indian Canyon Dr., www.wangsinthedesert.com, 3pm-close daily) has a popular happy hour that is especially happy on Friday with locals and weekend visitors.

Even if you're not staying at the romantically stylish La Serena Villas, you can enjoy the rooftop ambience of ★ **Sugar High** (339 South Belardo Rd., 844/932-8044, www.sugarhighpalmsprings.com, usually open noon-9pm daily depending on weather, call to confirm). The rooftop lounge is part of the on-site Azúcar restaurant and offers a full drink program and all the atmosphere you can soak up. Outdoor fireplace, boho chic pillows, twinkling strands of lights, and deep couches that are hard to leave behind (literally) make this a lovely spot for an appetizer or evening's end.

The dark-wood, galley-style hole-in-the-wall **Shanghai Red's Bar & Grill** (233 S. Indian Canyon Dr., 760/322-9293, www.fishermans.com, 4pm-10pm Mon.-Thurs., 4pm-11:30pm Fri., 11am-11:30pm Sat., 11am-10pm Sun.) is the unlikely home to some of the best fish tacos known to man. It's a great low-key place to pair said tacos with an icy beer (with a full seafood menu available as well). Happy hour specials and live music on the patio on weekends make this a fun hang for locals and visitors.

SOUTH PALM SPRINGS

★ **Melvyn's** (Ingleside Inn, 200 W. Ramon Rd., 760/325-2323, www.inglesideinn.com, 6pm-2am daily), the iconic Palm Springs lounge, is still going as strong as its popular Rat Pack days. Nestled in the elegant Spanish Revival-style Ingleside Inn, it sports an old Hollywood Regency decor, chandeliers, and decadently upholstered booths. The lounge has undergone a recent update, bringing it gracefully into this era while saving everything you like about the old. The lounge gets going most nights, fueled by live piano music and martinis that often inspire dancing on the tiny dance floor. Order a gimlet and enjoy the people watching.

One of the last remaining Rat Pack hangouts in Palm Springs, the **Purple Room Supper Club** (1900 E. Palm Canyon Dr., www.purpleroompalmsprings.com, 4pm-close Tues.-Sun.) is an old-school supper club and lounge that opened in 1960 in the Club Trinidad Resort. Nightly music and comedy shows accompany a surf and turf menu. Happy hour and late-night drinks are available in the 1960s-era lounge.

★ **The Reef** (411 E. Palm Canyon Dr., 760/656-3839, www.thereefpalmsprings.com, 1pm-1am Mon.-Fri., 10am-1am Sat., 10am-midnight Sun.) tiki bar recently opened in the most tiki of locations: the Caliente Tropics Hotel, a historic Polynesian-themed resort with an iconic, A-frame entrance and hand-carved tikis dotting the tropical grounds. The Reef took over the space once held by the Conga Room, a Rat Pack haunt back in the day, and tiki-fied it to the max. It's good for daytime (pool views), happy hour, or late night (there is also a late night happy hour) and offers an arsenal of fruity bevvies and a food menu with salads, burgers, and entrées.

Located in the Ace Hotel, the **Amigo Room** (701 E. Palm Canyon Dr., 760/325-9900, www.acehotel.com/palmsprings, 9am-2am daily) is the perfect purveyor of the Ace Hotel's brand of cool, with a retro dark styling. The bar is open day and night. Daytime it also serves the packed outdoor pool scene. Nighttime brings deejays and theme nights. The crowd skews young and über-hip, but don't be put off. If you like karaoke, live music, trivia, or a dark bar with a good soundtrack, you might end up here at some point.

If you're wondering, the name **Dead or Alive Bar** (150 E. Palm Canyon Dr., www.deadoralivebar.com, 5pm-2am daily) refers to the game where people guess if a celebrity has passed or not. It filled in a gap in the Palm Springs bar offerings when it opened its beer and wine bar in February 2016. They offer a curated beer and wine list in a darkly lit, converted storefront. Sip a beer from one of their ceramic beer mugs in the comfort of a handwoven bar stool. The bar is also conveniently located next to **El Mirasol** (140 E. Palm Canyon Dr., 760/323-0721) Mexican restaurant, if you're hungry.

As a culture on vacation in Palm Springs, we demand craft cocktails. Many bars promise, but few deliver well enough to justify the hefty price tag. ★ **Seymour's** (233 E. Palm Canyon Drive, 760/892-900, 6pm-midnight Sun., 6pm-midnight Tues.-Thurs., 6pm-2am Fri.-Sat.) is an exception. They may even have the best cocktails in town. Located behind the curtain at Mr. Lyon's Steakhouse, the intimate space has barstools you will want to take home, and enthusiastic and knowledgeable bartenders. They show us the difference between a drink and a libation.

Gay Bars and Clubs

All bars and nightlife venues in Palm Springs are gay-friendly; however, there are a range of bars geared specifically toward a gay clientele. Choose from dance clubs, cafés with cabaret performances, and themed deejay or karaoke nights.

UPTOWN DESIGN DISTRICT AND NORTH PALM SPRINGS

Located in North Palm Springs, **Toucan's Tiki Lounge** (2100 N. Palm Canyon Dr., 760/416-7584, www.toucanstikilounge.com, 2pm-2am Mon.-Tues., 2pm-midnight Wed., 2pm-2am Thurs.-Fri., noon-2am Sat.-Sun.) is a fun and friendly gay cocktail bar adorned with tropical tiki touches and a round bar that slings sugary drinks to fuel a lively dance floor. Drag shows and other special events offer plenty of entertainment.

CENTRAL PALM SPRINGS AND DOWNTOWN / ARENAS ROAD

Arenas Road is known as for its gay bar-hopping scene. In this area just east of Indian Canyon Drive, several bars are clustered within walking distance, with more a few blocks north.

Oscar's Café and Bar (125 E. Tahquitz Canyon Way, #108, 760/325-1188, www.oscarspalmsprings.com, 11am-9pm Mon., Wed. and Thurs., 4pm-9pm Fri., 4pm-10pm Sat., 9am-8pm Sun.) has a casual patio for drinking and dining; the spot is open for dinner as well as drag brunch on Saturday and Sunday. They offer a daily happy hour (4pm-7pm) and a popular Sunday tea dance (4pm-close) as well as cabaret and live music.

Streetbar (224 E. Arenas Rd., 760/320-1266, www.psstreetbar.com, 10am-2am Mon.-Fri, 6am-2am Sat., 6am-midnight Sun.) is a Palm Springs fixture that caters to a gay, male clientele. The divey central bar is offset by a chandelier and club lighting. In addition to daily drink specials, there's something going on every night of the week—from karaoke to deejay nights and live performances.

The long-running **Hunters** (302 E. Arenas Rd., 760/323-0700, www.hunterspalmsprings.com, 10am-2am daily, happy hour 10am-7pm daily) is a gay club that draws a mostly male crowd for drink specials, deejays, dancing, and weekly entertainment.

The newly re-branded **QuadZ** (200 S. Indian Canyon Dr., www.spurline.com, 2:30pm-2am Mon.-Thurs., noon-2am Fri.-Sun.) is the old Spurline, a popular neighborhood sing-along spot with strong drinks and theme nights, including show tunes, retro, cowboy country, and karaoke cabaret. The low-key bar draws a primarily male crowd, but all are welcome.

Chill Bar Palm Springs (217 E. Arenas Rd., 760/327-1079, www.chillbarpalmsprings.com, 10am-2am daily) is a gay cocktail bar and nightclub in a sleekly designed contemporary space with an outdoor patio. The adjoining Scorpion Room has karaoke, deejays, dancing, and themed nights.

1

2

3

4

Blackbook Bar (315 E. Arenas Rd, 760/832-8497, noon-late Mon.-Fri., 11am-late Sat. and Sun.) is a newcomer on the Arenas stretch of gay bars. The industrial-chic space spills out onto a street-front patio. If you've been out making the rounds, they also have a solid food menu. People rave about the Nashville fried chicken.

Casino

Palm Springs' proximity to tribal lands (Morongo Band of Mission Indians and the Agua Caliente Band of Cahuilla Indians) means that there are several deluxe casino resorts in the Coachella Valley. The **Spa Resort Casino** (401 E. Amado Rd., 888/999-1995, www.sparesortcasino.com, 24 hours) is the only casino in downtown Palm Springs. It only partially lives up to its name—the casino is open, but the spa and hotel closed in July 2015. The casino offers slots and table games, a 24-hour deli, lounge, and steak house (dinner only 5pm-10pm Sun.-Thurs., 5pm-11pm Fri.-Sat.). Casino resort lodging is available at their sister resort in Rancho Mirage (www.hotwatercasino.com).

THE ARTS

The **Annenberg Theater** (101 N. Museum Dr., www.psmuseum.org/annenberg-theater), housed within the Palm Springs Art Museum, hosts live professional performances in its 433-seat state-of-the-art theater. The Annenberg Theater combines the visual and performing arts to feature a yearly series showcasing theater, dance, music, and mixed media works. Order tickets online on the website or call the **box office** (760/325-4490, 10am-4pm Wed.-Fri., hours vary based on performance schedules).

FESTIVALS AND EVENTS

Modernism Week

Modernism Week (www.modernismweek.com, Feb.) is Palm Springs' signature annual event, celebrating mid-century modern architecture, design, and culture over two nonstop weekends every February. Modernism Week fosters appreciation for Palm Springs' shining modernist history while encouraging a fresh approach and thinking about design, art, fashion, and sustainable modern living. The festival features more than 250 events, including signature home tours with a chance to peek into some of Palm Springs' fabulous historic houses, a modernism show and sale, modern garden tours, architectural double-decker bus tours (including sunset tours of illuminated mid-century classic buildings), nightly parties (soiree at Frank Sinatra's estate, anyone?), walking and bike tours, lectures and cocktail hour discussions, fashion events, a vintage travel trailer exhibition, films, music, and more. Modernism Week hosts a **Fall Preview** (Oct.), a mini Modernism Week to kick off Palm Springs' social and recreation season. Check online for highlights, recommendations, and ongoing news.

Tickets (up to $150) for Modernism Week (on sale Nov. 1) and the Fall Preview (on sale Aug. 1) are sold online for individual events. Tickets sell out quickly, especially for the popular house tours.

Splash House

The pool party to end all pool parties is the annual **Splash House** (www.splashhouse.com, June and Aug.), a three-day electronic dance music and pool party held in Palm Springs two weekends a year. Three host hotels (the Saguaro, The Riviera, and the Renaissance) form ground zero for Splash House, with deejays and daytime events; shuttles run between the host hotels. A general admission wristband (from $120) gets you access to the pools and events at the hotels as well as the shuttle. General admission tickets can be purchased separately or as a package with hotel rooms. Late-night parties are held off-site at unique Palm Springs locations, such as the Palm Springs Air Museum. Tickets for the off-site parties are sold separately (from $40).

1: the bar at Melvyn's Restaurant **2:** the exterior of Melvyn's Restaurant and Lounge **3:** Bootlegger Tiki **4:** The Rowan Hotel in downtown Palm Springs

TOP EXPERIENCE

Mid-Century Modernism

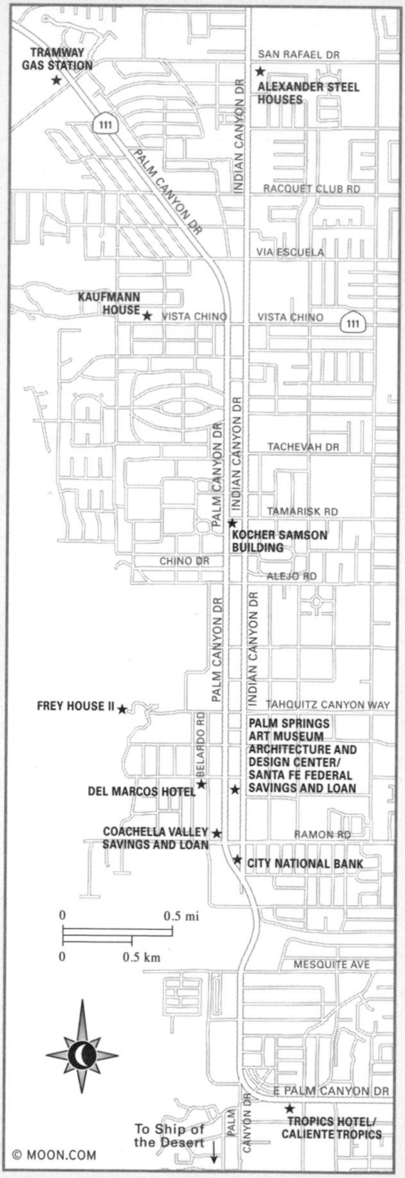

In the 1930s, celebrities streamed from Los Angeles to Palm Springs, acquiring second homes to hide in and party away the winter season. This laid-back desert lifestyle allowed architects the creative freedom to explore modernist materials, designing structures inspired by the clean lines of the desert. The 1950s and 1960s were the height of modernist design. Throughout the city are design examples from noted architects Albert Frey, E. Stewart Williams, William Cody, Donald Wexler, John Lautner, and Richard Neutra. A visit to Palm Springs is a trip back in time. Don't miss these Rat Pack-era abodes, whimsical desert structures, and modernist design examples from noted architects.

The Palm Springs Visitors Center sells a mid-century modern map ($5) highlighting civic buildings, inns and hotels, celebrity homes, and other exceptional residences. Interior tours of some gems are available during **Modernism Week** (www.modernismweek.com, Feb.). The following are listed from north to south:

- **Tramway Gas Station** (2901 N. Palm Canyon Dr.): This 1965 gas station once serviced the Palm Springs Aerial Tramway. Now the **Palm Springs Visitors Center,** it features iconic lines and a soaring roofline designed by Albert Frey with Robson Chambers.

- **Alexander Steel Houses** (btw. E. Molino Rd. and N. Sunnyview Dr.): Designed by Donald Wexler and Richard Harrison and built in 1960-1962 by the George Alexander Construction company, these seven prefabricated homes use light-gauge steel to frame glass walls that afford striking mountain views.

- **Kaufmann House** (470 W. Vista Chino): Designed by Richard Neutra in 1946-1947 for Edgar Kaufmann Sr. (who had also commissioned Frank Lloyd Wright to design Fallingwater), this private residence has been impeccably restored.
- **Kocher Samson Building** (766 N. Palm Canyon Drive): Albert Frey's first commercial structure, bringing Palm Springs into the international modernism movement, is located in the now Uptown Design District.
- **Frey House II** (686 Palisades Dr.): This 1963 rectangular glass box sits tucked on a hillside 220 feet above the desert floor and was constructed around a giant boulder.
- **Del Marcos Hotel** (225 W. Baristo Rd.): Designed by William F. Cody in 1947, the Del Marcos was ahead of its time, featuring post-and-beam construction with organic, natural materials including redwood and stone. The angular lines highlight interior garden rooms that form a U-shape around the pool, all complete with mountain views.
- **Santa Fe Federal Savings and Loan** (300 S. Palm Canyon Dr.): Now the **Palm Springs Art Museum Architecture and Design Center,** this iconic 1961 structure has been impeccably restored. Note the elevated concrete foundation and aluminum solar screens.
- **Coachella Valley Savings and Loan** (499 S. Palm Canyon Dr.): Designed by architect E. Stewart Williams in 1960, the structure (now Chase Bank) stands out with its arched facade and vertical bronze siding.
- **City National Bank** (588 S. Palm Canyon Dr.): Designed in 1959 by Rudi Baumfeld of Victor Gruen Associates, this current Bank of America is striking for its curved exterior and blue mosaic tile.
- **Palm Springs City Hall** (3200 E. Tahquitz Canyon Way): Built in 1952-1957 with diverse architectural elements, the building represents a stylistic collaboration between architects John Porter Clark, Albert Frey, Robson C. Chambers, and E. Stewart Williams. Noted features include a portico with a circular cutout encompassing two palm trees.
- **Ship of the Desert** (1995 S. Camino Monte): Designed in 1936 by Los Angeles architects Eric Webster and Adrian Wilson, this streamlined nautical house gets its name from the prow-front living room. Bedroom suites can only be accessed by an exterior redwood deck. (The home is currently owned by fashion designer Trina Turk.)
- **Tropics Hotel** (411 E. Palm Canyon Dr.): Now the **Caliente Tropics,** the 1964 Polynesian-themed resort still retains some of its fun and kitschy tiki elements.
- **Elrod House** (2175 Southridge Dr.): The 1968 residence of interior designer Arthur Elrod features bold concrete circles, movable walls, a fully retracting glass living room wall, and an infinity pool. Designed by architect John Lautner, it was featured in the 1971 James Bond thriller *Diamonds Are Forever.*

PALM SPRINGS CULTURAL CENTER FILM FESTIVALS

Camelot Theatres, part of the Palm Springs Cultural Center (2300 E. Baristo Rd., 760/325-6565, www.palmspringsculturalcenter.org) is home to many of Palm Springs' film festivals, including the prestigious **Palm Springs International Film Festival** (www.psfilmfest.org, Jan.). The original Camelot Theatre opened in 1967 and closed in 1992 during tough economic times. In 1999, patrons of the arts Ric and Rozene Supple purchased and renovated the theater. They dedicated it to the Palm Springs Cultural Center in 2018.

Palm Springs International Film Festival is a well-established destination film festival that draws more than 135,000 filmgoers every January. The festival features more than 200 films from 78 countries over 12 days of events and film screenings, including the prestigious Film Awards Gala. Advance **tickets** go on sale in December and can be purchased online, by phone (800/898-7256, 9am-5pm Mon.-Fri.), and in person at Festival Ticket and Information Center (Courtyard Plaza, 777 E. Tahquitz Canyon Way), Camelot Theatres (2300 E. Baristo Rd.), during business hours. The **Palm Springs International ShortFest** (www.psfilmfest.org) also happens every June.

American Documentary Film Festival (www.americandocumentaryfilmfestival.com, Apr.) showcases films from around the globe that focus on making an impact through real stories with real issues. First held in 2012, the nonprofit festival screens more than 100 documentaries during its five-day annual run. Tickets to individual screenings, many with Q&As, as well as tickets to the opening night gala and festival passes are available online ($11). Films are screened in venues in Palm Springs, Rancho Mirage, and Palm Desert.

Started in 2008, **Cinema Diverse** (www.palmspringsculturalcenter.org, Sept.) is a Palm Springs gay and lesbian film festival held annually in September. The festival showcases feature films, short films, and new media as well as a series of after-parties in popular Palm Springs bars and restaurants. Tickets are available online (individual tickets $13.25, all-access pass $159).

The **Arthur Lyons Film Noir Festival** (palmspringsculturalcenter.org, May) showcases a mix of black-and-white, film noir B classics and obscure vintage gems. The festival was founded in 2000 by Arthur Lyons, the late mystery author and Palm Springs community leader.

LGBT Events

Palm Springs is a year-round LGBT vacation destination with hotels and nightlife that cater exclusively to the LGBT community.

Pride Weekend happens annually on one weekend in November to celebrate lesbian, gay, bisexual, and transgender diversity. There are host hotels for centralized gathering and party zones, but the entire town of Palm Springs fills up for a celebratory weekend. Festivities include a block party and parade (www.pspride.org, Nov.).

Established in 1991, **The Dinah** (locations vary, www.thedinah.com, Apr.) is the self-proclaimed largest queer girl party music festival in the world. This four-day, four-night annual getaway catering to the lesbian community takes Palm Springs by storm every April. It kicks off with a massive opening party on Thursday night and continues its deluge of celebrity-studded events and parties throughout the weekend. The event features deejays, including celebrity guest deejays, dancers, daytime pool parties, live concerts, comedy, and nightclub parties throughout the weekend. The festival is based in a few of the larger Palm Springs hotels and is where the daytime pool parties take place. Stay at one of the featured hotel sponsors to make sure you are at the center of the action. Tickets are available on The Dinah website with **weekend package deals** ($239-500) or tickets to **individual events** ($30-80).

The **White Party** (locations vary, www.jeffreysanker.com, Apr.) is a massive gay dance party for male couples and singles. The three-day, three-night festival is held annually every April (not the same weekend as The Dinah). It kicks off Friday at noon and goes strong until 7am Monday morning, with daytime pool parties, deejays, live performances, and themed nighttime events. White Party festival's main event happens on Saturday night—a 10-hour dance party with multiple levels, dancers, special effects, and huge sound system. The White Party Ferris Wheel and fireworks display choreographed to a deejay music remix add even more spark to the event. White Party is centered in several host hotels in Palm Springs. **Weekend passes** ($379-455) are available on the White Party website, or you can buy tickets to **individual events** ($40-160).

Shopping

Palm Springs is known for its mid-century antiquing and stylish desert home furnishings.

TOP EXPERIENCE

UPTOWN DESIGN DISTRICT AND NORTH PALM SPRINGS

The sleek Uptown Design District has the highest concentration of mid-mod shopping in Palm Springs. Stroll colorful North Palm Canyon Drive between Vista Chino (north end) and Alejo (south end) to find vintage and new retro home furnishings, art, gifts, clothing, and fashion accessories.

★ Vintage

Just north of Vista Chino, **Modernway** (745 N. Palm Canyon Dr., 760/320-5455, www.psmodernway.com, noon-5pm Thurs.-Mon.) is a well-established and well-regarded Palm Springs vintage retail outlet specializing in mid-century modern furnishings from the 1950s, '60s, and '70s.

The elegant building that now houses **The Shops at Thirteen Forty-Five** (1345 N. Palm Canyon Dr., 760/464-0480, www.towneps.com, 11am-5pm Thurs.-Sun.) is a historic mid-century building designed by iconic architect E. Stewart Williams in 1955. Inside, a collective of 13 unique shops feature vintage and new furniture, home accessories, and art. **Soukie Modern** (www.soukiemodern.com) offers Moroccan-inspired, handcrafted home textiles, including rugs, home accessories, furniture, wedding blankets, and bags, while the curated vintage shop **Lindy California** (www.lindycalifornia.com) sells pedigreed decor and jewelry finds. And **Towne Palm Springs** (www.towneps.com) features vintage and modern furniture, accessories, and art.

Fully outfit the lanai in time for your retro cocktail party with vintage household items from **Dazzles** (1035 N. Palm Canyon Dr., 760/327-1446, www.visitpalmsprings.com, noon-5pm Wed., Fri-Mon.), a cheerful treasure trove stuffed into a defunct mid-century hotel. Oh, and be sure to outfit yourself, too—the collection of Bakelite and colorful costume jewelry is unparalleled.

After visiting **A La MOD** (844 N. Palm Canyon Dr., 760/327-0707, www.alamodps.com, 10:30am-5pm Mon.-Sat., noon-4pm Sun.), with its room after groovy room of impeccable vintage furnishings, you might just wish you could move in here instead of trying to update your own place to be this stylish. Couches, lamps, tables, chairs, bookends—one of each, please.

The large glass front of **Christopher Anthony Ltd.** (800 N. Palm Canyon Dr., 760/322-0600, www.christopheranthonyltd.com, 10am-6pm Mon., Wed.-Sat., noon-5pm Sun.) encourages window shopping with its eye-catching collection of high-end, mid-century home collectibles and an original line of retro-inspired lighting and furnishings. From sleek 1960s lounge chairs to abstract paintings, it's everything you need to seriously step up your household game.

Flow Modern Design (768 N. Palm Canyon Dr., 760/322-0768, www.flowmodern.com, 10:30am-5:30pm Mon. and Wed.-Sat., noon-5pm Sun.) is both a shop and gallery specializing in carefully selected mid-century modern fine furniture, art, jewelry, and accessories, including silver and brass pieces. Favorites include Milo Baughman, Arthur Elrod, and Scandinavian Glass and Rosenthal Studio Pieces. Flow Modern is a 1st Dibs dealer, a leading marketplace for globally selected rare and beautiful objects. The gallery features rotating exhibits of photography, painting, and sculpture.

Vintage cuff links? Check. Chunky necklaces? Check. Animal curios, curvy lamps, and massive multicolored glassware collection? Check, check, and check. Find it all at **Bon Vivant** (766 N. Palm Canyon Dr., 760/534-3197, www.gmcb.com/shop, 10am-5pm Thurs.-Mon.), situated in the street level floor of the original Albert Frey-designed Kocher-Samson building.

Gift and Home

Pelago (901 N. Palm Canyon Dr. #101, 760/322-3999, www.pelagopalmsprings.com, 10am-5pm Mon.-Fri., 10am-6pm Sat., 11am-5pm Sun.) offers a tempting array of vibrantly colored home and fashion accessories, including place, floor, and table mats. It's a good place to stock up on gifts for yourself and others.

Find original retro-style art, prints, books, and other merchandise evocative of atomic-era Palm Springs by the artist Shag (aka Josh Agle) at **Shag: The Store** (725 N. Palm Canyon Dr., 760/322-3400, www.shagthestore.com, 10am-5pm Mon.-Thurs., 10am-8pm Fri.-Sat.).

BKB Art + Design (388 N. Palm Canyon Dr., 760/821-3764, https://bkbceramics.com, 11am-3pm Mon. and Fri., 11am-5pm Sat. and Sun.) brings the spirit of the high desert to the low desert. Artists from Joshua Tree-area studios supply the chic store with a curated collection of contemporary art, including weavings, ceramic planters, mugs, painted tiles, and clothing.

Fashion

Iconic Atomic (1103 N. Palm Canyon Drive, 760/322-0777, www.iconicatomic.com, 10am-6pm Thurs.-Mon.) is a cheerful shop specializing in vintage clothing and accessories as well as bonus housewares from the 1960s and '70s. You might find party dresses, sport coats, tiki ware, vintage magazines, or furniture.

Local fashion design star Trina Turk has come to be synonymous with California chic. Her flagship store, **Trina Turk** (891 and 895-897 N. Palm Canyon Dr., 760/416-2856, www.trinaturk.com, 10am-6pm Mon.-Sat., 11am-5pm Sun.) occupies a luxurious glass-walled corner space originally designed by Albert Frey. The revamped modernist bohemian location features women's apparel, accessories, and Mr. Turk menswear.

★ **Elizabeth and Prince** (800 N. Palm Canyon Dr., Suite A, 760/992-5800, www.elizabethandprince.com, 10am-5pm daily) is an elegant boutique offering a curated collection of chic, modern clothing brands, and accessories. New York transplants, co-owners Analisa and Shawn Holoubek are slowly expanding their stylish empire from their original location in La Quinta to boutiques in Palm Desert and Palm Springs. Their hand-selected collection includes designers like Ulla Johnson, Humanoid, and Raquel Allegra.

Should you find yourself in a fashion emergency while on vacation, **The Frippery** (664 N. Palm Canyon Dr., 760/699-5365, www.thefrippery.com, 11am-5pm Thurs.-Sat., 11am-4pm Wed. and Sun.) has vintage finery for many different desert scenarios from resort lounging in Palm Springs to boulder gazing in Joshua Tree. Their collection ranges from mod to bohemian with accessories to complete your look.

1: the Uptown Design District **2:** Escena Golf Club

1

2

CENTRAL PALM SPRINGS AND DOWNTOWN

The main downtown drag, which runs along Palm Canyon Drive from Alejo Road to Ramon Road, tends to be much more touristy than the Design District. Since 2015, downtown Palm Springs has seen a lot of corporate development: the seven-story Kimpton Rowan Hotel, a giant fancy Starbucks, Tommy Bahama Restaurant and bar, West Elm, and H&M now mingle with small mom-and-pop shops. While downtown doesn't constitute a shopping destination, some of the stores are fun to browse, and you can find gifts, ice cream, bathing suits, fast fashion, and skin products that may also come in handy for your vacation predicament. Filtering down from the design district, a few shops showcase contemporary home decor and vintage finds.

Every Thursday, the downtown blocks of Palm Canyon Drive close to vehicles and open to **Villagefest** (www.villagefest.org, 6pm-10pm Thurs. Oct.-May, 7pm-10pm Thurs. June-Sept.). Over 180 vendors display art, sell handcrafted items, and set up food booths, and many shops, galleries, and restaurants stay open late.

Accessories

When my sunglasses broke on the first day of my Palm Springs vacation, I squinted up and down Palm Springs' downtown until I stumbled upon **Sunglasses of Palm Springs** (152 N. Palm Canyon Dr., 760/322-1344, 10am-3pm Mon.-Fri., 10am-9pm Sat., 10am-5pm Sun.). A store that may have moderate standing in a normal shopping area, in Palm Springs, where the sun blazes 300 days of the year, it can make or break your vacation. Whether you want to refresh your style or save yourself with this desert necessity, they have a great selection of styles and price points from Ray Ban to Prada.

Vintage

Palm Canyon Galleria (457 N. Palm Canyon Dr., 760/323-4576, 11am-5pm Thurs.-Mon.) is an antiques collective that brings together six shops to feature 20th-century home furnishings, ceramics, metal craft, art, and international design.

Gift and Home

★ **Destination PSP** (170 N. Palm Canyon Dr., 760/354-9154, www.destinationpsp.com, 9am-8pm Sun.-Wed., 9am-10pm Thurs., 9am-9pm Fri.-Sat.) offers a colorful and wide-ranging array of originally designed merchandise for the Palm Springs lifestyle, including swim apparel, towels, and housewares such as serving trays and coasters, decor, and gifts. This is a great place to pick up souvenirs and contemporary mid-century-inspired pieces for gift giving and living.

Sports and Recreation

DAY SPAS

Many of Palm Springs' larger resort hotels offer spa services, including massage and skin and body treatments. A few have standout day spas with services such as deep tissue massage, raw botanical treatments, or private pools. They cater to guests and non-guests, individuals and couples; a few are good for spa parties or groups. The town of Desert Hot Springs 12 miles north (a 20-minute drive) has a cluster of spa hotels with swimming pools and hot tubs that are fed by the natural hot mineral springs for which the town is named. The Coachella Valley to the south has luxurious destination spas located within several of the valley's major resorts.

Part of the classic Avalon Hotel, **Estrella Spa** (415 S. Belardo Rd., www.avalonpalmsprings.com, 760/318-3000, 9am-5:30pm Sun.-Thurs., 9am-7pm Fri.-Sat.), is located in a garden hacienda with access to an outdoor hot tub with shaded day beds, massage cabanas, fitness center, Vichy steam shower, and private courtyards. They offer a full, customizable treatment menu from body scrubs and facials to massage, nails, and reflexology. Estrella Spa is good for groups and spa parties; they also offer beauty stations for hair and makeup.

Book any spa treatment at **L'Horizon Hotel and Spa** (1050 E. Palm Canyon, 760/323-1858, www.lhorizonpalmsprings.com, 9am-6pm Sun.-Thurs., 9am-8pm Fri.-Sat.) for entry to the elegantly intimate indoor-outdoor space, including swimming pool, private outdoor showers, and white canvas cabanas. Aromatherapy massages, revitalizing body treatments and wraps, and facials are complemented by a fresh juice bar and poolside cocktail bar.

The hip Ace Hotel features organic treatments with raw botanical products in its **Feel Good Spa** (701 E. Palm Canyon Dr., 760/866-6188, www.acehotel.com, feelgoodspa@acehotel.com, by appointment 9am-6pm Sun.-Thurs., 9am-8pm Fri.-Sat.). Body treatments range from body masks and reflexology to massage and facials and can be booked for individuals and groups. The spa is located poolside with easy access to the popular swimming pool and open-air bar.

The **Palm Springs Yacht Club** spa (Parker Hotel, 4200 E. Palm Canyon Dr., 760/770-5000, 9am-7pm Mon.-Thurs., 8am-7pm Fri.-Sun.) is its own destination within the sprawling Parker Hotel grounds, offering massages, facials and waxing, scrubs and wraps, and natural nail services. A nautical blue-and-white design launches your spa voyage into a sea of pampering consisting of an idyllic indoor pool, 15 private treatment rooms, private outdoor deck for post-massage cocktails, and garden paths.

GOLF

Palm Springs is a golfing destination with its moderate winter temperatures and spectacular mountain views. Within Palm Springs proper, there are a few standout courses for visitors. The Coachella Valley to the east and south is a golfing mecca, boasting more than 100 golf courses. Many of these are located within hotel resorts so you enjoy the best of all worlds.

Most golf courses maintain online booking for tee times on their website. Pricing is dynamic, reflecting real-time conditions, including weather, demand, and other market factors.

Booking Resources

Stand-By Golf (760/321-2665, www.standbygolf.com, 7am-7pm daily) is a comprehensive booking site that is able to search for tee times in all Coachella Valley communities, including Palm Springs, Cathedral City, Rancho Mirage, Palm Desert, Indian Wells, La Quinta, and Indio. You can search by desired tee time, price range, and course. Book directly through their website.

Golf Now (800/752-9020, www.golfnow.com, 5am-5pm) offers an online tee time retail service for Palm Springs and other international golfing destinations. Search for daily available tee times to book online through their website (www.golfnow.com) or by phone.

Public Courses

Escena Golf Club (1100 Clubhouse View Dr., 760/778-2737, www.escenagolf.com, 6:30am-9pm daily, $34-109) is as much about the setting as it is about golf. The dramatic mountain backdrop, palm trees, and native landscaping make the public 18-hole, par 72 championship golf course spanning 172 acres. Golf club rentals are available ($65 pp), and there are an on-site **bar and grill** (6:30am-9pm daily) and pro shop. Tee times can book quickly on weekends.

The **Indian Canyons Golf Resort** (1097 Murray Canyon Dr., 760/833-8700, www.indiancanyonsgolf.com, $45-125) maintains two distinct golf courses set on 550 acres of Native American tribal property; both are 18-hole championship courses. The classic par 72 North Course plays 6,943 yards set in the canyon district and is surrounded on three sides by the San Jacinto Mountains. The course, designed by noted architect William F. Bell, dates to 1961 and winds through historic mid-century properties, including some originally owned by Walt Disney. The famous Walt Disney fountain acts as a water hazard and visual centerpiece, shooting water jets more than 100 feet high.

The par 72 South Course was redesigned in 2004. The 6,582-yard championship course features four large lakes, five par 5 holes, rolling mounds, fairways, and hundreds of native palm trees important to the Agua Caliente tribe. There are on-site club rentals, a pro shop, and restaurant.

Tahquitz Creek Golf Course (1885 Golf Club Dr., 760/328-1005, www.tahquitzgolfresort.com, 6am-6pm daily) is a public course offering a pro shop, bar and grill, and two courses. The Legend Course was designed in 1957 and offers a traditional country club-style golf experience. The 18-hole regulation golf course plays more than 6,800 yards and meanders through historic neighborhoods with undulating "push up" greens. The Resort Course is a par 36 regulation course designed in 1995. It features environmentally friendly design elements, including the use of drought-tolerant native landscaping, reclaimed irrigation, and reclaimed materials for mounding. The Resort plays more than 6,700 yards and offers tees for various handicaps to create a fair playing field. Rental clubs are available ($55 before twilight; $30 after twilight).

HIKING

Although it may be difficult to tear yourself away from the hotel swimming pool, Palm Springs offers some good hiking opportunities in its surrounding canyons and mountains. A few trails leave directly from near the Palm Springs Art Museum, climbing into the foothills and offering views of Palm Springs and the Coachella Valley. Locals treat these as workout trails, but in addition to the health benefits, they pay off with sweeping views.

Palm Springs

Trails in Palm Springs are exposed and are best hiked **October-March,** when temperatures are more moderate. If hiking other times of the year, start very early (plan to finish by 9am-10am during summer) and make sure you are off the trail before the heat of the day. Carry plenty of water, sunscreen, and a hat for shade.

PALM SPRINGS MUSEUM TRAIL

Distance: 2 miles round-trip
Duration: 1.5-2 hours
Elevation gain: 1,000 feet
Effort: Moderate
Trailhead: North parking lot of the Palm Springs Art Museum
Directions: From the Palm Springs Visitors Center, head south on N. Palm Canyon Drive for 2.9 miles. Turn right on Tahquitz Canyon Drive. Drive one block, then turn right on North Museum Drive. Pass the Palm Springs Art Museum on your left and make a left into the north parking lot. The signed trailhead begins from the parking lot.

Don't let the two-mile round-trip distance or the quaint trail name fool you. This is an intensely steep hike. The payoff is the bird's-eye view of downtown Palm Springs.

From the **Palm Springs Art Museum** (101 N. Museum Dr.), the trail starts with a bang in a series of tightly wound switchbacks that navigate the rocky hillside and never let up until the summit. (Stick to the main trail and avoid social trails that cut switchbacks and cause erosion.) The summit is marked by a picnic table, where you can have a triumphant slug of water or a snack as you look out over the modernist lines of Palm Springs below. Just beyond the summit, the trail intersects with the five-mile **North Lykken Trail** that continues north and south above Palm Springs. The Museum Trail also links up with the Skyline Trail, the backbone of the infamous Cactus to Clouds Hike that takes intrepid hikers a grueling 22 miles up to 10,400 feet in elevation from the desert floor to the peak of Mount San Jacinto in one day.

SOUTH CARL LYKKEN TRAIL

Distance: 6 miles round-trip to Tahquitz Canyon overlook (out-and-back along same route)
Duration: 2-3 hours
Elevation gain: 1,000 feet
Effort: Moderate
Trailhead: S. Palm Canyon Drive
Directions: From the Palm Springs Visitors Center, take N. Palm Canyon Drive south for 6.4 miles; continue straight when it turns into S. Palm Canyon Drive. The signed trailhead is on the west (right) side of S. Palm Canyon Drive just south of Canyon Heights Road.

This exposed hike into the toothy hills outlining the west side of Palm Springs offers excellent views of Palm Springs with a bonus peek into Tahquitz Canyon. The trail is in a neighborhood and is used by locals during the early morning hours and cooler winter months. There is a good reason—rewarding climbs give way to expansive city views as the trail levels out and winds along a north and east-facing ridge.

The trail begins at a **signed trailhead** near the road at 550 feet in elevation. It heads west before beginning a series of switchbacks up to a lookout point, checking in at 1,170 feet. From here the trail levels out, winding along the rocky hillside before climbing again to top out at 1,550 feet above **Tahquitz Canyon.** This is a good turnaround point, marked by picnic tables, and you can return the way you came.

It is also possible to continue the trail down a steep drop to street level, where it intersects with a second trailhead at the end of W. Mesquite Avenue. You can arrange for a car shuttle from here or, as one enterprising hiker suggested, call a cab or rideshare to get back to your hotel.

This trail is completely exposed. Carry enough **water,** and make sure you start early and are off the trail no later than midmorning in summer months. The good news is that even if you are not able to make it to the final turnaround point, the continuous views mean that hiking almost any length of the trail will be a satisfying experience.

ARABY TRAIL

Distance: 3 miles round-trip
Duration: 2 hours
Elevation gain: 800 feet
Effort: Moderate
Trailhead: South Palm Springs at Rim Road/Southridge Road. Parking area is on the right, past the turnoff from Highway 111.

The Araby Trail reaches excellent heights above the city of Palm Springs, winding past celebrity homes and offering expansive views of the town and the windmills to the north. This is a popular neighborhood exercise trail, and it does provide a great workout while rewarding with interesting views and architecture.

From the parking area, the trail cuts switchbacks steeply up the rocky hillside to the south, passing famed architect John Lautner's dramatic **Elrod House** with its circular bladed rooftop. (This is where part of the 1971 James Bond thriller *Diamonds Are Forever* was filmed.) Next door is the groovy bachelor pad of actor **Steve McQueen.** Continue climbing the steep switchbacks and you'll pass the crowning rooflines of yet another celebrity house and architectural wonder: The **Bob Hope Residence,** a massive domed structure designed by John Lautner that sits perched on the hillside. It is the highest structure in Palm Springs. The trail winds to a ridge above his house, a good place to turn around and return.

★ Indian Canyons

The **Indian Canyons** (760/323-6018, www.indian-canyons.com, 8am-5pm daily Oct.-June; 8am-5pm Fri.-Sun. July-Sept., day use $9-11) refer to the rugged, scenic canyons that burrow into the flanks of the San Jacinto Mountains in the southwest corner of Palm Springs. The steep, often snowcapped San Jacintos feed the seasonal streams that transform the rocky canyons in spring. Natural fan palm oases and groundwater feed perennial pools and streams year-round, making the canyons a haven

Indian Canyons:

from the surrounding arid landscape and a delight for hikers.

The Indian Canyons are sacred to the Agua Caliente Band of Cahuilla Indians who own and manage the land. Ancestors of the Agua Caliente Cahuilla settled Tahquitz, Andreas, Murray, Palm, and Chino Canyons, establishing villages and irrigating and planting crops. The Agua Caliente own 32,000 acres spread across desert and mountains in the Palm Springs area. Tahquitz and three other canyons are listed on the National Register of Historic Places, while Palm Canyon boasts the world's largest California fan palm oasis.

These trails are best hiked **October-March** due to soaring temperatures. You have the best chance of encountering the seasonal snowmelt streams that feed these canyons in early spring. However, since the canyons offer short hikes with some shade, visiting the canyons at other times of the year is also worthwhile. When it is hot, start early (the canyons open at 8am year-round). Seasonal **ranger talks** are open to the public and are held at the Trading Post (10am Mon.-Thurs.) and at Andreas Canyon (1pm). Ranger-led interpretive hikes are also available October-June (10am-11:30am and 1pm-2:30pm).

GETTING THERE

A **Trading Post** and ranger station on South Palm Canyon Drive is the hub for exploring Andreas, Murray, and Palm Canyons. The Trading Post has hiking maps, drinks and snacks, books, jewelry, and Indian pottery, baskets, and weaving. Restrooms and parking are available. To get there from the Palm Springs Visitors Center (2901 N. Palm Canyon Dr.), head south on Palm Canyon Drive for nine miles until the road ends at the Trading Post and Palm Canyon overlook. Visitors will pass through a toll gate to pay the entrance fee prior to reaching the Trading Post.

The entrance to **Tahquitz Canyon** (www.tahquitzcanyon.com) is from the Tahquitz Visitors Center, where water, maps, parking, and restrooms are available. From the Palm Springs Visitors Center (2901 N. Palm Canyon Dr.), head south on Palm Canyon Drive for 3.8 miles and turn right on Mesquite Avenue. The road ends at the **Tahquitz Canyon Visitors Center** (500 W. Mesquite Ave.) in 0.4 mile.

TAHQUITZ CANYON

Distance: 2 miles round-trip
Duration: 1 hour
Elevation gain: 240 feet
Effort: Easy
Trailhead: Tahquitz Canyon Visitors Center

Tahquitz Canyon is the most popular trail in the Indian Canyons, and for good reason. This moderate two-mile loop winds through a scenic, rocky canyon full of native vegetation across an ancient **Cahuilla village site** to end at Tahquitz Falls, a rare **desert waterfall.** At the visitors center, pay your fee and pick up a Tahquitz Canyon trail guide for interpretive descriptions of historic and scenic points along the trail. (Water is also available for purchase.)

The trail follows a seasonal creek dependent on snowmelt from the San Jacinto Mountains. The best time to hike is **February-April** for more moderate canyon temperatures and the highest chance of water in the canyon. On the way back you'll have wide views of Palm Springs and the Coachella Valley to the east.

LOWER PALM CANYON TRAIL

Distance: 2.2 miles round-trip
Duration: 1 hour
Elevation gain: 100 feet
Effort: Easy
Trailhead: Trading Post and scenic overlook for Palm Canyon
Directions: From the Palm Springs Visitors Center (2901 N. Palm Canyon Dr.), head south for nine miles until Palm Canyon Drive ends at the Trading Post and Palm Canyon overlook.

You'll catch the views of the world's largest fan palm oasis, hundreds of green palms clustered improbably at the bottom of a rocky gorge,

1: Palm Springs Museum Trailhead 2: the Indian Canyons 3: Tahquitz Creek 4: well-watered Murray Canyon in the Indian Canyons

PALM SPRINGS
Welcome to the
Museum Trailhead
1

2

3

4

before strolling down to the canyon floor to be dwarfed by their primordial trunks. Fifteen miles long, Palm Canyon marks the divide between the Santa Rosa and San Jacinto Mountains. It offers stunning contrasts—the lush proliferation of palms set against the craggy canyon walls and arid desert.

A graded trail winds down into the canyon from the **Palm Canyon overlook.** The trail wanders through mammoth palms offering shaggy seclusion and shade. Depending on the season and snowmelt, you'll come across secret pools and intermittent streams studded with boulders. The canyon feels mysterious and Jurassic—it wouldn't seem out of place to catch a glimpse of a dinosaur strolling along. You'll follow a trail on the right side of the canyon above the level of the streambed for about 0.7 mile, continuing through spectacular palm groves. At 0.7 mile the trail crosses to the left side of the canyon, an easy or more difficult task depending on water flow in the canyon. Soon (after a mile total), the palms become less dense and the trail becomes exposed, forking with the **East Fork** and **Victor Trails**. This is a good turnaround point if your goal was to experience the palm oasis. Return the way you came (the full trail travels 15 miles one-way). Seasonal **ranger-led hikes** (10am Fri.-Sun. Oct.-June) are also available.

ANDREAS CANYON LOOP

Distance: 2 miles round-trip
Duration: 1 hour
Elevation gain: 50 feet
Effort: Easy
Trailhead: A picnic area and trailheads for Andreas and Murray Canyons
Directions: From the intersection of S. Palm Canyon Drive and Highway 111, continue south for under 3 miles, following signs for Indian Canyons. After the toll, take the road to the right for 0.7 mile until it ends. Start by hiking the right (north) side of the canyon to follow the creek.

The trail through lovely Andreas Canyon follows a permanent creek through hundreds of native California fan palms. Secluded pools and striking rock formations make this well worth the small amount of effort the hike requires. Until the late 1800s, the Cahuilla used the creek to irrigate crops of melons, corn, and pumpkins. The turnaround point for this scenic desert stroll is a fence blocking off land for the **Andreas Canyon Club**. The secretive and exclusive club was formed in 1923. Members bought land from the Southern Pacific Railroad and built a series of rock houses (22 in all) into the craggy hills to blend in with the desert landscape. A clubhouse was built in 1925. Prior to procuring the land, members camped in the canyon's streambed in rock caches. The return route on the left side of the canyon follows a high ridge south of the stream. Seasonal **ranger-led hikes** (1pm Fri.-Sun. Oct.-June) are also available.

MURRAY CANYON

Distance: 4 miles round-trip
Duration: 2 hours
Elevation gain: 500 feet
Effort: Moderate
Trailhead: A picnic area and trailheads for Andreas and Murray Canyons
Directions: From the intersection of S. Palm Canyon Drive and Highway 111, continue south for under 3 miles, following signs for Indian Canyons. After the toll, take the road to the right for 0.7 mile until it ends.

The winding trail through Murray Canyon offers a longer chance to explore a palm-filled canyon than its scenic neighbor Andreas.

The trail begins at the parking area for Andreas and Murray Canyons and heads south before entering **Murray Canyon** proper. It delves into the lower edges of the San Jacinto Mountains, providing views of its soaring cliffs as you meander through the palm-enclosed, stream-crossed canyon. The second half of the trail requires hopping back and forth across a picturesque stream that varies in intensity depending on the season. California fan palms are abundant and mixed in with a scattering of cacti, desert willows, and cottonwoods. A series of gentle cascades (**Seven Sisters Waterfall**) marks the end of the hike. Return the way you came.

★ Mount San Jacinto State Park

The granite peaks of the San Jacinto Mountains may be a world away from the sunbaked desert floor, but the miracle of engineering that is the **Palm Springs Aerial Tramway** (www.pstramway.com) was designed to allow visitors to reach the cool mountain air in about 10 minutes.

The tramway leaves from Valley Station on the desert floor (elevation 2,643 feet) and lifts visitors on a dizzying ride via suspended cable cars to traverse the length of rugged Chino Canyon, alighting in a crisp alpine climate at Mountain Station (elevation 8,516 feet) in **Mount San Jacinto State Park** (951/659-2607, www.parks.ca.gov). From Mountain Station, a network of trails (totaling 54 miles within the 14,000-acre wilderness) leads to pine forests, meadows, and striking views. Stop at the **Long Valley Ranger Station** (0.25 mile west of Mountain Station) for maps and info. All trails (except the Long Valley Discovery Trail and Desert View Trail) require that you check in and complete a **day-use permit.**

Because of the drastic change in elevation, the hiking season generally runs **April–November.** Keep in mind that temperatures may be very cold, and trails may be impassable due to snow and ice. Expect a 30- to 40-degree temperature difference from the valley floor.

LONG VALLEY DISCOVERY TRAIL

Distance: 0.6 mile round-trip
Duration: 0.5 hour
Elevation gain: Negligible
Effort: Easy
Trailhead: Upper Terminal Mountain Station via the Palm Springs Aerial Tramway

This easy, level nature trail lies outside the back entrance of **Mountain Station,** after a thrilling lift from the **Palm Springs Aerial Tramway** to the top of Mount San Jacinto State Park. The signed trail starts at the bottom of the walkway and follows a 0.6-mile loop through pine forest and past a gorgeous meadow with interpretive signs providing an introduction to the park's plants and animals.

DESERT VIEW TRAIL

Distance: 1.6 miles round-trip
Duration: 1 hour
Elevation gain: 160 feet
Effort: Easy-moderate
Trailhead: Upper Terminal Mountain Station via the Palm Springs Aerial Tramway. Exit Mountain Station via the back entrance. The signed trail starts at the bottom of the walkway leading to trails, wilderness, and a ranger station.

Slightly longer than the Long Valley Discovery Trail, this trail offers another option from the **Mountain Station** after your **tram ride** to the top. Enjoy the striking contrasts between this fresh alpine haven and the austere desert below via an easy to moderate loop trail that clocks in at less than two miles. The trail, which can be hiked clockwise or counterclockwise, undulates through rich pine forest, passing five rocky lookouts (notches) that give way to sweeping views of the Coachella Valley below. Each notch gives a different panoramic perspective and up close views of colorful rock outcroppings.

ROUND VALLEY LOOP TO WELLMAN DIVIDE

Distance: 4.5-6.5 miles round-trip
Duration: 3-4 hours
Elevation gain: 1,300 feet
Effort: Moderate
Trailhead: Long Valley Ranger Station
Directions: Take the Palm Springs Aerial Tramway to the Upper Terminal Mountain Station. From Mountain Station, the Ranger Station is 0.25 mile to the west. Check in and complete a day-use pass before beginning your hike.

Hike the Round Valley Loop with lovely Round Valley and its luxuriant meadow as your destination (4.5 miles round-trip) or tack on a steep addendum (6.5 miles round-trip) to see the spectacular views from Wellman Divide.

From the Long Valley Ranger Station, follow the well-marked trail (**Low Trail** on maps) southeast toward Round Valley. The trail climbs steadily through pine forests. In early summer you may be crossing or traveling alongside bubbling seasonal snowmelt streams. At 1.8 miles the trail splits. Continue right toward Round Valley and the meadow. You will reach **Round Valley** at 2.1 miles; it's a satisfying destination. Many people use it as an overnight spot, camping at the Round Valley **backcountry campground** or Tamarack Valley to the north.

Continuing from Round Valley the trail gets real, climbing 660 feet over one mile. The views from **Wellman Divide** make the short and steep trek worth it. They're spectacular, casting a visual net toward venerable Tahquitz Peak and deeper over the Santa Rosa Mountains. From here it's only 2.7 miles to San Jacinto Peak.

Assuming you've had enough for the day (continuing on to San Jacinto Peak will add an additional 5.4 miles round-trip), return 0.3 mile to a trail junction past Round Valley. Mix it up by taking the right loop (**High Trail** on maps). This will add a mere 0.3 mile to your hike but will vary your return scenery and give you unexpected views of Mountain Station as you descend the last mile to the ranger station.

SAN JACINTO PEAK

Distance: 12 miles round-trip
Duration: 6 hours
Elevation gain: 2,300 feet
Effort: Strenuous
Trailhead: Long Valley Ranger Station
Directions: Take the Palm Springs Aerial Tramway to the Upper Terminal Mountain Station. From Mountain Station, the Ranger Station is 0.25 mile to the west. Check in and complete a day-use pass before beginning your hike.

Naturalist John Muir proclaimed the view from San Jacinto Peak to be one of the most sublime on earth. Topographically, it makes sense. San Jacinto Peak is the highest peak in the San Jacinto Mountains and one of the most prominent peaks in the contiguous United States, its north escarpment rising 10,000 feet in seven miles from the San Gorgonio Pass and its low desert wind farms. The peak towers over Palm Springs to the west and the mountain village of Idyllwild to the south. The vistas from the top are amazing, taking in the Coachella Valley, Salton Sea, and looking north to the impressive San Bernardino Mountains and lofty San Gorgonio Mountain.

There are several routes to San Jacinto Peak, including from the town of Idyllwild. The most direct (and shortest) route begins from the top of the Palm Springs Aerial Tramway. From the Long Valley Ranger Station, follow the well-marked trail (**Low Trail** on maps) southeast toward Round Valley. The trail winds up steadily through pine forests. In early summer if there has been a good season of winter snowfall, you may come across lively seasonal streams. At 1.8 miles the trail splits. Continue right toward Round Valley, reaching **Round Valley** at 2.1 miles. From here the trail begins to climb more seriously toward Wellman Divide, climbing 660 feet over the course of one mile. Take in the spectacular views from **Wellman Divide;** Tahquitz Peak and the Santa Rosa Mountains are in your sights. From here it's only 2.7 miles to San Jacinto Peak. Follow the trail north toward San Jacinto Peak as it switchbacks steeply and the views grow increasingly sweeping. Just below the peak (0.3 mile) the trail splits again. Follow the steep trail up to the giant granite massif that is **San Jacinto Peak**. Soak in the views from the steep (and sometimes windy) pinnacle.

Return the way you came. After Round Valley you will reach a split with the Low and High Trails. Both return to the Long Valley Ranger Station. The **High Trail** (right split) adds a small amount of mileage (0.3 mile), but it takes you over ground you haven't covered. The good news: either way you're close to some well-earned food, drinks, and continued views (from the comfort of a chair) at Mountain Station.

BIKING

Many hotels offer complimentary cruiser bikes for touring Palm Springs. Scenic bike paths thread along the base of the rocky foothills and through Palm Springs' historic neighborhoods, past old Rat Pack-era haunts with architectural pedigree and storied histories.

If you want to get more serious about biking, **Big Wheel Tours** (www.bwbtours.com, rentals $12-20 hourly, $25-60 half day, $35-80 per day, $70-195 half week, $90-295 weekly, tours $105-250) offers bike rentals and guided tours. Biking is best **October-May.** Summers can be way too hot. If you do bike in summer, start early and return no later than midmorning.

For cruising around town, a network of paved bike paths traverses Palm Springs, extending from Indian Canyon Drive northeast of the Palm Springs Visitors Center south toward the Indian Canyons and Murray Canyon Drive and southeast to Golf Club Drive. There are several types of bike paths: Class One (road-separated trails with exclusive right-of-way for bicycles and pedestrians), Class Two (striped lanes for one-way bike travel on city streets), and Class Three (signed trails that share roads with motor vehicles and no on-street striping).

Bike Paths

CITYWIDE TOUR

For a great introduction to town, take the **Citywide Tour** (13 miles). This ride brings you on a wide loop around Palm Springs, from residential neighborhoods to golf courses and country clubs to civic buildings. Start on the north end of town at Palm Canyon Drive and Tachevah Drive. The trail begins by heading west toward the mountains to explore historic residential neighborhoods, including Las Palmas. It then heads south, skirting the foothills of the San Jacinto Mountains and passing the Palm Springs Art Museum. The trail continues south to weave through the country clubs and golf course on the south end of town. On the return, the loop makes an arc through the eastern side of town paralleling the Palm Springs International Airport and some of Palm Springs' civic buildings.

DOWNTOWN TOUR

Cruise around downtown Palm Springs on the **Downtown Tour** (3 miles), a quieter take on Palm Springs' bustling center. Begin at Palm Canyon Drive and Alejo. The first part of the loop runs along the foot of the mountains along Belardo Road. It parallels the main downtown thoroughfares of Palm Canyon Drive and Indian Canyon Drive and dips past the Palm Springs Art Museum. The route continues down to Ramon Road, where it begins its northward return path at the north/south Calle El Segundo.

DEEPWELL TOUR

For an easy and scenic trip, try the **Deepwell Tour** (3.5 miles). This route begins at Mesquite Avenue and Sunrise Way to follow Calle Palo Fiera and Camino Real south (with a quick eastward jog on E. Palm Canyon Dr.) to take you through the palm-lined residential streets of one of the city's older neighborhoods on the south end of town. The loop returns via LaVerne and Sunrise Way to connect again with Mesquite Avenue.

Bike Rentals

Many hotels offer complimentary cruiser bikes for tooling around town. If your hotel does not have bikes or if you would like a mountain, road, tandem, or electric bike, they are available for rent at two locations.

BIKE Palm Springs Bike Rentals (194 S. Indian Canyon, 760/832-8912, www.bikepsrentals.com, 8am-5pm daily Oct.-June, 8am-10am July-Sept.) is located in downtown Palm Springs next to Hotel Zoso. They rent premium cruisers ($25 for four hours, $35 per day), road bikes with carbon forks ($35 for up to four hours, $50 per day), full-suspension mountain bikes ($50 for up to four hours, $65 per day), tandems ($40 for four hours, $50 per day), electric bikes ($44 for four hours, $60 per day), as well as child bikes and bike carriers ($15 for four hours, $20 per day). Rentals include free maps with touring routes, locks, and helmets.

Big Wheel Tours (760/779-1837, www.bwbtours.com, tours daily 8am-8pm, summer hours vary, rentals by reservation) features KHS and Benno brand bicycles for rent in the

Palm Springs area. Cruisers, mountain bikes, hybrids, and road bikes are available for rent by the hour ($12-18), half day ($25-40), full day ($35-60), and week ($90-195). Big Wheel Tours is based in Palm Desert, 15 miles southeast of Palm Springs in the Coachella Valley, but their bikes are available for delivery ($25 per delivery; $35 west of Gene Autry in Palm Springs; call to reserve).

Big Wheel Tours also offers bike tours (four hours, departs 8am and 1pm daily Oct.-May, 7am daily June-Sept., $105 pp). Its **Earthquake Canyon Express Tour** for beginner to intermediate riders travels the San Andreas fault zone along the Colorado and Mojave Desert transition with views of the Salton Sea. The Indian Canyon Bike and Hike offers a 10-mile round-trip excursion through some of Palm Springs historic neighborhoods combined with a scenic nature walk in well-watered Andreas Canyon. Customized Palm Springs mountain bike tours are also available (4-6 hours, $105-185 pp).

HORSEBACK RIDING

Beyond its reputation as a sleek resort town, Palm Springs has a Wild West side. The last of the traditional ranch-style inns offering city slickers an escape to simpler times is the historic **Smoke Tree Stables** (2500 S. Toledo Ave., 760/327-1372, www.smoketreestables.com, Oct.-May, $120 pp). Established in 1927, they offer guided horseback trail rides that allow you to experience the striking Palm Springs desert. Trips follow more than 150 miles of riding trails along the mountain foothills surrounding Palm Springs and through the palm oasis-filled Indian Canyons.

Rides are offered hourly during the season. Reservations are not necessary (rides are first-come, first-served), but you should call prior to your ride to confirm times, weather, and availability, and plan to arrive at least 30 minutes prior to departure. **One-hour trail rides** (8am-2pm every hour, $60 pp) follow a trail along the base of the Santa Rosa Mountains. **Murray Canyon Haul Rides** (9am, 11am, and 1pm daily, $120) follow the streams and palms of Andreas and Murray Canyons. Private guided trail rides ($50 per guide per hour) are available by advance reservation.

PARKS

Palm Springs is nestled near such spectacular wilderness parks as Joshua Tree National Park and Mount San Jacinto State Park, and time adventuring outdoors is best spent in these destination spots; however, a skate park and dog park near Palm Springs' downtown fill a niche.

The **Palm Springs Skate Park** (Sunrise Plaza, 401 S. Pavilion Way, 760/656-0024, noon-10pm Mon.-Fri., 9am-10pm Sat.-Sun.) taps into Southern California's history of pool skating to offer bowls for smooth, fast skating with several feet of vertical walls, pool coping, and transitions. The skate park also features street skating elements like rails, pyramids, stairs, ramps, and quarter pipes. Actual skaters were consulted in the building of this park with a fun and genuine result for board and in-line skaters of all skill levels.

The leash-free 1.5-acre **Palm Springs Dog Park** (N. Civic Dr., 760/323-8117, www.palmspringsca.gov, 6am-10pm daily, closed noon-3pm Tues. and Fri.) is behind City Hall. Separate areas for large and small dogs offer your pets a place to run free. Park benches, shade canopies, and drinking fountains round out the amenities.

Food

UPTOWN DESIGN DISTRICT AND NORTH PALM SPRINGS

Breakfast, Brunch, and Coffee

Billy Reed's Restaurant Bakery & Bar (1800 N. Palm Canyon Dr., 760/325-1946, www.billyreedspalmsprings.com, 8am-9pm daily, $8-29) resembles a Wild West saloon and bordello as seen through a fanciful 1970s lens, which, even if it didn't occur to you beforehand, might be exactly what you want in your brunch spot. Biscuits and gravy, omelets, country fried steak, tuna salad sandwiches, and daily soups are served anytime from their extensive menu filled with all-American classics. It's one of the many nice things about Palm Springs that someone can have a quirky idea, execute it, and then turn it into a comfortable favorite, where people forget about the quirk factor and simply enjoy their prime rib, fresh strawberry pie, and mimosas under chandelier lighting.

Brave the sidewalk line and start your day at ★ **Cheeky's** (622 N. Palm Canyon Dr., 760/327-7595, www.cheekysps.com, 8am-2pm daily, $7-13) for one of the most popular brunches in town. The sunny spot with a patio offers a seasonal, locally-sourced menu that changes weekly, plus classics like Blondie's eggs Benedict with bacon, arugula, and a cheddar scone; Cheeky's BLT with jalapeno bacon and pesto fries; signature housemade cinnamon rolls; and a bacon flight. Their array of breakfast drinks includes spicy Bloody Marys, fresh-pressed green juice, and white peach mimosas.

★ **Ernest Coffee** (1101 N. Palm Canyon Dr., 760/318-4154, www.ernestcoffee.com, 6am-7pm daily) is a wonderful way to start the day. This chic space has polished concrete floors, plenty of natural light, warm wood tables, and splashes of bright color. They serve the Portland-originated Stumptown coffee and fresh, locally baked pastries. They also offer an excellent list of beer, wine, and a few small plates, including cheese and charcuterie. It shares the space with the Bootlegger Tiki Bar next door. The coffee shop is named after Ernest Raymond Beaumont Gantt, better known as Don the Beachcomber, who opened the Palm Springs location of the famed tiki bar (Don the Beachcomber) in 1953. Only adults 21 and over are permitted due to their liquor license.

The original location of **Koffi** (515 N. Palm Dr., 760/416-2244, www.kofficoffee.com, 6am-7pm daily) has been gracing Palm Springs with its strong brews since 2008. The fresh, small-batch house blends are fragrantly ferried up from a roasting facility in the Coachella Valley. Food is an afterthought: standard coffee shop offerings, including scones and muffins and such. Come here for the fresh high octane, convenient location, and friendly service.

Locals' favorite ★ **Rick's Restaurant** (1973 N. Palm Canyon Dr., 760/416-0090, 6am-2pm Mon.-Fri., 6am-3pm Sat. and Sun., $8-19) doesn't do anything on a small scale. Breakfast and lunch diner classics are served in heaping and well-executed quantities. Ignore the questionable 1980s decor at this American-style diner and dig into their giant pancakes (crispy on the edges), giant cinnamon rolls, or omelets for breakfast. Order a side of the excellent bacon to go with anything. Lunch transitions into salads, cold and hot sandwiches (including Cuban pressed sandwiches), and hot plates with American and Cuban specialties.

California Cuisine

Maybe only in Palm Springs does an upscale, retro, tropical-themed restaurant with mood lighting and a neon color scheme not only make sense but also seem like a great idea. The ★ **The Tropicale Restaurant and Coral Seas Lounge** (330 E. Amado

Rd., 760/866-1952, www.thetropicale.com, 4pm-10pm Sun.-Thurs., 4pm-11pm Fri.-Sat., brunch 11am-2:45pm Sat.-Sun., $13-32) serves a very eclectic menu with a focus on Pacific Rim plates. Pizzas and sandwiches are thrown in for good measure. Deep banquette booths, chandeliers, and a buzzing tropical patio and bar are a throwback to the dinner clubs and themed cocktail bars Palm Springs does so well.

Trio (707 N. Palm Canyon Dr., 760/864-8746, www.triopalmsprings.com, 11am-10pm Mon.-Thurs., 11am-11pm Fri., 10am-11pm Sat., 10am-10pm Sun.) taps into Palm Springs' signature party persona with its splashy lighting, historic mid-century setting, lively bar, and crowd-pleasing entrées (comfort food meets California contemporary) from seared ahi tuna to mushroom linguine. Specialty cocktails are fresh, fruity, and seasonal. Be sure to make a reservation, especially on weekends. This place is popular with both locals and tourists and can be packed with groups and bachelorette parties.

Workshop Kitchen and Bar (800 N. Palm Canyon Dr., 760/459-3451, www.workshoppalmsprings.com, 5pm-10pm Sun.-Thurs., 5pm-11pm Fri.-Sat., $29-38, 10am-2pm Sun., brunch) shines most as a temple to outstanding architecture and design. The bones of the 1926 Spanish Colonial have been laid bare and recast with sleek concrete booths, a communal table, and long strands of custom lighting emphasizing the ceiling's height and the striking symmetry of the space. The soaring wood ceiling trusses have housed a bank, furniture store, and myriad other incarnations before its 2012 redesign—which snagged the prestigious 2015 James Beard Foundation Award for best restaurant design or renovation in North America. Consider it part of your touristic duty to, at least, have a carefully crafted cocktail at the altarlike bar. Soak in the space with drinks like the white rum and lime Hemingway Special or the vodka and pineapple Palm Springer. The restaurant is open for dinner, serving richly nuanced small and large plates—from house-made pâté to seared scallops. Sunday brunch features plates like Jidori chicken and waffles, and lobster breakfast burrito.

Part of the former Cary Grant estate, **Copley's** (621 N. Palm Canyon Dr., 760/327-9555, www.copleyspalmsprings.com, 5:30pm-close daily Oct.-mid-June, mid-June-Sept. closed Mondays, $22-39) offers new American fine dining in a romantic setting. The candlelit patio has the choicest seating and a stone fireplace. Entrées are geared toward the meat eater, with perfectly executed steaks, duck, fish, and lamb. A fleeting happy hour at the tiny bar brings the restaurant pricing within reach for one hour on weekdays.

Make a reservation or prepare to wait for weekend meals at **Jake's** (664 N. Palm Canyon Dr., 760/327-4400, www.jakespalmsprings.com, 11am-2:45pm lunch Tues.-Fri., 10am-2:45pm brunch Sat. and Sun; 5pm-8:45pm dinner Tues.-Thurs., 5:30pm-9:45pm dinner Fri.-Sat. $20-32). It's a popular bistro with a fun patio scene. The extensive menu has every variation of new American, Southwest, and Mediterranean-influenced dishes you can dream up. Servings are fresh and manageable, which allows you to save room for their bakery case. Specialty cocktails are crowd-pleasers with a twist by category: the Marys, ritas, sparklers, refreshers, and virgins.

American

Situated in the hip ARRIVE hotel, **Draughtsman** (1501 N. Palm Canyon Dr., 760/407-1744, draughtsmanpalmsprings.com, 11am-1am, $13-24) is as classy as a sports bar can get. Sleek glass architecture with roll up garage doors to take advantage of the weather and stylish vinyl booths meld with vegan cauliflower "McNuggets," spicy tuna nachos, burgers, and comfort entrées like chicken pot pie. DirecTV brings in the Sunday games, while cornhole and other games entertain on the expansive patio with mountain views.

1: the sleek Ernest Coffee in the Uptown Design District **2:** Rick's Restaurant **3:** Eight4Nine Restaurant and Lounge **4:** lively brunch at Pinocchio in the Desert

1

RESTAURANT
QUALITY FOOD YOU CAN TASTE
2

3

ATM
All Day Happy Hour
Bottomless Champagne $3.95
Well Drinks & Well Martini from $2.95
Martini Burger $9.95
Great Espresso Bar
All Day Breakfast & Lunch available!
4

Italian and Pizza

Birba (622 N. Palm Canyon Dr., 760/327-5678, www.birbaps.com, 5pm-11pm Wed.-Thurs. and Sun., 5pm-midnight Fri.-Sat., $10-29) offers a modern take on Italian classics, serving up small plates and wood-fired pizzas topped with savory toppings from braised greens to meatballs. Dinner is served on the bustling patio and a long indoor bar. The place is popular and can feel like a dinner mill, cranking diners through on busy nights. Make reservations online in advance and stick with the basics: pizza and beer or wine.

Mexican

It's Palm Springs. Chances are you've spent a hard day at the pool or enjoying some festive event. **El Mirasol** (266 E. Via Altamira, 760/459-3136, 11am-10pm daily, $12-20), located in the Los Arboles Hotel, offers the type of Mexican comfort food that can easily hit the spot. The signature smoky Doña Diabla sauce accompanies every meal in liter bottles. Strong margaritas and a charming patio make an easy choice for anyone staying in the hotel. The restaurant also serves poolside during the day. El Mirasol has a second location in **South Palm Springs** (140 E. Palm Canyon Dr., 760/323-0721).

Sushi

Reservations are recommended for dinner at ★ **Sandfish** (1556 N. Palm Canyon Dr, 760/537-1022, https://sandfishps.com, 4:30pm-10pm Sun.-Thurs., 4:30pm-11pm Fri.-Sat., $17-22), one of Palm Springs' newest offerings. Chef-owner Engin Onural has drawn from around the globe to create a buzzy spot with Japanese sushi and seafood uniquely paired with an extensive whiskey list. The menu is served against a stylishly spare Scandinavian interior.

Sweets

Ice Cream & Shop(pe) (part of ARRIVE hotel, 1551 N. Palm Canyon Dr. Suite A, 760/507-4005, https://icecreamandshop.com, noon-11pm Sun.-Thurs., noon-midnight Fri.-Sat., $3-8) offers an array of gourmet ice creams with scrumptious options like Mexican chocolate, pomegranate chip, and salty caramel. They offer 16 flavors daily, including vegan sorbets and ice creams. They also stock a selection of fun gifts.

CENTRAL PALM SPRINGS AND DOWNTOWN

Breakfast, Brunch, and Coffee

★ **Pinocchio in the Desert** (134 E. Tahquitz Canyon Way, 760/322-3776, www.pinocchiops.com, 7:30am-2pm daily, $7-17) is a full-on party. By somewhere around noon, the eggs and hash browns are flying onto packed tables in the kitschy setting, and the cheap bottomless mimosas are flowing. The patio gets cranked up to a feyer pitch, fanned by the pink fringed umbrellas, speedy service, and drink specials. It would be difficult to maintain such a pace, so they do everyone a favor and close at 2pm every day.

Once you manage to find the French-inspired **Farm** (6 La Plaza, La Plaza Shopping Center, 760/322-2724, 9am-2pm daily 6pm-9pm Fri. -Sat., $10-16) tucked down a walkway and nestled past a wedding chapel, it oozes charm. Farmhouse-style wooden tables are scattered under a shady canopy. Brunch-goers enjoy a new American and Provencal-inspired menu with French press coffee, mimosas, chicken and mushroom crepes, banana French toast, and other brunch specialties. Farm prides itself on its menu. Translation: they do not allow substitutions, and the food can take a while. Be prepared to choose something and relax. Friday and Saturday adds dinner with a five-course chef's-choice prix-fixe ($52) that varies daily.

The newest location of **Koffi** (650 E. Tahquitz Canyon Way, 760/318-0145, www.kofficoffee.com, 6am-6pm daily) is located in central Palm Springs near the Convention Center and hotels. They serve the same fresh small-batch house blends roasted in the Coachella Valley and standard coffee shop fare as their other locations. The large patio and setting in Kaptur Plaza add panache—a Class 1 historic site designed by famed architect Hugh Kaptur in the mid-1970s.

California Cuisine

The bright and airy **Lulu California Bistro** (200 S. Palm Canyon Dr., 760/327-5858, www.lulupalmsprings.com, 8am-11pm Sun.-Thurs., 8am-1am Fri.-Sat., $10-30) is a no-brainer with its central location on the downtown strip. The sprawling menu is solid, offering salads, panini, pastas, and entrées. The tiered dining areas, central bar with 12 hours of happy hour daily, and efficient service make for a buzzing scene.

Eight4Nine Restaurant and Lounge (849 N. Palm Canyon Dr., 760/325-8490, www.eight4nine.com, 11am-3pm and 5pm-10pm Mon.-Thurs., 11am-3pm and 5pm-11pm Fri., 9am-3pm and 5pm-11pm Sat., 9am-3pm and 5pm-10pm Sun., $16-22) offers a striking white decor for its restaurant and lounge. In 1954 the building housed the Palm Springs Post Office. Now, the contemporary, crisp white space is accented with colorful art and jewel tones. The restaurant offers fresh California nouveau classics with sea, land, and farm mains, featuring salads, sandwiches, and entrées like sourdough crusted Chilean sea bass as well as brunch items like lobster roll eggs Benedict. Dinner offers choices ranging from a poblano chili relleno to grass-fed New York strip steak. The lounge stays open all day, offering a bar menu every day from 11am to close. An outdoor patio offers mountain views.

★ **Shanghai Red's Bar & Grill** (235 S. Indian Canyon Dr., 760/322-9293, www.fishermans.com, 5pm-10pm Mon.-Thurs., 5pm-11:30pm Fri.-Sat., bar opens at 4pm $5-35) offers some of the finest fish tacos out there. Anthony Bourdain said so himself. Located inside the Fisherman's Market & Grill Restaurant Complex, this dark hole-in-the-wall consists of a long wooden bar and a few tables. The small space allows the person cooking behind the counter to whip up your fluffy shrimp and fish tacos doused with pico de gallo, shredded cabbage, and white sauce, and hand them straight over to you without further ado. The menu also includes a full array of steamed, grilled, and fried seafood, soups, salads, and pastas. There is live music on the patio on weekends.

Bring your parents, your mom, your partner, your mom's partner, your business friend, your oldest friend, or all of the above to ★ **Spencer's** (701 W. Baristo Rd., 760/327-3446, www.spencersrestaurant.com, 8am-2:30pm and 5pm-10pm daily, brunch 8am-2:30pm Sun., $10-40), a Palm Springs mainstay. Tucked away in the historic Palm Springs Tennis Club, Spencer's exemplifies Palm Springs upscale resort style for the clientele and decor. The restaurant serves new American and French Pacific Rim-influenced dishes. Brunch is the best meal for the value here and a fun place to see and be seen. Dinner is more romantic, while lunch is fit for the power set.

Juniper Table (100 W. Tahquitz Canyon Way, 760/904-5032, www.junipertable.com, 7am-3pm and 5pm-9pm daily, $9-24 breakfast and lunch, $14-29 dinner) serves a Mediterranean-inspired menu at this casual indoor-outdoor café on the ground floor of The Rowan Hotel. The hotel is designed to be inclusive of the neighborhood, and Juniper Table exemplifies that, opening onto a downtown art-filled square. The all-day menu features hot and cold breakfast from yogurt and granola to vanilla custard French toast and sausage and kale frittata. Lunch features salads and sandwiches. Dinner adds share plates and mains like branzino and rice pilaf and pasta primavera. They pour draft wines and craft beers as well as cocktails.

American

Two things: Dutch crunch bread and Bomb Sauce. **The Sandwich Spot** (240 N. Palm Canyon Dr., 760/778-7900, www.sandwichspotpalmsprings.com, 11am-6pm daily, $8) serves up a smorgasbord of hefty sandwiches with provocative names like the MILF (cranberry, chicken, cheese, veggies) and the Dreamkiller (crunchy veggies and cheese). Choose a bread (did I mention the Dutch crunch?) and a sauce (Bomb or Secret) and dig into one of their gooey, crunchy, flavorful sandwiches.

Tyler's Burgers (149 S. Indian Canyon Dr., 760/325-2990, www.tylersburgers.com, 11am-4pm Mon.-Sat., $6-12) is Americana nostalgia made fresh. The small, casual café is set in an old 1936 Greyhound Bus depot, but the patio provides people watching for the very current Palm Springs. The menu features classic all-American fare—burgers (obviously), sandwich classics (egg and chicken salad, BLT, and others), soups, and chili. Veggie options include a veggie burger and grilled cheese. Come for the burgers, stay for the coleslaw—they're known for it. Beer and wine are also available.

Sherman's Deli and Bakery (401 E. Tahquitz Canyon Way, 760/325-1199, 7am-9pm daily, $8-19), a beloved Palm Springs tradition since 1963, is a kosher-style deli serving up mile-high sandwiches and heaping plates. The staggering menu includes deli sandwiches, soups and salads, appetizers, chef specialties, breakfast, plates and platters, deluxe dinners, and a kids' menu. Oh, and save room for their arsenal of fluffy cream pies, cakes, and pastries for dessert.

Stock your Airbnb or hotel with gourmet provisions from **On the Mark** (777 N. Palm Canyon Dr., 760/832-8892, www.onthemarkpalmsprings.com, 10am-5pm daily). They have an excellent selection of meats, cheeses, and pickled goods for your poolside Bloody Mary tray or charcuterie plate. Their specialty wine and beer selection is far superior to the typical liquor store selections around Palm Springs. They also offer a sandwich menu.

Asian

The low-key hip **Rooster and the Pig** (356 S. Indian Canyon Dr., 760/832-6691, www.roosterandthepig.com, 5pm-9pm Wed.-Mon., $9-19) is a small, progressive Vietnamese American restaurant. The menu features appetizers like pork belly and charred brussels sprouts; fresh, tangy salads; spring rolls; and larger-format dishes like crispy whole fish, a rice noodle bowl, and a Banh mi burger. These are served family-style and recommended for sharing. The menu is accompanied by a small but good selection of beer, wine, and cocktails. There can be lines to get in, but they generally move quickly.

European

A sleek, modern spot tucked into an unassuming corner location in downtown, **Johanne's** (196 S. Indian Canyon Dr., 760/778-0017, www.johannesrestaurants.com, 5pm-10pm Tues.-Thurs. and Sun., 5pm-10:30pm Fri.-Sat., hours vary seasonally, $20-40) offers a fresh continental menu in an airy, upscale setting. The Austrian chef-run kitchen puts out sophisticated versions of Austrian and Pacific Rim specialties, including schnitzel and seared scallops. The menu can be pricey, but they also offer a bar menu that includes several of their signature schnitzels served in a bright bar that offers a view into the street and good downtown people watching.

Le Vallauris (385 W. Tahquitz Canyon Way, 760/325-5059, www.levallauris.com, 11:30am-2:30pm and 5pm-10:30pm daily, $20-48) delivers elegant French dishes from duck to lobster ravioli with a setting to match. The formal, old-world dining and romantic patio add up to a choice evening. Special prix fixe menus are offered from time to time and are worthwhile for the indulgent range and value.

4 Saints (100 W. Tahquitz Canyon Way, 760/392-2020, www.4saintspalmsprings.com, dinner 5:30pm-10pm Sun.-Thurs., 5:30pm-11pm Fri.-Sat., bar 5:30pm-11pm Sun.-Thurs., 5:30pm-midnight Fri.-Sat., $29-68) offers a rarified dining experience on the rooftop of The Rowan. The selling point here is the stunning, high-design space with views of the mountains and city. The menu features creative global cuisine in portions that can be miniscule. The good service, well-poured drinks, and setting balance out the experience.

Italian and Pizza

The family-owned **Johnny Costa's** (440 S. Palm Canyon Dr., 760/325-4556, www.johnnycostaspalmsprings.com, 5pm-10:30pm Mon.-Sat., $20-30) has been serving classic Italian specialties since 1976. Sink into a deep booth and dinner lighting at this low-key spot with an old-school feel. They offer a large and satisfying menu with a wide range of dishes—steak, veal, chicken, seafood, and pastas. Try the Steak Sinatra (the restaurant founder cooked for Sinatra at his estate) or comforting choices like linguine with clams and baked eggplant parmigiana.

Mexican

★ **Rio Azul** (350 S. Indian Canyon Dr., 760/992-5641, www.rioazulpalmsprings.com, 11am-9pm Mon.-Thurs., 11am-10pm Fri.-Sat., 10am-9pm Sun., $12-22) goes a huge step beyond the status quo of the refried bean, rice, and bubbling cheese plate of formulaic Mexican restaurants. They do offer this standard fare (we practically demand it as vacationing Americans), but their menu gets way more complex and nuanced with house specialties like the traditional Yucatan Cochinita Pibil (slow-roasted pork in banana leaf), grilled quail, and seafood enchiladas. They kill it with their skinny margarita: organic tequila, fresh lime, agave, and a sweet and salty chili rim. The space is vibrant with wood booths, good lighting, and a separate bar area. They offer a Desert Divas Drag Brunch on Sundays with tickets available on their website ($25).

SOUTH PALM SPRINGS

Breakfast, Brunch, and Coffee

With three locations, **Koffi** (1700 S. Camino Real, 760/322-7776, www.kofficoffee.com, 5:30am-7:30pm daily) is positioned to give you your fix wherever you are. This location (the others are in the Uptown Design District and central Palm Springs) offers a much-needed jolt to the guests staying at the cluster of party and relaxation hotels in South Palm Springs. Come for the coffee and leave with a better attitude. They offer basic breakfast survival food—muffins, scones, and the like.

The choice to go to **Elmer's Pancake House** (1030 E. Palm Canyon Dr., 760/327-8419, www.eatatelmers.com, 6am-9pm daily, $7-15) is as solid as its massive breakfast plates. Part of a Pacific Northwest diner chain dating from 1960, Elmer's makes its one California star appearance in Palm Springs. The service is good in this family-style retro diner with canted ceilings and plenty of windows. They serve all the breakfast favorites as well as their signature German pancakes. Lunch and dinner offer up sandwiches, soups, salads, and comfort food entrées straight out of Twin Peaks diner territory.

California Cuisine

Kiyosaku (Plaza Del Sol Shopping Center, 1555 S. Palm Canyon Dr., 760/327-6601, www.kiyosakusushi.menutoeat.com, 5:30pm-9pm Thurs.-Mon., $17-30) sushi is the real deal—traditional, family owned, and high quality. Instead of trendy rolls, the husband and wife team focus on excellent sushi and sashimi—he makes the sushi, she serves it in full kimono. (Yes, it's sushi in the desert, but they know what they're doing.) Beer, wine, and sake are served.

American

The new owners of ★ **Mr. Lyon's** (233 E. Palm Canyon Dr., 760/327-1551, www.mrlyonsps.com, 5pm-11pm Tues.-Sat., 4pm-9pm Sun., $32-59) breathed new life into an old establishment, creating a sleekly designed upscale steak house with a modern twist. Dry, aged beef and prime rib are house specialties, with seafood and veggie options available. The dark, friendly bar offers classic cocktails and a lounge menu with items like a burger and moules frites ($10-20).

The Barn Kitchen (1330 E. Palm Canyon Drive, 760/327-2300, sparrowslodge.com, lunch $12-15, dinner market price) refers to the wood-beamed open-air restaurant and bar on site at the Sparrows Lodge. On Wednesdays and Saturdays, they offer a family-style supper for hotel guests and others if there is available space. Offerings by Chef Gabriel Woo change weekly, but "Chicken Wednesday" and "Steak Saturdays" typically feature a salad, main course, and desert. Advance reservations are required. Call for details.

Located inside the Ace Hotel, ★ **King's Highway** (701 E. Palm Canyon Dr., 760/969-5789, www.acehotel.com, 7am-3pm, 5:30pm-11pm daily, $7-15 brunch, $11-27 dinner) offers reimagined locally sourced nouveau American classics in an airy space with Naugahyde booths and original terrazzo floors. This roadside diner that was formerly a Denny's has a breakfast and lunch menu that features classics like the breakfast burrito and silver dollar pancakes alongside fresh salads and classic American sandwiches, while dinner adds entrées like grilled salmon and steak frites.

The upscale diner fare at ★ **Norma's** (4200 E. Palm Canyon Dr., 760/770-5000, www.theparkerpalmsprings.com, 7am-10pm daily, $18-26) is pricey but worth it. Within The Parker Palm Springs, the stylish comfy eatery offers perfectly executed breakfast and lunch with specialties like a fruit-stuffed waffle or crab Louie salad. Dinner brings out indulgent comfort classics like lobster mac and cheese, and spaghetti and meatballs. Bonus: you can ogle the hotel's chic Jonathan Adler design and wander the manicured *Alice in Wonderland* garden grounds of the Parker.

European

Central European meets Mediterranean cuisine in the cozy, well-appointed atmosphere of ★ **Miro's** (Plaza Del Sol Shopping Center, 1555 S. Palm Canyon Dr., 760/323-5199, www.mirospalmsprings.com, 5pm-9:30pm Tues.-Sun., $28-39). The skilled kitchen staff takes basic ingredients like whole Mediterranean sea bass, cabbage, beef, mushrooms, and Yukon Gold potatoes and practices some magical cooking alchemy to turn every piping plate into a nuanced blend of satisfying goodness. Try dishes like beef Stroganoff, osso buco, scallops, and schnitzel paired with their (should-be-trade-secret) cabbage salad and a choice from the extensive wine list. The service is truly refined without being stuffy. Tip: Make a reservation! Even if you have to make it on your phone before you walk through the doors.

Italian and Pizza

The Chicago-inspired ★ **Guiseppe's Pizza and Pasta** (Smoke Tree Village Shopping Center, 1775 E. Palm Canyon Dr., 760/537-1890, www.giuseppesps.com, 11am-9pm Sun.-Thurs., 11am-9:30pm Fri.-Sat., $15-20) is a fresher version of a generations-old comfortable neighborhood joint. The warm space has exposed brick walls, a relaxed dining room, and cozy bar. It's good for families, friends, or dates. Try the pan or thin-crust pizzas (their eggplant pizza is award-winning for good reason) as well as pastas (from mushroom ravioli to shrimp scampi linguine). Gluten-free options are also available.

Mexican

The casual **El Mirasol** (140 E. Palm Canyon Dr., 760/323-0721, www.elmirasolrestaurants.com, 11am-9:30pm Mon.-Thurs., 8am-10pm Fri.-Sun., $12-20) is a great walkable option for the handful of hotels stretching along this section of South Palm Canyon Drive. They serve up plates of comfort food and strong margaritas in their stripped-down dining room and patio. The signature smoky Doña Diabla sauce accompanies every meal in liter bottles. El Mirasol has a second location in the **Los Arboles Hotel** (266 E Via Altamira).

Mediterranean

Located in the Caliente Tropics Hotel, **Evzin** (411 E. Palm Canyon Drive, 760/656-8764, https://evzincuisine.com, lunch 11am-4pm daily, dinner 5pm-9pm Mon.-Thurs., 5pm-10pm Fri.-Sun., $12-42) offers fresh, high-quality Mediterranean cuisine for lunch and dinner. Husband and wife team chef-owners John and Maria Tsoutis have filled a dining niche in the hotel itself and have also created a destination with well-executed classics like shawarma spiced chicken and falafel and Spanish fideo with chorizo, gulf shrimp, and mussels.

Vegetarian

The chef-owner of the popular Native Foods plant-based chain has branched out with **Chef Tanya's Kitchen** (706 S. Eugene Rd, 760/832-9007, www.cheftanyapetrovna.com, $9-14), billing itself as a Cuban vegan deli. You're right to wonder how this can be, but they pull it off. Sandwiches like their signature slow-roasted citrus and garlic seitan El Cubano or Chupacabra chicken defy the imagination. The deli-style eatery features sandwiches, salads, and sides, and is good for a casual lunch or pickup. Also great for pickup, their Wednesday dinner entrées, which rotate weekly and can be reserved ahead of time.

Palm Springs has the original location of the **Native Foods** (Smoke Tree Village Shopping Center, 1775 E. Palm Canyon Dr., #420, 760/416-0070, www.nativefoods.com, 11am-9pm daily, $8-12) vegan chain. They offer freshly made plant-based mock meat and other vegan fare in a fast-casual setting. Go guilty pleasure with the popular Chicken Run Ranch Burger (their most popular item) or chili cheese fries (it's okay—it's vegan!). They also serve a creative selection of burgers, sandwiches, bowls, and salads, magically whipping whole foods like kale and quinoa into beloved creations like the Reuben and taco salad.

Sweets

Kreem (170 E. Palm Canyon Dr, 760/699-8129, www.ilovekreem.com, 11am-9pm Sun.-Thurs., 11am-10pm Fri.-Sat., $4-9) adds a sweet spot to the small business stretch of south Palm Springs with artisanal ice creams and coffee by Portland-based Heart Coffee Roasters. They use high-quality organic dairy to make six daily flavors as well as seasonal options with flavors like mint chip and lemon meringue pie. They also craft a good selection of vegan flavors. "Canine cones" are offered for pets.

Accommodations

HOTELS

October-May is when lodging rates are at their highest, and hotels can book weeks in advance (prices dip in January, when temperatures are colder). Rates especially skyrocket in **March** and **April**, when thousands of revelers flock to Palm Springs and the Coachella Valley for a number of large-scale events and festivals. Hotels can be booked *months* in advance—although with the sheer number of hotels in the area, last-minute reservations will likely be available at a few places. **Summer** is the low season due to soaring desert temperatures. But if your main goal is to lounge in a pool, there are great hotel rates to be had June-September. Rates vacillate widely based on market pricing. The same room at one hotel could vary by hundreds of dollars depending on the weekend or time of year. In addition, mid-week rates can drop by more than half. If your timing is flexible, many hotels are within pricing reach.

Uptown Design District and North Palm Springs

$150-250

Infusion Beach Club (1900 N. Palm Canyon Drive, 760/799-9969, infusisonbcps.com, $175-290) opened in 2018 and fills some gaps that Palm Springs' exclusive boutique, adults-only hotel scene leaves open. The 62-room hotel offers a low-key and relatively affordable hang that allows children. It doesn't skimp on amenities either. A spacious pool with cabanas, city cruiser bikes, on-site food and drinks for poolside (or room-side), and text service make for a comfortable stay as do the spare rustic modern rooms with refrigerators, toiletries, and flat-screen TVs. Children and pets are permitted.

The star of the cozy boutique **Avanti Hotel** (354 E. Stevens Rd., 760/327-3866, www.avantihotelps.com, $180-250) is its small kidney-shaped pool sunk into a central courtyard ringed by potted flowers, greenery, and 10 hotel rooms. Quarters are intimate and peaceful with rooms opening directly poolside, offering mountain views and most with private patios. The rooms tend to be comfortable as opposed to stylish, but you're likely to find everything you need, including snacks, water, televisions, and kitchenettes. The hotel also offers complimentary continental breakfast, happy hour, and cruiser bikes. There is a hot tub on site. The hotel is dog-friendly. Only adults 21 and over are permitted.

Once you go past the unassuming concrete facade of the **Skylark Hotel** (1466 N. Palm Canyon Dr., 760/322-2267, www.skylarkps.com, $200-220), the inside is bursting with color. A rainbow of lounge chairs rings the inviting pool and hot tub and offer spectacular views of the San Jacinto Mountains. The hotel was originally constructed in 1955 and retains its mid-century exterior while offering newly furnished, updated, and contemporary poolside hotel rooms. Sundays can be a scene at the Skylark pool, with mimosas and party tunes playing over the hotel's sound system. Continental breakfast is included. The blend of fun, easy style and value makes the Skylark a solid choice. Children are allowed, but pets are not.

The historic, hacienda-style **Los Arboles Hotel** (784 N. Indian Canyon Dr., 760/459-3605, www.losarboleshotel.com, $150-220) has 21 Spanish-tiled rooms, a pool garnished with lush greenery, and the on-site El Mirasol Mexican restaurant. There's clearly no reason to leave the grounds. All 21 spacious rooms are set in single-story stucco with red-tile roofs just steps from the pool. It's a peaceful place to read, nap, or drink margaritas poolside.

Situated in the center of the Uptown Design District, **Alcazar** (622 N. Palm Canyon Dr., 760/318-9850, www.alcazarpalmsprings.com, $170-330) is a hip and relaxing 34-room boutique hotel with Spanish Colonial red-tile roofs and a sleek, modern sensibility. Mountain and poolside king rooms and poolside and courtyard queen rooms are available, including some suites with whirlpool tubs and kitchenettes and some with patios. Rooms feature Italian linens and flat-screen TVs. A resort fee covers the amenities of a saltwater pool, hot tub, and loaner townie bikes. Alcazar also boasts two of Palm Springs' favorite restaurants: **Cheeky's** (760/327-7595, www.cheekysps.com, 8am-2pm Wed.-Mon.) for a farm to table brunch and **Birba** (760/327-5678, www.birbaps.com, 5pm-11pm Wed.-Thurs. and Sun., 5pm-midnight Fri.-Sat.) for pizza and cocktails. The complimentary continental breakfast comes from Cheeky's. The hotel allows children.

OVER $250

It took new owners and a vision to strip away years of paint and bougainvillea, revealing the Albert Frey-designed modernist classic that is ★ **The Monkey Tree Hotel** (2388 East Racquet Club Road, 760/322-6059, www.themonkeytreehotel.com). This 16-room desert gem opened in 1960 as a stylish getaway with a star-studded roster, including Lucille Ball and Desi Arnaz, Spencer Tracey and Katherine Hepburn, and even JFK and Marilyn Monroe (hotel staff can point out the suite where they stayed guarded by the secret service). Albert Frey's attention to the surrounding landscape is apparent in the courtyard of the hotel: floating in the sun-drenched, heated saltwater pool, you can zone out on the sharp ledges of the San Jacinto Mountains framed by low-angled rooflines. Lest you think this is some austere getaway, there is nothing minimalist about the hospitality here. Among the myriad amenities, the property boasts four pools varying in size and temperature, a truly good house-made

1: uniquely shaped hot tub at the Skylark Hotel
2: Los Arboles Hotel

1

2
LOS ARBOLES HOTEL
Palm Springs. Ca.

continental breakfast, poolside sodas and pool floats, and in-room snacks and water. All this for reasonable (by Palm Springs' inflated standards) rates and no resort fees. Check out the Jungle Room with its original leopard print wallpaper and private patio (Eric Clapton's favorite back in the day). The hotel does not allow children under 14 or pets.

The Palm Springs Hotel (2135 N. Palm Canyon Dr., 760/459-1255, https://thepalmspringshotel.com, from $300, no resort fees) is a small boutique hotel with larger-than-life themed rooms. The Presley, The Deluxe Sinatra, and The Retro Raquel feature iconic retro pop art as well as all the modern amenities, including Direct TV, Keurig, and fast Wi-Fi. Courtyard rooms and suites, some with patios, ring the central pool. The hotel allows children but not pets.

I wish the Irwin Schuman-designed **Riviera Palm Springs** (1600 N. Indian Canyon Dr., 760/327-8311, www.rivierapalmsprings.com, $260-300) lived up to its Palm Springs royalty pedigree, but even in its current incarnation there is luxury, history, and plenty of amenity to be had. It opened in 1959 as the city's first resort hotel and played a key role in Palm Springs history as a glamour celebrity destination. The hotel was renovated in 2006 and continues as a deluxe resort with 398 rooms and 73 suites (although you're more likely to see bachelorette parties rather than celebrities basking around the pool). Hotel amenities include two resort pools (with pool bars), a spa and fitness center, two lounges, and an on-site restaurant. The hotel permits children and is dog-friendly.

It's true that the ★ **ARRIVE** hotel (1551 N. Palm Canyon Dr., 760/507-1650, https://arrivehotels.com, from $300) was the subject of an *LA Times* article titled "How hipster is this new Palm Springs hotel? You check in at the bar." Putting that aside, the hotel has a lot going for it even if it is trying to out-hipster the Ace (former reigning champ). A butterfly roofline lifts the hotel into Palm Springs' mid-century architectural pedigree, while rusted steel and natural elements anchor the hotel in the 21st century. The 32 hotel rooms have small private patios, Apple TV, and Malin+Goetz bath products. Lots of sunlight and flow between inside and outside create a seamless backdrop for a buzzy social scene fueled by on-site coffee, ice cream, cocktails, and food. Cartel Coffee (6am-6pm) offers espresso, filter drip, tea, and pastries. Ice Cream & Shop(pe) is a combination ice cream parlor with 16 gourmet flavors (including vegan) and fun gifts (noon-11pm Sun.-Thurs., noon-midnight Fri.-Sat.). The menu at Wexler's Deli (8am-9pm daily) features lox, pastrami sandwiches, and all day breakfast. The Draughtsman (11am-1am Mon.-Sat., 10am-1am Sun., happy hour 3pm-6pm daily) has rotating taps, craft cocktails, and gastropub fare. The hotel allows dogs. There is no strict adults-only policy in place, however, they have a no more than two-person per room policy, which puts a damper on family travel.

Colony Palms Hotel (572 N. Indian Canyon Dr., 760/969-1800, www.colonypalmshotel.com, from $350 plus $40 resort fee) was opened in 1936 as the Colonial House by reputed mobster Al Wertheimer, member of the Detroit-based Purple Gang. The private hotel hosted a number of illicit activities, including gambling, a speakeasy, and a brothel that's entered via a secret staircase. Since then, Colony Palms has classed things up. This 56-room luxury boutique hotel features Mediterranean-style decor with designer guest rooms (some with fireplaces and clawfoot tubs), courtyards for relaxing, a heated outdoor pool, hot tub, a Moroccan spa, gym, meeting space, and concierge. The Purple Palm Restaurant and Bar gives a nod to the old days. Children are allowed and dogs are welcomed.

Located in the prestigious Movie Colony neighborhood of Palm Springs, **Triada Palm Springs** (640 N. Indian Canyon Dr., 760/844-7000, www.triadapalmsprings.com, from $330) is a Spanish hacienda-style boutique hotel featuring 56 Mediterranean-style rooms. Some of the rooms have patios, making them feel like private villas. Two pools and an on-site upscale restaurant and bar round out the luxury experience. Children are allowed.

Central Palm Springs and Downtown

$100-150

The spelling of the ★ **Orbit In** (562 W. Arenas Rd., 760/323-3585, www.orbitin.com, $209-269) is intentional. Coming from your travels to land amid the atomic-style furnishings of this mid-century boutique hotel will truly feel as if you just orbited in. The Orbit In is actually two properties on the same block. Herb Burns, who introduced Palm Springs to the luxury, ultramodern motor court inn, built both the Orbit In and **The Hideaway** (370 W. Arenas Rd., 760/323-3585, www.orbitin.com, $209-269). They both feature large studio-style rooms with sitting areas and kitchenettes surrounding a saltwater pool. The **Orbit In** is funkier, with nine poolside rooms, terrazzo bar, hot tub, and vintage orange sun umbrellas. The Hideaway is sleeker and more muted with 10 poolside studios and great mountain views. At "Orbitini Hour" (5pm), guests of both properties gather at the Orbit In to chat over fruity Orbitinis.

The classic mid-century **Desert Hills** (601 W. Arenas Rd., 760/325-2777, www.deserthills.com, from $160) hearken back to a time when vacationers had their priorities straight and chose Palm Springs for extended vacations, often wintering here. The apartment-style hotel was built in 1956 and features 14 casual, stylish rooms, some with kitchens and patios, stretching out around a central pool and hot tub. A three-night minimum encourages quiet relaxation with nothing to do but chat with other hotel guests or contemplate the mountains, another dip in the pool, some light reading, or what you'll be cooking up on the property grill for dinner. Guests also have access to the Palm Springs Tennis Club and loaner bicycles. The hotel does not allow pets and only adults 21 and over are permitted.

Founded in the 1920s, historic **Casa Cody** (175 S. Cahuilla Rd., 760/320-9346, www.casacody.com, $180-280) is the oldest operating hotel in Palm Springs. The romantic adobe inn has 29 Southwestern-inspired rooms and studios as well as one-two bedrooms with tile or hardwood floors, many with private patios and fireplaces. Amenities include two outdoor pools and daily breakfast. Children and pets are allowed.

OVER $250

The stone and redwood ★ **Del Marcos Hotel** (225 W. Baristo Rd., 760/325-6902, www.delmarcoshotel.com, $300-400) welcomes guests through its boldly angled entrance to a bright lobby with white terrazzo floors and floor-to-ceiling glass looking out to the saltwater pool. Designed in 1947 by William Cody, the hotel received a historic designation for its post-WWII modern resort design. The Del Marcos's 17 suites are impeccably styled with individual charm from the Eames Poolside Suite with terrazzo floors and Eames furnishings to the Desert Oasis Deluxe with a tiki bar and private patio. Beach cruisers are available for tooling around town. A daily complimentary happy hour is a nice touch.

The ★ **Avalon Hotel** (415 S. Belardo Rd., 760/320-4117, www.avalonpalmsprings.com, from $400), is a Palm Springs luxury classic. The 68 guest rooms and bungalows wind through manicured property. Mediterranean exteriors give way to retro Regency-style interiors sporting a white, black, and yellow motif. The rooms are fun and over the top design-wise—wingback chairs, flocked wallpaper, and chandeliers galore. There are three pools on the premises; two are adults only, while one is open to families. The hotel's on-site restaurant, Chi-Chi, offers breakfast, lunch, dinner, and poolside drink service. The lobby bar offers signature cocktails. The hotel allows children and even offers complimentary cribs on request.

At seven stories, ★ **The Rowan** (100 W. Tahquitz Canyon Way, 760/904-5015, from $350) is a stylish anchor for Palm Springs' downtown strip. The open lobby soars with high ceilings and two-story windows, giving views of the San Jacinto Mountains. You have the same striking mountain views from room balconies and the hotel's signature rooftop pool (the only one in Palm Springs). The multiple stories defy traditional low-slung Palm Springs architecture (locals complain that it steals the views from everyone else), but the hotel's sleekly elegant design acknowledges its location in a mid-century mecca. A daily complimentary happy hour in the lobby provides some low key mingling for a clientele that ranges from Palm Springs weekenders to families to business travelers. The hotel's 153 rooms and suites offer up lots of amenities, including open spa-style showers, Malin+Goetz bath products, robes, USB plugs, and fast Wi-Fi. The property boasts a rooftop pool and pool bar, lobby bar, exercise room, and two on-site restaurants: Juniper Table (7am-9pm daily) for coffee, pastries, salads, snacks, and dinner, and 4 Saints (5:30pm-10pm Sun. Thurs., 5:30pm-11pm Fri.-Sat., bar open one hour later) for a Mediterranean-focused seasonal dinner menu. Hotel allows children and pets.

The Willows (412 W. Tahquitz Canyon Way, 760/320-0771, www.thewillowspalmsprings.com, $400-700) offers a romantic and elegant retreat in a former private mansion built in 1924. The historic Mediterranean-style eight-room inn is designed for seclusion and luxury: guests are pampered with a three-course breakfast, evening wine and hors d'oeuvres, and fresh fruit. The historic setting maintains a heated pool and hot tub. Rooms are beautifully appointed with traditional antiques but also include modern amenities like flat-screen TVs. A two-night minimum is required on weekends; there are no resort fees.

★ **Holiday House** (200 W. Arenas Rd, 760/320-8866, https://holidayhouseps.com, $400-500) is making its tour in the best-of design lists for good reason: a 1951 Palm Springs classic is newly re-invigorated into a fun, high-design 28-room boutique hotel with a fresh blue and white theme and easy-going hospitality. It originally opened in 1951 as a sleek luxury hotel designed by Herbert H. Burns, one of the definers of Palm Springs' mid-century modern style. After many incarnations, the team behind the rustic chic Sparrows Lodge made it shine, revealing clear lines and a livable style. Check-in is in the open lobby/bar hung with original artwork by Liechtenstein and Mr. Brainwash among others, convenient for your welcome glass of rosé. The bright rooms have custom blue and white textiles, oversized showers, and an impeccable minibar. A firepit, citrus trees, polka-dot cruiser bikes for loan, and central swimming pool ensure you won't want to leave the grounds. Continental breakfast is included, and there is on-site dining at The Pantry (sharing the bar space) with an Americana-style menu of salads and sandwiches (11am-4pm). A bar stays open until 11pm. Only adults 21 and over are permitted. Pets are allowed.

The Rossi (375 W. Arenas Rd, 760/325-7100, https://therossihotel.com, $400-500) offers 11 luxury suites in a secluded setting dating from the 1920s. Individually designed suites offer private patios and hot tubs, some with separate living rooms and kitchenettes. The hotel is a mix of old-school charm and new-school amenities: rooms boast luxury linens and bath products, mini fridges and HDTV. Grounds have lush foliage and a common courtyard with two swimming pools.

The ★ **Korakia Pensione** (257 S. Patencio Rd., 760/864-6411, www.korakia.com, from $479) was built as a Moroccan-inspired artist retreat in 1924 and continues in this spirit as its incarnation as a stylish bed-and-breakfast resort. The 28 suites, studios, and bungalows are housed in two restored villas set on 1.5 acres of fountains. Many have private balconies or patios. Enter through the keyhole-shaped grand entrance flanked by ornately carved Moorish wooden doors. Moroccan fountains, a stone waterfall, and stone courtyard complete the outside vibe, while the wood-beamed ceilings and antiques of the rooms ooze good taste. Guests under 13 are not permitted.

If you've dreamed about traveling the world in luxury when you grew up, a version of ★ **La Serena Villas** (339 S. Belardo Rd, 760/832-8044) might have figured in your imagination. The secluded boutique hotel's 18 guest villas are set on an acre of landscaped grounds, walking distance to downtown shops and restaurants. Originally built in 1933, the property was redeveloped as a luxury hotel in 2016. Rooms and suites have private patios with firepits, claw-foot tubs, and built-in benches. The on-site restaurant, Azucar, is a destination even for non-hotel guests, offering poolside dining and a contemporary California menu (think fish tacos, salmon with goat cheese risotto) for lunch and dinner daily (lunch 11am-3pm daily, $10-20; dinner 5pm-9pm Sun.-Thurs., 5pm-10pm Fri.-Sat., $25-38). Sugar High rooftop bar pours libations from specialty margaritas to sparkling rose. Breakfast is included for guests in the form of a breakfast basket delivered to your room. Only adults 21 and over are permitted. Pets are allowed.

South Palm Springs

$150-250

Visiting the newly restored ★ **Ingleside Inn** (200 W. Ramon Rd, 760/325-0046, https://inglesideinn.com, from $229) is like weekending at your sophisticated friend's swimming pool estate. Which is exactly how the property was designed. Built in 1925 as a private home for the Birge family of the Pierce Arrow Motor Car Company, the home was opened as an elite hotel in 1939 by Ruth Hardy, Palm Springs' first councilwoman. Melvyn Haber, New York businessman, took over in 1975 and made **Melvyn's Restaurant and Lounge** the elegantly upbeat nighttime scene with serious Hollywood Rat Pack cred that continues to draw a crowd. In 2016, the San Francisco-based PlumpJack Group restored the hotel to highlight its Spanish Colonial Revival bones, giving Melvyn's dining room and lounge a skillful face-lift that still evokes old Palm Springs glamour. Some of the 30 guest rooms offer sitting areas, private patios, and gas fireplaces. Service is understated but there when you need it. Most importantly at happy hour you can have martini service delivered to your guest room or suite. In theory, you could leave the grounds to drink, dine, swim, or relax elsewhere, but you know the saying, "just because you can do something doesn't mean you should." The hotel is adults 21 and over only and allows pets.

Sunny hospitality is what sets apart the ★ **Hotel California** (424 E. Palm Canyon Dr., 760/322-8855, www.palmspringshotelcalifornia.com, $120-180). The historic Spanish Mission-style hotel was originally constructed in 1942. Recently updated rooms have a comfortable, rustic decor with Spanish tile floors, flat-screen TVs, and kitchenettes. King, queen, double queen, and suites are available. The communal space boasts a relaxing pool, lush greenery, hot tub, cruiser bikes, common kitchen, and grill. Bring your own supplies and relax for the weekend. The hotel is adults 21 and over only.

Caliente Tropics (411 E. Palm Canyon Dr., 760/327-1391, www.calientetropics.com, from $250) was once one of the hippest games in town with its A-frame entrance, tiki swank style, Congo Room Steak House, and Rat Pack clientele. Times have changed, but the bones of the place are still there. Manage your expectations and this Polynesian-styled hotel may pleasantly surprise you. It offers 91 basic budget rooms with king-size beds or double queens as well as suites. Service can be unpolished, but the large pool, manicured grounds dotted with tikis, and affordable rooms make it worth the stay. Afternoon weekends at the pool can be a zoo. Mornings and evenings are more mellow. Nighttime brings out the lit tiki torches. The crowds are a downside, but on the plus, the hotel is family-friendly, and the pool is large. An on-site tiki bar and Mediterranean restaurant seriously ups the hotel's game. The Reef pours tropical cocktails with a satisfying bar food menu (1pm-1am Mon.-Fri., 10am-1am Sat., 10am-midnight Sun.). Evzin dishes Mediterranean specialties in a sleek space (lunch 11am-4pm daily, dinner 5pm-9pm

1

2

3

4

Mon.-Thurs., 5pm-10pm Fri.-Sun., $12-24). The hotel allows children.

OVER $250

Villa Royale (1620 S. Indian Trail, 760/327-2314, https://villaroyale.com, from $315) offers a vibrant 38-villa hideaway with lush foliage, three swimming pools, and intimate on-site bar and restaurant. Originally constructed in 1947, the California ranch-style hotel for the Hollywood set is a redesigned study in well-balanced contrasts. Spanish tile and warm wood are offset by striking splashes of pop art in guest rooms. A romantic wood and marble bar offers bright cocktails. Lush foliage contrasts with the stark mountain views. Guest rooms are poolside rooms with mountain views and fully stocked in-room dry bars. Suites are one or two bedrooms with a separate living area, some with a private patio, fireplace, or cocktail bar. Del Rey, the intimate on-site bar and restaurant, offers craft cocktails and small Mediterranean-inspired plates. Hotel is adults 21 and over only and is pet friendly.

The 1950s-inspired decor of the **Desert Riviera** (610 E. Palm Canyon Dr., 760/327-5314, www.desertrivierahotel.com, $190 with two-night minimum) maintains some of the mid-century charm of this 1951 hotel. A pool, hot tub, firepit, outdoor gas grills, communal kitchen, and loaner bikes make the Desert Riviera an oasis of fun times. The 11 rooms (double queen, king, suites, and studios) are warmly inviting.

The **Ace Hotel** (701 E. Palm Canyon Dr., 760/325-9900, www.acehotel.com, $160-350) has a pitch-perfect hipness with its mid-century, vintage-inspired style. This 176-room renovated hotel, spa, and resort (formerly a Westward Ho with a Denny's) offers two pools and a hot tub. The Ace Swim Club Pool has one of the major pool scenes in Palm Springs, with regular deejays and events. The quieter Commune Pool has a more mellow and family-oriented vibe. The on-site Amigo Room bar serves poolside drinks and late-night atmosphere. The Kings Highway Diner offers a poolside menu and a day and evening menu in its roadside diner setting. Standard double, king, suites, and patio rooms feature clean, stylish design, flat-screen TVs and MP3 plug-ins. Some rooms offer vintage furniture, record players, or outdoor fireplaces. Children are allowed. There is an on-site gym and spa. Pets are also allowed for a fee.

The ★ **Sparrows Lodge** (1330 E. Palm Canyon Dr., 760/327-2300, http://sparrowslodge.com, $230-380) is an impeccably restored 1950s retreat. Originally constructed in 1952 as the Red Barn, a hangout for the Hollywood elite, the lodge was restored to its original charm in 2013. Concrete and pebble-inlaid floors, exposed wood-beamed ceilings, open showers, and private patios grace the 20 poolside rooms and garden cottages. They're furnished with high-end rustic design classics like butterfly chairs and Swiss Army blankets. Imagine rustic mountain lodge meets mid-century ranch with a page from spare, traditional Japanese design. The vibe is understated and hip. It manages to exceed expectations and blend in with the landscape. A central pool and hot tub make for a simple and relaxing scene. The barn-style communal area serves beer, wine, and specialty drinks, including a refreshing house-made sangria. The continental breakfast of muffins, yogurt, granola, fruit, and French press coffee is as well thought out as everything else. Rooms are double occupancy and are restricted to guests over 21 only. Pets are allowed for a fee.

Jonathan Adler redesigned ★ **The Parker Palm Springs** (4200 E. Palm Canyon Dr., 760/770-5000, www.theparkerpalmsprings.com, $260-400), which began life in 1959 as California's first Holiday Inn. It's hard to make that mental leap as you wander the sumptuous 13 garden acres with two pools, poolside bar, firepit, tennis courts, croquet lawn, and luxury retro-hip suites. In the lobby, chandeliers

1: Spanish mission-style Hotel California **2:** Orbit In **3:** the reinvigorated 1951 Holiday House **4:** the Ingleside Inn Courtyard hearkening back to the original estate merge with Moroccan-inspired antiques for a richly eccentric boho chic. Patio, suite, and estate rooms are available. Hefty resort fees cover valet parking and bellman service at this upscale resort. Food and drink offerings include a lobby bar, **Norma's** (7am-3pm and 5pm-10pm daily), perfectly executed upscale diner fare, and **Mister Parker's** (6pm-close Wed.-Sun.), a posh French bistro. Wine bar **Counter Reformation** offers an impeccably curated wine list and sophisticated small bites like fresh shucked oysters and beef carpaccio with a truffle chimichurri in a Paris-inspired setting (3pm-11pm daily, $11-16).

Designed in 1952 by renowned architect William F. Cody, **L'Horizon Hotel** (1050 E. Palm Canyon Dr., 760/323-1858, www.lhorizonpalmsprings.com, from $485) has recaptured its glamour as a celebrity destination of the 1950s and 1960s. This low-slung hotel was newly redesigned by Steve Hermann around 25 well-appointed guest bungalows, angled wood beams, and long, low architecture that highlights the mountain panoramas. This exclusive luxury resort features an intimate landscaped setting, infinity pool, spa treatments, on-site dining, and bar. The hotel is adults 21 and over only.

LGBT HOTELS

Nearly all hotels in Palm Springs, from small boutique inns to large resorts, are gay-friendly. In addition, there are several that cater exclusively to gay, male clientele, with accommodations that range from clothing-optional resorts to secluded retreats. There are no women-only resorts.

Uptown Design District and North Palm Springs

A former gay, male hotel **East Canyon Hotel & Spa** (288 E. Camino Monte Vista, 760/320-1928, www.eastcanyonps.com, $199-299, three-night minimum) changed ownership in 2017 and is now open to LGBTQ, straight, and all friendly couples. Lush grounds and an oversized heated swimming pool create a secluded retreat feel. Nightly, poolside happy hour lends a sense of community. Accommodations include queen and king suites. The hotel is adults 18 and over only.

South Palm Springs/Warm Sands Neighborhood

The Warm Sands neighborhood is the mecca for gay resorts and hotels. Strictly defined, the neighborhood is located east of Palm Canyon Drive bounded by Ramon Road to the north and East Sunny Dunes Road to the south. However, other gay resorts in the area extend south down to East Mesquite. More generally, the area is located south of downtown and before the curve where South Palm Canyon Drive becomes East Palm Canyon Drive.

El Mirasol Villas (525 Warm Sands Dr., 760/327 5913, www.elmirasol.com, $129-329) is a California ranch-style hotel originally built by Howard Hughes in the 1940s and operating as a gay male clothing-optional resort since 1975. Two swimming pools, a 10-person hot tub, outdoor shower, and eucalyptus steam room are on a property with citrus trees and fountains. The hotel offers studio rooms with king-size beds. Deluxe studios and suites add private patios.

Vista Grande Resort (574 S. Warm Sands Dr, 760/322-2404, vistagranderesort.com, from $209) features three swimming pools, a 16-person spa, lagoon, and waterfall for a sexy but laid-back vibe at this clothing-optional men's resort. The lush grounds make up for the slightly dated digs. The 29-room resort offers two-bedroom friend accommodations with separate entrances and studios for solo travelers as well as one-bedroom apartments and suites. Breakfast, lunch, and dinner served on-site.

The Hacienda at Warm Sands (586 Warm Sands Dr., 760-327-8111, thehacienda.com, from $384) is a small, upscale, luxury, gay male resort offering nine suites with separate living and bedroom areas and one patio room. Amenities include two pools, a hot tub, and an outdoor fireplace set in the landscaped grounds with mountain views. Rates include an expanded continental breakfast and catered lunch.

INNdulge (601 S. Grenfall Rd., 760/327-1408, inndulge.com, $145-225) is a lively gay men's clothing-optional resort offering Thursday pizza, evening social hours, and weekend pool parties. A saltwater pool (heated and chilled as needed) and 12-person hot tub are in the central courtyard. Guest rooms have king-size beds and refrigerators, some add full kitchens. Continental breakfast and complimentary local gym access included.

The stylish **Santiago** (650 E. San Lorenzo Rd., 760/322-1300, www.santiagoresort.com, $189-245) is a male-only, swimsuit-optional resort featuring chic, modern rooms, and landscaped grounds. The resort is warmly styled: suites have Spanish tile floors, king beds, and woven rugs. Hammocks, a firepit, and courtyard fountain complement the native landscaping. A pool and lounging area complete the tranquil atmosphere.

Set on a classic 1950s property, **Escape Resort** (641 E. San Lorenzo Rd., 760/325-5269, www.escapepalmsprings.com, $179-209) is a laid-back, clothing-optional resort catering to gay singles and couples. A heated pool (cooled in summer) and hot tub are at the center of the manicured grounds. Join fellow guests and owners for weekend social hour. The 12 rooms are sleekly styled; some come with full-size refrigerators and sitting areas.

La Dolce Vita (1491 S. Via Soledad, 760/325-2686, www.ladolcevitaresort.com, $179-209) is a swimsuit-optional, gay men's resort offering a relaxing oasis in a Spanish hacienda-style inn. Its 18 guest rooms surround two swimming pools. Amenities include an on-site spa for professional spa treatments, a hot tub, steam room, continental breakfast, and weekend social hours. The rooms and suites feature hardwood floors, double French doors, and private patios.

VACATION RENTALS

In addition to its many hotel options, Palm Springs has some stunning vacation rentals available through third party booking sites like Airbnb and Vrbo. The city has strict guidelines limiting vacation rentals, so they have not proliferated and taken over the hotel scene. Instead, they tend to be special lodging options with historic pedigree—homes, estates, or small historic boutique hotels turned into single-party rentals. Some are small and intimate, while others are good for larger festive gatherings involving you and sixteen of your closest friends.

Uptown Design District and North Palm Springs

The **Racquet Club** listing refers to an original Meiselman-designed, two-bedroom mid-century home located in the Racquet Club Estates neighborhood of North Palm Springs (thedesertcollective.com). The gorgeous two-bedroom sits on a private landscaped yard with a saltwater pool, hammocks, BBQ, and a teepee (sure, why not). The impeccably designed home was featured in Sunset Magazine: the interior is light and breezy, furnished with vintage and original furniture and art from the 1950s to the present. A wall of sliding doors creates a seamless example of California indoor-outdoor living.

With a location directly behind Bootlegger Tiki Bar and Ernest Coffee you've got both your morning and evening bases covered. **The Twist** (140 W. Vía Lola, 415/744-1475, http://thetwistps.com, from $128) features classic Palm Springs architecture in a sleek white building that comes to life with splashes of mod color and design. The 17 vacation rentals range from studios to 2-bedrooms with private balconies or patios, some with outdoor gas firepits. Grounds include a central pool, hot tub, mini golf, stainless steel grill, and complimentary beach cruisers. When hotels in Palm Springs book up, you may be able to sneak into one of these. Or plan ahead and take over the place.

The **Kocher-Samson** building is arguably where it all began (stayatthefrey.com, $149). Before the era of the high-design boutique luxury hotels with custom textiles, pop art, opulent bath products, and hand-crafted minibars, there was the Kocher Samson building. Albert Frey, the godfather of desert modernism, designed the building intended as a utilitarian insurance building, and its spare lines and desert backdrop put Palm Springs on the map (and in textbooks) for its place in international modernism. Miraculously, this building still stands; architecture geeks make pilgrimages to it. Even more miraculously, you can stay in it. Bright and sunny and newly restored, this original 1934 Albert Frey-designed Class 1 historic site shines as a modernist time capsule. Black-and-white photos from the building's design era make it looks like it's in the middle of nowhere. Today, it's in the middle of everything. Walk to bars, restaurants, and shopping. Or kick back on the deep patio with a cold beverage and people watch. Your space is an upstairs apartment designed for one or two on the main stretch of the Uptown Design District. The interior is spare and functional, exactly as Frey intended it, but the current hosts have made sure you have everything you need for Palm Springs' high standard of comfort: full original period kitchen, comfortable queen bed, Wi-Fi, and swimming pool access.

Central Palm Springs and Downtown

Within the historic Old Las Palmas neighborhood, the ★ **Coral Sands Inn** (210 W. Stevens Rd., 760/325-4900, www.coralsandspalmsprings.com, from $1,100) is cinematic with its bright-pink facade, neon sign, and six themed rooms. Lounging by the kidney-shaped pool with the mountain backdrop, you'll feel like you're starring in the best road trip movie of the summer. Ruby Montana is a warm hostess, an avid collector with a cult following. She dreamed up and furnished the kitschy rooms, including the western Yippy Ky Yo Ky Yay Rodeo Room and the Liberace Room. It's a fun place to lounge the weekend away, and the inn is also available to rent out for special events for you and your friends. The motel primarily books as a vacation rental through Airbnb, with six separate rooms and bathrooms plus three small kitchens and a central pool. Individual rooms may be available by calling.

In addition to the Coral Sands Inn, Ruby Montana also has other properties nearby. ★ **Casa Redonda** is a gorgeous 1937 Spanish-style hacienda. It was originally built for two sisters who each took a wing of the house. The space has two, two-bedroom mirror image stand-alone bungalows and a casita (side house)—enough to comfortably sleep 10. Spanish tile floors, period furnishings, rooftop cocktail decks, and unobstructed views of the mountains make this a stunning and relaxing getaway. It's billed as a restored 1937 hacienda-style compound. Reservations are available on Vrbo.

The Amado (1821 E. Amado Rd., 760/537-0053, www.theamado.com, $175) is a classic mid-century gem, offering boutique accommodations. The five-unit complex features five king suites with private kitchens, bathrooms, dining rooms, and living rooms. A two-bedroom suite takes it up a notch with the addition of a vintage gas fireplace and full bath. Desert-chic styling, polished concrete floors, a central courtyard, barbeques, and plenty of lounging opportunities make this contemporary retreat a good bet. Book one room or the whole property ($1,350) for you and your friends.

South Palm Springs

Take over your own swanky hotel complete with central pool, hot tub, kitchen, and indoor fireplace. **The Marley** (598 S. Grenfall Rd, from $1,195) is an entire historic nine-bedroom hotel that can accommodate up to 16 guests to lounge in style and privacy. Splashes of color and pop art make the sleek white and polished concrete space festive. More splashing can be had in the commercial-grade pool and hot tub with iconic mountain and palm tree views. The hotel accommodates one group at a time. The hotel allows children.

A collection of flats from an era when people wintered in Palm Springs, **The Wesley** (711 S. Riverside Dr., 424/523-5310, www.wesleypalmsprings.com, from $127) accommodations range from deluxe studios to two-bedroom, two-bath flats furnished in fun mid-century style. Most feature private garden patios. A central pool and hot tub as well as gas grills complete the outdoor living scenario. It is an adults only accommodation.

Desert Star (1611 S. Calle Palo Fierro, www.desertstarpalmsprings.com, from $155) is a small, mid-century modern oasis offering four stylish and bright studio apartments surrounding a central heated saltwater pool and outdoor firepit. Kitchens and private patios ensure you won't have to leave the property. The property was designed by Howard Lapham, Palm Springs architect, and completed in 1956. The bones of the place are great and continue to shine. Children are not permitted.

Transportation and Services

GETTING THERE

The two major airports closest to Palm Springs are in Los Angeles to the west and San Diego to the southwest; however, the Palm Springs Airport, located two miles east of downtown Palm Springs, is worth looking into to eliminate the intense traffic slog from LA or San Diego.

Air

The tiny **Palm Springs Airport** (PSP, 3400 E. Tahquitz Canyon Way, 760/318-3800, www.palmspringsca.gov) is a public airport that is served by 11 airlines. Connections are available from cities worldwide. The airport serves nonstop markets from 10 major airline hubs. If you are flying into the Palm Springs Airport, several hotels offer airport shuttle service, including the Saguaro Palm Springs, the Smoke Tree Ranch, and corporate hotels like the Hyatt, Omni, Hilton, and Marriott. The major car rental carriers are located here, including Enterprise, Hertz, Dollar, and Alamo. Uber and Lyft ride shares are also available for airport pickup.

Los Angeles International Airport (LAX, 1 World Way, Los Angeles, 424/646-5252, www.lawa.org) has its advantages and disadvantages to fly into. Advantages: it's a major international airport with many carriers and flight options. All the major rental car companies are nearby, with regular shuttles from the airport. Disadvantage: LAX can be very congested.

The **San Diego International Airport** (SAN, 3225 N. Harbor Dr., San Diego, 619/400-2404, www.san.org) is a busy single-runway airport located three miles northwest of downtown San Diego. Its major carriers include Southwest, American, United, Alaska, and Delta. A consolidated rental car center on the north side of the airport serves many major car rental car companies and makes it easy to rent a car from the airport.

Ontario Airport (ONT, Ontario, 909/937-2700, www.flyontario.com/) is a medium-hub, full-service airport located 70 miles west of Palm Springs. Ontario Airport has all the major rental car companies on-site. It's big enough to have affordable flights with good time options and small enough to make it easy to navigate. From the Ontario airport, the drive to Palm Springs is slightly over an hour via I-10 east. You can avoid the congestion of the other major airports altogether and cut your drive time in half.

Car

Without heavy traffic, the drive from Los Angeles can take under two hours via I-10. Getting out of LA can be a slog, though, so you may need to factor in extra time (up to five hours) if driving from LA. **From Los Angeles,** take I-10 east for approximately 100 miles. The 210 and 60 freeways can sometimes provide good eastbound alternatives if I-10 is jammed. They eventually join up with I-10 before Palm Springs. After approximately 100 miles, exit off I-10 to take Highway 111 south toward Palm Springs. Highway 111B continues south to reach the Palm Springs city limit in just over 10 miles, turning into North Palm Canyon Drive, the main road through Palm Springs.

If traffic cooperates, the drive from San Diego takes just over two hours. **From San Diego,** take I-15 north (the same interstate that goes to Las Vegas) for about 50 miles. When I-15 splits off with I-215, follow the I-215N and signs for Riverside/San Bernardino. Follow I-215N for 30 miles until it intersects with CA-60. Take the exit for CA-60 heading east for 18 miles. Merge onto I-10 east and continue for another 18 miles until the CA-111 exit toward Palm Springs. Highway 111B continues south to reach the Palm Springs city limit in just over 10 miles, turning into North Palm Canyon Drive, the main road through Palm Springs.

Public Transit

The enterprising **Flixbus** (www.flixbus.com, from $9.99) is a German-based transportation start-up with no-frills, affordable bus service connecting major international cities. Direct bus routes run daily between downtown Los Angeles and Palm Springs. Provided all goes well (your bus shows up on time), this is the best option for public transportation.

Another option is to take **Amtrak** (800/872-7245, www.amtrak.com) via a combination train and bus from Los Angeles in a route that runs daily and takes three-four hours. The route begins from Union Station in downtown Los Angeles, taking the *Pacific Surfliner* train line. After a transfer, an Amtrak California Thruway Bus completes the journey at the Palm Springs Amtrak stop in North Palm Springs (North Indian Canyon Drive and Palm Springs Station Road, no amenities) 3.4 miles north of the Palm Springs Visitors Center. Other stops on the Thruway route include Cabazon at the Morongo Casino Resort and Spa (49500 Seminole Dr., Cabazon) as well as two stops in the Coachella Valley: Palm Desert at the Palm Desert Westfield Mall (72-840 Highway 111, Palm Desert) and the La Quinta Town Center (Highway 111 and Adams, La Quinta).

There are no Greyhound stations directly in Palm Springs.

GETTING AROUND

Central Palm Springs is extremely easy to get around in. The main concentration of hotels and businesses span a 4.5-mile stretch. It's easy to plan much of your vacation to be walkable. In addition, many hotels provide free cruiser-style bicycles to guests, and Palm Springs has wide streets as well as bike lanes. Most hotels require bikes to be back before dark.

Shuttles

The city offers a free shuttle called the **Buzz Bus** (www.sunline.org/buzzisback, every 20 minutes noon-10pm Thurs.-Sat., free). The cheerfully painted shuttle is air-conditioned and wheelchair-friendly. It has its own stops along the two main streets (Palm Canyon and Indian Canyon). The bus runs from Via Escuela in the Uptown Design District to Smoke Tree in South Palm Springs.

Ride Shares and Taxis

Palm Springs is swarming with **Uber** (www.uber.com) and **Lyft** (www.lyft.com) ride shares, making this the best way to get from one end of town to the other. There are also a few taxi services that serve Palm Springs and the Coachella Valley. **Desert City Cab** (760/328-3000, www.desertcitycab.com) offers 24-hour service to the entire Coachella Valley, including Palm Springs. **Yellow Cab of the Desert** (760/340-8294, www.yellowcabofthedesert.com) is based in Palm Desert and serves Palm Springs, Cathedral City, Rancho Mirage, La Quinta, Indio, and Indian Wells.

SERVICES

The first building you will pass on entering Palm Springs is the **Palm Springs Visitors Center** (2901 N. Palm Canyon Dr.,

760/778-8418, www.visitpalmsprings.com, 9am-5pm daily). The iconic building was designed in 1965 by renowned architect Albert Frey as a gas station for the Palm Springs Aerial Tramway. The fully staffed visitors center has a wealth of books and maps about the historic city. Other resources include the official Palm Springs tourism website (www.visitpalmsprings.com), which is helpful for planning. For a gay tourism perspective, check out www.visitgaypalmsprings.com for recommendations on lodging, dining, and activities.

The Coachella Valley

The Coachella Valley sprawls southeast from Palm Springs. This suburban desert is flanked by the San Jacinto Mountains on its southwest border, and Joshua Tree National Park and the San Bernardino Mountains bound the northwest edge. It's primarily residential, a checkerboard of gated communities and golf courses. It trends northwest to southeast all the way to the Salton Sea, and while not a destination, there are a few stops worth making. In the middle of it all is the surprising Thousand Palms Oasis Preserve, a literal oasis with shining palms and shaded pools set against a heat-baked landscape.

PLANNING YOUR TIME

The sights in the Coachella Valley are **day trip** options or short drives from Palm Springs for sightseeing, recreation, dining, and casino accommodations. Towns and cities include **Desert Hot Springs** (a small mid-century resort community with hotel and spa opportunities), **Thousand Palms, Palm Desert,** and **Indio,** most of which can be accessed from I-10.

SIGHTS

★ Cabot's Pueblo Museum

Cabot Yerxa is the man responsible for the fascinating Hopi-inspired 35-room pueblo, an artistic masterpiece he built entirely out of found materials between 1941 and 1950. **Cabot's Pueblo Museum** (67616 E. Desert View Ave., Desert Hot Springs, 760/329-7610, www.cabotsmuseum.org, 9am-4pm Tues.-Sun. Oct.-May, 9am-1pm Wed.-Sat.

Cabot's Pueblo Museum, a Hopi-inspired masterpiece built of found materials

June-Sept., tours $13) offers guided tours of the home's interior, but you don't have to take the tour to visit the trading post and grounds, which include beautifully weathered outbuildings, a meditation garden, a well house, and "Waokiya," a 43-foot-tall Native American sculpture carved from a fallen cedar. Tickets are available online and in-person and close one hour before tour start times.

Living Desert Zoo and Gardens

The **Living Desert Zoo and Gardens** (47900 Portola Ave., Palm Desert, 760/346-5694, www.livingdesert.org, 9am-5pm daily Oct.-May, 8am-1pm daily June-Sept., $20 adults, $10 children 3-12) is a desert botanical garden and zoo with an amusement park feel. Paved paths wind through exhibits representing major desert regions. The place is a huge draw for families and can be very crowded on weekends and holidays.

Shields Date Garden

In the 1920s, Highway 111 was lined with date farms all vying for motoring tourists' patronage. **Shields Date Garden** (80-225 Hwy. 111, Indio, 760/347-0996, www.shieldsdategarden.com, 8am-4pm daily, $5) is the last one standing. This family-friendly roadside attraction features a gift shop with free date samples, packaged dates, date milk shakes, and other gifts. A film, *The Romance and Sex Life of the Date,* chronicles the history of the date farm and, well, how these delicious dates come to be. Visitors can wander through the date gardens and oasis, which has strangely been reenvisioned as a biblical sculpture garden complete with famous biblical scenes. There is also the on-site **Café at Shields** (760/775-0902, 8am-3pm daily, $12-15) offering breakfast, lunch, beer, and wine.

Palm Springs Art Museum in Palm Desert

Palm Springs Art Museum in Palm Desert (72-567 Highway 111, Palm Desert, 760/346-5600, www.psmuseum.org, 10am-5pm Tues.-Sun., free) is a branch of the acclaimed Palm Springs Art Museum. It opened in 2012 in the newly constructed Galen building, an architecturally significant, high-performance green structure. The interior houses four separate galleries as well as space for lectures, films, and educational events. The Faye Sarkowsky Sculpture Garden is set on four acres surrounding the building with 10 significant sculpture works set amid landscaped gardens, water features, native plants, and walkways.

ENTERTAINMENT AND EVENTS

Casinos

Tucked at the foot of the San Jacinto Mountains 18 miles west of Palm Springs, **Morongo Casino Resort and Spa** (49500 Seminole Dr., Cabazon, 951/849-3080, www.morongocasinoresort.com) offers 150,000 square feet of Las Vegas-style gaming in a high-rise luxury resort hotel. The Tukwet Canyon Golf Club, a professional bowling center, and a range of dining options are also on-site.

The sleek **Agua Caliente Casino Resort Spa** (32-250 Bob Hope Dr., Rancho Mirage, 760/321-2000, www.hotwatercasino.com) is 10 miles southeast of Palm Springs just off I-10. This upscale resort features a concert theater and lounge for entertainment with a second lounge offering specialty cocktails. The casino houses a selection of casino table games, slots, a live poker room, and a high-limit room. Dining options include a high-end steak house, two cafés, a deli, and a buffet.

Festivals and Events

★ COACHELLA VALLEY MUSIC AND ARTS FESTIVAL

The **Coachella Valley Music and Arts Festival** (www.coachella.com, Apr.), known simply as Coachella (as in "Dude, are you going to Coachella this year? The lineup looks rad!") is an annual music festival held every April on the Empire Polo Club fields in the Coachella Valley. From folk rock to power pop to hip-hop to electronic music, the festival draws big names and huge numbers of fans. Past headliners have included cultural icons like The Beastie Boys, Radiohead, Bjork, The Black Keys, Red Hot Chili Peppers, Outkast, and Jack White. People come from far and wide to attend. The festival is so popular that it offers the same lineup two weekends back to back in April. Tickets are highly competitive to get and sell out within hours of going on sale in January. The crowd skews youngish, but it can be a fun time for anyone due to their predictably excellent band lineup. They don't shy away from the "art" aspect of the festival either, featuring a few choice Burning Man-level technology and sculpture installations. On-site camping is available, including stylish tepees all set up for you. Outside the festival, local hotels as far as Palm Springs 25 miles away book quickly. For transportation to and from the festival (if you're not camping on the grounds), prepaid and reserved shuttles are available at pickup points throughout the Coachella Valley and Palm Springs.

STAGECOACH FESTIVAL

The **Stagecoach Festival** (www.stagecoachfestival.com, end of Apr.) takes the Coachella Festival's place on those same polo fields to throw a massive outdoor country music festival at the end of April. Acts range from mainstream to outlaw country, old-timers to new blood, with some big names gracing the festival's three stages. Since its beginning in 2007, the festival has been on the rise. Past Stagecoach lineups have featured Merle Haggard, Emmylou Harris, Dwight Yoakam, and Hank Williams Jr. The three-day lineup (Fri.-Sun.) is all-ages and draws thousands of festivalgoers. Accommodations are tight and should be booked well in advance. There is limited on-site RV camping that fills up months ahead of time. Beyond this, visitors rely on campgrounds and hotels in the area outside the festival grounds. Shuttles (with prepaid weekend shuttle passes) transport festivalgoers from designated hotel shuttle stops in the Coachella Valley and Palm Springs.

SHOPPING

Shops on Perez Road

The hotbed of mid-century home furnishing shopping may be in Palm Springs, but Cathedral City's shops on Perez Road have a few offerings. Set in an unassuming strip mall north of Highway 111, a short series of vintage design stores make for a destination in the otherwise uninspired suburban sprawl. **Hedge** (68-929 Perez Rd., Ste. F, Cathedral City, 760/770-0090, www.hedgepalmsprings.com, noon-5pm Thurs.-Sun.) displays a curated collection of pristine mid-century furniture and housewares, including chairs, patio furniture, lamps, ashtrays, art, sculpture, and pottery. The collection at **Hom** (68929 Perez Rd., Ste. G, H, I, 760/770-4447, www.at-homps.com, 10am-5pm Mon.-Sat., 11am-5pm Sun.) spans three suites chock full of vintage furniture, lamps, and art from mid-century to the 1960s and 1970s. An upstairs loft is stocked with vintage records favoring lounge and feel-good rock. **Spaces** (68-929 Perez Rd., 760/770-5333, 11am-5pm Wed.-Sat. noon-5pm Sun.) feels like a cluttered estate sale stuffed with glassware, furniture, and housewares. You're sure to find a treasure. The limited number of items at **JP Denmark** (68-929 Perez Rd., Ste. N, 760/408-9147, www.jpantik.com, call for hours) gives good clues as to the quality and price range of this shop featuring vintage Danish modern furniture and accents.

The Fine Art of Design (73717 Hwy. 111, Palm Desert, 760-565-7388, www.thefineartofdesign.com, 11am-4pm Fri.-Sat., 11am-3pm Sun.) in Palm Desert features a vintage collection of designer gems unparalleled in Palm Springs or the Coachella Valley. This is not your average vintage shop: they specialize in couture classics from shiny Halston wraps to Alexander McQueen dresses as well as wedding dresses, shoes, jewelry, and handbags. Hours can be limited, but they also open by appointment.

Shops on El Paseo

The **El Paseo Shopping District** (73-061

El Paseo, Palm Desert, 760/341-4058, www.elpaseocatalogue.com, shops open daily) is the Rodeo Drive, Beverly Hills, of Palm Desert. The walkable outdoor six-block area features luxury shopping set against landscaped desert gardens and mountain views. High-end brands like Ralph Lauren, Burberry, and Gucci, and staples such as Pottery Barn mingle with designer boutiques and restaurants to create a destination. The upscale shopping district begins on El Paseo Drive between Highway 74 and Sage Lane. Complimentary valet parking is provided. The shopping and dining district continues another four blocks to the east where Hotel Paseo anchors one end.

RECREATION

★ Thousand Palms Oasis Preserve

The 20,114-acre **Thousand Palms Oasis Preserve** (29200 Thousand Palms Canyon Rd., Thousand Palms, 760/343-1234, www.coachellavalleypreserve.org, 7am-6pm daily May-Sept. 7am-5pm daily Oct.-Apr.) is hidden unexpectedly in the middle of the suburban Coachella Valley, protecting a fragile and diversely beautiful desert habitat in an area otherwise overrun by suburban sprawl. Shaped by the San Andreas fault zone, the landscape features both rocky, barren ridges and lush oases. Across the preserve, clusters of native California fan palms flash in the glaring sun, protecting hidden pools. A **visitors center** (760/343-2733, hours vary, closed June-Aug.) offers maps and information in the Palm House, a picturesque rustic cabin. The preserve is closed to all pets and bikes. The preserve parking area cannot accommodate large vehicles like RVs.

HIKING

The preserve is a peaceful and striking destination, good for a picnic or a hike on more than 28 miles of trails (closed to dogs and bikes). The most popular hike is the **McCallum Trail** (two miles round-trip), an easy, level trail cross-desert to a spectacular series of oasis pools. To extend the hike, continue onto the Moon Country Loop and wind through Colorado River Desert, by contrast barren and desolate (four miles round-trip in combination with the McCallum Trail and oasis).

GETTING THERE

The preserve is located east of Palm Springs and north of I-10. From Palm Springs, follow Ramon Road east to Thousand Palms Canyon Road. Turn left (north) and continue along Thousand Palms Canyon Road to Preserve turn-off, a short dirt road that leads to the visitors center parking lot. Note that services here are limited.

Santa Rosa and San Jacinto Mountains National Monument

The **Santa Rosa and San Jacinto Mountains National Monument** (www.blm.gov and www.fs.usda.gov) encompasses the mountain ranges to the west of the Coachella Valley towering above the desert floor. With its highest elevation reaching 10,834 feet, it provides a spectacular, sometimes snowcapped, backdrop to the desert communities. An array of destinations and hikes—from lush palm oases to rugged peaks, wilderness areas, and a scenic section of the Pacific Crest Trail—makes the national monument an outstanding destination.

The monument spans more than 280,000 acres, extending from the Coachella Valley to the alpine hamlet of Idyllwild near Mount San Jacinto State Park. The vast sprawl encompasses two federal wilderness areas (Santa Rosa and San Jacinto), the San Jacinto Ranger District, and public BLM lands within the California Desert Conservation Area. The monument's extensive network of trails and backcountry can be accessed from Idyllwild and the Coachella Valley.

The ranger-staffed **visitors center** (51-500 Hwy. 74, Palm Desert, 760/862-9984, Oct. 1-Apr. 30, 8:30am-noon and 12:30pm-4pm Thurs.-Mon., May 1-Sept. 30 8am-noon and 12:30-3:30pm Thurs.-Mon.) is your best resource for exploring this region, with maps and books for hikes and recreation. The visitors center is in the Coachella Valley four miles south of Highway 111 in the town of Palm Desert. Interpretive trails ranging from 0.2 mile to 2.5 miles leave from the visitors center and wind through the desert landscape.

Golf

The Coachella Valley is a golfing mecca. Moderate year-round temperatures and spectacular mountain views have given rise to a wealth of golf courses and clubs throughout the valley. Golfing is a lifestyle as well as a destination in the Coachella Valley, and there are a number of courses open to the public, including municipal courses, semiprivate clubs, and resort facilities. Courses vary widely for a range of skill levels and price points, from basic courses for knocking around to luxury resort settings to PGA Classic courses. Many courses enforce dress codes.

To immerse yourself into a golfing vacation, stay at one of the Coachella Valley's numerous resorts. Most golf courses maintain online booking for tee times on their website. Pricing for many courses is dynamic, reflecting real-time conditions including weather, demand, and other market factors. Other booking resources include Stand-By Golf and Golf Now. **Stand-By Golf** (760/321-2665, www.standbygolf.com, 7am-7pm daily) is a comprehensive booking site that is able to search for tee times in all Coachella Valley communities, including Palm Springs, Cathedral City, Rancho Mirage, Palm Desert, Indian Wells, La Quinta, and Indio. You can search by desired tee time, price range, and course. Book directly through this website 365 days a year. **Golf Now** (800/752-9020, www.golfnow.com, 5am-5pm daily) offers an online tee time retail service for Palm Springs and other international golfing destinations.

The **Westin Mission Hills Golf Resort & Spa** (760/328-3198, www.playmissionhills.com, $60-109) is a resort facility in Rancho Mirage with two golf courses available for public guests as well as resort guests. The **Gary Player Signature Course** (70705 Ramon Rd., Rancho Mirage) is straightforward with wide fairways, while the **Pete Dye Course** (71501 Dinah Shore Dr., Rancho Mirage) is more difficult with challenging greens. Amenities include shared golf carts and a pro shop. The resort also offers a golf academy, daily clinics, private lessons, and golf schools.

Also in Rancho Mirage, **Omni Rancho Las Palmas Resort & Spa** (42-000 Bob Hope Dr., 760/568-2727, www.omnihotels.com, $59-99) has three distinct layouts across a 27-hole championship course characterized by a gently rolling terrain with palm trees and six lakes.

Desert Willow Golf Resort (38995 Desert Willow Dr., 760/346-0015, www.desertwillow.com, from $63) in Palm Desert offers two 18-hole regulation courses featuring desert landscaping, large lakes, and bunkers. Amenities include a golf academy, complete practice facility ($30 pp), PGA instruction, a restaurant with patio dining, and a full-service pro shop. Golf club rentals are available. Sunrise and prime tee times run $75 (includes two sleeves of golf balls), and twilight and sunset tee times $45 (no golf balls).

JW Marriott Desert Springs Resort & Spa (74855 Country Club Dr., 760/341-1756, ext. 1, www.marriott.com, $99-160) is a luxury golf resort in the city of Palm Desert that encompasses 36 holes across two championship layouts—the Palms Course (par 72) and Valley Course (par 54). Resort amenities include a clubhouse and golf shop, rentals and lessons, driving range and putting green, golf program available for juniors, and a Kids Golf-4-Free program.

The **Indian Wells Golf Resort** (44500 Indian Wells Ln., www.indianwellsgolfresort.com, $49-109) offers two 18-hole courses: the Celebrity course and the Players course. The Celebrity course features undulating fairways, split-level lakes, waterfalls, brooks, and floral details. The Players course features wide playing corridors and sculpted bunkers. Resort amenities include a driving range, practice greens, power carts, locker rooms and showers, a golf performance center, a golf academy, bar and grill, and clubhouse. Accommodations, golf packages, and rental clubs and shoes are available.

A former home course of the PGA, **SilverRock Resort** (79179 Ahmanson Ln., 888/600-7272 or 760/777-8884, www.silverrock.org, call for rates) in La Quinta features an 18-hole regulation golf course that sprawls over 200 acres with water features and native bunkers. The Clubhouse is a historic, renovated ranch hacienda situated amid rocky outcroppings. Amenities include a grill-style restaurant.

La Quinta Resort (50200 Ave. Vista Bonita, 760/564-4111, www.laquintaresort.com, $49-109) offers two 18-hole regulation golf courses—the Dunes Course with traditional Scottish design and the Mountain Course known for its dramatic mountain backdrop and challenging course. Both courses are open to resort and public guests. Golf amenities include the Mountain Dunes clubhouse with a grill-style restaurant and a golf shop (6am-6pm daily). Fees include shared cart and unlimited day-of-play use of practice facilities. The resort also offers resort accommodations and golf packages. Golf club rentals are available.

Three 18-hole regulation PGA West golf courses are also part of the luxurious La Quinta Resort ($89-179). **PGA West Greg Norman** features 60 acres of fairways and nine ponds spanning 18 acres. The world-famous **PGA West TPC Stadium Course** is considered to be one of the greatest 100 courses in the world and has been viewed on TV by millions. The **PGA West Jack Nicklaus** is a more manageable version of the PGA West TPC. Both courses are open to resort and public guests. Tee time reservations are available online. Fees include shared cart and unlimited day-of-play use of practice facilities. Other amenities include two clubhouses with restaurants and golf shops.

Tennis

Like golf, tennis is a big draw to Palm Springs and the Coachella Valley. The lovely weather and year-round sun put Palm Springs on the map even before golf became a favorite pastime. There are a number of public, semiprivate, and resort facilities open to the public.

Indian Wells Tennis Garden (78200 Miles Ave., Indian Wells, 760/200-8200, www.iwtg.net, 8am-8pm Mon.-Fri., 8am-5pm Sat.-Sun. Oct. 1-May 31; 7am-noon and 5pm-9pm Mon.-Fri., 7am-noon Sat.-Sun. June 1-Sept. 30) is the second-largest tennis stadium in the world. The full-service tennis club features 29 concrete courts, 23 lighted courts, locker rooms, a fitness area, and a pro shop. A regular calendar of private lessons, group lessons, clinics, and camps are available for both adults and juniors. Additional services include ball-machine rental ($30), racquet stringing and repairs, and game arrangements.

Spas and Hot Mineral Springs

There is no shortage of opportunity to luxuriate in hot water in the Coachella Valley. The town of Desert Hot Springs, developed over natural hot- and cold-water aquifers, is a haven for spa hounds who flock to the dozens of hotels that have tapped into these rich mineral aquifers to fill their swimming pools and hot tubs. Further south, in the Coachella Valley south of Palm Springs, big resorts offer on-site spas that specialize in body treatments and give access to a range of amenities.

Desert Hot Springs Spa Hotel (11740 Mesquite Ave., Desert Hot Springs, 760/673-8689, www.dhsspa.com, 8am-10pm daily, $5-10 day pass) takes a quantity-over-quality approach. A day pass gets you access to the 1940s resort hotel's eight mineral pools in a large, palm-studded courtyard. The hotel also has an on-site café and sports bar. The hotel is well known as a party spot and has live music on weekends.

The charming Moroccan-themed **El Morocco Inn** (66810 4th St., Desert Hot Springs, 760/288-2527, www.elmoroccoinn.com, 9am-4pm daily, $50 pp or free with one-hour spa treatment) offers a huge covered hot spa, outdoor mineral pool, sauna, and a range of spa services, including massages, scrubs, masks, facials, and detoxifying treatments for guests and nonguests.

The **Miracle Springs Resort & Spa** (10625 Palm Dr., Desert Hot Springs, 760/251-6000, www.miraclesprings.com, 9am-6pm daily, age 21 and over only, $14) offers eight pools and spas for day use. They also have an on-site salon (manicures and pedicures) and a full-service spas. The on-site Capri restaurant serves breakfast, lunch, and dinner, and has a full bar and poolside lunch service.

At **The Spring Resort & Spa** (12699 Reposo Way, Desert Hot Springs, 760/251-6700, www.the-spring.com, call for reservations 7:45am-8:45pm, with spa services only, from $125-285) guests receive day spa services with two hours' use of the resorts three mineral pools heated to different temperatures. They offer several different packages combining massages, scrubs, and wraps from 1.5 to 3 hours.

The quiet **Tuscan Springs Hotel & Spa** (68187 Club Cir., Desert Hot Springs, 760/251-0189, www.tuscansprings.com, $45 for four hours) offers mineral pool day use (free when purchasing any treatment from the on-site La Bella Spa).

The setting at family-friendly **Sam's Family Spa Hot Water Resort** (70875 Dillon Rd., Desert Hot Springs, 760/329-6457, www.samsfamilyspa.com, $18 Mon.-Fri., $25 Sat.-Sun. and holidays) includes a spring-fed swimming pool and a series of hot mineral pools tucked amid palm trees in a parklike setting.

If you're looking for something outside of Desert Hot Springs, **The Spa at Desert Springs**, located in the JW Marriott Desert Springs Resort & Spa in Palm Desert (74-855 Country Club Dr., Palm Desert, 760/341-1874, www.marriott.com, $45 per day) offers unlimited use of their heated outdoor saltwater pool, sauna, steam room, whirlpools, fitness equipment, and lounges (both co-ed and gender separated). Book a spa treatment at $80 or over and use of the amenities is included.

ACCOMMODATIONS

Resort accommodations in the Coachella Valley tend to go big. Major hotel chains like JW Marriott and the Omni, tribally-owned luxury casino hotels, and a few sleek new or refurbished properties offer grand amenity-filled resorts with multiple swimming pools, onsite restaurants, and other perks. The exception is the small town of Desert Hot Springs, where the lodging tends to be more like an understated Palm Springs, with mid-century architecture and quiet courtyard pools.

Desert Hot Springs

Situated along the San Andreas fault line, Desert Hot Springs' claim to fame is the abundance of hot natural mineral springs that propelled the development of the town's spas and resorts. The 1950s were the heyday, and some of the operating boutique hotels sport the clean lines and neon signs of desert resort mid-century architecture. Desert Hot Springs has never achieved the popularity of nearby Palm Springs. The town has seen growth in recent years but much of it in the form of newer residences. Desert Hot Springs' spas are mixed in amid the more recent housing. The town attracts snowbirds and other visitors looking for a more low-key and affordable experience than Palm Springs. Its spas range from retro-hip to sleekly luxurious.

Many hotels in Desert Hot Springs offer day-use services for nonhotel guests. For a fee that varies by hotel, visitors can enjoy the cold mineral pools, hot spas, or spa treatments and massages at a range of hotels in Desert Hot Springs from tranquil retreats to party spots.

The Casablanca-inspired digs at ★ **El Morocco Inn** (66810 4th St., 760/288-2527, www.elmorroccoinn.com, from $180) walk the line between luxurious, kitschy, and chic. The hotel is strewn with extravagant Moroccan lamps that the owner brings back from his travels. Rooms in this hideaway feature canopy beds, while the hotel spoils guests with complimentary mint tea, snacks, breakfast, and a nightly "Morocco-tini" hour.

Desert Hot Springs

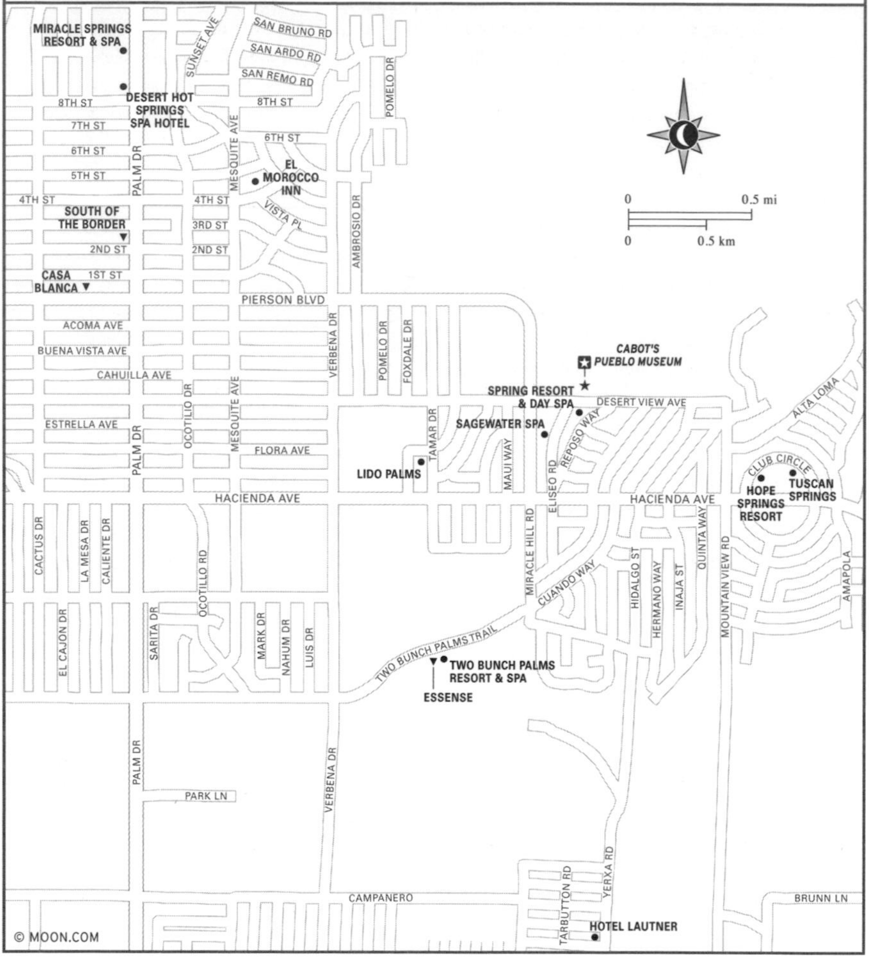

There's also a desert garden with hammocks, a bocce ball court, a relaxation tent, and a movie and game library. The pool and gigantic covered spa are open 24 hours daily.

Lido Palms (12801 Tamar Dr., 760/329-6033, www.lidopalms.com, from $170) offers a chance to relax and rejuvenate. The nine-room mid-century retreat opens onto a neatly landscaped courtyard with ocotillos, yuccas, agaves, barrel cacti, and palms. Inside, slightly dated rooms feature tile floors, full kitchens, and fluffy robes. Amenities include a pool, a hot tub, and a spa that are open 24/7, plus a grill for guest use on-site. Children and pets are not permitted.

The upscale modernist **Sagewater Spa** (12689 Eliseo Rd., 760/220-1554, www.sagewaterspa.com, $219-349) offers a restful and serene experience. The seven guest rooms have views and full kitchens.

Spare mid-century style and desert chic meet over polished concrete floors at **Hope**

Springs Resort (68075 Club Circle Dr., 760/329-4003, www.hopespringsresort.com, $200-250), which offers 10 rooms with king-size beds (four rooms include kitchens) that open onto a communal pool and spa. Guests take advantage of the continental breakfast, communal kitchen, and grill, which means you never have to leave. Children and pets are not permitted.

Contemporary The **Spring Resort & Day Spa** (12699 Reposo Way, 760/251-6700, www.the-spring.com, $259-369) offers 12 understated guest rooms in view of the San Jacinto Mountains. Most rooms surround the courtyard pool and include rainfall showerheads and Egyptian cotton linens. Guests can look forward to a complimentary breakfast, a firepit, and three mineral pools.

Set on 77 lush acres, **Two Bunch Palms Resort & Spa** (67425 Two Bunch Palms Trail, 760/329-8791, www.twobunchpalms.com, from $395) offers charm dating back to 1930. Choose from the original "Grotto" rooms with king beds, or "Soulstice" rooms, which come in a range of layouts with either a king bed or two double beds; some rooms have patios or courtyards. Amenities include two mineral springs pools, a shaded "grotto" for soaking, and tennis courts, as well as the on-site farm to table restaurant **Essense.**

Iconic architectural home turned desert oasis, the **Hotel Lautner** (67710 San Antonio St., 760/832-5288, www.hotellautner.com, $295) was designed by John Lautner in 1947 and features concrete, redwood, lots of glass, and skylights. Four private vacation rental units with a boutique luxury feel offer private patios, share a communal space with a saltwater plunge pool, a firepit lounge, and a grilling area.

Coachella Valley

In the land of shining swimming pools, the town of Palm Springs is the primary destination with its mid-century architectural treasures and small, high-design luxury boutique hotels. But the sunshine continues beyond the boundaries of Palm Springs, and the Coachella Valley provides a whole different vacation experience that is bigger, grander, resort-ier and child-friendlier. If you want swimming pool options, tee times, 38,000-square-foot spa facilities, on-site restaurants, outdoor bars, family-friendly rooms and amenities that compel you to stay on the premises for your entire stay, you may want to shift your vacation digs south to the Coachella Valley. The kids will love **Splashtopia**, a 2-acre water playground complete with lazy river, sandy beach, two 100-foot waterslides, and sprinklers. Need some adult time? An adults-only pool with poolside drink and food service, cliffside hot tub and cabanas are also on-site. The 240-acre **Omni Rancho Las Palmas Resort & Spa** (42-000 Bob Hope Dr., Rancho Mirage, 760/568-2727, www.omnihotels.com, $330-400) has been fully revitalized from its original Hollywood heyday in the 1950s as the Desert Air Hotel & Resort. It boasts 444 guest rooms, a 27-hole golf course, tennis courts, full-service spa, and on-site bars and restaurants in addition to the water park.

At the **JW Marriott Desert Springs Resort & Spa** you can take a boat ride to dinner. A mini ferry leaves from the hotel lobby and lands water-side at the Mikado Japanese Steakhouse (74855 Country Club Dr., Palm Desert, 760/341-1756, www.marriott.com, $250-500). This lavish touch is one of many at the extensive luxury hotel featuring waterways traversed with gondolas, an island populated by pink flamingos, five outdoor pools, a spa, two golf courses, six restaurants, and tennis courts. Oh, yes, and they have hotel rooms. Contemporary guest rooms offer luxurious bedding and bathrooms, plus LCD flat-screen TVs and mini fridges; some rooms have private balconies.

Hotel Paseo (45-400 Larkspur Ln., Palm Desert. 760/340-9001, from $265) opened in 2018 next to the upscale El Paseo shopping district (known as the Rodeo Drive of the Desert), creating a destination hub for upscale shopping, dining, and lounging. The sleek luxury hotel differs from the mega-resorts that the Coachella Valley is known for. Instead

1

2

of offering everything, it prides itself on one well-appointed restaurant, spa, and swimming pool. The hotel's format is open and airy. encouraging you to explore the nearby shopping, art, restaurants, tennis, golf, hiking, and natural beauty nearby.

A dazzling redesign by renowned interior designer Martyn Lawrence Bullard transformed the historic the **Sands Hotel & Spa** (44-985 Province Way, Indian Wells, 760/321-3771, sandshotelandspa.com, from $265) from a nondescript stucco hotel into a luxurious destination with Moroccan influences and a mid-century vibe. Service at the hotel can fall short of the high bar set by the design; however its charms are many. The hotel offers 46 guest rooms, each uniquely designed with different color combinations, hand-crafted furniture, and custom textiles, many with private patios or balconies. They have taken the concept of the in-room minibar to the next level with vintage crystal stemware and premixed cocktails rivaling ones from the actual bar. Bathrooms are luxurious with Acqua di Parma bath amenities and open showers with soaking tubs. The on site Pink Cabana restaurant and bar serves breakfast, lunch, and dinner. Adults 18 and over only for the hotel.

The historic **La Quinta Resort** (50200 Ave. Vista Bonita, La Quinta, 760/564-4111, www.laquintaresort.com, from $180) is a restored desert hideaway dating to 1926 with a long list of Hollywood A-listers in its roster. The Spanish revival-style resort is set on 45 acres and features six golf courses, tennis courts, six restaurants, a swimming pool, a gym, and a spa. Cozy casitas offer mini fridges and LCD flat-screen TVs; some rooms have fireplaces. Upgrades and suites can add hot tubs, private patios, and sitting areas. Villas are also available.

Casino Hotels

You can't miss the sweeping architecture of the **Morongo Casino Resort and Spa** (49500 Seminole Dr., Cabazon, 951/849-3080, www.morongocasinoresort.com, from $239) as you slog your way east from Los Angeles on Interstate 10 toward Palm Springs. The impressive facade hides a self-contained 44-acre oasis designed to make you forget about your day-to-day as you float on the lazy river or enjoy 150,000 square feet of gaming. The high-rise luxury resort hotel has 310 rooms and suites. Some rooms have views of the mountains. Perks included in your resort fee: Wi-Fi, flat-screen TVs, stocked minibars, the Oasis pool (lazy river, sandy beach, hot tubs), shuttle to nearby outlets, access to Tukwet Canyon Golf Club, fitness center, professional bowling center, and plenty of dining options on site.

If you want Las Vegas without the long highway drive, the **Agua Caliente Casino Resort Spa** (32-250 Bob Hope Dr., Rancho Mirage, 760/321-2000, www.hotwatercasino.com, from $250) is a good option. The resort has a full calendar of entertainment, a high-end steak house, the obligatory buffet, and a full-service casino with slot machines, table games, a poker room, and high limit rooms. For daytime, two outdoor pools, cabana rentals, and an outdoor bar and grill will keep you lounging. Deluxe rooms offer 42-inch flat-screen TVs, Wi-Fi, robes, and oversize sunken tubs, while suites will garner you parlors, a wet bar, and jetted whirlpool tubs.

FOOD

Desert Hot Springs

There are dining options in Desert Hot Springs but few are destination-worthy. It's worth it to drive (or ride share) to Palm Springs 12 miles south or take advantage of the kitchens and barbecues provided in some of the resorts. If you want to stick close to your hotel, casual Mexican is usually a crowd pleaser, or Desert Hot Springs offers one upscale farm to table restaurant worth a try.

Serving up Mexican specialties and smoky salsa in a setting with colorful decor, **Casa Blanca** (66370 Pierson Blvd., 760/251-5922, www.casablancamenu.com, 7:30am-10pm

1: Hotel Paseo in Palm Desert 2: the revitalized, luxurious Sands Hotel & Spa in Indian Wells

daily, $6-18) is a popular choice for locals and visitors. Try the signature spinach enchiladas.

You can also enjoy the traditional Mexican plates and deep booths at **South of the Border** (11719 Palm Dr., 760/251-4000, 11am-9:30pm Sun.-Thurs., 11am-10pm Fri.-Sat., $9-12). This spot delivers satisfying Mexican comfort food in the form of hearty combination plates, cheese-covered enchiladas, and steak, chicken, and shrimp house specials served up in an eccentric atmosphere with carved wood seating, hanging lights, and oil paintings.

Essense (67425 Two Bunch Palms Trail, 760/329-8791, www.twobunchpalms.com, 7:30am-9pm Sun.-Thurs., 7:30am-10pm Fri.-Sat.) is the farm to table restaurant in the Two Bunch Palms Resort, offering brunch options from house-made granola to eggs Benedict to organic chicken pho ($8-32), and dinner specialties such as vegan lasagna and filet mignon with lump crab ($22-48). Specialty cocktails, wines, local and organic beers, and snacks are served in the lounge.

The Coachella Valley

An unassuming location in a stucco strip mall in Cathedral City provides the simple backdrop for **Justin Eat & Drink's** (68784 E. Palm Canyon Dr., Cathedral City, 760/904-4093, www.justinrestaurant.com, 5pm-9pm Tues.-Sun.) fresh, innovative dishes that rival Palm Springs' foodie temples. The inventive cowboy fare defies categorization, but dishes like Cowboy Candy (candied jalapenos, cream cheese, and crostini) and grass-fed Angus beef with honeynut squash, pepitas, and ancho butter stand out in the desert. Reservations recommended.

Upscale prime rib with a heavy dose of ye olden times, English pub **Lord Fletcher's** (70385 Hwy. 111, Rancho Mirage, 760/328-1161, www.lordfletcher.com, 5:30pm-10pm Tues.-Sat., $28-48) specializes in upscale classic English fare from prime rib to chicken and dumplings set amid an impressive collection of English bric-a-brac and antiques. Sit at Frank Sinatra's favorite table near the fireplace, adorned with a painting of Ol' Blue Eyes himself. Lord Fletcher's also offers a pub menu served bar-side (from 5pm, $5-15). Reservations are recommended.

Wilma and Frieda's (73575 El Paseo #2310, Palm Desert, 760/773-2807, https://wilmafrieda.com, 8am-3pm daily, $9-17) offers brunch classics in its original location in Palm Desert including the post-brunch coma inducing banana caramel French toast and griddled meatloaf and eggs. Look for the Palm Desert spot on the second floor in the El Paseo shopping district. A second location in Palm Springs adds dinner (155 S. Palm Canyon Dr., Suite A21-A27, 760/992-5080, 8am-3pm Sun.-Wed., 8am-9pm Thurs.-Sat., dinner $13-22).

An old-school American diner, **Keedy's Fountain Grill** (Palms to Pines Shopping Center, 73633 Hwy. 111, Palm Desert, 760/346-6492, 5:30am-3pm daily, $7-13) has been getting folks fed since 1957. This mostly locals spot is slinging omelets, burgers, and other American diner fare at the coffee counter and stripped-down dining room.

Light and bright ★ **AC3** (45350 Larkspur Ln., Palm Desert, 760/340-6069, www.ac3palmdesert.com, 7am-11pm daily, breakfast and lunch $10-20, dinner $22-37) offers creative nouveau-American food in a modern, airy space with verve. The restaurant is adjacent to the El Paseo Shopping District, so their spacious patio is a perfect place to refresh during your shopping outing. Black truffle pommes frites accompany fresh salads like the lobster cobb or burgers like the AC3 Kobe beef for lunch, while dinner adds sophisticated Mediterranean-inspired mains. The restaurant opened as part of the boutique luxury Hotel Paseo, but it stands on its own.

Part of the newly revitalized 1950s Sands Hotel and Spa, **The Pink Cabana** restaurant (44-985 Province Way, Indian Wells, 8am-9pm Sun.-Thurs., 8am-10pm Fri.-Sat., brunch $9-21, lunch $12-29, dinner $18-42) offers a dreamy, poolside café setting with a vintage Parisian feel and whimsical tropical touches. Small bites, salads, and large plates draw from French classics by way of California.

Around 5 pm, the long-timers from the surrounding Indian Wells communities and a smattering of tourists start to roll into the dining room for dinner. At 10pm, some of them may still be there on the dance floor. An Indian Wells staple since 1965, ★ **The Nest** (75188 CA-111, Indian Wells, 760/346-2314, www.gotothenest.com, 4pm-midnight Sun.-Thurs., 4pm-1:30am Fri.-Sat., $23-57) offers a full-service restaurant and lively venue with live music, drinks, and dancing nightly. Their restaurant features American specialties like steaks, pastas, and seafood as well as traditional family recipes, including cabbage rolls and moussaka. They also offer an excellent pared-down version of their dining room menu at the bar with happy hour prices and smaller portions. The restaurant is connected to the Sands Hotel, but they operate as strictly separate businesses.

On the edge of the Coachella polo fields where the Coachella Music Festival is held, **Tack Room Tavern** (81800 Avenue 51, Indio, 760/347-9985, www.empirepoloevents.com, 3pm-12:30am Mon., 11am-12:30am Tues.-Sat., 9am-12:30am Sun., $11-15) is open to the public. This fun local watering hole with a patio and saddle bar seats serves excellent sandwiches, burgers, and salads, drawing everyone from ladies sipping manhattans to dudes chanting over the big game.

Head to **Jackalope Ranch** (80400 Hwy. 111, Indio, 760/342-1999, www.thejackaloperanch.com, 11:30am-10pm Sun.-Wed., 11:30am-midnight Thurs.-Sat., $11-39) for BBQ, steaks, and seafood served in a stone lodge with a saloon, outdoor bar, and live music.

TRANSPORTATION AND SERVICES

The Coachella Valley sprawls southeast of Palm Springs, encompassing the towns of Desert Hot Springs, Cathedral City, Rancho Mirage, Thousand Palms, Palm Desert, Indian Wells, La Quinta, Indio, and Coachella, all of which are accessed from I-10. A car is the only way to navigate this region surrounding Palm Springs.

Car

Desert Hot Springs is located north of Palm Springs and I-10. To get here, follow North Indian Canyon Drive north from Palm Springs or take Highway 62 north from I-10 and turn east on Pierson Boulevard.

Cathedral City abuts Palm Springs to the east and is accessible via I-10 by following Vista Chino or Ramon Road east from Palm Springs. Continuing east, **Rancho Mirage** is the next in line, accessible from I-10 via Bob Hope Drive or along Highway 111 from Palm Springs.

Thousand Palms and **Palm Desert** sandwich I-10 north and south (respectively). Monterey Avenue (Exit 131) from I-10 links the two.

Tiny **Indian Wells** sits off Highway 111 between Palm Desert and La Quinta. To get here from Palm Springs, follow Highway 111 east. To get here from I-10, exit at Cook Street (Exit 134) or Washington Street (Exit 137) and drive south to Highway 111.

As Highway 111 continues its journey east, it passes through **La Quinta, Indio,** and **Coachella** to connect with Business I-10 in Indio. Note that Business I-10 continues south, merging with Highway 111 and Highway 86 north of Mecca and toward the Salton Sea. To continue on I-10 east and the South Entrance to Joshua Tree, turn northeast on Dillon Road to I-10.

THE SALTON SEA

On clear days, standing on a high peak in Joshua Tree National Park or a rugged ridge near Idyllwild, you'll see an enormous body of blue water shimmering to the south. This is the Salton Sea, deep in the arid Colorado Desert, directly on the San Andreas fault, and covering a massive area 35 miles long and 15 miles wide. In this desert valley, where summer temperatures often top 115°F and the average rainfall is less than three inches, the story of the Salton Sea is a saga of boom and

Pleasures and Plagues

beach and yacht club on the Salton Sea designed by famed architect Albert Frey

The Salton Sea occupies the ancient Salton Sink, which acted as a flood basin for the Colorado River over thousands of years. The river would overflow its banks, running along dry flood channels, fill the sink with a temporary lake, and then disappear. Native American oral history tells of a lake around 1600-1700. Between 1824 and 1904 the river flooded the basin no fewer than eight times. All this flooding and evaporating created a nutrient-rich soil, and in the early 1900s, the California Development Company tried to cash in by developing an industry of year-round irrigated agriculture. By the end of 1904, 10,000 settlers were farming the newly irrigated land. The success was short-lived. By 1905, the irrigation channels had silted up, and engineers made an infamous cut into the bank of the Colorado River to try to increase flow. You could say they succeeded. However, the water that flowed out crashed through the engineered canal creating a raging torrent that swamped the Salton Basin in successive floods for two years before the deluge was stopped. Witnesses described huge waterfalls 20, 40, and 80 feet high. The Salton Sea was born.

Recreation became the fledgling industry. In fact, one of the original settlers, Captain Charles E. Davis, set the region on its course. He had fortuitously built his early camp in 1898 on top of an extinct volcano near what would become the shores of the Salton Sea. After the flooding, the site of his camp became Mullet Island. Hell's Kitchen was the name of the café, dance hall, and boat landing he built in 1908. By the late 1920s the Salton Sea was well on its way to becoming a wildly popular recreation destination. Tourists flocked to the shores of the "Salton Rivera" for fishing, boating, waterskiing, swimming, golf, and partying. Albert Frey, an architect who pioneered the desert modernist aesthetic, was responsible for the distinct lines of the **Salton Bay Yacht Club** and the nautical-themed **North Shore Beach and Yacht Club** in 1958.

In the late 1970s the sea's popularity began to sink with the rise of the sea and flooding due to agricultural runoff and above-average rainfall. By the early 1980s most of the planned vacation communities around the Salton Sea were abandoned. With no natural outlet, the saline levels of the Salton Sea have continued to rise, causing problems with the sea life and birds who depend on the lake.

bust, a disaster turned happy accident turned disaster again as a combination of ancient geography and contemporary folly created the perfect storm—or in this case, flood.

Today the Salton Sea is a strangely beautiful place, surrounded by the stark Chocolate Mountains and the semi-ghost towns of once-vibrant resort communities. Photographers come here to capture the abandonment and decay, while road-trippers marvel at the juxtaposition of natural beauty and desolation. The communities still exist, though they are mostly abandoned. Some are home to those who were stuck when the Salton Sea crashed, while others became a refuge for eccentrics, artists, and those looking to live off-the-grid in an out-of-the-way place.

For the best documentary about the Salton Sea, watch *Pleasures & Plagues on the Salton Sea*, narrated by John Waters.

Mecca, Bombay Beach, and Slab City

There are still some functioning businesses from the old days. One enterprising family opened the **International Banana Museum** (98775 Hwy. 111, Mecca, 619/840-1429, www.internationalbananamuseum.com, call for seasonal hours) on the site of the bar and tackle shop they had owned since 1958 during the Salton Sea's heyday.

In the town of Bombay Beach, the **Ski Inn** (9596 Avenue A, Niland, 760/354-1285, 10am-midnight daily, cash only) is operated by owners Jane and Wendell and has achieved cult status among dive bars, claiming the lowest bar in the Western Hemisphere at 223 feet below sea level. On any given day, old-timers, locals, OHV riders, and the occasional curious visitor sip cold beers in the dim coolness of the bar.

In the 1930s military operations moved in but were all decommissioned by the mid-1990s. The remains of one World War II Marine base near the town of Niland has since been taken over as a recreational vehicle squat called **Slab City**. Today it attracts artists, snowbirds, and wanderers who live off the grid. Just outside the boundary of Slab City, **Salvation Mountain** (www.salvationmountaininc.org) is an adobe and straw painted visionary sculpture created by outsider artist Leonard Knight from 1980 to his death in 2011. The bright colors and spiritual text convey his universal message that "God is Love." Within Slab City, the artist community of **East Jesus** (http://eastjesus.org) has received attention for its impressive sculpture installations.

Getting There

When it comes to accommodations, food, and services around the Salton Sea, lower your expectations now. This is a remote desert region and services are very, very few. Fill up the gas tank in Palm Springs or Indio before heading out here, and bring water and food.

From Palm Springs, take I-10 south for 24 miles to the split with Highway 86. To reach Salton City on the west side, follow Highway 86 south for 37 miles. To reach Bombay Beach on the east side, take Highway 111 south for 40 miles. Plan at least one hour for either drive.

The San Jacinto Mountains

Follow Highway 243 or Highway 74 up from the Coachella Valley desert floor and in under an hour you will find yourself in the much cooler San Jacinto Mountains. Originally the summer home of Cahuilla Indians migrating from the desert valleys below, the area began to be settled by homesteaders in the 1890s. Logging and tourism became the primary industry. Tourism won out, and now most of the land surrounding Idyllwild is protected through the Mount San Jacinto State Park, Santa Rosa and San Jacinto Mountains National Monument, and San Bernardino National Forest. In the 1960s and 1970s, an influx of hippies to the area changed the cultural fabric in Idyllwild. Browse the boutique shops in the town center now, and you'll find cowboy hats as well as healing crystals.

Planning Your Time

Summer is the high season with visitors taking advantage of cooler temperatures, campgrounds, and hiking trails. **Winter** brings snow tourism. Community events such as Jazz in the Pines (July) and the Art Walk and Wine Tasting (Oct.) give folks an excuse to visit year-round.

MOUNT SAN JACINTO STATE PARK AND WILDERNESS

Subalpine forests, granite peaks, and mountain meadows quilt the 14,000-acre **Mount**

San Jacinto State Park and Wilderness (www.parks.ca.gov and www.fs.usda.gov) in the heart of the San Jacinto Mountains. Craggy San Jacinto Peak, the highest peak in the park and the second highest in the San Jacinto Range (after Mount San Gorgonio), reaches nearly 11,000 feet and is snowcapped for much of the year. The steep mountain escarpments of the San Jacinto Range plunge 9,000 feet in less than four miles on the northeast side down to the desert floor.

Hiking trails offer sweeping views toward Palm Springs and over 100 miles to the southeast and the Salton Sea. It's a destination for day hiking, backpacking, snowshoeing, and camping. The famous Pacific Crest Trail (PCT), a continuous 2,650-mile trail system that runs from Mexico to Canada, passes through the San Jacinto Mountains, and Idyllwild is a destination for PCT hikers.

The two main jumping-off points for hiking and camping in the state park and wilderness are the town of Idyllwild and the Palm Springs Aerial Tramway.

A **Forest Adventure Pass** is required to park at trailheads and day-use areas. Adventure Passes are available at the Idyllwild Ranger Station or at **Nomad Ventures** (54415 N Circle Dr., 951/659-4853, www.nomadventures.com, 9am-5pm Thurs.-Mon.) as well as at other ranger stations and retailers throughout the San Bernardino, Angeles, and Los Padres National Forests. Rules regarding where Adventure Passes are required are somewhat in flux (pay attention to signage; the default is that Adventure Passes are required).

Hiking

Hundreds of miles of hiking trails for all ability levels are accessible from the town of Idyllwild. Due to the short growing season and popularity of the area, there is a **wilderness permit** system in place. *Everyone must obtain a wilderness permit prior to day hiking or overnight camping.* Day-use permits are free and available at the **Idyllwild Ranger Station** (54270 Pine Crest Ave., 909/382-2921, 8am-4pm Fri.-Tues.). They are also available at the entrance station for **Idyllwild Campground** (25905 Hwy. 243) in San Jacinto State Park. Outside of business hours you can complete a form available on the porch of the campground's ranger station and drop it in the drop box. If you are hiking from the Palm Springs Aerial Tramway, permits are available at the strategically located Long Valley Ranger Station once you arrive at the top.

views from the Ernie Maxwell Scenic Trail

In 2017, forest fires damaged the trail system in the Mount San Jacinto State Park and Wilderness region near the town of Idyllwild. Several trails, including the South Ridge Trail to Tahquitz Peak are closed indefinitely for forest regeneration and trail rebuilding. *Check in at the local ranger station for a hiking permit and current trail conditions before embarking on your hike.* Skirting barriers and entering closed areas prolongs damage and can result in tickets and fines.

ERNIE MAXWELL SCENIC TRAIL

Distance: 5.3 miles round-trip
Duration: 2-3 hours
Elevation gain: 550 feet
Effort: Easy
Trailhead: Tahquitz View Drive at the end of a dirt road on the south end of Idyllwild
Directions: From the Idyllwild Ranger Station (Hwy. 243 and Pine Crest Ave. in Idyllwild), head south on Highway 243 for 0.7 mile. Turn left onto Saunders Meadow Road just past the Mile High Café and before the Idyllwild School. Follow Saunders Meadow Road for 0.8 mile then turn left onto signed Pine Avenue. After 0.1 mile turn right onto the signed Tahquitz View Road. The trailhead is in 0.6 mile. The pavement ends 0.2 mile into Tahquitz View Drive, and the road forks. Follow the left fork signed for the Ernie Maxwell Scenic Trail. The trailhead is signed on the right. Park along the dirt road.

First off, here's a pro tip: Hike the trail starting from the dirt road trailhead in Idyllwild. This way, you will gain elevation on the beginning stretch and have an easier return.

A gentle elevation gain through a mostly shaded forested trail makes this a good choice for a leisurely but satisfying hike. (This is a good pre-brunch Sunday morning hike.) Starting from the **Tahquitz View Drive** trailhead, the path climbs gently through a mix of Jeffrey, ponderosa, and Coulter pines all the way to the **Humber Park** trailhead. The trail provides intermittent views toward Idyllwild and the southwest. The real highlight here is the immersive forest experience and the mellow grades. The trail is particularly nice in **September** and **October.** Once you reach the Humber Park trailhead, turn around and return the way you came.

DEVIL'S SLIDE

Distance: 5 miles
Duration: 2-3 hours
Elevation gain: 1,300 feet
Effort: Moderate
Trailhead: Humber Park
Directions: To get there from the Idyllwild Ranger Station, head northeast on Pine Crest Avenue for 0.6 mile. Turn left onto Fern Valley Road and continue for 1.8 miles until you reach Humber Park. The trail begins on the upper level of the parking area.

The Devil's Slide trail offers a scenic climb through idyllic forest. It's a nice day hike on its own merits, but it's also a key connector trail that leads to the PCT as well as routes to San Jacinto Peak and Tahquitz Peak. This busy trail can be congested; **hike in the morning** to beat some of the traffic as well as catch cooler temperatures. Much of the trail is exposed to direct sunlight after noon.

The trail begins in the upper parking level of **Humber Park.** A short climb quickly gives way to stunning views of Tahquitz Rock, a local landmark sometimes called **Lily Rock.** As the trail continues to climb, you'll have views of Idyllwild and Strawberry Valley to the southwest. You'll climb steadily all the way to **Saddle Junction.** Although Saddle Junction isn't really a destination in and of itself, it's a good goal for a hike that really is about the journey. Return the way you came or continue on to Tahquitz Peak (8.6 miles round-trip), San Jacinto Peak (16 miles round-trip), or an array of other backpacking or day-hiking destinations.

TAHQUITZ PEAK (CONTINUING VIA DEVIL'S SLIDE TRAIL)

Distance: 8.6 miles
Duration: 5 hours
Elevation gain: 2,800 feet
Effort: Strenuous
Trailhead: Humber Park

This striking granite crag can be seen on the drive in from Highway 243. It stands sentinel over the town, and you'll catch glimpses of it from different vantage points. In addition to experiencing breathtaking views and a trip to a historic, furnished fire tower, if you kick off your time in Idyllwild with this spectacular hike, you'll get to feel a sense of smug accomplishment every time you look up.

After wildfires swept the region around Idyllwild in 2017, the South Ridge Trail to Tahquitz Peak closed, leaving the Devil's Slide Trail as the next best option for reaching the peak. It adds a mile and an additional 700 feet of elevation gain than the more direct South Ridge Trail, but it achieves the same lofty peak.

Follow the Devil's Slide Trail to Saddle Junction. From this five-way junction, turn right onto the PCT heading south. You will have a slight break from climbing before the trail ascends through pine forest. The climb continues along a ridge, the Desert Divide, with views into the Coachella Valley. After 1.3 miles along the PCT, turn right onto an access trail and begin the final climb. When you come to a junction with the South Ridge Trail, stay to the right for the last rocky stretch before the lookout tower comes into view.

Climb the steps up to the deck of the lookout tower to get an eyeful. The tower was used historically as a fire lookout, positioned because of its 360-degree views. It has been preserved with historic furnishings, and volunteers maintain the space and greet hikers at the top on some weekends in season (May-Nov.). It adds an extra layer of richness to the experience to tap into some of the region's history and pick the volunteers' brains about trails and surrounding geography as well as enjoy the natural beauty. From the lookout tower deck, the Coachella Valley sprawls to the east, bounded by Joshua Tree National Park and the Little San Bernardino and Cottonwood Mountains. To the north, Marion Mountain looms, blocking views of San Jacinto Peak and the Palm Springs Aerial Tramway. To the southeast, the views extend as far as the Salton Sea.

Winter Sports

While Mount San Jacinto State Park was never developed for skiing (a boon, as this allowed the wilderness to be preserved and the mountain town of Idyllwild to remain peaceful), cross-country skiing and snowshoeing are accessible from Mountain Station at the top of the Palm Springs Aerial Tramway. A **Winter Adventure Center** (10am-4pm Mon. and Thurs.-Fri., 9am-4pm Sat.-Sun, hours and season vary) is open whenever there is snow. The center offers cross-country ski packages (skis, poles, and boots, $21 per day) and snowshoe packages ($18 per day). Mount San Jacinto State Park is also a good destination for families who just want some fun snow frolicking. Snow camping is even available at the hike-in campgrounds along the state park and wilderness network of trails.

There are also sledding opportunities at **Idyllwild County Park** (54000 Riverside County Playground Rd., 951/659-2656, www.rivcoparks.org, open sunrise-sunset).

IDYLLWILD

Idyllwild is a charming mountain town, a forest island nestled one mile high in the San Jacinto Mountains, surrounded by the outlying desert. The artsy, rustic community sits nestled amid pines, cedars, manzanitas, and scenic rock outcroppings. Picturesque cabins with A-frame roofs hint at snow, an exciting proposition in contrast with the sleekly flat mid-century desert dwellings below. Seasonal streams and hiking trails crisscross the hills. Inns with chainsaw-carved wildlife sculptures and fireplaces welcome visitors escaping the heat and traffic of the urban areas below.

The adjacent communities of Fern Valley, Pine Cove, and Idyllwild are generally grouped together and are all considered "Idyllwild."

Shopping

Many shops here can feel like they're caught in a time warp catering to the New Age hippie

Idyllwild

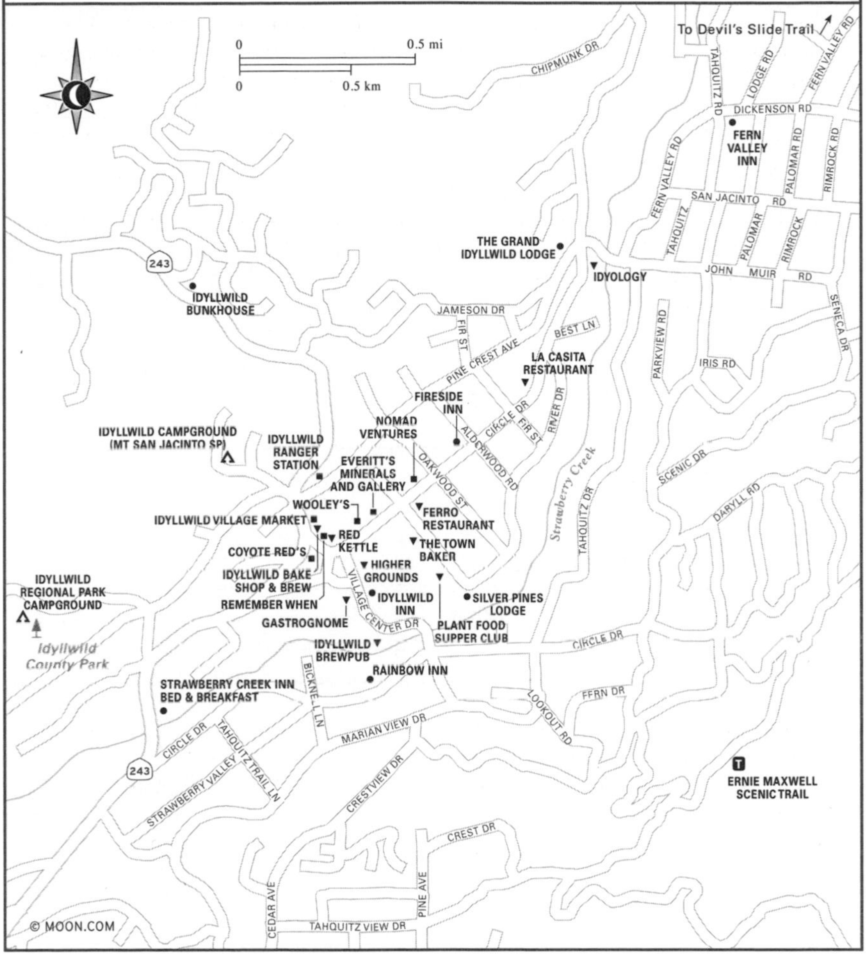

at heart, while other boutique shops cover a range of specialties, including gifts, sweets, art, clothing, and outdoor gear. The majority of the shops in Idyllwild are clustered in a three-block radius on North Circle Drive, where it intersects with Highway 243. An Idyllwild town website (idyllwildvisitorscenter.com) provides a town business directory, including shopping, dining, and lodging.

Nomad Ventures (54415 N. Circle Dr., 951/659-4853, www.nomadventures.com, 9am-5pm Thurs.-Mon.) provides outdoor gear and equipment covering climbing, mountaineering, backpacking, hiking, trail running, and kayaking. There is a second location in Joshua Tree (61795 Twentynine Palms Hwy., 760/366-4684, 9am-7pm daily in summer).

Wooley's (54274 N. Circle Dr., 951/659-0017, www.wooleys.com, 10:30am-5pm daily) offers sheepskin products, including sheepskin slippers, boots, and seat covers. They also stock clothing, cowboy hats, and winter hats—great if you're caught in the cooler temperatures of Idyllwild and need to make an emergency fashion purchase. Home furnishings include high-quality cowhide rugs, lambskin throws, and pillows.

Everitt's Minerals and Gallery (54300 N. Circle Dr., 951/659-7075, www.everittsminerals.com, 11am-5pm daily, but hours can vary) sells handmade jewelry and designs, exotic mineral specimens, rare fossils, and antique Japanese woodblock prints. Their gallery features 14 local and semi-local artists with fine art media, including ceramics, sculpture, and painting.

Coyote Red's (54225 N. Circle Dr, 951/659-2305, 11am-4pm Mon.-Thurs., 11am-5pm Fri., 10am-5pm Sat., 10am-4pm Sun.) is a gourmet country store featuring beef jerky and hot sauce. Their signature chipotle sauce rivals the best of them.

Remember When (54225 N. Circle Dr., 951/659-6456, 11am-4pm Sun., Mon, Thurs., Fri., 10am-5pm Sat.) stocks nostalgic sweets, sodas, and toys. Their almost 200 specialty sodas, throwback candies, and selection of simple toys are fun for the family.

Idyllwild Village Market (2600 Hwy. 243, 951/659-3800, idyllwildvillagemarket.com, 7am-10pm daily) has come a long way in recent years, from a bare-bones convenience grocery to the gourmet goods shop that vacationers want to stock their cabin weekends. They offer a full grocery plus deli, beer, liquor, and pizza.

Accommodations

The aesthetic here is rustic, and hotel accommodations range from boutique mountain lodges with elaborate amenities to frayed cabin motels with charming exteriors and interiors that have seen better days. A host of cabin rentals through third party rental sites offer a range from romantic, two-person hideaways with hot tubs to expansive properties for larger groups. Hotels and motels put you closer to town and walking to restaurants, bars, and shopping. Cabins can make for a more secluded weekend. Make reservations in advance, as Idyllwild can book up completely on popular event weekends.

CABINS

In addition to rentals through Airbnb, Vrbo, Homeaway, or other vacation rental platforms, **Idyllwild Vacation Cabins** (54380 N. Circle Dr., 951/663-0527, www.idyllwildvacationcabins.com, office hours 7am-10pm Mon.-Fri., Sat.-Sun. by appointment) is a locally based company with a large selection of rental cabins. You can search by preference: pet friendly, with views, with hot tubs, on a creek, and price. Cabins are searchable and bookable on their website, but they also have an actual, physical location in Idyllwild's downtown and an actual, real live human in their office who can assist with booking. The office is convenient for last minute bookings when your day trip turns into a weekend getaway, and they also offer centralized management assistance.

MOTELS

For a budget motel, the **Bluebird Cottage Inn** (26620 Saddle Dr., 951/659-2696, www.bluebirdcottageinn.com, $75-205) has character. The cabin-style motel dates to 1957. Its 17 units include studio lodge rooms, duplexes, triplexes, and one two-bedroom cabin. Amenities range from basic rooms to kitchens, fireplaces, and hot tubs. The inn is located on the south end of town about a 20-minute walk or less than a five-minute drive to the town center.

The **Idyllwild Bunkhouse** (25525 CA Hwy. 243, 951/659-2201, idyllwildbunkhouse.com, $109-169) offers camping-themed rooms with knotty pine interiors and several room configurations that make the rustic boutique motel couple- or family-friendly. Queen bedrooms, two-room suites, queen plus twin bedrooms, and downstairs queen plus twin loft rooms all come with kitchenettes and private balconies with forest views. A continental breakfast is delivered to your door each morning. Other amenities include DirecTV and Wi-Fi. The hotel is located along Hwy 243 less than a mile north of town, a two-minute drive or a 15-minute walk to the town center.

LODGES AND CABINS

Silver Pines Lodge (25955 Cedar St., 951/659-4335, $71-129) is a classic mountain inn built in 1923, and it has been the Silver Pines Lodge since 1952. The main lodge has a pitch-perfect exterior and is stuffed full of leather couches, antlers, and other lodge-like furnishings. Silver Pines offers 13 rooms—five connected to the lodge and eight stand-alone cabins, duplexes, or triplexes. The lodges and cabins are a little worse for the wear but clean with decent amenities. Most rooms have fireplaces, and about half have kitchens. Private porches or decks offer peaceful reflection over seasonal Strawberry Creek unless the Town Hall next door is hosting a community event (including daily Jazzercise). The good news is that you're in the center of town with easy walking to restaurants and shops. The lodge also offers six new units at the **Silver Pines Village** 100 yards away.

The family-owned ★ **Idyllwild Inn** (54300 Village Center Dr., 888/659-2552, www.idyllwildinn.com, $107-160) dates from 1904 and is a favorite of PCT hikers and repeat visitors. Set on five wooded acres in the center of town, it features cabins, suites, and theme rooms. Its 12 one- and two-bedroom rustic cabins are original with knotty pine paneling, fireplaces, and private decks. Cabin #9 is carved with historic graffiti dating to the 1950s. Eight new rustic cabins are family-friendly with queen beds and sleeper sofas. New rustic suites offer hot tubs, queen beds, and sleeper sofas. Eight themed rooms are a relatively recent addition.

Make sure you know what your spirit animal (or tree) is before you make reservations at **The Fireside Inn** (54540 N. Circle Dr., 951/659-2966, www.thefiresideinn.com, $119-210). They offer seven lightly themed duplex cottages and a separate 1930s lodge, all with fireplaces and most with kitchens. The inn is set in a residential neighborhood in the center of town within easy walking distance to shops and restaurants. The red-and-white cottage-style **Fern Valley Inn** (25240 Fern Valley Rd., 951/659-8100, www.fernvalleyinn.com, $100-140) dates to 1950 and offers charming cottages set amid garden pathways with a chicken coop. Of the 10 cottages, six are duplexes and four are private cottages. Each has a queen-size bed, wood-burning stove or fireplace, refrigerator, and basic cable TV. Some have full kitchens. Some units have an additional sofa sleeper for a maximum occupancy of four persons. The inn is situated in the upper part of Idyllwild in the quieter Fern Valley neighborhood and close to Humber Park hiking trails. The town center is a five-minute drive or 20-minute walk.

BED-AND-BREAKFASTS

Too much rustic got you down? See no difference between staying in a mountain cabin and camping? **The Grand Idyllwild Lodge** (54820 Pinecrest Rd., 951/659-2383, www.grandidyllwildlodge.com, $265-315) might be the place for you. The Craftsman-style boutique lodge is situated at the top of the town in Fern Valley close to Aroma and Idyology restaurants and Humber Park hiking trails. They offer seven king suites and two queen guest rooms with private entrances, decks, gourmet breakfast, fireplaces, flat-screen smart TVs, gym, Swedish-style sauna, and spa services.

The Craftsman-style **Rainbow Inn** (54420 S. Circle Dr., 951/659-0111, www.rainbowinn.com, $125-165) offers five well-appointed rooms with rustic elegant design. They feature Wi-Fi, cable TV, DVD players, mini fridges, and coffee makers, and some also offer hot tubs and fireplaces; all have private baths. The inn is in the center of town.

Nine rustic, individually decorated rooms make up the **Strawberry Creek Inn** (26370 Hwy. 243, 951/659-3202, www.strawberrycreekinn.com, $197-207). The cozy rooms, including courtyard, queen, and fireplace suites, have Wi-Fi, private bathrooms, and TVs. Some also offer private decks, fireplaces, or canopy beds. A full, homemade breakfast is included. The two-story

Strawberry Cottage on the property features a private entrance, full kitchen, and whirlpool tub. The inn is located in the center of town.

On the south side of Idyllwild, a 20-minute walk to the town center, **Quiet Creek Inn** (26345 Delano Dr., 951/468-4208, www.quietcreekinn.com, from $187) encompasses seven secluded acres along seasonal Strawberry Creek. Studio cabins feature queen and king beds with fireplaces and private decks plus Wi-Fi, refrigerators, and microwaves. One-bedroom suites add a private bedroom with king or queen bed plus kitchenettes.

Camping

There are many great camping options in and around Idyllwild, from developed camping close to town to remoter sites. Note: Fire restrictions may be in effect during fire season (summer months), and campfires may not be allowed at local campgrounds. Campgrounds may be closed intermittently due to drought and fire conditions. Check for current conditions.

Mount San Jacinto State Park (www.parks.ca.gov) operates two campgrounds near Idyllwild: Idyllwild Campground and Stone Creek Campground. Winter storms in 2019 closed both of these campgrounds indefinitely. Check for current conditions.

Mount San Jacinto State Park's **Idyllwild Campground** (25905 Hwy. 243, 951/659-2607, www.reservecalifornia.com, year-round, $25) has 33 sites under a canopy of pine and dotted with manzanitas for tent camping, RVs, and trailers. Showers, flush toilets, water, picnic tables, and fire rings are on-site. Since the site is walking distance to Idyllwild shops and restaurants, campers can spend time enjoying the stars instead of washing dishes. Reservations at Idyllwild Campground are managed by Mount San Jacinto State Park (www.parks.ca.gov).

Stone Creek Campground (Hwy. 243, www.reservecalifornia.com, May 1-October 31, $20) is off Highway 243, about six miles north of Idyllwild. The campground offers 50 sites for tent camping, as well as trailer and RV sites (no hookups or dump stations). Amenities include fire rings, picnic tables, water, and vault toilets. Reservations at Stone Creek are managed by Mount San Jacinto State Park (www.parks.ca.gov).

Idyllwild Regional Park Campground (54000 Riverside County Playground Rd., 951/659-2656, www.rivcoparks.org, $33) is less than a mile south of the state park campground. Its 88 sites are situated under shaded pine forest and are available year-round for tent, RV, and trailer camping. Amenities include picnic tables, fire rings, flush toilets, and showers. Designated accessible sites are 1, 23, and 39. These sites also have a grill. Reservations are accepted April through October; November to March, the park has sites 1-6 available for first-come, first-served camping. The park also offers a nature center and interpretive trails and is walking distance to shops and restaurants. Other seasonal campgrounds are open in summer only; these are in the vicinity of the Stone Creek Campground and are operated by the **San Bernardino National Forest** (909/382-2921, www.fs.usda.gov).

At **Fern Basin** (reserve at www.recreation.gov, May-Sept., $10-34), about 6.5 miles north of Idyllwild, 22 sites are set amid manzanitas, oaks, and conifers at 6,400 feet. Amenities include vault toilets, fire rings, and picnic tables, but there is no drinking water.

Up the road from Fern Basin, **Marion Mountain Campground** (reserve at www.recreation.gov, June-Nov., $10-34) has 24 campsites set in two loops amid a cedar and ponderosa pine forest. Amenities include vault toilets, fire rings, drinking water, and picnic tables. Marion Mountain is located about seven miles north of Idyllwild.

Dark Canyon Campground (first-come, first-served, May-Sept., $12) has 12 shaded tent-only campsites set next to a seasonal creek at 5,900 feet elevation. Amenities include vault toilets, fire rings, drinking water, and picnic tables. Dark Canyon is located about eight miles north of Idyllwild.

Boulder Basin Campground (reserve at www.recreation.gov, end of May-mid-October, $10) is a secluded forested campground pitched at 7,300 feet elevation. The campground is accessed via a dirt road from Hwy 243 eight miles north of Idyllwild. The road is rough and steep; high clearance is recommended, although 4WD is usually not necessary. Allow extra time for this five-mile stretch. The campground offers 16 shaded tent-only campsites with vault toilets, fire rings, and picnic tables. There is no drinking water available. There are bouldering opportunities nearby, and the campground is popular with rock climbers, hikers, and campers who like the solitude. A hike from the campground via dirt road takes you to the Black Mountain Lookout Tower with spectacular views of the area.

Food

BREAKFAST AND COFFEE

The family-run **Idyllwild Bake Shop and Brew** (54200 N. Circle Dr., 951/659-4145, 6:30am-4pm Mon.-Thurs., 6:30am-5pm Fri., 7am-5pm Sat., 7am-4pm Sun., $4-13) bakes breakfast pastries and savory items on-site with fresh coffee and fresh-squeezed juice to wash them down. For a little later in the day they switch gears to grilled sandwiches, craft beers, and wine.

If you want the classic, cozy coffee shop vibe where you can hang out and take advantage of Wi-Fi, **Higher Grounds Coffee** (54245 N. Circle Dr., 951/659-1379, idyllwildcoffeeroasters.com/higher-grounds, 6am-7pm Sun.-Thurs., 6am-9pm Fri.-Sat.) is the place to go. The coffee is locally sourced and organic by Idyllwild Coffee Roasters. Food is standard fare, including bagels and muffins.

The **Town Baker** (54385 N. Circle Dr., 951/659-8606, 6:30am-noon Mon., 6:30am-2pm Thurs.-Fri., 7am-3pm Sat., 7am-2pm Sun., $6-10) serves up fresh coffee, breakfast plates, and baked goods to take out or enjoy in the cheerful cottage setting. People rave about the pecan sticky buns. Pro tip: They also offer prepackaged sandwiches and sides to grab and go on your mountain adventures.

The ★ **Red Kettle** (54220 N. Circle Dr., 951/659-4063, http://perrysredkettle.com, 7am-2pm daily, $8-11) is a great place to fuel up before a hike or to savor a casual weekend. They serve up classic American breakfasts like country ham and eggs and lunch specials like chili, burgers, soups, and salads in a quaint cottage setting.

ECLECTIC

Chandeliers, upholstered parlor furniture, and sepia lighting make **Idyology** (54905 N. Circle Dr., 951/659-5962, www.idyology.org, 4pm-midnight Mon.-Fri., noon-2am Sat, 8am-midnight Sun., $8-15) a perfect place to cozy up with a craft beer, glass of wine, or specialty cocktail. They offer a full food menu that ranges from American comfort food to vegan fare, but the food is wildly hit-or-miss. The bar stays open later than the restaurant and is a popular hangout for tourists and locals. They have a live music calendar, adding to the festivities.

The burgers are perfectly executed, the fries are hot, and the beers are cold at this stripped down watering hole, pub, and café. **The Lumber Mill** (25985 Hwy. 243, 951/659-0315, www.lumbermillidyllwild.com, 11am-midnight daily $11-16) offers burgers, sandwiches, chili, appetizers, and a full bar.

★ **Plant Food Supper Club** (54241 Ridgeview Dr., 11am-8pm Wed.-Sat., 11am-4pm Sun.-Mon., $9-18) is the sceney vegan brainchild of chef-owner Kelly Johnston-Gibson. She started this culinary adventure for small, select dinner parties on the back deck of her Idyllwild cabin and has since grown it into a bustling business with live music and a patio brunch in the town center. Both visitors and locals frequent her lovely A-frame location, established 2016, which offers a full brunch, lunch, and dinner menu as well as organic wines, craft beers, fresh juices, smoothies, and tonics. Menu items range from banana pancakes and breakfast tacos to a grilled tempeh Reuben and sweet potato enchiladas verde.

SILVER PINES LODGE
25955
CREEKSIDE CABINS
1

Idyllwild Inn
2

IDYOLOGY
TODAY
LUNCH
TONIGHT
DINNER
LIVE MUSIC
3

RESTAURANT
GASTROGNOME
4

★ **Idyllwild Brewpub** (54423 Village Center Dr., 951/659-0163, www.idyllwildbrewpub.com, noon-9pm Mon.-Thurs., noon-10pm Fri., 11am-10pm Sat., 11am-8pm Sun., $10-18) brought Idyllwild into the 21st century (in a good way) for food and drink with the 2016 opening of this lively gastropub. They offer a full menu of competently brewed English, Belgian, U.S., and Canadian style brews as well as a full bar. The menu offers hearty shareable snacks like brisket nachos and buffalo wings and mains including burgers and fish and chips. The upstairs location has an indoor space with tables and a long bar and an outdoor patio with forest views. It is both family- and party-friendly.

Take a 1970s ski lodge and spruce it up with design tips from *The Hobbit,* and you've got ★ **Gastrognome** (54381 Ridge View Dr., 951/659-5055, www.gastrognome.com, 10am-9pm Sun.-Thurs., 10am-9:30pm Fri.-Sat., winter hours vary, call for availability, $10-34), the picturesque favorite of locals and visitors. A lengthy dinner menu features fish, chicken, lamb, steaks, and pasta dishes. The lunch menu is equally daunting with sandwiches, fish, seafood, pastas, vegetarian options, and steaks. When in doubt, the French onion soup is a solid choice. The charm of the restaurant might be its biggest selling point, but the food is generally well executed. Reservations are recommended for dinner on weekends.

ITALIAN

Ferro Restaurant (25840 Cedar St., 951/659-0700, www.ferrorestaurant.com, 4pm-9pm Mon.-Tues., 4pm-9pm Thurs., 4pm-10pm Fri., 11:30am-10pm Sat., 11:30am-9pm Sun.; appetizers 4pm-5pm, $10-34) offers a lovely alfresco dining experience with a patio, pine canopy, and Edison lights, with live music some nights (they also offer indoor seating). The wood-oven pizza is a good choice; the dough is excellent. The outdoor pizza oven with bar seating gives you front row seats. The menu also features pasta, pizza, and panini for lunch, and pasta, risotto, polenta, seafood, chicken, steaks, and small plates for dinner. Reservations are recommended for dinner.

1: the historic Silver Pines Lodge in Idyllwild
2: Idyllwild Inn 3: Idyology, a great spot for cocktails 4: the mountain charm of Idyllwild's Gastrognome restaurant

MEXICAN

In the Fern Valley neighborhood, ★ **La Casita Mexican Restaurant** (54650 N. Circle Dr., 951/659-6038, www.idyllwildlacasita.com, 11am-9pm daily summer, 11am-8pm daily winter, $10-20) anchors the other end of town with satisfying plates of Mexican food and margaritas served in a rustic, wood-paneled setting with a large patio. Located near the entrance to the hiking trails in Humber Park, the small restaurant can get packed.

Transportation

There is no public transportation available in Idyllwild—no buses, taxis, or ride-sharing services. Idyllwild is a small town of less than three miles from end to end, and it is easy to get around by driving or walking. The town center has sidewalks and lighting, and if you are staying directly in town, it is no problem to do everything on foot.

Outside the town center the sidewalks and lighting disappear. Both Highways 243 and 74 have steady traffic, and it can be a little nerve-wracking to be a pedestrian walking along the narrow shoulders of these dark roads at night. Carry a flashlight so that you are visible to drivers.

CAR

The town of Idyllwild is located in the San Jacinto Mountains above Palm Springs. To get here from Palm Springs, take N. Palm Canyon Drive (Hwy. 111) north to I-10. Take I-10 west for three miles to the town of Banning. At Banning, take Highway 243 and drive 25 twisting mountain miles south to the town center. Note that Highway 243 may close due to snow or other inclement weather.

From the Coachella Valley, take Highway 74 west (from its intersection with Hwy. 111) and continue onto Highway 243 north to reach Idyllwild in 41 miles.

Joshua Tree and the Hi-Desert

The stunning, alien landscape of Joshua Tree

both startles and charms.

Powerful geologic forces have whipped the rocks here into twisted shapes and scrambled boulder piles. Among the eroded chaos, spiky Joshua trees reach out in unpredictable angles, forming jagged, moody backdrops against dusty desert roads. This is the Mojave, the high desert: gorgeous in spring and fall, brutal in summer, and dusted by snow in winter.

Farther south the landscape changes yet again, straddling the boundary between the Mojave and Sonoran Deserts. The lower-elevation Sonoran sits austere and arid, with wide alluvial fans to guard its mountain canyons. Instead of Joshua trees, creosote bushes

Highlights

Look for ★ to find recommended sights, activities, dining, and lodging.

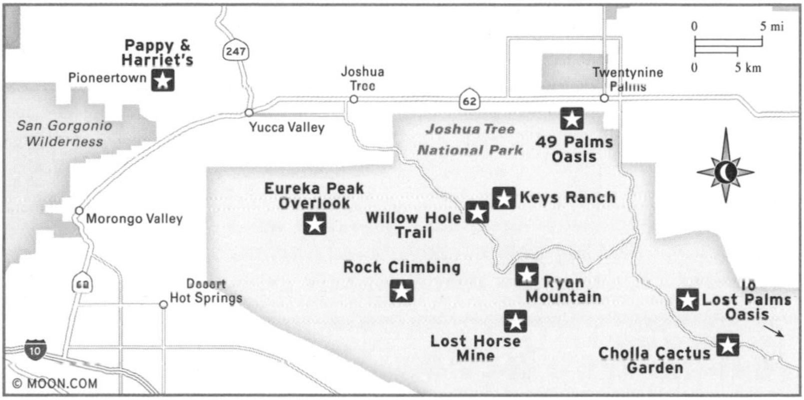

★ **Eureka Peak Overlook:** While everyone crowds the popular Key's View overlook, this lightly visited peak offers equally spectacular views (page 119).

★ **Keys Ranch:** Take a ranger-guided tour of the ranch house, buildings, and grounds owned by one of Joshua Tree's most colorful characters (page 120).

★ **Cholla Cactus Garden:** A brigade of fuzzy, multihued cacti stretch out to form this surreal desert garden (page 123).

★ **Ryan Mountain:** A vigorous hike leads to panoramic views of the Pinto Basin, Hidden Valley, and the Wonderland of Rocks (page 135).

★ **Lost Horse Mine:** Follow an old mining road to this well-preserved stamp mill with rock house ruins and stunning views toward Queen Valley (page 129).

★ **Willow Hole Trail:** This easy trek delves into the heart of the wildly eroded Wonderland of Rocks (page 130).

★ **49 Palms Oasis:** Hike to this mirage-like fan palm oasis (page 138).

★ **Lost Palms Oasis:** From lush Cottonwood Spring, this trail crosses desert ridges to a secluded oasis of fan palms, with detours to mine ruins and panoramic views (page 140).

★ **Rock Climbing:** The park's boulder-strewn oasis makes it a world-class destination for rock climbers (page 140).

★ **Pappy & Harriet's:** Built as part of a Wild West film set, this historic restaurant and saloon serves up excellent barbecue and live music (page 153).

and spindly ocotillos dot the pristine desert wilderness.

Joshua Tree's surreal appeal draws casual day-trippers, spring wildflower hounds, serious hikers, and hard-core rock climbers in droves, all wanting to experience its beauty and strangeness. The park's location near major urban centers like Palm Springs and Los Angeles contributes to its popularity, as does its easy access for locals living in the gateway towns of Joshua Tree and Twentynine Palms. The tiny towns surrounding the park are filled with outsider art, alien-inspired feats of aeronautical engineering, and some of the best live music around.

PLANNING YOUR TIME

Joshua Tree is doable as a **day trip** from Palm Springs; it's about one hour to the Joshua Tree Visitors Center at the West Entrance. (From Los Angeles, plan 3-4 hours for the drive and definitely spend the night.) Some visitors only spend one day in the park, and most of that in the car driving the Park Boulevard loop into, and then out of, each entrance station. Such limited time affords equally limited exposure to how much the park has to offer—and that involves getting out of the car and onto the trail. Do yourself a favor and plan to spend at least an overnight; **3-5 days** are even better. If you want to explore further, a side trip to the newly established Sand to Snow National Monument lets you sample the dramatic topography of the area.

Plan your visit during the cooler months of **October-April** (although these are also the most crowded). If you're **camping,** make a reservation well ahead of time to snag a coveted site in the park. Visitors seeking accommodations with luxuries such as running water should book a room at one of the multiple lodging options in the towns surrounding the park entrances—**Yucca Valley, Joshua Tree,** and **Twentynine Palms.**

You'll need a **car,** a full tank of gas, and plenty of patience driving the long distances both on the park roads and between the desert towns. Bring all the **water** you'll need to drink, clean with, or bathe in (at least two gallons per day of drinking water), as there are no services inside the park.

Joshua Tree National Park

Joshua Tree National Park (www.nps.gov/jotr, open daily year-round, $30 per vehicle, $25 per motorcycle $15 for bike or on foot, $55 annual pass) is famous for its large stands of Joshua trees and scenic desert landscape. Wildly eroded rocks make the park a world-class rock climbing destination. Most visitors spend their time on the west side of the park, where the only paved road access (Park Boulevard) exists. From the West Entrance near the town of Joshua Tree, Park Boulevard delves deep into Hidden Valley (the most popular section of the park, filled with trailheads and campgrounds) to emerge in the town of Twentynine Palms. While the Black Rock Canyon area and Indian Cove offer developed (and reservable) campgrounds, their access does not extend farther into the park. At the South Entrance, Cottonwood Spring offers a less-visited glimpse of the park's Sonoran Desert geography.

VISITORS CENTERS

Joshua Tree Visitors Center

The **Joshua Tree Visitors Center** (6554 Park Blvd., Joshua Tree, 760/366-1855, 8am-5pm daily) is in the town of Joshua Tree on Park Boulevard before the western park entrance.

Previous: the Joshua Tree Saloon; *Yucca brevifolia* flowers in Joshua Tree; jumbo rocks in Joshua Tree National Park.

Joshua Tree and the Hi-Desert

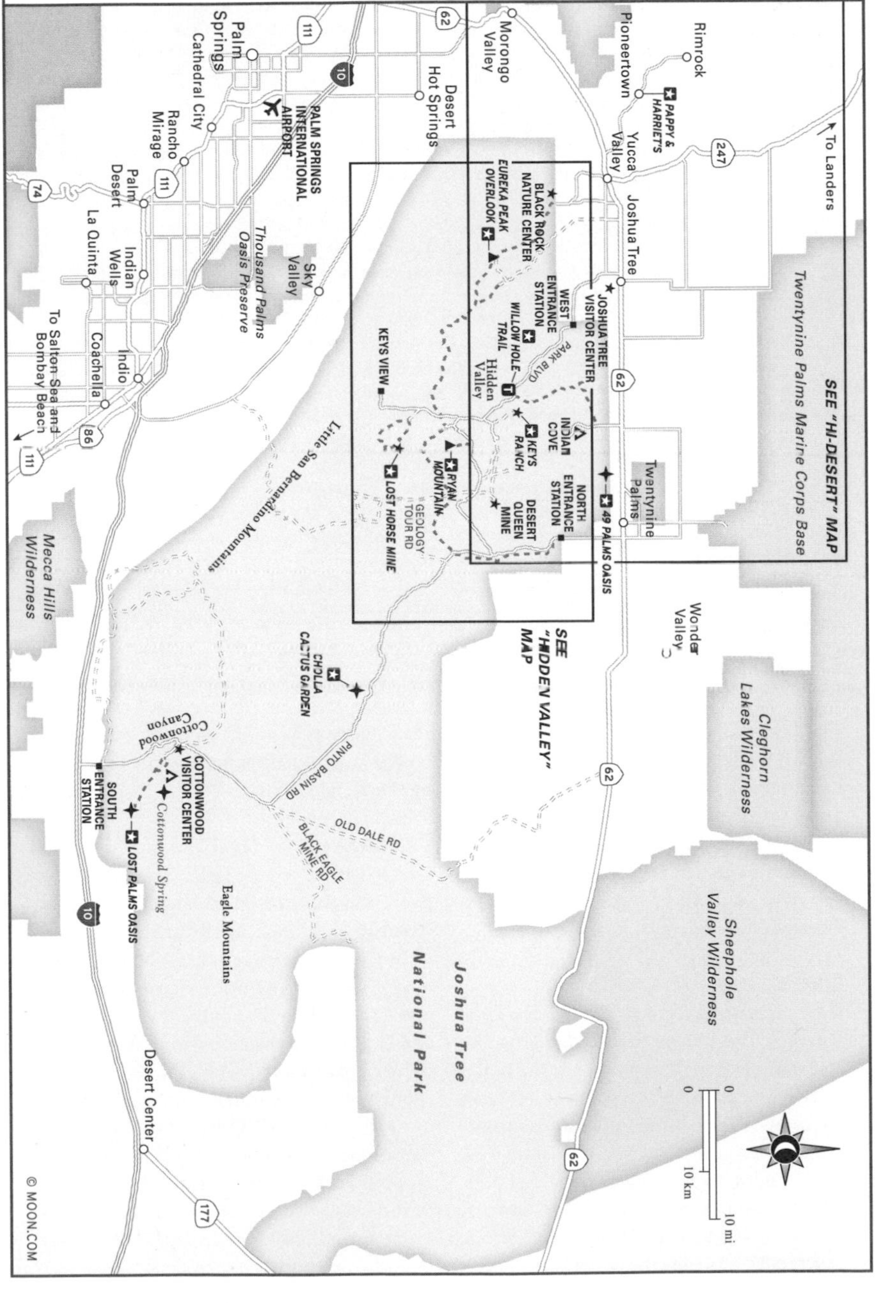

Joshua Tree in One Day

Even with limited time, it's still possible to soak in many of the parks' sights and wonders. Start in the **Indian Cove** area with an invigorating and scenic hike to the **49 Palms Oasis** (3 miles) for your first taste of the hidden wonders Joshua Tree National Park has in store. The two-hour hike winds up a rocky canyon with views of the town of Twentynine Palms before emerging above a natural palm oasis tucked into the craggy hills.

After the hike, drive east on Highway 62, making your way to the park's less-crowded **North Entrance.** Stop by the **Oasis Visitors Center** for a great selection of books, maps, and information, then head southeast on Park Boulevard to make a loop through the park from east to west. From here on out, it's all about the journey as you marvel at the passing landscape.

On Park Boulevard, drive 10 miles west (20 minutes) to **Queen Valley,** an excellent destination thanks to its boulder-strewn and Joshua tree-filled landscape and history. A series of networked hiking trails lead to ranching sites, mining remains, and the site of Native American settlements. The trail to the **Wall Street Mill** (3 miles round-trip, 1.5 hours) leads to a well-preserved ore-processing mill dating from the 1930s, while the remains of the **Desert Queen Mine** (1-3 miles, 0.5 hour) clings to the steep side of Desert Queen Wash. The **Lucky Boy Vista** loop (3.6 miles, 2 hours) traverses an ancient Native American village with views of Hidden Valley. **Barker Dam** (1.3 miles, 0.5 hour) is a popular nature trail leading to the edge of the Wonderland of Rocks and a ranch-era dam created on the site of a Native American settlement. Bring your lunch and picnic at nearby Split Rock or Live Oak picnic areas.

Cap off your time wandering the canyons with a perspective-building drive to popular **Keys View.** This scenic overlook gives sweeping panoramas of the park's southwest, taking in the Santa Rosa Mountains, San Andreas fault, Palm Springs, San Jacinto Peak, and San Gorgonio Peak. The paved observation point is wheelchair-accessible.

For a last hurrah, meander your way northwest along **Park Boulevard** toward the **West Entrance,** passing through the impressive rock formations of **Hidden Valley** on your way; plan one hour for the drive.

This fully staffed visitors center offers a well-stocked bookstore with travel guides, nature guides, maps, and gifts. There are restrooms and a café. The **Park Rock Café** (760/366-8200, 8am-5pm daily) is right next door and serves sandwiches, soups, salads, espresso, beer, wine, smoothies, and boxed lunches for dining in or as takeout.

Oasis Visitors Center

Oasis Visitors Center (74485 National Park Dr., Twentynine Palms, 760/367-5500, 8:30am-5pm daily) is en route to the park's North Entrance in the gateway town of Twentynine Palms. The fully staffed visitors center offers a well-stocked bookstore with travel guides, nature guides, maps, and gifts. Water, restrooms with flush toilets, and picnic tables are also available. A short 0.5-mile interpretive trail from the visitors center leads to the Oasis of Mara, a historic fan palm oasis with a large standing pool originally settled by the Serrano Indians.

Cottonwood Visitors Center

Located at the remote South Entrance to the park, the **Cottonwood Visitors Center** (Cottonwood Spring Rd., 8:30am-4pm daily) provides check-in for visitors entering through the more sparsely traveled South Entrance. The fully staffed visitors center offers a bookstore with travel guides, nature guides, maps, and gifts. Water, restrooms with flush toilets, and picnic tables are also available. A short botanical garden interpretive loop leaves from the visitors center. The visitors center is convenient to the Cottonwood Campground as well as Cottonwood Spring and the Hidden Palms Oasis hiking trail.

Black Rock Nature Center

The **Black Rock Nature Center** (9800 Black Rock Canyon Rd., Yucca Valley, 760/367-3001, 8am-4pm Sat.-Thurs., 8am-8pm Fri. Oct.-May) is a small visitors center used primarily as a check-in for campers heading to the Black Rock Canyon Campground and other visitors to the Black Rock Canyon area. Several trails lead from here, including ones to Warren Peak and the Panorama Loop through the Little San Bernardino Mountains. The ranger-staffed center has maps, books, and nature guides for purchase. Park entrance fees may also be paid here.

Twentynine Palms Visitors Center

Located en route to the North Entrance, the **Twentynine Palms Visitors Center and Gallery** (6847 Adobe Rd., Twentynine Palms, 760/361-1805, 10am-4pm daily fall-spring,) welcomes you to the gateway town of Twentynine Palms and Joshua Tree National Park. The visitors center and gallery features maps, brochures, local books, Wi-Fi, a gift shop, electric car charging station, a community art gallery, and the Twentynine Palms Chamber of Commerce.

ENTRANCE STATIONS

There are three main entrances into the park:

The **West Entrance** (5 miles south of Hwy. 62 and Park Blvd.) is accessed from the gateway town of Joshua Tree and sees the heaviest volume of visitors. Lines can be long on busy weekends. Visitors to the park go through a ranger-staffed entrance kiosk to pay entrance fees ($30, $55 annual pass), while season pass-holders are often offered a shorter line. Restrooms are available.

The **North Entrance** (3 miles south of Hwy. 62 and Utah Trail) is located in the gateway town of Twentynine Palms and sees slightly less traffic and shorter lines. Visitors pass through a ranger-staffed kiosk to pay entrance fees. Restrooms are available.

The **South Entrance** (off I-10, 25 miles east of Indio in the Coachella Valley) accesses Cottonwood Spring and sees the fewest visitors. There is no entrance kiosk; instead, visitors entering from the south should stop at the ranger station to pay fees and gather information. Restrooms and maps are available.

TOP EXPERIENCE

DRIVING TOURS

For a paved introduction to Joshua Tree National Park, drive Park Boulevard to access the park's highlights. If you want to get off the pavement, Joshua Tree has several rugged backcountry roads that are best for four-wheel drive vehicles. Many of these roads make for some good biking routes as well. There are also graded dirt roads that still offer scenery and some seclusion but can be navigated by most passenger cars. Note that the speed limit on park roads is 45 mph or lower.

Black Rock Canyon

COVINGTON FLATS
10.9 MILES

The series of dirt roads in **Covington Flats** gives access to the sweeping views from Eureka Peak, several hiking trails (including the Upper Covington Flats section of the California Riding and Hiking Trail), and some of the largest stands of Joshua trees, junipers, and piñon pines in the park. Covington Flats is situated between Black Rock Canyon and the town of Joshua Tree in the northwestern section of the park. Compared to other sections of the park, this area is lightly traveled and makes for some pleasant scenery watching. The dirt road is also good for mountain biking.

To access Covington Flats, take La Contenta Road south from Highway 62 in Yucca Valley. A 10.9-mile drive leads to Eureka Peak and spectacular views of Palm Springs, the Morongo Basin, and the San Jacinto Mountains. The Covington Flats area has signed intersections that make it easy to navigate; while there is occasional sand, the dirt roads are navigable by most cars despite some elevation gain near Eureka Peak. To

Joshua Tree National Park Visitor Cen
Park Rock Café
CAFE
DELI
ESPRESSO
CAFE
Park Rock Café
GOOD FOOD
FREE WI FI
Park Rock Café
1

Joshua Tree National Park
2

3

4

reach **Eureka Peak,** follow La Contenta Road south from its intersection with Highway 62 in Yucca Valley; the road quickly turns to dirt. After driving 7.8 miles, look for a signed intersection that directs you right toward Eureka Peak. As the road begins to climb, continue straight to a picnic area and the trailhead access in 0.9 mile. At 9.6 miles, another right turn takes you to a small parking area within a few hundred yards of the peak. A left turn here leads south to Upper Covington Flats and access to the **California Riding and Hiking Trail.**

Hidden Valley

PARK BOULEVARD
25 MILES

Park Boulevard takes you through the park's most spectacular scenery in a 25-mile loop beginning at the West Entrance in Joshua Tree and ending at the North Entrance in Twentynine Palms (you can also do this in reverse). You will pass the fantastical formations of the Wonderland of Rocks and have the opportunity to explore a number of short interpretive trails, some with picnic areas. A detour to Keys View affords a landscape panorama. If you only have a few hours or one day, this is your drive. The paved main road is also a good place to take road bikes.

QUEEN VALLEY
13.4 MILES

In **Queen Valley,** a series of short dirt roads totaling 13.4 miles connects **Barker Dam** with the **Pine City** backcountry area. Steeped in ranching lore and Native American history, the Queen Valley area also gives rise to thick stands of Joshua trees. The one-lane dirt roads (**Queen Valley Road, Bighorn Pass Road, and O'Dell Road**) are accessible to most vehicles, though the narrow roads might make it a tight squeeze for passing. The dirt road is also good for mountain biking.

GEOLOGY TOUR ROAD
18 MILES

Geology Tour Road (passenger cars okay for the first 5 miles, then 4WD beyond) is a pleasant 18-mile backcountry drive that descends south into the broad Pleasant Valley and an ancient dry lake. Along the way it gives long views of the dramatic erosion and uplift that have formed Joshua Tree's unique geologic phenomena. This is a good road to take mountain bikes on as well. Pick up a free interpretive pamphlet from the Joshua Tree Visitors Center, which details the route with 16 numbered points of interest. (They're also available from a small metal box at the start of the drive.)

Begin from a signed intersection on Park Boulevard about two miles west of **Jumbo Rocks Campground.** The dirt road knifes south into Pleasant Valley, situated between the Hexie Mountains and Little San Bernardino Mountains. Sights along the way include stark **Malapai Hill,** distinct for its black basalt formation, and Pleasant Valley, with its heavily oxidized rocks (called desert varnish), and the Blue Cut earthquake fault.

As stark as the landscape may seem, the drive will take you past places that saw human—not just geologic—action. **Squaw Tank** (Stop 9) was dammed with concrete by ranchers who were really just bolstering a watering source used by Native Americans in the area for centuries. **Pleasant Valley** (Stop 10) was once home to a periodic lake and cattle-ranching operation when the area was wetter and full of grasses, again on the site of land historically used by indigenous groups. The steep Hexie Mountains are riddled with **mining shafts** (Stop 12) that date to the late 1800s and early 1900s.

The first five miles of graded dirt road to Squaw Tank are passable by most cars (no RVs) during dry weather. (During wet weather, don't go beyond Squaw Tank in any vehicle, as the road can become flooded or

1: Joshua Tree Visitors Center at the national park's west entrance **2:** Oasis Visitors Center in 29 Palms **3:** views of Malapai Hill and Pleasant Valley from the Geology Tour Road **4:** dirt road through the scenic Queen Valley

Hidden Valley

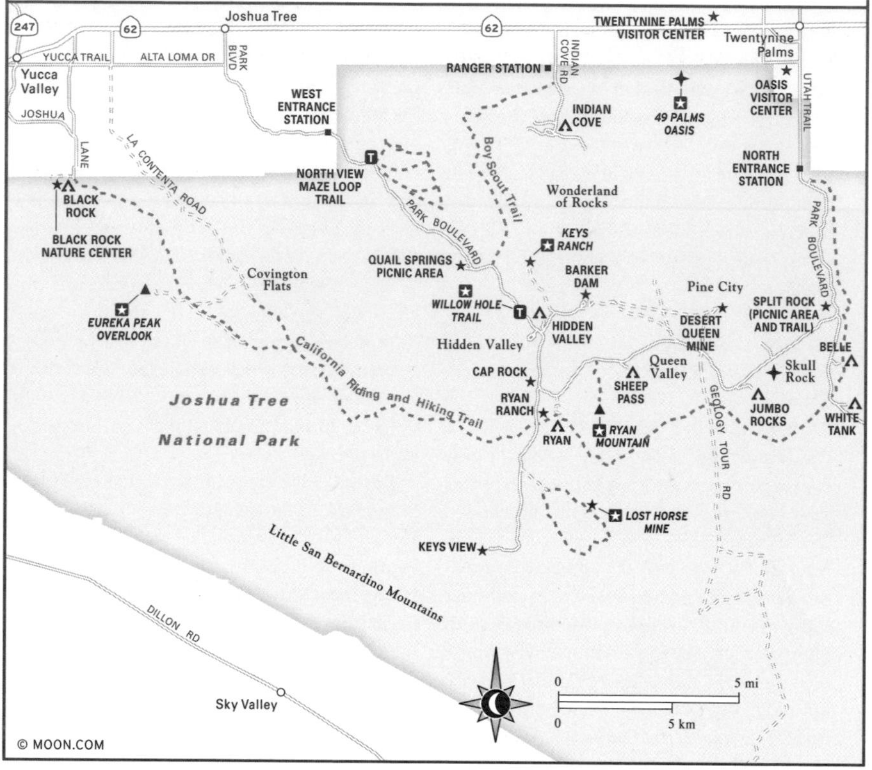

impassable.) Beyond Squaw Tank, the road is labeled **four-wheel drive only** by the park service due to deep ruts, sand, and steep grades. There are some rough spots, but you may be able to handle the drive in a compact SUV, depending upon your backroad driving experience and the current road conditions. Past Squaw Tank the road completes a one-way loop clockwise along the Hexie Mountain foothills and through Pleasant Valley. From this point you're committed to the drive, a leisurely round-trip that can take up to **two hours**.

BERDOO CANYON ROAD (4WD)
15.4 MILES

Stemming from the southern tip of the Geology Tour Road, **Berdoo Canyon Road** continues 15.4 miles south to end beyond the park boundary at **Dillon Road** in the Coachella Valley. The unmaintained road heads through Pleasant Canyon and then navigates rugged Berdoo Canyon to the southern park boundary. Outside the park boundary, the final 3.9 miles of the road passes the remains of **Berdoo Camp,** established for builders of the California Aqueduct in the 1930s. Berdoo Canyon Road requires **high-clearance 4WD.**

Cottonwood Spring
PINTO BASIN ROAD
30 MILES

Joshua Tree National Park is uniquely split across two deserts: the Mojave in the more popular northern section, characterized by the park's signature Joshua trees and monzonite granite boulders, and the Sonoran (or Colorado) Desert to the south, with austere broad valleys and washes—creosote and smoke trees dot the terrain. To beat the crowds and watch the drama of the landscape unfold slowly, start your drive at the south park entrance and Cottonwood Visitor Center. The paved highway cuts north through the arid Pinto Basin for 30 miles, with the Eagle Mountains to the east and Hexie Mountains to the west. Look for the spindly talons of a large ocotillo patch and the deceptively fuzzy-looking cholla cactus garden at just under 20 miles into your drive. Pinto Basin Road connects with Park Boulevard, the main park drive, at 30 miles. Continuing north, it is eight miles to the Oasis Visitors Center. The paved road is also a good place to take road bikes.

OLD DALE ROAD (4WD) 23 MILES

The **Old Dale Road** begins at a signed intersection on Pinto Basin Road, 6.5 miles north of Cottonwood Visitors Center. This rugged 23-mile unmaintained jeep trail crosses the Pinto Basin for 11 miles, then crawls beyond the park boundary into the eastern hills of the Pinto Mountains and a nest of old mines that make up the **Old Dale Mining District.** (A number of side roads split off to these sites.) The Old Dale Mining District drew prospectors looking for gold from as early as 1881. At peak production in 1898, there were as many as 3,000 miners in the region. Production limped along on a small scale until 1939 and the outbreak of World War II. Today the historic mining district is located on BLM land. The main road eventually spills north out onto Highway 62, 15 miles east of the town of Twentynine Palms.

BLACK EAGLE MINE ROAD (4WD) 9 MILES

The **Black Eagle Mine Road** shares its start with the Old Dale Road off Pinto Basin Road, 6.5 miles north of the Cottonwood Visitors Center. The road strikes east across the Pinto Basin and into the northwest Eagle Mountains, where it ends at a barricade at the park boundary at just over nine miles. The road continues beyond the barricade on BLM land near several old mining sites.

SIGHTS

Black Rock Canyon

The Black Rock Canyon region is in the northwest corner of Joshua Tree, with a campground and several great hikes as well as easy access to the shops and restaurants of the Yucca Valley. The Black Rock area is characterized by craggy rolling peaks and piñons, juniper, and oak trees, giving it a different feel from the more popular Hidden Valley section of Joshua Tree. Though the Black Rock Canyon area is located near the West Entrance, there is no direct access into the center of the park.

★ EUREKA PEAK OVERLOOK

At 5,521 feet, **Eureka Peak Overlook** offers panoramic views of Joshua Tree and surrounding valleys. Not only are the views spectacular, Eureka Peak is way less crowded than the very popular Keys View, a paved, drive-up viewpoint in the middle of the heavily visited central section of the park. From the summit, the Coachella Valley, Desert Hot Springs, and the San Jacinto Mountains (including the often snowcapped San Jacinto Peak) lie to the southwest, while views to the north take in the Morongo Valley. Look east into the park and you'll glimpse into the Wonderland of Rocks.

Of course, there's a catch: Eureka Peak is not accessed via the park's main entrances. Instead, entry is via a graded dirt road from Yucca Valley (near the Black Rock Canyon Campground) that leads into Covington Flats, ending within a few hundred yards of the peak. It's also possible to hike to Eureka Peak via the trail from Covington Flats (8 miles round-trip) or the Black Rock Canyon Campground (10 miles round-trip).

From Highway 62 (29 Palms Highway) in the town of Yucca Valley, take La Contenta

Wonderland of Rocks

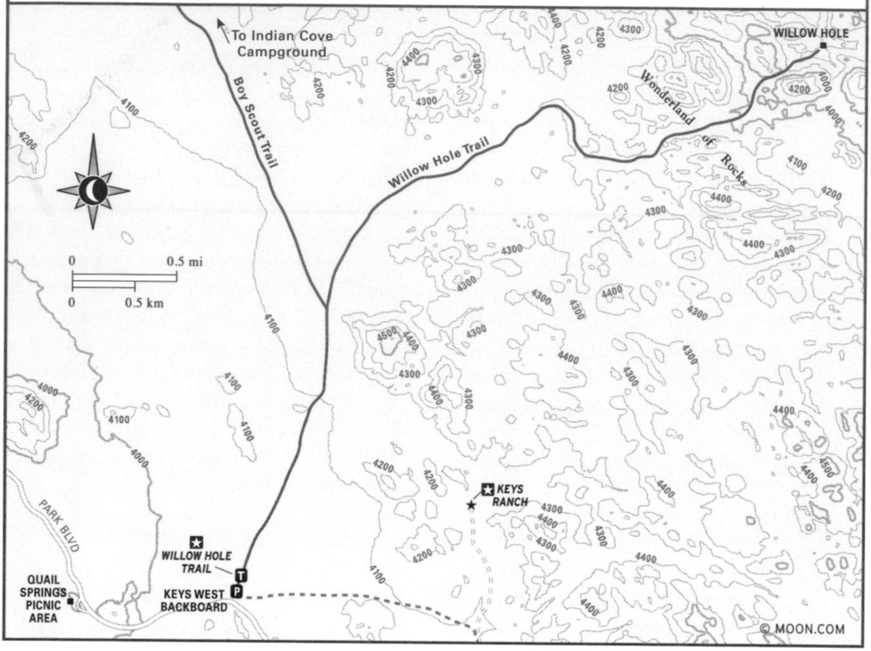

Road south. The road quickly becomes dirt and has some sandy places. In normal weather conditions, it should be passable for most two-wheel drive cars. At 7.8 miles, turn right toward Eureka Peak. At 9.6 miles, turn right again toward Eureka Peak (signed). At 10.9 miles, you will reach a small parking area a few hundred yards below the peak.

Hidden Valley

From the park's West Entrance in Joshua Tree, Park Boulevard travels 25 miles southeast, making a loop with the North Entrance in Twentynine Palms. This paved stretch is the most popular region of the park, with access to Queen Valley, Hidden Valley, Quail Springs, the Wonderland of Rocks, as well as the majority of campgrounds and trailheads.

★ KEYS RANCH

Colorful homesteader, rancher, and miner Bill Keys was an industrious and resourceful pack rat who fashioned a homestead and a life in the isolated desert. From 1917 to 1969, he and his family carved out a desert domain that included a ranch house, a schoolhouse, a store, and a workshop. Today, visitors can tour the well-preserved ruins of the Desert Queen Ranch, now listed on the National Register of Historic Places.

From October through May, park rangers lead 90-minute guided tours of **Keys Ranch** (by reservation only: call 760/367-5522 9am-4:30pm daily, $10 over age 12, $5 children age 6-11, children under 6 free). This popular tour guides you to a preserved historic homestead near the Hidden Valley Campground. The schedule varies, but tours are usually held once daily Friday-Sunday and offer your only peek at these historic remains.

WONDERLAND OF ROCKS

Dubbed the **Wonderland of Rocks,** for reasons that quickly become apparent, this region is characterized by a wildly eroded maze of striking granite rock formations studded with secret basins, gorgeous views, and history. The Wonderland of Rocks covers the area southeast of Indian Cove Campground and northeast of Hidden Valley Campground. Its compelling rock formations are visible to the east and north while driving along Park Boulevard, the main park road. Indian Cove Campground and the parking area for the Barker Dam Nature Trail are the closest driving points into the belly of the beast. The area lures rock climbers and hikers. Four trails (Barker Dam Loop, Boy Scout Trail, Willow Hole, and Wonderland Wash) knife short distances into the Wonderland of Rocks. Rock climbing use trails are signed and established.

RYAN RANCH

Ryan Ranch was named after the Ryan brothers, Thomas and J. D., "Jep," who bought interest in the nearby Lost Horse Mine and set up camp at the Lost Horse Well at the base of Ryan Mountain. The homestead ruins date to 1896, but the region had been used by Native Americans prior to the mining era thanks to the availability of water in the area. A short 0.5-mile stroll leads to remains of the ranch and its adobe bunkhouse, windmill, and outbuildings. A deeper search of the area reveals a pioneer cemetery and evidence of Native American habitation, including grinding stones. This interpretive site is accessed from a pullout on Park Boulevard between the Ryan Mountain trailhead and the turnoff for Ryan Campground.

KEYS VIEW

Impressive views spill from the lip of windswept **Keys View,** an observation point in the Little San Bernardino Mountains. Take in a panorama that stretches to the Salton Sea, Santa Rosa Mountains, San Andreas fault, Palm Springs, San Jacinto Peak, and San Gorgonio Peak. The paved observation point is also wheelchair-accessible. Find it seven miles south of the Hidden Valley Campground, a... Boulevard alon...

QUEEN VALL...

Queen Valley i... Tree's greatest h... mining ruins, N... scenic hikes, and... roads crisscrosse... through one of th... trees in the park... large gold operati... Queen Mine, to way humbler affairs marked by the rusty remains of tent encampments. Evidence of Native American settlements dot the boulder-strewn landscape. Established hiking trails follow a series of old mining roads to the **Desert Queen Mine, Lucky Boy Vista,** and the **Wall Street Mine.** To reach the Queen Valley area, follow the unpaved Queen Valley Road or Desert Queen Mine Road east to their terminus at Pine City.

Cottonwood Spring

Located near the South Entrance to the park (off Pinto Basin Road, north of I-10), the Cottonwood region encompasses a visitor center, campground, and several hiking trails. **Cottonwood Spring** itself is a fan palm oasis named for a surprising crop of native cottonwood trees that are mixed into the luxuriant vegetation surrounding the spring. Cottonwood Spring has served as a vital water source for centuries with Native American settlement signs around to prove it. One example of how few and far between such water sources are in the desert: One ill-fated Matt Riley started off with a friend from the Dale Mining District intending to refill their small shared canteen at the spring 25 miles away. Beaten down by the heat, the friend turned back and survived. Riley pressed on and died on July 4, 1905, within 200 yards of the spring. Your access is a lot easier today. Cottonwood Spring is located on a paved road past the Cottonwood Campground in the vicinity of the Cottonwood Visitors Center.

1

2

★ CHOLLA CACTUS GARDEN

Driving south through the endless landscape of the Pinto Basin, the **Cholla Cactus Garden** appears like an army of prickly planted teddy bears—their sheer numbers impress in this already surreal landscape. Though these cacti may look fuzzy, their multicolored arms are effective against predators. Urban legend-style photos show hapless visitors covered in cholla (aka jumping cactus), with segments that have attached themselves to those who got too close. You'll be fine if you keep your hands to yourself and use common sense. A small parking area allows visitors to stop and wander the 0.3-mile interpretive trail through a surreal crop of this strange flora. The trailhead for this nature walk is located 20 miles north of the Cottonwood Visitors Center on Pinto Basin Road.

HIKING

Joshua Tree offers fantastic hiking in an otherworldly landscape. The park has a range of hikes from easy nature trails to difficult cross-country adventures. Some of the longer trails lend themselves to backpacking (all backpackers overnighting in the backcountry must self-register for a free permit at any backcountry board).

Regardless of trail length, dehydration is the biggest factor while hiking in Joshua Tree. Always carry at least **two gallons of water per day per person,** especially during strenuous activities, and plan your hike to coincide with cooler times of the day, such as early morning or late afternoon.

Joshua Tree can be a confusing place for hikers as some trails are not well marked, and hikers veer off trail or follow washes instead of trails. Over time as more people follow these detours, the correct trail can become more difficult to follow. Always follow signs posted by the park service. Also, look for barriers made of natural materials (e.g., a line of rocks, a fallen Joshua tree). The park service uses these to maintain trails.

Black Rock Canyon

HI-VIEW NATURE TRAIL

Distance: 1.3 miles round-trip
Duration: 0.5 hour
Elevation gain: 320 feet
Effort: Easy
Trailhead: Near Black Rock Campground
Directions: Immediately before the entrance to Black Rock Campground, turn right onto a dirt road and drive 0.8 mile to a parking area.

For such a short trail, you'll be rewarded with panoramic views and desert knowledge. To hike the trail, follow the gentle grade clockwise. Take in the sweeping views of the Yucca Valley to the northeast, **Black Rock Canyon** and campground to the south, and the San Bernardino Mountains to the west. See if you can spot the highest peak in the San Bernardino Mountains, snowcapped San Gorgonio Mountain at 11,503 feet.

The trailhead can also be reached from a spur trail connecting from the **Black Rock Ranger Station**, where interpretive brochures are available.

PANORAMA LOOP

Distance: 7.4 miles round-trip (8.6 miles round-trip to Warren Peak)
Duration: 4-5 hours
Elevation gain: 1,120 feet
Effort: Strenuous
Trailhead: Black Rock Canyon Backcountry Board or the southern end of the campground near site #30
Directions: From Highway 62 in Yucca Valley, turn south onto Avalon / Palomar Avenue for 2.9 miles. Turn left onto Joshua Lane for 0.9 mile. Turn right then left to follow San Marino Drive. San Marino becomes Black Rock Canyon Road. Follow Black Rock Canyon Road 0.3 mile south of San Marino Road. Just before a split in the road, look for a small dirt parking area and the Black Rock Canyon Backcountry Board on the left, just past the campground entrance. Follow park signs.

Hike this crown of peaks—five in all—and you'll be rewarded with sweeping views extending from the Salton Sea to Mount San

---

1: brigade of cholla cactus along the Pinto Basin Road **2:** eroded granite creating a dramatic landscape in the Wonderland of Rocks

Black Rock Canyon

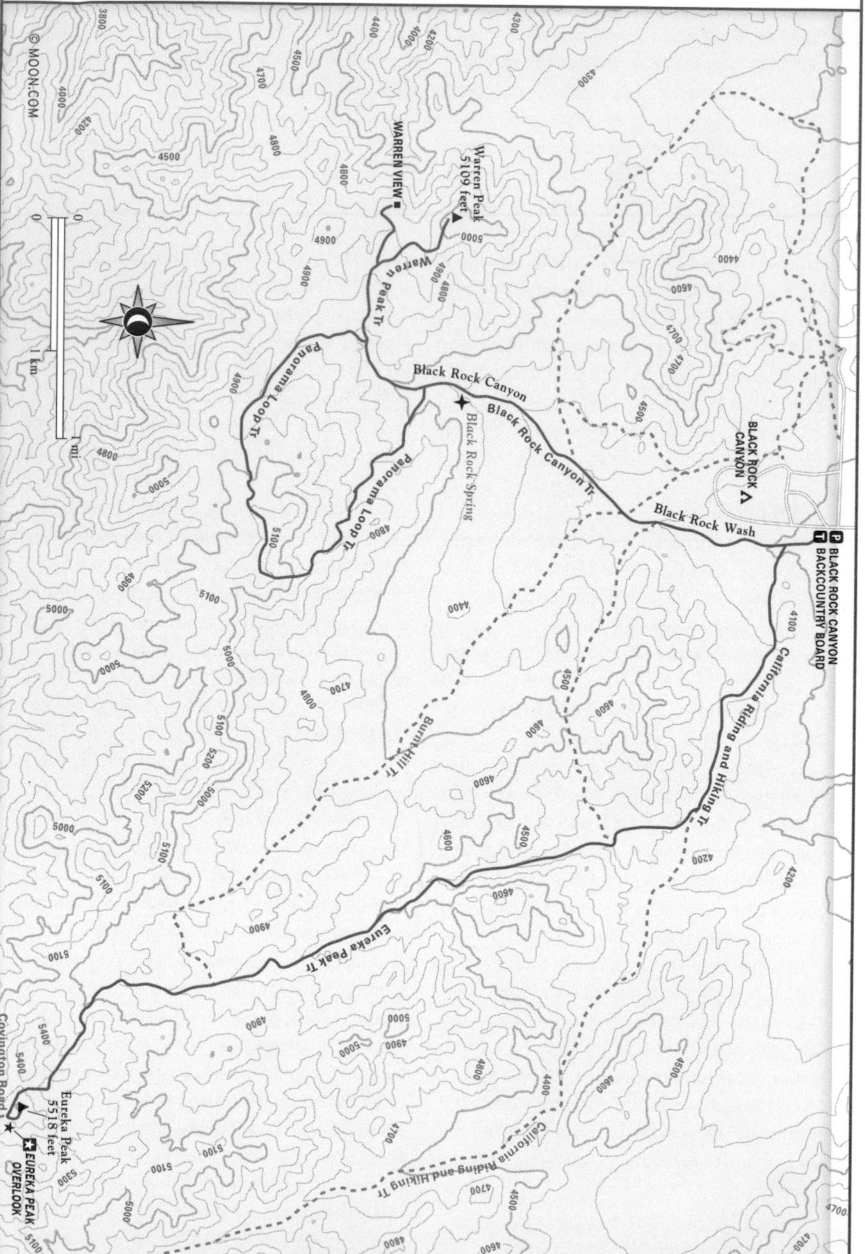
© MOON.COM
Warren Peak
5109 feet
WARREN VIEW
Warren Peak Tr
Panorama Loop Tr
Panorama Loop Tr
Black Rock Canyon
Black Rock Canyon Tr
Black Rock Spring
Black Rock Wash
BLACK ROCK CANYON
BLACK ROCK CANYON
BACKCOUNTRY BOARD
California Riding and Hiking Tr
Burnt Hill Tr
Eureka Peak Tr
California Riding and Hiking Tr
Covington Road
Eureka Peak
5518 feet
EUREKA PEAK
OVERLOOK
0
1 km
0
1 mi

Jacinto and the Yucca Valley. Starting from the well-marked trailhead, travel south along a sandy trail that can feel like walking on a desert beach. The trail splits at 0.3 mile; head right to follow a sign pointing toward **Black Rock Canyon.** For the next 0.5 mile, you'll hike Black Rock Wash through open desert and a Joshua tree forest framed by a serrated landscape of ridges and peaks. The trail is easy to follow but splits into smaller washes and use trails at times. Pay attention to official trail markers (**PL** for Panorama Loop; **WP** for Warren Peak), as well as stone boundaries that mark the trail.

At just under two miles, you'll reach the base of the foothills and **Black Rock Spring.** The spring usually does not have standing pools, but the ground may be damp. Oaks and other vegetation are abundant here (a good sign of water), and the area can be swarmed with flies, another giveaway. From Black Rock Spring, the trail narrows and cuts through the region's signature black rock formations.

At two miles the trail splits at a **signed intersection.** A straight left continues into the first loop entrance to hike the Panorama Loop clockwise, but we are going to follow the loop counterclockwise. (The trail can be hiked in either direction, but hiking it counterclockwise gives you a slightly gentler grade going uphill and a steeper hike downhill.) Stay right to reach the second loop entrance in 0.4 mile. From the **second intersection,** continuing straight (right) takes you to Warren Peak in 0.6 mile. (If you're up for it, I highly recommend this 1.2-mile round-trip detour to get the full eyeful and bragging rights. Six peaks in a day? Sure!) If you're only following the Panorama Loop, this will be a **left turn** at the intersection.

The three-mile Panorama Loop begins by climbing a steady grade through the foothills, following the remains of an old road. The grade tops out at a sharp ridge with spectacular views to the southeast across the Coachella Valley—you can see all the way to the Salton Sea on a clear day. Across the valley to the southwest are the impressive San Jacinto Mountains and Mount San Jacinto. At 5,154 feet, this ridge marks the highest point in the hike (including Warren Peak).

From here the trail continues to be one big reward as you wind your way along four more peaks on an open ridge that gives you an eyeful far across the Yucca Valley. Once you've made your way back down to the canyon floor (6.6 miles), turn right to follow the Black Rock Canyon wash the final two miles to the trailhead.

WARREN PEAK

Distance: 6 miles round-trip
Duration: 3-4 hours
Elevation gain: 1,070 feet
Effort: Strenuous
Trailhead: Black Rock Canyon Backcountry Board or from the southern end of the campground near site #30
Directions: From Highway 62 in Yucca Valley, turn south onto Avalon / Palomar Avenue for 2.9 miles. Turn left onto Joshua Lane for 0.9 mile. Turn right then left to follow San Marino Drive. San Marino becomes Black Rock Canyon Road. Take Black Rock Canyon Road 0.3 mile south of San Marino Road. Just before a split in the road, look for a small dirt parking area and the Black Rock Canyon Backcountry Board on the left just past the campground entrance. Follow park signs.

At 5,103 feet, Warren Peak is the 10th-highest peak in the park. Considering that the highest peak, Quail Mountain, clocks in only 713 feet higher at 5,814 feet, Warren Peak's ranking is more impressive than it might sound at first. The trail to Warren Peak manages to be a moderate hike with a huge view payoff.

Starting from the well-marked trailhead, follow the trail for the **Panorama Loop** (PL; see previous hike) to the second intersection where it junctions with the trail to Warren Peak (WP). Stay right to continue to **Warren Peak.** At the next intersection at 2.4 miles, stay straight (right). You're only 0.6 mile from Warren Peak, and it comes into clear view. The trail climbs steeply up to the knobby peak, where you're rewarded with panoramic views—the San Jacinto Mountains, Coachella Valley, Yucca Valley, and toward Hidden

Valley and the Wonderland of Rocks in the heart of Joshua Tree. When you're done basking in the views, return the way you came. A use trail exiting the peak dead-ends at a ridge; pay attention to where you entered the peak.

EUREKA PEAK

Distance: 10 miles round-trip
Duration: 4-5 hours
Elevation gain: 1,535 feet
Effort: Strenuous
Trailhead: Black Rock Canyon Campground
Directions: From Highway 62 in Yucca Valley, turn south onto Avalon / Palomar Avenue for 2.9 miles. Turn left onto Joshua Lane for 0.9 mile. Turn right then left to follow San Marino Drive. San Marino becomes Black Rock Canyon Road. Take Black Rock Canyon Road 0.3 mile south of San Marino Road. Just before a split in the road, look for a small dirt parking area and the Black Rock Canyon Backcountry Board on the left just past the campground entrance. Follow park signs.

You definitely need to be in an "it's all about the journey" mind-set to hike Eureka Peak. The journey is a pleasant one, leaving Black Rock Canyon to navigate a series of mountain canyons, finally arriving at Eureka Peak and its spectacular views of the San Jacinto Mountains and the Coachella Valley extending to the Salton Sea. However, after you've huffed and puffed your way to the top, you may be disappointed to find that a perfectly good dirt road, navigable by most vehicles, stops less than 0.2 mile from the peak. The idea may dawn on you that you could have had those same spectacular views in a much easier way. The road is lightly traveled, and your chances of solitude on the peak are good no matter how you get there.

For hiking purposes, a network of trails spiderwebs out from Black Rock Canyon, giving you various routes for reaching Eureka Peak. Beginning from the Black Rock Canyon Backcountry Board, follow the **California Riding and Hiking Trail** (CA R&H) for the first two miles. It quickly leaves the wash to climb into the foothills. Ignore a trail split at 1.5 miles to stay left on the CA R&H, climbing to an upper valley. At 1.9 miles, a signed junction indicates the **Eureka Peak Trail** (EP). Turn right to head up the wash. Continue to follow the main wash as it narrows and climbs, ignoring another junction at 2.3 miles. Intermittent signposts for the next two miles indicate that you're on the right path. At 4.3 miles, the trail twists up to the peak, arriving at a ridge just below the summit at 4.9 miles. Turn left for the 5,518-foot peak.

Retrace your steps when you're done basking in the views. It is also possible to turn the hike into a loop by taking **Covington Road** (the dirt road just south of the peak) to its intersection with the CA R&H. You can follow the CA R&H trail the whole way back to the Black Rock Canyon Backcountry Board.

Hidden Valley

This is the most popular area of the park, as it includes access to Queen Valley, Hidden Valley, Quail Springs, and the Wonderland of Rocks. Expect filled parking lots and plenty of company on the trails.

NORTH VIEW MAZE LOOP

Distance: 6.4 miles round-trip
Duration: 4 hours
Elevation gain: 400 feet
Effort: Moderate
Trailhead: Drive 1.7 miles south from the West Entrance (main park entrance in Joshua Tree). The trailhead is a small dirt parking area on your left. It gives access to the North View, Maze Loop, Window Rock, and Big Pine trails.

This hike combines the North View and Maze Loops for a spectacular loop trail through fantastical boulder formations, Joshua tree forest, craggy viewpoints, desert wash, and past a window rock. It is also lightly traveled compared to more popular hikes so add solitude to the mix of reasons to hike here. The trail starts out in a wash heading north toward low hills and a signed intersection. Head left/north to follow the North View Trail. The trail leaves the wash to wind into the hills, and you are quickly transported to a secluded rock amphitheater surrounded on all sides by towering formations. A few dips in the cracked

Hidden Valley

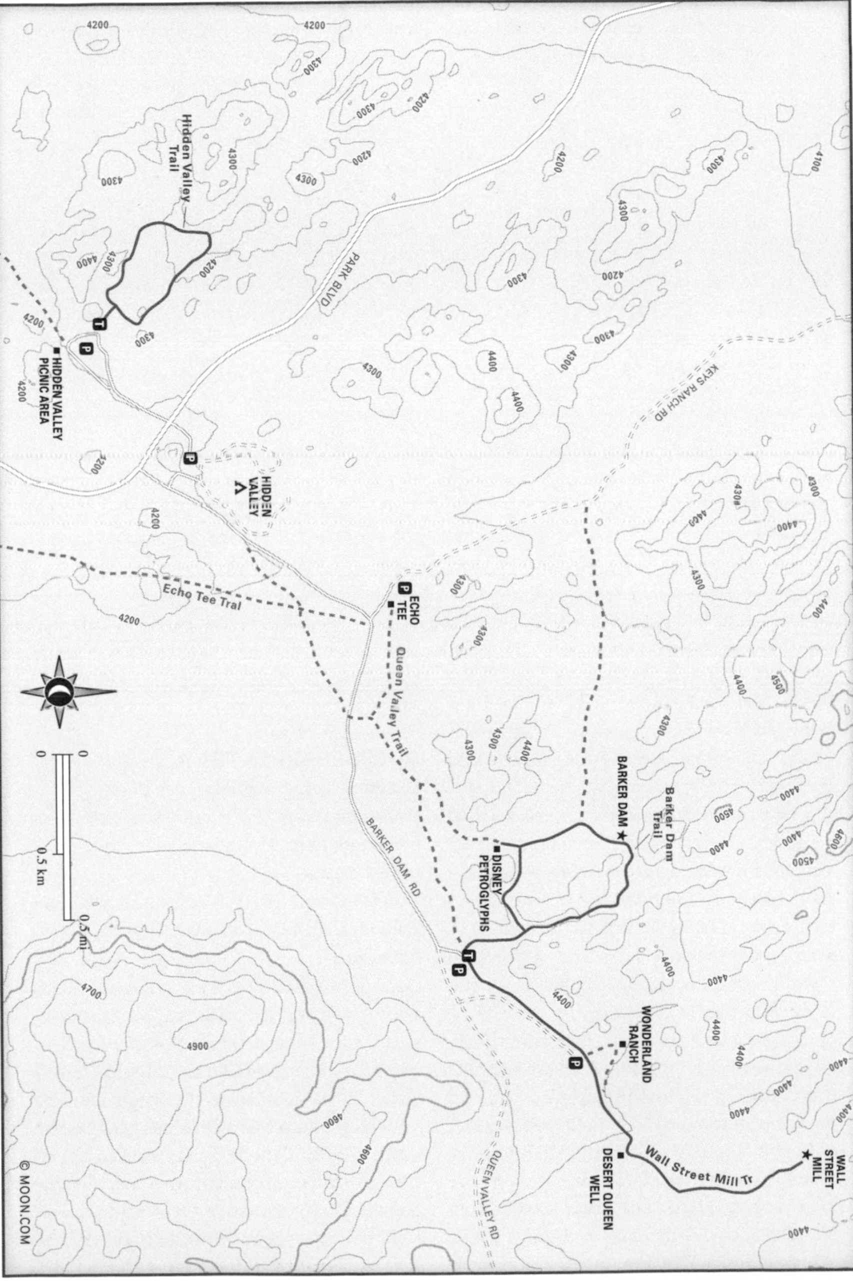
Hidden Valley Trail
PARK BLVD
HIDDEN VALLEY PICNIC AREA
HIDDEN VALLEY
Echo Tee Tral
ECHO TEE
Queen Valley Trail
KEYS RANCH RD
BARKER DAM RD
DISNEY PETROGLYPHS
BARKER DAM
Barker Dam Trail
WONDERLAND RANCH
DESERT QUEEN WELL
Wall Street Mill Tr
WALL STREET MILL
QUEEN VALLEY RD
0
0
0.5 km
0.5 mi
© MOON.COM

North View Maze Loop

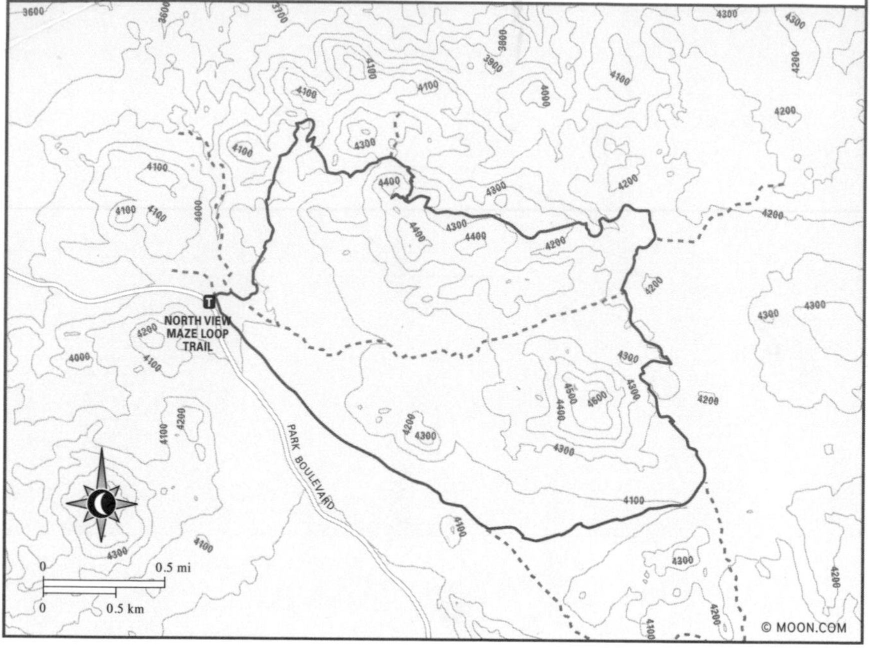

rock walls allow for glimpses of the desert below. Two spur trails (Copper Mountain View and West Hills) at about 1.7 miles allow you to catch more views both north and into the park.

The trail winds down to a deep wash at 2.5 miles. Cross it and be on the lookout for a signed intersection at 2.7 miles. Here, head right toward the Loop Trail. The next section continues generally south until it reaches the maze. Here the trail cuts directly through rectangular slabs of rock to emerge on flat desert floor on the other side.

Your next landmark will be Window Rock, a prominent peak in front of you as you continue south. Keep looking up, and you will see the eagle-shaped hole in the mountain, only visible from a distance. At an intersection, turn right to head west and continue the loop back to the parking area. (Continuing straight adds 1.9 miles as it loops around Window Rock.) The remaining stretch is an enjoyable flat walk through sparse Joshua Tree desert.

QUAIL SPRINGS TRAIL

Distance: 6 miles round-trip
Duration: 3 hours
Elevation gain: 243 feet
Effort: Moderate
Trailhead: Quail Springs Basin Picnic area; look for an unmarked eroded trail on the west side of the paved parking area.

Quail Springs Historic Trail, as it is named on some topo maps, strikes out through peaceful open desert, intersecting with historic routes like the Johnny Lang Canyon (original claimholder for the Lost Horse Mine) and connecting with a network of trails that extend to the west park entrance. It is also used to access **Quail Mountain,** the highest peak in Joshua Tree National Park at 5,814 feet.

The first three miles of the trail to the base of Quail Mountain are peaceful and

Lost Horse Mine

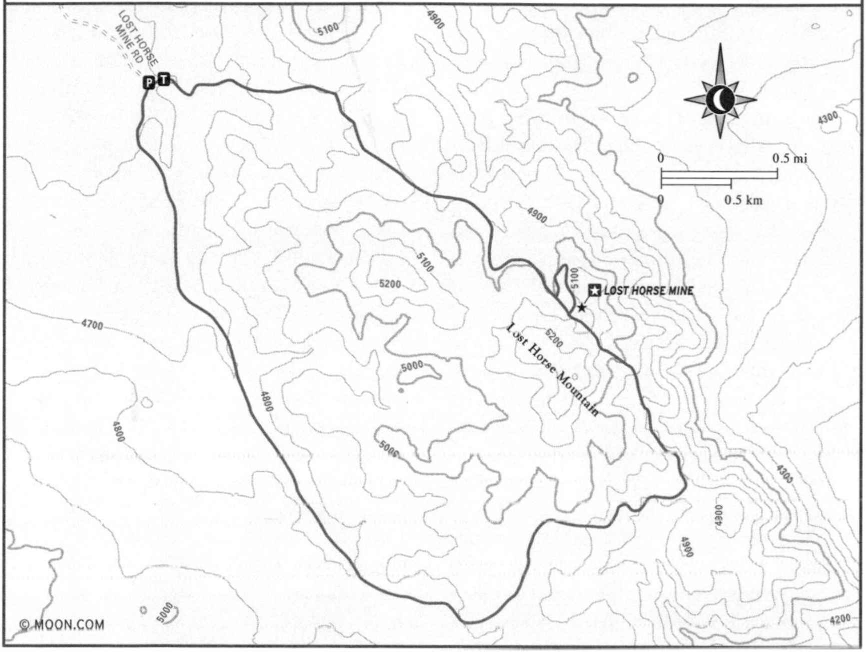

open, crossing what looks like a grassy plain that doesn't necessarily fit into our ideas of boulder-strewn Joshua Tree. The silvery husks of downed Joshua trees burned in a fire further add to the prehistoric savanna feel. The silence is punctuated by the occasional sound of a bird or a car along Park Boulevard, the main road within distant sight for most of the hike, making this place feel that much more secret.

From the picnic area, the trail is clearly defined. One mile in, the route splits with **Quail Springs wash,** and footprints are visible in both forks. Although the wash (right) will take you in generally the same direction as the trail (due west), the going is easier on the trail. Take the left fork to continue. At 2 miles, the trail crosses the access route to **Johnny Lang Canyon,** veering off to the south (left). Continue straight.

At 2.9 miles you will reach signs indicating that the area used to be **private property.** An out-of-place weathered parking curb as well as sun-silvered timber and metal odds and ends are strewn about. A pile of boulders a few hundred yards to the north marks the site of the 1920s **homestead of John Samuelson,** a Swedish immigrant who was ultimately denied his homestead claim in 1928 by the U.S. land office because of his Swedish heritage. His house burned down in the 1930s.

This is a good turnaround point, or you can continue to Quail Mountain or to eventually intersect with Park Boulevard near the West Entrance. (Note: To continue along the Quail Springs Trail requires maps, planning, and possibly a car shuttle at the other end.)

★ LOST HORSE MINE

Distance: 4-7.4 miles round-trip
Duration: 2-4 hours
Elevation gain: 450-570 feet
Effort: Moderate to strenuous (very steep, rocky grades climbing Lost Horse Mountain)

Trailhead: Far end of the dirt parking area at the end of Lost Horse Mine Road

Directions: From Park Boulevard take Keys View Road south for 2.4 miles. Turn left onto the signed Lost Horse Mine Road and follow it for 0.9 mile to the parking area.

One of the **best preserved mining sites** in Joshua Tree National Park, the beautifully weathered stamp mill at the Lost Horse Mine was in operation from 1894 to 1931. The mill's breadth and sturdy construction are a testament to the mine's success as one of the highest producing in Joshua Tree history. The first person to file a claim was Johnny Lang of local lore who, in Wild West campfire tale fashion, had recently had his horses stolen by a gang of local cattle rustlers. The mill and surrounding ruins (look for rock house foundations, equipment, and mining tunnels) are the highlight of the out-and-back hike, but the loop offers more surprises and history.

The signed loop trail is located in the middle of the parking lot and directs hikers counterclockwise. The trail climbs (gradually then steeper at 2.5 miles) around the flank of stark **Lost Horse Mountain** through a mix of Joshua trees, yucca, and juniper, following an old mining road. On the way it crosses paths with the **Optimist Mine;** only a picturesque stone chimney and scattered artifacts remain. Beyond these ruins the trail climbs precipitously, giving way to sweeping views toward the northeast, Wonderland of Rocks, and Queen Valley. At 4.7 miles the rocky trail hits the ridge below the Lost Horse Mountain Summit, and the **Lost Horse Mine** comes into view below. Take time to check out the area. Although the mill and tunnels are fenced off, remains of rock houses and artifacts make this an interesting place to explore. You've done the hard work—the way back is mostly downhill with pleasant views looking toward Lost Horse Valley. Keep an eye out for additional rock structure remains and mining artifacts.

★ WILLOW HOLE TRAIL

Distance: 7 miles round-trip

Duration: 3-4 hours

Elevation gain: Negligible

Effort: Moderate

Trailhead: Parking area for Boy Scout Trail

The Willow Hole Trail strikes into the heart of the Wonderland of Rocks. The flat, sandy track and lack of elevation gain mean that your main job is to admire the spectacular scenery. At 1.2 miles the trail splits at a signed intersection. The left fork continues as the **Boy Scout Trail,** ending at the **Indian Cove Campground** in another 6.4 miles. Most people hike the Boy Scout Trail as a shuttle hike with a car at either end. To continue on the **Willow Hole Trail,** stay to the right. The trail officially ends unceremoniously in 3.5 miles in a sandy, boulder-filled wash at so-named **Willow Hole.** As you may have guessed, Willow Hole itself is marked by a stand of willow trees. Depending on seasonal rains, the area can be filled with ephemeral pools of water.

BOY SCOUT TRAIL

Distance: 8 miles one-way (arrange a car shuttle at one end)

Duration: 4-5 hours

Elevation gain: 1,265 feet (mostly downhill)

Effort: Moderate

South Trailhead: South Keys West Backcountry Board 0.7 mile east of the Quail Springs picnic area

North Trailhead: Indian Cove Backcountry Board, near the Indian Cove Ranger Station

This scenic eight-mile trail skirts the western edge of the Wonderland of Rocks before it winds through sharp mountains and rocky canyons to end in open desert at the Indian Cove Backcountry Board. With the shifting landscape and elevation along the Boy Scout Trail, the plant zones transition so that you have the chance to move through classic Joshua tree forest and mesquite, piñon, and oak at the higher elevations, yucca and boulder gardens, and creosote and cholla at the lower altitudes. This hike is the **most popular overnight backpacking hike** in the park. The Wonderland of Rocks to the east is a day-use area only: campsites must be west of the Boy Scout Trail. Sections of the

Mining History

Word association for visitors to Joshua Tree National Park may evoke spiky Joshua trees, giant boulders, rock climbing, and otherworldly scenery; however, the region also has its share of mining history. Most of us know that the Gold Rush in California began in 1849, but when the gold began to play out in the Sierra Nevada Mountains, prospectors fanned into the deserts.

Mining activity began in the 1870s and peaked in the 1920s and 1930s. Joshua Tree became a National Monument in 1936, putting a slowdown on mining as sites came under the protection of the National Park Service. All the usual desert problems, including hot summers, scarce water, limited wood for fuel, and the remoteness of the region made it difficult to get provisions and equipment in and out and to sustain mining operations even though there was gold in the hills. Gold was the main commodity here, and some hardy souls persevered in finding it. Nearly 300 mines (288 by one scholarly study) were developed in the area that is now Joshua Tree National Park. Few of the mines were good producers, and many of these sites are humble and fading back into the desert, marked by mining tunnels, tailings, rusted can dumps, and cleared flat tent sites miners once called home. However, you can visit some of the park's best-preserved sites, with colorful histories, weathered structures, and scattered artifacts all set against the rugged scenery of Joshua Tree's washes and peaks.

A four-mile round-trip hike along the old mining road takes you to the impressive remains of the Lost Horse Mine, including a well-preserved stamp mill that once boomed out 24 hours a day as gold and silver ore was crushed.

A series of suspect circumstances landed the ownership of the Desert Queen Mine into the hands of an infamous local cattle rustler before rancher Bill Keys ended up with it. Access the picturesque gold mine ruins from a short trail.

With parts scavenged from the old mining site of Pinyon Well in Pleasant Valley, local rancher Bill Keys used the Wall Street Mill to mill ore for different miners in the area. A colorful collection of equipment and junk awaits along this three-mile round-trip hike.

The biggest drama surrounding the Mastodon Mine may be the striking views across the Cottonwood Mountains from this windswept gold mine. The mine is unique for its access to water at nearby Cottonwood Spring, used to feed the mine's processing at the Winona Mill. Cottonwoods and other non-native species at the site mark this time in history.

trail are indistinguishable or unmarked, especially through washes. Carry a topo map.

The trail begins as a pleasant stroll through Joshua trees along a well-defined sandy track along the western edge of the Wonderland of Rocks. At 1.3 miles the trail splits with the **Willow Hole Trail.** Follow the signed junction to the left.

From here the trail climbs slightly before leveling on a high plateau, and the vegetation transforms with piñon, juniper, oak, and cholla cactus. At 3.8 miles the trail continues into an open wash marked by a **signpost.** For the next half-mile the trail can be hard to follow through a series of washes. You'll pass a split with the **Big Pine Trail** on your left at 4 miles. Beyond the split, look out for an old concrete cattle trough as a landmark.

The trail exits the wash on the left at 4.4 miles and winds to the head of a deep canyon with austere desert views. From here the trail descends steeply to the canyon floor then heads right into the wash. Follow the rugged canyon for a mile, heading northeast. Yucca and barrel cactus line your way.

Exit the canyon at 6.2 miles, bearing right at a signpost. The trail spills into an open *bajada.* The final leg of the trail crosses open desert to end at the **Indian Cove** Backcountry Board.

HIDDEN VALLEY

Distance: 1 mile round-trip
Duration: 0.5 hour
Elevation gain: 20 feet
Effort: Easy

Trailhead: Hidden Valley Campground and picnic area

This one-mile loop passes through granite boulders to emerge in scenic **Hidden Valley,** once wetter, grassier, and used for cattle grazing during the ranching halcyon of the early-mid 1900s. The well-signed trail circles the small enclosed valley, delving into the monzogranite **boulder piles** with tempting bouldering opportunities.

BARKER DAM

Distance: 1.3 miles round-trip
Duration: 0.5 hour
Elevation gain: Negligible
Effort: Easy
Trailhead: Paved parking area and signed trailhead off of Hidden Valley Road

Located on the southern edge of the Wonderland of Rocks, the popular 1.3-mile loop trail winds through closely lined boulders to a small pond that can be dry at certain times of year. Ranchers dammed the natural pond for cattle, taking advantage of a site used by Native Americans for centuries. The trail is well marked and easy to follow.

The watering hole is now a stop for migrating birds, bighorn sheep, and other wildlife. This area is also home to the **Disney petroglyphs.** During shooting for a film in the 1960s, a film crew painted over existing Native American petroglyphs to make them more dramatic for the shoot, possibly adding some of their own—a cultural travesty.

WALL STREET MILL

Distance: 3 miles round-trip
Duration: 1.5 hours
Elevation gain: 23 feet
Effort: Easy
Trailhead: Barker Dam parking area; the trailhead for the Wall Street Mill is clearly signed.

When local rancher **Bill Keys** wanted to build a mill for processing ores from local mines, he scrounged an existing one and relocated it, tapping into the time-honored desert tradition of moving defunct mining cabins and structures to new, profitable locations. The mill was originally located at Pinyon Well and had been in operation since 1891. Keys rebuilt the mill and used it from 1932 to 1942 to mill ore for different miners in the area. The mill was used briefly in 1949 and again as late as 1966. When Keys died, the National Park Service took over the mill site and has done an excellent job of preserving it. In addition to the mill, you'll find **abandoned cars** and other equipment and **artifacts.** The site also used to house a bunkhouse, now gone.

To get to the mill, begin at the marked trailhead for the Wall Street Mill in the Barker Dam parking area. The trail veers east, clearly marked with stone trail boundaries and occasional arrows. In 0.3 mile the trail hits a second, smaller parking lot then picks up again on the left. At 0.5 mile an unexpected psychedelic pink marks the remains of the **Wonderland Ranch,** tempting exploration. A short side trip will lead you to the foundations, crumbling walls, and scattered artifacts of the ranch.

Another historic bonus awaits in the form of the **Desert Queen Well** ruins one mile into the hike. A tall windmill, once used to pump water, still stands over piles of weathered timbers and an old tank.

The **Wall Street Mill** is definitely the highlight. Leave time to admire the well and poke around the area.

WONDERLAND WASH

Distance: 2 miles round-trip
Duration: 1 hour
Elevation gain: 75 feet
Effort: Moderate
Trailhead: Barker Dam parking area. Begin at the signed trailhead for the Wall Street Mill.

A use trail past the Wonderland Ranch cuts into the Wonderland of Rocks via a secluded wash and ends at the Astro Domes, an impressive pair of granite monoliths popular with rock climbers. Begin at the signed trailhead for the Wall Street Mill. At 0.5 mile, an unexpected crumbling pink structure marks the scattered remains and crumbling walls of the Wonderland Ranch. To the left of the ruins, an unmaintained trail heads east through low boulders into the wash. On the other side, the trail follows the wash northeast. Although the trail dries up at times, follow the wash. You will occasionally have to scramble over low boulders or work your way through foliage. At 0.3 miles into the wash, cross the remains of a stone dam used by cattle ranchers. Continuing up the wash, you are surrounded by thriving desert vegetation and the striking rock formations of the Wonderland of Rocks. At 1 mile, look for the giant dome of white tank granite, outstanding for its monolithic, uncracked state in this maze of jumbled boulder piles. The trail dwindles beyond this, but it is possible to continue deeper into the Wonderland of Rocks. Otherwise, return the way you came.

PINE CITY SITE

Distance: 3 miles round-trip to Pine City; 4 miles round-trip to overlook of Pine Canyon
Duration: 2 hours
Elevation gain: 150 feet
Effort: Moderate
Trailhead: Parking area for Desert Queen Mine

"Site" not "city" is the operative word here. Pine City is long gone, marked by piñons and a few scattered mining tunnels. The highlights of this hike are the easy, open trail winding through classic Mojave Desert flora, picturesque boulders, and its location off the beaten path of Park Boulevard.

The trail starts at the end of the graded dirt Queen Valley Road, and although the trailhead is less than a mile from Park Boulevard, it offers more **solitude** than some of the more popular nearby hikes. The trail gains slight elevation as it heads toward the **Pine City site** (1.5 miles) or the **Pine Canyon overlook** (2 miles). The slight elevation makes this an easy desert trek but also gives rise to shifts in desert vegetation along the way. Hearty desert creosote gives way to yuccas and Joshua trees and eventually junipers and piñons. Cholla and barrel cacti also spike the landscape. At 1.3 miles you'll see your first pine trees interspersed in a picturesque bay of stacked monzonite boulders. The "city" itself is also marked by these pines at 1.5 miles. Here the trail splits slightly with the left (main) fork continuing another 0.5 mile to an overlook on the edge of Pine Canyon. The trail down into the canyon is unmaintained beyond the overlook. The right fork continues the extra few hundred yards to Pine City proper.

DESERT QUEEN MINE AND WASH

Distance: 1-7 miles round-trip
Duration: 1-5 hours
Elevation gain: 160-660 feet
Effort: Easy to strenuous
Trailhead: Pine City/Desert Queen Mine parking area

This steep, rugged wash in Queen Valley saw a lot of mining action from the 1890s until the 1960s. A short trek to the Desert Queen Mine reveals the rust-varnished equipment, mining tunnels, and massive tailings of a successful California gold mine. Continuing down the wash turns up more scattered mining debris and, eventually, scant remains of other, meaner mining camps, never as rich as the Desert Queen, hinting at a harsh life for miners scraping out a living.

To reach the Desert Queen Mine, take the **unsigned trail** from the Pine City parking area. At 0.3 mile you will see the picturesque remains of a **miner's stone cabin** on your right. Continuing straight, you will soon reach an overlook. This is a great stop or a destination. From the overlook, you can see across the wash to the mines on the hillside and the old road snaking along the rocky embankment. Tailings, the huge piles of silvery rock excavated from the mining tunnels, are mounded, monuments to mining, on the wash floor.

To get a closer look at the **Desert Queen Mine's** equipment and tunnels, backtrack to the stone house and follow the road down into the wash then back up to the mining site.

If this didn't satisfy your itch for exploration, a rugged hike through the wash brings you to a much smaller mining site. From the top of the Desert Queen Mine, return to the

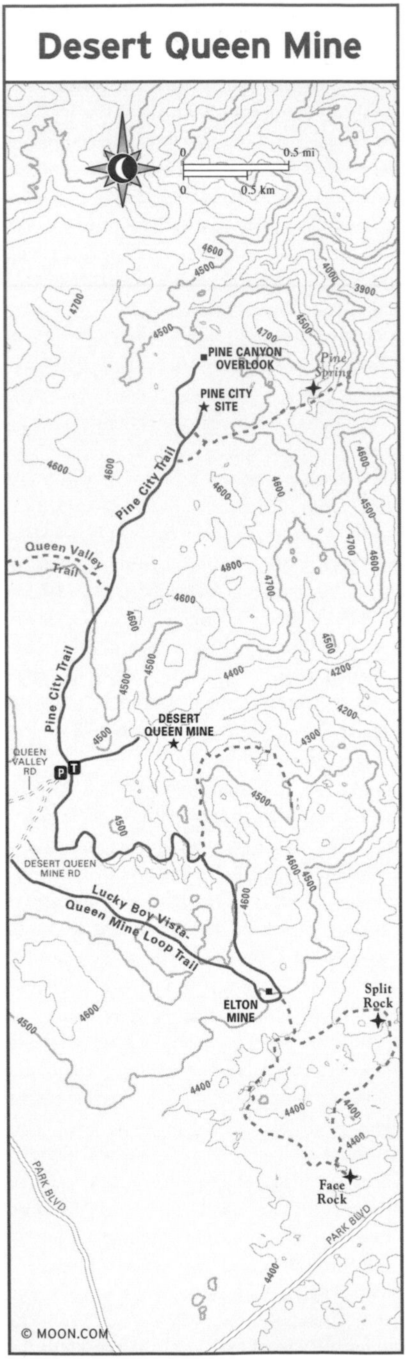

wash and turn right (north) to continue exploring the wash. After a few hundred yards, the canyon jogs and the hike trends generally east. The sandy-floored canyon is wild and scenic with steep walls, clusters of boulders, and scattered mining debris, testament to the power of desert floods. **Two boulder jams** block your way, but they are passable by use trails. After the second boulder jam, the wash widens, and you'll see tailings from the **Gold Hill Mine.** The miners' small tent community of John's Camp was located on a long, low shelf on the right side three miles from your starting point in the wash below the Desert Queen Mine. Return the way you came.

LUCKY BOY VISTA

Distance: 3.6 miles round-trip
Duration: 2 hours
Elevation gain: 150 feet
Effort: Moderate
Trailhead: Pine City/Desert Queen Mine parking area. Trailhead is unsigned at the south end of the parking area (on the right just past parking entrance).

What makes the Lucky Boy Vista such a nice hike is its combination of views, Native American history, mining history, solitude, and the pleasant walk through boulder-strewn desert piñon and yucca gardens. Heads up: there are a number of use trails, old mining roads, and washes crossing this area near the Desert Queen Mine, so it is easy to veer off your route if you're not paying attention. Carry a map and compass and know how to use them.

Start from the Pine City/Desert Queen Mine parking area. The sandy trail is clearly defined but unmarked. It starts by heading south then curves through a series of washes lined with striking stacked rock formations. Look for signs of the Native American village that once inhabited this site in the form of a pair of ***morteros*** along this stretch. At 0.8 mile, the trail forks. The left (north) trail heads toward the Desert Queen Mine and Wash. Rock scrambling is required. To reach the Lucky Boy Vista, turn right (south) and follow the trail. Continue to head south/

Ryan Mountain

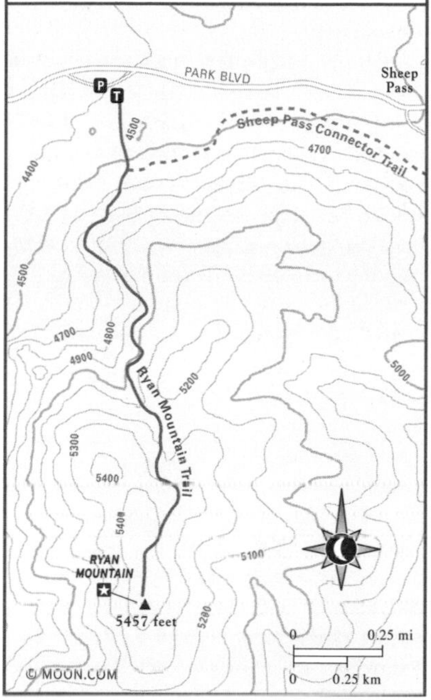

southeast over the next mile. You will pass through a **gate,** a holdover from the era of mines and private property. Beyond the gate, the trail forks and begins to climb slightly. Take the left fork to follow the old mining road. The **Elton Mine site** is easily identifiable from its shuttered mining tunnels at about 1.5 miles. The trail continues past the mine site to pause on a lofty plateau with views of Split Rock—the **Lucky Boy Vista.** Follow the return trail.

At 2.6 miles the trail forks at an easy-to-miss **No Camping post.** Stay straight (west) to complete the loop. Turning right will take you back to where you started the trail. At 3.1 miles you will reach the **Desert Queen Mine Road.** Turn right for the last half of a mile to complete the loop.

CAP ROCK

Distance: 0.4 mile round-trip
Duration: 0.5 hour
Elevation gain: Negligible
Effort: Easy
Trailhead: Parking area at intersection of Park Boulevard and Keys View Road

At first glance the Cap Rock nature trail seems like just another gorgeous destination—a flat, easy trail leads through whimsically eroded boulder formations, most notably a flat, cap-like rock balanced on top of a spectacular formation. But there are a few things that set this spot apart. First, it's **wheelchair-accessible.** The trail is wide, flat, and made of hard-packed sandy dirt. Second, although it may be hard to imagine with the paved parking area and interpretive signs, Cap Rock played backdrop to a rock-and-roll drama. In 1973, country rocker **Gram Parsons** died of a drug overdose at a motel in nearby Joshua Tree. His friends, trying to fulfill his wishes, brought his body out to Cap Rock and set it on fire so that he could be cremated in his beloved Joshua Tree. The site still attracts fans of the cult-famed rocker.

★ RYAN MOUNTAIN

Distance: 3 miles round-trip
Duration: 1.5 hours
Elevation gain: 1,070 feet
Effort: Moderate
Trailhead: Signed parking area on Park Boulevard east of Ryan Campground

Although only three miles round-trip, this trail climbs a little more than 1,000 feet in elevation over its 1.5-mile ascent to the summit. Hikers are rewarded with panoramic views from the 5,457-foot wind-scoured vantage point where a **giant cairn** marks the peak. Soak in views of Pinto Basin, Hidden Valley, Wonderland of Rocks, and a bird's-eye view of Ryan Ranch and the Lost Horse Well. This is one of the **most popular hikes in the park.** While it's short on solitude, it's long on vistas.

SKULL ROCK

Distance: 1.7 miles round-trip
Duration: 0.5-1 hour
Elevation gain: 157 feet

Effort: Easy

Trailhead: Parking for Skull Rock and the nature trail is located on Park Boulevard near the Jumbo Rocks Campground entrance. The trail begins to the right of the landmark Skull Rock.

Skull Rock, anthropomorphically named for its gaunt eye socket-like depressions, is a popular rock formation along Park Boulevard. The concave hollows, called *tafoni,* originally began as small pits. Over time they cyclically filled with rainwater and eroded. After your photo op at the skull, follow the 1.7-mile nature trail as it winds through the scenic boulder- and plant-strewn landscape. From the right side of the skull, the trail hooks over to **Jumbo Rocks Campground,** passing interpretive signs on desert ecology along the way. Turn right when you reach the campground. The trail follows the campground road until it intersects with Park Boulevard. It crosses the road to wind back through more boulders with views of the surrounding desert before it completes the loop at Skull Rock.

ARCH ROCK NATURE TRAIL

Distance: 0.5 mile round-trip

Duration: 0.5 hour

Elevation gain: 30 feet

Effort: Easy

Trailhead: White Tank Campground across from site #9

The highlight of this trail is a delicately eroded arch tucked into a boulder pile formation in the first third of the loop. The rest of the trail winds through **carved rock formations** to return to the starting point at **White Tank Campground.** Though the trail is short, several social trails split off from the official trail and can make it hard to follow. Pay attention to where you're going.

SPLIT ROCK LOOP

Distance: 2 miles round-trip

Duration: 1 hour

Elevation gain: 133 feet

Effort: Easy

Trailhead: From the north park entrance in Twentynine Palms, head south for 6.7 miles. Turn right into the signed Split Rock picnic area and park in the parking and picnic area at the end of the road. The trail begins next to a giant split rock at the north (far) end of the parking lot.

The family-friendly Split Rock Loop Trail allows you to immerse yourself in the details of the landscape. The hike starts from a small picnic area and winds for two miles through boulders and desert flora. Yucca, paddle cactus, and mesquite are interspersed with the boulders lining your pathway. Look for lizards sunning themselves on the sunbaked rocks.

CONTACT MINE

Distance: 4 miles round-trip

Duration: 2-3 hours

Elevation gain: 516 feet

Effort: Moderate

Trailhead: The unsigned trailhead is located 0.5 mile south of the North Entrance of the park (Twentynine Palms entrance) off of Utah Trail. Park in a turnout on the right (west) side of the road.

The hike to the Contact Mine offers austere desert views, solitude, and a glimpse into Palm Springs' mining history. The hike begins in a wide wash. Follow a series of red hiking signs to navigate this open, sandy terrain. In a few hundred yards, the trail takes a more solid shape as the wash leads to a hard-packed, rock-lined trail. This is the remains of the old mining road, still clearly etched into the landscape as it cuts through the steep hills. The hike slowly gains in elevation with views of the Pinto Mountains to the east and craggy peaks running south from Twentynine Palms. As the trail winds around each hill, you expect the mine to come into view. This feeling is even more pronounced since the trail is completely exposed. Hike early or in cooler weather. More than a mile and a half in, the mine finally comes into view on the hillside. It is a tantalizing sight. Enjoy this glimpse from a distance; the remains at the site are scant, but there is some machinery and debris from

1: an old road and the remains of the Desert Queen Mine **2:** anthropomorphic Skull Rock **3:** 49 Palms Oasis

1

2

3

this old gold and silver mine dating to the early 1900s.

Indian Cove

★ 49 PALMS OASIS

Distance: 3 miles round-trip
Duration: 2-3 hours
Elevation gain: 360 feet
Effort: Moderate
Trailhead: The trailhead is accessed from a parking area at the end of Canyon Road, about 1.7 miles east of Indian Cove Road, off of Hwy. 62.
Directions: From Hwy. 62, turn right onto Canyon Road, signed for 49 Palms Oasis. (Note: It is only signed heading east.) A small animal hospital on Hwy. 62 is a good landmark. Follow Canyon Road (signed for 49 Palms Oasis) for 1.7 miles to the trailhead.

This natural oasis surrounded by **native fan palms** secluded in a rocky canyon is a striking destination. From the trailhead, the trail climbs up over a ridge and then winds down through arid hills. The trail is easy to follow, passing through a flinty landscape that gives no indication of its secret oasis until you are close. You'll see the oasis from a distance, nestled against the jagged hills, before you reach it. There are only 158 fan palm oases in North America, and five in Joshua Tree; this is clearly a special place, used historically by Cahuilla Indians and offering precious habitat for bighorn sheep, quail, and coyotes. Tread lightly in this fragile ecosystem.

CALIFORNIA RIDING AND HIKING TRAIL

The California Riding and Hiking Trail is a continuous **36-mile trail system** cutting across piñon and juniper forests, Joshua tree stands, and creosote-strewn lowlands in the main western section of the park. Long on views and solitude, this trail can be hiked as a **three-day backpacking trip** or broken into smaller day or overnight hikes. For backpacking, you will want to cache water. You must register at designated backcountry boards if you plan to stay out overnight.

There are **six main trailheads** anchoring **five trail sections.** For thru-hiking, the trail is best hiked west to east.

- Section 1: **Black Rock Canyon Trailhead to Upper Covington Flats.** Starting from the Black Rock Canyon Campground, this 7.5-mile section of the trail hooks through creosote lowlands before it climbs 1,000 feet, gaining the steepest elevation of the entire hike, to 5,130 feet. From here, the trail rolls downhill to Upper Covington Flats.
- Section 2: **Upper Covington Flats to Keys View.** This is the remotest section of the trail, and the trail here can be overgrown. Its 10.8 miles traverse a series of washes and ridges offering panoramic views before descending into the Joshua tree groves of Juniper Flats and then the Lost Horse Valley to end at Keys View trailhead. Nearby Ryan Campground also provides trail access on the eastern end of this section.
- Section 3: **Ryan Ranch to Geology Tour Road.** This 6.5-mile section of the trail veers close to the ruins of Ryan Ranch and the Lost Horse Well south of Ryan Mountain before climbing to the Geology Tour Road trailhead.
- Section 4: **Geology Tour Road to Pinto Basin.** From Geology Tour Road, the next section is the shortest, clocking in at 4.4 miles to end up at the Pinto Basin Trailhead (Twin Tanks parking between Belle and White Tank Campground). Its manageable distance and light elevation gain make it a candidate for a day hike. Views of Jumbo Rocks and the Pinto Basin make it worth the effort.
- Section 5: **Pinto Basin to North Entrance.** The final 7.3-mile stretch skirts Belle Campground and offers sweeping views of Twentynine Palms as it continues north to end just south of the north park entrance.

Cottonwood Spring

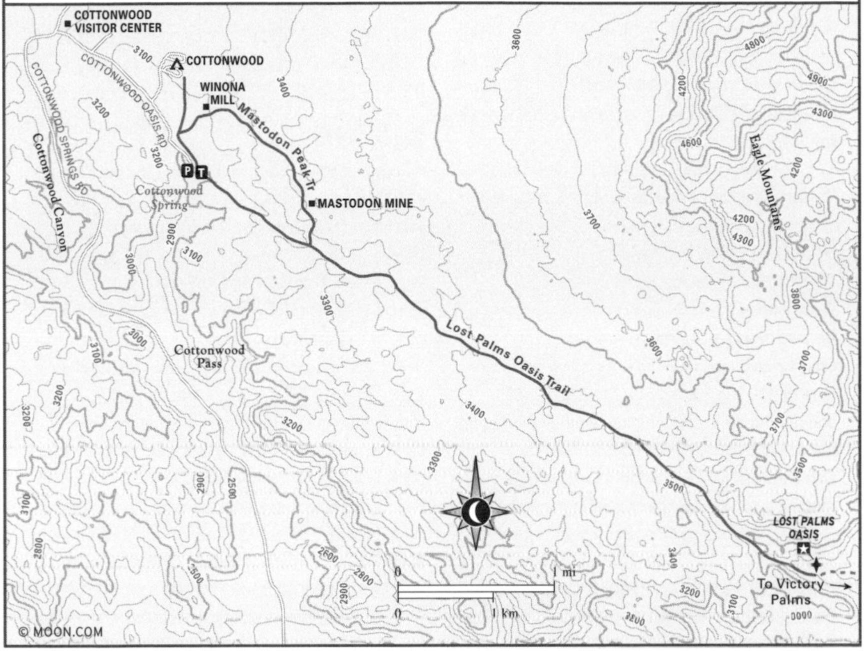

Cottonwood Spring

MASTODON PEAK

Distance: 3 miles round-trip

Duration: 1.5-2 hours

Elevation gain: 375 feet

Effort: Moderate

Trailhead: The trail begins at a nature trail a few yards east of the Cottonwood Spring sign and staircase; campers follow a signed trail from the eastern end of Loop A.

Directions: From the Cottonwood Visitors Center, continue 1.2 miles southeast on the Cottonwood Campground road until it dead-ends at Cottonwood Spring.

Mastodon's rocky peak crowns this loop hike and affords dramatic desert views stretching toward the Eagle Mountains, San Jacinto Mountains, and as far as the Salton Sea. On the way, the preserved remains of the Mastodon Mine add some historical spice to the trail. The peak was named by miners for its resemblance to the prehistoric creature. If you spend enough time in the desert sun, it's possible you'll start to see dubious shapes in the rocks too.

The Mastodon Peak loop is very well-signed and clearly established. It begins on a nature trail that leaves from the parking area and heads northwest to a junction at 0.5 mile. Turn right (left leads to the campground) to continue toward the base of the foothills. Just past the junction, concrete foundations mark the site of the old **Winona Mill.** From the base of the mountains, the trail climbs toward the peak and the remains of the **Mastodon Mine** clinging to the hillside below the peak at 1.4 miles. From the mine, there are sweeping views toward the west and the Cottonwood Mountains. George Hulsey operated the gold mine from 1919 to 1932. He was also responsible for building the Winona Mill, used to process ore from the Mastodon Mine and other claims to the north in the Dale Mining

District. Continue the loop down the mountain. At the base of the hills the trail forks. To complete the loop, turn right. (A left turn will take you to the Lost Palms Oasis in approximately 3 miles.) The loop has a strong finish at scenic **Cottonwood Spring.** From the spring, follow the staircase up to the parking lot.

For a longer hike, combine a trip to the Lost Palms Oasis for a spectacular 9.5-mile trek.

★ LOST PALMS OASIS

Distance: 7.5 miles round-trip
Duration: 4-5 hours
Elevation gain: 460 feet
Effort: Moderate
Trailhead: The trail begins at a staircase leading down to Cottonwood Spring; campers follow a signed trail from the eastern end of Loop A.
Directions: From the Cottonwood Visitors Center, continue 1.2 miles southeast on the Cottonwood Campground road until it dead-ends at Cottonwood Spring.

This trail undulates through striking desert scenery before dropping down to a secluded canyon and the largest collection of fan palms in the park.

The trail is straightforward, making a beeline to the southeast along a well-marked and well-signed route. It starts from scenic **Cottonwood Spring** and ripples over an up-and-down landscape dominated by a series of ridges and washes. The trail is almost completely exposed, flanked by interesting desert gardens, including barrel cacti, ocotillos, and desert willows.

The trail edges into the foothills of the Eagle Mountains before emerging to overlook a steep canyon and the Lost Palms Oasis, tucked on a rugged canyon hillside. The name makes sense in this remote place. The **Lost Palms Oasis** is a watering hole for bighorn sheep and other wildlife. Over the next 100 yards, a steep trail continues to the boulder- and palm-strewn canyon floor. Shaded and peaceful, this is a great place to take a break before your return. If you're still feeling like exploring, continue to follow the trail down the canyon. One mile of picking your way and rock scrambling will bring you to another fan palm stand—the **Victory Palms.**

For a longer hike, add the loop to Mastodon Peak and the Mastodon Mine (adds two miles) for a total 9.5-mile hike.

BIKING

Biking within Joshua Tree National Park is confined to roads that are open to vehicles, but there are some good rides along the park's paved and backcountry roads. For road biking, **Park Boulevard** offers a great route through the park's most spectacular scenery. The paved road runs 25 miles from the West Entrance in Joshua Tree to the North Entrance in Twentynine Palms, with many opportunities for shorter stretches in between. **Pinto Basin Road,** the other main park road, cuts through the Pinto Basin's open desert with scenery that's less rewarding than Park Boulevard but also more lightly traveled. It runs 30 miles from its start four miles south of the North Entrance.

For mountain biking, the short series of dirt roads crossing **Queen Valley** (the Hidden Valley area between Barker Dam and the Pine City Backcountry Board) totals 13.4 miles and offers scenic rides through large stands of Joshua trees. The **Geology Tour Road** stretches slightly downhill for its first 5.4 miles to Squaw Tank; beyond this, it loops six miles through Pleasant Valley. Be cautious as the road is sandy and rutted at points.

There are no bike rentals available in Joshua Tree National Park. Located near the West Entrance in the town of Joshua Tree, **Joshua Tree Bicycle Shop** (6416 Hallee Rd., Joshua Tree, 760/366-3377, www.joshuatreebicycleshop.com, 10am-6pm Mon.-Sat., $20 per hour, $65 per day) is a full-service bike shop that rents bikes and offers repairs and ride recommendations.

★ ROCK CLIMBING

From rock stars to beginners, climbers of all levels are drawn to the park's traditional-style crack, slab, and steep-face climbing and its

TOP EXPERIENCE

Rock Climbing in Joshua Tree

Joshua Tree's unique desert landscape drives thousands of visitors a year to tackle its signature monzogranite boulders and striking rock formations. When other climbing meccas like Yosemite are covered in winter snow and ice, climbers flock to the scene in "J-Tree" (as it's called by this adventure-driven subculture).

Joshua Tree as an international climbing destination built slowly, starting about a decade after it became a national monument in 1936. The first rock climbing groups were organized through the Sierra Club's rock-climbing section and met casually to climb in Joshua Tree and nearby areas like Idyllwild. Through the 1950s and 1960s, some of the pioneers of the sport began testing the vertical geological expanses of the region and themselves as they sought a connection with the landscape away from mainstream civilization.

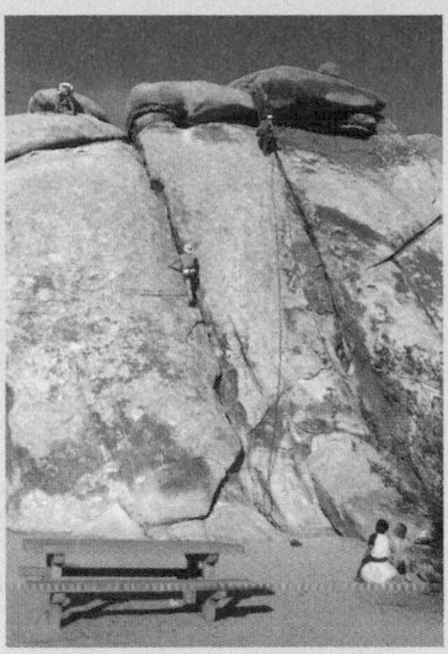

watching climbers at Quail Springs picnic area

The action grew slowly, with these early pioneers establishing and naming first ascents and recording climbs. The gear also started to improve, initially designed and fabricated by climbers to sell out of their vans, some of whom went on to found companies like Black Diamond, Patagonia, and North Face. As the vertical frontier expanded, Joshua Tree established itself as the perfect winter climbing destination while the tight-knit climbing communities pushed to new heights. The community continues to evolve as climbers make the pilgrimage to Joshua Tree. Today, it's hard to go anywhere in the northwestern section of the park without seeing someone rock climbing. Here are a few spots where you can watch the action (or get in on it).

- The **Quail Springs** picnic area has another, more adventurous side. While families picnic at this scenic spot, rock climbers tackle popular formations like Trashcan Rock, Hound Rocks, and the White Cliffs of Dover.
- **Intersection Rock** at the turnoff to Hidden Valley Campground is a classic, with over two dozen routes established by a handful of pioneering climbers in the 1960s.
- **Hidden Valley Campground** has a high concentration of quality routes, meaning you don't have to leave your campsite to experience some of Joshua Tree's finest.
- A use trail along the scenic **Wonderland Wash** in the Wonderland of Rocks region leads to the Astro Domes, a destination heavy on solitude, and a scenic journey to reach the dual granite monoliths.
- **Cap Rock** has a lot going for it: a place in rock and roll history (Gram Parsons), a good selection of routes for beginning climbers, a great boulder circuit, and some of the most classic boulder problems in Joshua Tree.
- There are many classic climbing routes at the Jumbo Rocks Campground, but **Conan's Corridor**, a short walk northwest from the end of the loop, presents some interesting challenges.
- While you can't climb the official Split Rock itself, the **Split Rock region** offers many routes next to an easy-to-access picnic area and loop trail.

vast array of climbs. More than 400 climbing formations and more than 8,000 recognized climbs make it a world-class destination.

To keep an ear to the ground about closed routes and any other climbing info, **Climber's Coffee** (Hidden Valley Campground, 8am-10am Sat.-Sun. mid-Oct.-Apr.) offers the opportunity to meet Joshua Tree's climbing ranger and share information with other climbers.

There are many great rock climbing guides sold in the park's visitors centers, as well as outfitters outside the park. Classic guides include *The Trad Guide to Joshua Tree* by Charlie and Diane Winger and a number of guides by rock climber and author Randy Vogel (*Rock Climbing Joshua Tree, Rock Climbing Joshua Tree West*). More recent books on the market include *Joshua Tree Rock Climbs* by Robert Miramontes and Bob Gaines's *Best Climbs Joshua Tree National Park.*

Climbing Guides

To get in on the action as a first-timer or experienced climber looking to hone your skills, you may want to take a group class or a private guided climb through one of several outfitters in the area. The NPS website (www.nps.gov) has a full list of permitted guides. **Joshua Tree Rock Climbing School** (760/366-4745, www.joshuatreerockclimbing.com) offers year-round rock climbing classes and private guided outings. **Cliffhanger Guides** (6551 Park Blvd, 209/743-8363, www.cliffhangerguides.com, 8am-6pm daily) maintains a brick-and-mortar presence on Park Blvd. to help book your custom guided rock climbing adventures with half-day and full-day rates for up to 10 people. **Vertical Adventures** (800/514-8785, www.vertical-adventures.com) is available for one- to multi-day courses, as well as private instruction and guided climbing in Joshua Tree National Park and Idyllwild's Tahquitz and Suicide Rocks from May to September. **Climbing Life Guides** (760/780-8868, www.joshuatreeclimbinglifeguides.com) are available for guiding rock climbing and technical climbing instruction for up to six people. **Joshua Tree Guides** (www.joshuatreeguides.com) offers private guided climbs for beginners through advanced climbers for half and full days, as well as guided weekend trips.

Outfitters and Gear

To gear up for your rock climbing (or other) adventures, check out one of the three outfits located on the main drag in Joshua Tree close to the intersection of Park Boulevard and Highway 62.

Nomad Ventures (61795 Twentynine Palms Hwy., Joshua Tree, 760/366-4684, www.nomadventures.com, 8am-6pm Sun.-Thurs., 8am-8pm Fri.-Sun., summer hours vary) is the most extensively stocked of the Joshua Tree outfitters, with a huge selection of climbing gear, an assortment of camping and hiking gear, and a wide selection of guidebooks (including rock climbing guides).

Coyote Corner (6535 Park Blvd., Joshua Tree, 760/366-9683, www.joshuatreevillage.com, 9am-6pm Sun.-Thurs., 9am -7pm Fri.-Sat.) is eclectically stocked with gifts and gear ranging from T-shirts, jewelry, novelty items, and books to camping, hiking, and rock climbing gear. The best part? Showers! For about $5, you can buy a hot shower, quite a bonus considering none of Joshua Tree's campgrounds have showers.

Joshua Tree Outfitters (61707 Twentynine Palms Hwy., Joshua Tree, 760/366-1848, 9am-5pm daily) mainly specializes in camping gear rentals, including tents, sleeping bags, coolers, camp stoves, water containers, and lanterns. They also rent rock climbing guides and bouldering pads and offer gear repair. Their retail space is sparsely stocked, but it has a few high-quality clothing items and miscellaneous gear, maps, and books.

HORSEBACK RIDING

With more than 250 miles of equestrian trails and trail corridors, horseback riding is a great way to experience Joshua Tree National Park if you bring your own horse. Two campgrounds offer equestrian camping with overnight areas for stock animals: **Ryan Campground** (760/367-5545, $15, no water, closed in summer), in centrally located Hidden Valley, and **Black Rock Canyon** (877/444-6777, www.recreation.gov, $20, water available) in Joshua Tree's northwest corner. Reservations are required.

Both campgrounds lie along the continuous 36-mile **California Riding and Hiking Trail** that extends through Joshua tree forests, washes, canyons, and open lands from northwestern Black Rock Canyon east to the North Entrance. Popular areas for equestrian users include trails near the West Entrance and Black Rock Canyon. Horse trail maps are available for download from the park website (www.nps.gov/jotr). Special **permits** (760/367-5545) are required for camping with stock in the backcountry.

If you're not bringing your own horse, **Joshua Tree Ranch** (760/366-5357, www.joshuatreevillage.com, $35 per hour pp) offers guided private and group trail rides from their ranch, located less than two miles from the park's West Entrance.

CAMPING

There are no hotels or lodges inside the park boundaries. The closest lodgings are just outside the park in the gateway towns of Joshua Tree, Yucca Valley (both via the West Entrance), and Twentynine Palms (at the North Entrance).

Inside the Park

There are seven NPS campgrounds located within the park boundaries, two of which—**Black Rock Campground** and **Indian Cove Campground**—accept seasonal reservations October through May. The other five campgrounds are first-come, first-served year-round. Campgrounds in Joshua Tree start to fill up on Thursday mornings most weekends **October-May,** beginning with the more popular and centrally located campsites like Hidden Valley, Jumbo Rocks, and Ryan Campground, which have sites tucked in among Joshua Tree's famous boulders and Joshua trees. By Thursday evening, your options are limited. If you can't make it into the park by Thursday afternoon, and you don't have a reservation, better have a contingency plan. Fortunately, there is overflow camping and private camping available outside the park boundaries. In summer, all campgrounds are first-come, first-served.

Only three campgrounds—Black Rock, Indian Cove, and Cottonwood—have **drinking water.** Even if you are staying at one of these campgrounds, it is wise to bring at least two gallons of water (per person per day) with you into the park.

There are no RV hookups at any of the park campgrounds. Black Rock and Cottonwood Campgrounds have RV-accessible potable water and dump stations, and there are spaces that can accommodate trailers under 25 feet at Hidden Valley and White Tank Campgrounds.

BLACK ROCK CANYON CAMPGROUND

Black Rock Canyon Campground (99 sites, 877/444-6777, www.recreation.gov, $20) is in the northwest corner of Joshua Tree, just south of the town of Yucca Valley. Black Rock Canyon has a distinct geographic feel; instead of boulder jumbles, you'll find rolling hills dotted with Joshua trees and yuccas. This is a good campground for first-time visitors, as **drinking water** is available, and the location offers easy access to Yucca Valley for supplies. This campground also offers limited equestrian sites (by reservation only), and trailer and RV sites with water fill-up and dump stations are also available. Campground amenities include drinking water, flush toilets, picnic tables, fire rings, and a small visitors center with maps and guides.

The road in dead-ends at the campground, and there is no driving access into the rest of the park. A series of hiking trails, including the short Hi-View Nature Trail, the view-filled Eureka Peak, Panorama Loop, and Warren

Campgrounds at-a-Glance

	Location	Sites	Reservations	Amenities
Black Rock Canyon	Black Rock Canyon 4,000′	99	reservation only Oct.-May; first-come, first-served June-Sept.	tent, RV, and equestrian sites; drinking water, flush toilets, dump station
Hidden Valley	Hidden Valley 4,200′	44	first-come, first-served year-round	tent and RV sites; vault toilets; no drinking water
Ryan	Hidden Valley 4,300′	31	first-come, first-served year-round	tent and equestrian sites; vault toilets; no drinking water
Sheep Pass	Hidden Valley 4,300′	6	required year-round	Group-only tent sites; vault toilets; no drinking water
Jumbo Rocks	Hidden Valley 4,400′	124	reservation only Oct.-May; first-come, first-served June-Sept.	tent and RV sites; vault toilets; no drinking water
Belle	Hidden Valley 3,800′	18	first-come, first-served Oct.-May, may close in summer	tent sites; vault toilets; no drinking water
White Tank	Hidden Valley 3,800′	15	first-come, first-served Oct.-May, may close in summer	tent and RV sites; vault toilets; no drinking water
Indian Cove	Indian Cove 3,200′	101	reservation only Oct.-May; first-come, first-served June-Sept.	tent and RV sites; access to drinking water; vault toilets
Cottonwood	Cottonwood Spring 3,000′	62	reservation only Oct.-May; first-come, first-served June-Sept.	tent, RV, and group sites; drinking water, flush toilets, dump station

Peak trails, leave from the campground and offer access into the park by foot. The trailhead for the 35-mile California Riding and Hiking Trail also starts at the campground.

Reservations are required online (www.recreation.gov) from October through May up to six months in advance. To get there from Highway 62 in Yucca Valley, turn south on Joshua Lane and drive five miles into the park.

HIDDEN VALLEY

Central **Hidden Valley** (44 sites, first-come, first-served year-round, $15) tends to be the most difficult campground to get a spot in. On the southern end of the Wonderland of Rocks, the campground is popular with rock climbers...and everyone else. Its sites are picturesquely set amidst Joshua Tree's signature boulders, and you are right in the heart of the park. The campground can accommodate trailers and RVs (under 25 feet), and amenities include vault toilets, fire rings, and picnic tables. There is **no drinking water.**

Reservations are not accepted. To reach Hidden Valley from the Joshua Tree Visitors Center on Highway 62, turn south onto Park Boulevard and continue 14 miles to the intersection with Barker Dam Road. The campground will be to the left.

RYAN CAMPGROUND

Ryan Campground (31 sites, first-come, first-served year-round, $15) is a scenic campground centrally located between Hidden

Valley and Jumbo Rocks with campsites interspersed among boulders and Joshua trees. The adjoining **Ryan Horse Camp** (760/367-5545, $15) offers four equestrian sites by reservation only from October through May. Amenities include vault toilets, fire rings, and picnic tables. There is **no drinking water.**

Reservations are not accepted. To reach Ryan Campground from the Joshua Tree Visitors Center on Highway 62, follow Park Boulevard south for 27 miles, passing the Hidden Valley Campground. Immediately past the Keys View Road turn-off, the campground will appear on the right.

SHEEP PASS GROUP CAMP

Towering rock formations and Joshua trees surround **Sheep Pass Group Camp** (6 sites, 877/444-6777, www.recreation.gov, $35-50), a tent-only group campground centrally located off of Park Boulevard in between Ryan and Jumbo Rocks Campgrounds. Amenities include vault toilets, fire rings, and picnic tables. There is **no drinking water.**

Reservations are required and can be made up to one year in advance. The campground is 18 miles south of the West Entrance and 16 miles south of the North Entrance.

JUMBO ROCKS

Jumbo Rocks (124 sites, reservation-only Oct.-May, first-come, first-served June-Sept., $15) is the largest campground in the park. Despite its size, sites fill up quickly thanks to a convenient location along Park Boulevard and access to plentiful rock climbing opportunities as well as the Skull Rock Nature Trail. Popular sites are scenically tucked into the large rock formations for which the campground is named, but the sheer volume of sites leaves little privacy. This lends the place the feel of a small village, which may be good for families or groups. Amenities include vault toilets, fire rings, and picnic tables. There is **no drinking water.**

Reservations are required October-May. To reach Jumbo Rocks from the North Entrance in Twentynine Palms, follow Utah Trail south as it becomes Park Boulevard and continue southwest for eight miles. From the West Entrance in Joshua Tree, it is a drive of about 24 miles.

BELLE CAMPGROUND

Belle Campground (18 sites, first-come, first-served Oct.-May, $15) is a small, low-key campground with cozy sites tucked amid a pile of rock formations. Amenities include vault toilets, fire rings, and picnic tables. There is **no drinking water.**

Reservations are not accepted. To reach Belle from the North Entrance in Twentynine Palms, follow Utah Trail south as it becomes Park Boulevard and continue about 5 miles to the junction with Pinto Basin Road. Follow Pinto Basin Road 1.5 miles south, turning left onto Belle Campground Road.

WHITE TANK

The smallest campground in the park, **White Tank** (15 sites, first-come, first-served year-round, $15) is a laid-back campground with sites tucked in amid scattered rock formations. Sites can accommodate trailers and RVs (under 25 feet). Amenities include vault toilets, fire rings, and picnic tables. There is **no drinking water.**

Reservations are not accepted. White Tank is located just south of Belle Campground along Pinto Basin Road, about 7.4 miles south of the North Entrance.

INDIAN COVE

Indian Cove (101 sites, reservation only Oct.-May, first-come, first-served June-Sept., $20) **accepts reservations** (877/444-6777, www.recreation.gov, Oct.-May) *and* it has **drinking water available** at the ranger station just two miles away. The sites are tucked into spectacular boulder formations and offer both group and RV (under 25 feet) camping options. Indian Cove sits on the northern edge of the Wonderland of Rocks and is popular with rock climbers; the north end of the popular Boy Scout Trail also begins here. Amenities

1

2

include vault toilets, fire rings, and picnic tables, and access to drinking water.

The campground is located off Highway 62, between the towns of Joshua Tree and Twentynine Palms, and is accessed via Indian Cove Road South. The road dead-ends at the campground, so there is no vehicle access into the rest of the park. The nearest park entrance is the North Entrance in Twentynine Palms.

COTTONWOOD CAMPGROUND

The area around **Cottonwood Campground** (62 sites, reservation only Oct.-May, first-come, first-served June-Sept., $20) is much more lightly visited than the Hidden Valley region, which makes finding a site here slightly less competitive whether booking online in the high season or vying for a first-come, first-served spot in the off season. The campsites are scattered across an open desert dotted with creosote. Though there is little to divide them, the sites are nicely spaced and offer some privacy. The nearby Cottonwood Visitors Center is a fully stocked visitors center and bookstore, while hiking trails to scenic Lost Palms Oasis and Mastodon Peak depart directly from the campground. There are also trailer and RV sites with water fill-up and a dump station. The **Cottonwood Group Campground** (3 sites, 877/444-6777, www.recreation.gov, $35-40) provides tent-only sites by reservation. Amenities include flush toilets, fire rings, picnic tables, and **drinking water.**

Reservations are required October-May. Cottonwood Campground is located in the Pinto Basin at the South Entrance to the park. From I-10 south of the park, take Cottonwood Spring Road north for about 10 miles. At the Cottonwood Visitors Center, turn right onto Cottonwood Oasis Road and continue 7.5 miles to the campground on the left.

Outside the Park

Campgrounds in the park fill quickly October through May. Outside the park, options include backcountry camping on BLM land or at a privately owned RV park in Joshua Tree. Enterprising land owners have also begun offering camping or glamping on private land, available through booking platforms like www.hipcamp.com or www.airbnb.com.

JOSHUA TREE

★ **Joshua Tree Lake RV and Campground** (2601 Sunfair Rd., Joshua Tree, 760/366-1213, www.joshuatreelake.com, first-come, first-served, $10 pp tent sites, $4 children 12 and under; $25-40 RV sites, reservations accepted) is 14 miles north of the West Entrance. The well-maintained property offers tent and RV camping in open desert. The sites include picnic tables and firepits, and the campground has a small fishing lake, a camp store with firewood and basic supplies, RV hookups, hot showers, flush toilets, and a playground.

BLM CAMPING

Overflow camping is available on **Bureau of Land Management** (BLM, www.nps.gov/jotr) land both north and south of the park. Consider this camping your last resort. Plan ahead with a campground reservation or alternate lodging plan. Note that BLM camping includes no amenities (toilets, water, firepits, or drinking water). Fires are allowed in self-contained metal firepits (provide your own) in the overflow camping south of the park but are not allowed on BLM camping north of the park. Bring your own firewood.

For camping **north of the park:** Drive four miles east of Park Boulevard on Highway 62 and turn left (north) on Sunfair Road. Continue two miles to Broadway, then turn right (east) on Broadway, where the pavement ends. Drive one mile to a one-lane, unmarked dirt road (Cascade) at a line of telephone poles running north and south. Turn left (north) onto Cascade and drive 0.5-mile until you pass a single-lane, unmarked dirt road. Camping is allowed on the right (east) side of

1: Jumbo Rocks campground **2:** White Tank campground

that road for 0.5-mile beginning with the unmarked dirt road.

For camping **south of the park:** Drive six miles south of the Cottonwood Visitors Center, passing the park boundary sign. Just beyond the aqueduct, turn right or left on the unmarked water district road. Camping is allowed south of the water district road west and east of the Cottonwood Road. South of I-10, Cottonwood Road turns into Box Canyon Road; camping is allowed south of I-10 on both the east and west sides of Box Canyon Road.

TRANSPORTATION AND SERVICES

The West Entrance to Joshua Tree National Park is located 40 miles north of Palm Springs (about an hour's drive) and 145 miles east of Los Angeles (plan 3-4 hours for the drive from LA, Friday afternoons can take up to 4-5 hours from LA). The North Entrance near Twentynine Palms is 16 miles farther east along Highway 62. The South Entrance is located about 60 miles (one hour) east of Palm Springs along I-10 and 160 miles (four hours) east of Los Angeles. All roads and entrance stations are open year-round, weather permitting.

Car

For exploring Joshua Tree National Park, it is best to **have your own vehicle** for getting to the park and for transportation between gateway towns in the region. Within the park a pilot shuttle program began in fall of 2018 with transportation to some of the park's highlights. To reach the **West Entrance** from I-10 near Palm Springs, head north on Highway 62 for about 30 miles to the town of Joshua Tree. Turn south on Park Boulevard and follow the road into the park. To reach the **North Entrance** near Twentynine Palms, continue east on Highway 62 for 16 more miles and turn south on Utah Trail. To reach the **South Entrance,** follow I-10 east for 60 miles to Cottonwood Spring Road and turn north.

Several major car rental agencies are available in nearby Palm Springs. Car rentals in Yucca Valley are available from **Enterprise** (57250 29 Palms Hwy., 760/369-0515, www.enterprise.com, 8am-12pm, 1pm -6pm Mon.-Fri., 9am-noon Sat.).

Yucca Valley is also the best place to fuel up before entering the park. Within the park, there are frequent free parking areas near sights and major trailheads.

Shuttle

A pilot shuttle, The Roadrunner (www.nps.gov, 8am-5pm daily, free), began in 2018 for transportation within Joshua Tree National Park. It leaves from the north park entrance in Twentynine Palms and travels along Park Boulevard, the main park thoroughfare, with stops at the popular sights, hikes and campgrounds.

Air

The closest airport is the **Palm Springs Airport** (PSP, 3400 E. Tahquitz Canyon Way, Palm Springs, 760/318-3800, www.palmspringsca.gov), served by 11 airlines. The major car rental carriers are located here, including Enterprise, Avis, Hertz, Dollar, and Alamo.

Services

Services are more conspicuous in their absence. There is **no food** available inside the park. There are good dining options in the gateway towns along the edge of the park, including Yucca Valley, Joshua Tree, and Twentynine Palms. There are also chain grocery stores in the towns of Twentynine Palms and Yucca Valley.

Water is not widely available within the park; bring at least two gallons per person per day with you. Within the park, water may be available at the West Entrance ($0.25 fee), the Black Rock Campground, the Indian Cove Ranger Station, the Oasis Visitors Center in Twentynine Palms, and Cottonwood Campground at the south end of the park.

There is **limited cell service** in the park. Emergency phones are located at the Indian Cove Ranger Station and at the Hidden Valley Campground. In the event of an emergency, dial 911 or call 909/383-5651.

Ranger Programs

Park rangers offer guided hikes, evening programs, and patio talks—many geared toward families—to connect you with Joshua Tree's geography and history. Locations, subject matter, and times vary seasonally. The ranger program schedule is available for download on the park website (www.nps.gov/jotr), or you can pick up a copy at any visitors center.

Hi-Desert

Dotting the northern border of Joshua Tree National Park are several small towns and sights worthy of a visit in their own right. Creative and unusual works of outsider art here express the desert's remoteness and wild freedom, all of which is accompanied by a "desert rock" soundtrack composed of talented musicians performing nightly on stages across the scenic valley.

Orientation

The High Desert refers to higher elevation areas of the Mojave Desert located between 2,000 and 4,000 feet (distinguished from low desert areas like Palm Springs) and encompass areas of LA County to the northwest of Joshua Tree to Victorville and Barstow to the north. The term *Hi-Desert* breaks out the towns in the Morongo Basin along the northern border of Joshua Tree National Park, including Yucca Valley, Joshua Tree, and Twentynine Palms as well as the park itself.

The mostly residential town of **Morongo Valley**, 21 miles west of the park's main West Entrance, has a gas station, a restaurant and saloon, a small breakfast café, and the destination-worthy **Cactus Mart**. Most visitors pass through it on the way to Joshua Tree. It is also positioned on the "sand" section of the Sand to Snow National Monument.

The town of **Yucca Valley,** located 13 miles west of the park's main West Entrance, is the largest town in this area. Funky boutiques and vintage stores compete with big-box stores, grocery stores, and chain hotels for the character of the place. These reminders of 21st-century suburban living feel strangely out of place against the timeless beauty of the desert. However, if you need services, Yucca Valley will likely have what you need. Its proximity to Pappy & Harriet's makes it a magnet for artists and musicians.

Pioneertown, 5 miles to the north of Yucca Valley, refers to both the Wild West town built as a movie set and the surrounding neighborhood. It is mostly known for **Pappy & Harriet's,** the wildly popular venue, restaurant, and roadhouse. Pioneertown also has a few lodge-style hotels and a growing number of vacation rentals.

The tiny outpost of **Landers,** located along Highway 247/Old Woman Springs Road 15 miles north of Highway 62 in Yucca Valley, gets a mention for its destination-worthy restaurant **La Copine** as well as the **Integratron,** a brewing company, and unique lodging.

The town of **Joshua Tree,** seven miles to the east, is a small artsy outpost that welcomes visitors through the park's main West Entrance, which is located five miles south. A cluster of charming restaurants (and a saloon) as well as outfitters, gift shops, and hotels offer a picturesque getaway with a laid-back desert vibe.

Fifteen miles east of Joshua Tree, the town of **Twentynine Palms** gives passage to Joshua Tree National Park's quieter North Entrance. The historic 29 Palms Inn anchors the tourism experience here. The small town

Hi-Desert

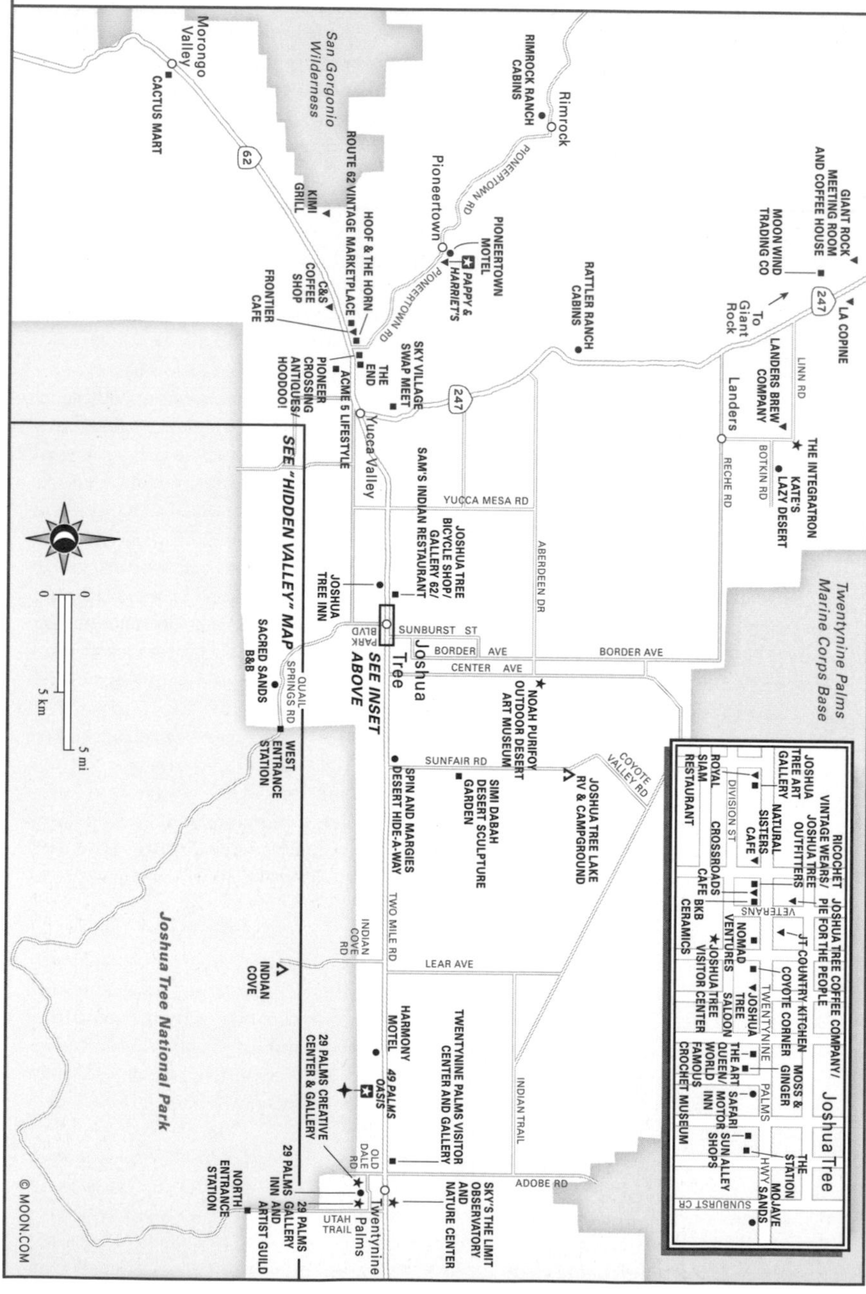
Morongo Valley
CACTUS MART
San Gorgonio Wilderness
62
ROUTE 62 VINTAGE MARKETPLACE
KIMI GRILL
HOOF & THE HORN
C&S COFFEE SHOP
FRONTIER CAFE
PIONEER CROSSING ANTIQUES/ HOODOO!
ACME 5 LIFESTYLE
THE END
SKY VILLAGE SWAP MEET
Yucca Valley
Rimrock
RIMROCK RANCH CABINS
PIONEERTOWN RD
Pioneertown
PIONEERTOWN MOTEL
PAPPY & HARRIET'S
RATTLER RANCH CABINS
247
GIANT ROCK MEETING ROOM AND COFFEE HOUSE
MOON WIND TRADING CO
To Giant Rock
LA COPINE
LINN RD
LANDERS BREW COMPANY
Landers
THE INTEGRATRON
KATE'S LAZY DESERT
BOTKIN RD
RECHE RD
YUCCA MESA RD
SAM'S INDIAN RESTAURANT
JOSHUA TREE BICYCLE SHOP/ GALLERY 62/
JOSHUA TREE INN
ABERDEEN DR
SUNBURST ST
PARK BLVD
Joshua Tree
BORDER AVE
CENTER AVE
SEE INSET ABOVE
SEE "HIDDEN VALLEY" MAP
SACRED SANDS B&B
QUAIL SPRINGS RD
WEST ENTRANCE STATION
NOAH PURIFOY OUTDOOR DESERT ART MUSEUM
SUNFAIR RD
COYOTE VALLEY RD
JOSHUA TREE LAKE RV & CAMPGROUND
SIMI DABAH DESERT SCULPTURE GARDEN
SPIN AND MARGIES DESERT HIDE-A-WAY
TWO MILE RD
Twentynine Palms Marine Corps Base
INDIAN COVE RD
INDIAN COVE
LEAR AVE
Joshua Tree National Park
HARMONY MOTEL
49 PALMS OASIS
TWENTYNINE PALMS VISITOR CENTER AND GALLERY
INDIAN TRAIL
29 PALMS CREATIVE CENTER & GALLERY
OLD DALE RD
ADOBE RD
SKY'S THE LIMIT OBSERVATORY AND NATURE CENTER
Twentynine Palms
UTAH TRAIL
29 PALMS GALLERY
29 PALMS INN AND ARTIST GUILD
NORTH ENTRANCE STATION
0 5 mi
0 5 km
© MOON.COM
Joshua Tree
RICOCHET VINTAGE WEARS/ JOSHUA TREE OUTFITTERS
JOSHUA TREE COFFEE COMPANY/ PIE FOR THE PEOPLE
JOSHUA TREE ART GALLERY
NATURAL SISTERS CAFE
ROYAL SIAM RESTAURANT
DIVISION ST
CROSSROADS CAFE
BKB CERAMICS
VETERANS
NOMAD VENTURES
JT COUNTRY KITCHEN
JOSHUA TREE VISITOR CENTER
COYOTE CORNER
JOSHUA TREE SALOON
TWENTYNINE PALMS
THE ART QUEEN/ WORLD FAMOUS CROCHET MUSEUM
MOSS & GINGER
SAFARI MOTOR INN
SUN ALLEY SHOPS
THE STATION
MOJAVE SANDS
HWY
SUNBURST CR

is scattered across open desert. It's home to a military base and a few functional businesses, including inexpensive motels, a grocery store, and gas stations.

More of a state of mind than a town, **Wonder Valley** is home to the dusty Palms roadhouse and venue, a collection of historic jackrabbit homesteads in varying states of rehabilitation, and secluded cabin and home rentals for visitors to the park.

SIGHTS

The Integratron

George Van Tassel (1910-1978) held respectable jobs as an aeronautical engineer for Lockheed Douglas Aircraft and as a test pilot for Hughes Aviation, but arguably his real life's work was as an inventor and UFO advocate.

Van Tassel was the engineer behind the **Integratron** (2477 Belfield Blvd., Landers, 760/364-3126, www.integratron.com, $35-40 by appointment only, private $300-1,300), a spherical all-wood dome originally intended as an electrostatic generator to promote cellular rejuvenation and time travel. An avowed alien contactee, Van Tassel claimed that extraterrestrials from Venus gave him the formula to build the structure. The building's ship-tight wood construction and dome shape imbued it with an amazing sound resonance.

The current owners of the Integratron haven't yet figured out how to tap into the structure's time travel aspects, but they are intent on rejuvenation (at least for the soul). The only way to visit the Integratron is by reserving a private or "pop-up" **sound bath** (by appointment only). Sound baths last one hour and include 25 minutes of crystal bowl harmonies followed by recorded music for relaxation and meditation. Reserving a sound bath also gives you access to the structure's grounds and a display about the history of the Integratron.

GIANT ROCK

Tens of thousands of people attended George Van Tassel's annual Spacecraft Conventions held at **Giant Rock** (three miles north of the Integratron), the largest freestanding boulder in the world, coming in at seven stories high and covering 5,800 square feet of ground. The spiritually powerful place was a sacred Native American site and meeting place for local tribes until the 1900s.

Van Tassel used to hold weekly meditations in rooms underneath Giant Rock that had originally been dug by a local prospector.

the Integratron in Landers

From the 1950s to the 1970s, Van Tassel used these meditations to try to attract UFOs. He was eventually successful (according to him) in 1953, when a saucer from the planet Venus landed, and he was invited onto the ship and given the formula for the Integratron. Sadly, a visit to Giant Rock today shows a sad disrespect for nature and history: broken glass litters the ground and graffiti detracts from the impressive landmark.

GETTING THERE

The Integratron is located in Landers, north of the town of Yucca Valley. From the intersection of Highways 62 and 246 (Old Woman Springs Rd.), turn left onto Highway 247 and head north for 10.6 miles. Turn right (west) onto Reche Road and continue 2.3 miles. Turn left (north) onto Belfield Boulevard and continue 2 miles to the Integratron.

Noah Purifoy Outdoor Desert Art Museum

Artist Noah Purifoy (1917-2004) used found items to create assemblage sculpture that was dubbed "Junk Dada." The title feels dead-on. In the surreal **Noah Purifoy Outdoor Desert Art Museum** (63030 Blair Ln., Joshua Tree, www.noahpurifoy.com, sunrise-sunset daily, free but donations appreciated), metal, plywood, porcelain, paper, cotton, and glass are twisted and stacked into sculptures spread across 10 acres of an otherworldly artscape.

Born in 1917 in Snow Hill, Alabama, Purifoy was almost 40 when he received his BFA from Chouinard Art Institute (now California Institute of the Arts). He was the school's first full-time African American student. He spent much of his life in Los Angeles working in public policy and cofounding the Watts Towers Art Center. Using found objects to create sculpture, Purifoy devoted himself to art and social change to become a pivotal American artist.

Purifoy launched his career as a sculptor with his collection *66 Signs of Neon* (1966), assembled from the charred wreckage of debris he collected from the 1965 Watts Riots in Los Angeles. In the late 1980s, he moved to Joshua Tree full-time, creating large-scale art on the Mojave Desert floor.

The sculptures in this outdoor desert museum are whimsical, political, and comical, with broken pieces and discarded junk mended into recognizable shapes. Made from cheap plywood and gaudy paint, the interior of the brightly colored *Carousel* is jammed with computer monitors, discarded office machinery, and analog artifacts. Other sculptures, such as *Shelter* and *Theater*, are reminiscent of abandoned mining camps and Wild West towns, resuscitated once again into a cobbled together reminder of the American Dream scattered across rocky desert.

In 2015, several of Purifoy's sculptures were featured in an exhibition at the Los Angeles County Museum of Art. It's a testament to the strength of his sculpture that the pieces held their own even when removed from their desert context and featured in a more sterile museum space.

GETTING THERE

From Highway 62 in the town of Joshua Tree, turn north onto Yucca Mesa Road and drive four miles to Aberdeen Drive. Turn right (east) and continue another four miles to Center Street. Turn left (north) onto Center Street and make the next right onto Blair Lane (dirt road).

Pioneertown

Created as a Wild West movie set in 1946, **Pioneertown** (Pioneertown Rd.) was founded by Hollywood investors as a frontier town that served as a backdrop for Western movies. Some of the big names that helped establish Pioneertown included Roy Rogers, Gene Autry, Russell Hayden, and the Sons of the Pioneers (which gave Pioneertown its name). The 1940s and 1950s saw Pioneertown as a popular filming destination, with more than 50 films and television shows featuring the stables, saloons, jails, and shops of the main street. As part of the setup, a functioning motel provided quarters for the Hollywood set who were there for filming. When not filming, Pioneertown did double duty as a roadside attraction and tourist spot. Visitors came for the ice cream parlor, the bowling alley, and the motel.

The adjacent **Pappy & Harriet's Pioneertown Palace** (53688 Pioneertown Rd., 760/365-5956, www.pappyandharriets.com) was originally part of the set as a dusty cantina facade. It was eventually turned into a functioning cantina that served as a biker burrito bar from 1972 to 1982. In 1982, the cantina debuted as "Pappy & Harriet's Pioneertown Palace."

Today Pioneertown continues as a family-friendly attraction. Visitors can wander the main street, taking in the frontier buildings. The original sound stage has been restored and now features live music some weekend afternoons. Visitors can also browse a handful of **retail shops** (open weekends) that feature gifts, soap, and pottery. And of course, no Wild West town would be complete without a staged **gunfight,** available on Mane Street most weekends.

GETTING THERE

Pioneertown is located four miles north of Yucca Valley. From the intersection of Highway 62 and Pioneertown Road, turn left to head north for four miles. Pioneertown's Mane Street is located adjacent to Pappy & Harriet's Pioneertown Palace, and the two share parking.

Sky's the Limit Observatory and Nature Center (29 Palms)

Joshua Tree is just far enough away from light-filled Los Angeles to be a world away when it comes to clear, dark skies. Of course, you can kick back at your campsite or cabin and admire the stars. For more guided stargazing, the **Sky's the Limit Observatory and Nature Center** (9697 Utah Trail, Twentynine Palms, www.skysthelimit29.org, free) offers casual viewing parties on Saturday nights (not on full moon or close to full moon nights) in 29 Palms just outside the north entrance to Joshua Tree National Park. Astronomers set up telescopes trained on different objects in the night sky and invite the public, answering questions about the celestial bodies on the other end of the telescopes. Some astronomers use laser pointers to identify constellations. Hours vary for nighttime viewing events throughout the year, typically, from approximately sunset to three hours after sunset. Check the website calendar for a schedule. Docents are at Sky's the Limit every Saturday 10am-2pm, when visitors can explore the orrery (scale model of the solar system) and nature garden. The campus is always open.

ENTERTAINMENT AND EVENTS

Live Music Venues

There are many good reasons to go to the **Joshua Tree Saloon** (61835 29 Palms Hwy., Joshua Tree, 760/366-2250, www.thejoshuatreesaloon.com, 7am-midnight Sun.-Thurs., 7am-2am Fri.-Sat., $10-20). The fact that they have live music to accompany their well-executed menu, good service, and array of cold bevvies adds another reason to the list. From open-mic and karaoke on the weekdays to live bands rocking out on weekends to mellow acoustic accompaniment at brunch, the Joshua Tree Saloon knows how to make the atmosphere festive. The Yard, their outdoor patio, is open on weekends (weather permitting) with live music, barbecue, and an outdoor bar. They allow pets, and it's also a good spot for kids. Check the calendar on the saloon's website for a full listing of music and events.

★ PAPPY & HARRIET'S

You don't need a festival to hear great live music at **Pappy & Harriet's** (53688 Pioneertown Rd., Pioneertown, 760/365-5956, www.pappyandharriets.com, 11am-2am Thurs.-Sun., 5pm-2am Mon., cover charge varies). Set amid historic Pioneertown, originally built as a Wild West movie set, the saloon, venue, and restaurant boast an impressive music lineup that stands up to

1

W E W
C L
L O
M E

2

3

PAPPY & HARRIET'S
PIONEERTOWN
PALACE
NO OUTSIDE ALCOHOL or FOOD

4

offerings in Los Angeles and San Diego. Weekends bring heavy-hitting bands in rock and roll genres from sludgy desert rock to Americana-influenced. Sundays (no cover) are chill with The Sunday Band, a rotating star-studded mix of local musicians and the occasional surprise guest. Musicians are excited to play here, and you can feel that energy in this intimate space.

You're never sure what you're going to get at the weather-beaten roadhouse that is **The Palms Restaurant** (83131 Amboy Rd., Wonder Valley, 760/361-2810, 3pm-6pm Thurs., 3pm-9:30pm Fri., 3pm-8pm Sat., 9am-6pm Sun.), but it won't be boring. Whether you're sipping icy cold, dirt-cheap PBR (think $2 drafts) with the locals on a laid-back Sunday or there for a weekend festival held out back on the rickety stage in the scrubby, open desert, there's a certain charm to this dusty outpost with the out-of-tune piano. Live music is on the weekends, but music and events are sporadic; check the Facebook page or call if seeing music is your main goal. Be advised: They're not afraid of the experimental and music that tends toward the neo-psychedelic and out-there.

The limited menu features bar food (with veggie options) that's better than it has any right to be considering this place looks like the patron saint of abandoned homesteads.

Set in a historic 1948 roadhouse close to the Integratron, **Landers Brew Company** (1388 Golden Slipper Ln., 760/623-6300, 3pm-12am Tues., 5pm-12am Wed., 5pm-2am Thurs., 12pm-2am Fri.-Sat., 12pm-10pm Sun.) keeps up the roadhouse tradition with cold beers and live music. They offer a low-key hang with 24 draft beers, a pool table, an outdoor patio, live music, and karaoke and deejay nights. Check their Facebook page for events. Only adults twenty-one and over are permitted.

1: Noah Purifoy Outdoor Desert Art Museum **2:** entrance to the Noah Purifoy Outdoor Desert Art Museum **3:** Pioneertown, originally built as a Wild West movie set **4:** Pappy & Harriet's Pioneertown Palace

Live Music Events

"The Desert is Freedom, Music is Power, & Community is Crucial" reads the tagline for the **Joshua Tree Music Festival** (www.joshuatreemusicfestival.com, May and Oct., $50-190), a four-day outdoor, independently produced music festival held twice yearly at the **Joshua Tree Lake RV and Campground** (2601 Sunfair Rd., Joshua Tree, 760/366-1213, www.joshuatreelake.com). This musical carpet ride takes place in an intimate setting outside the park boundary with the open desert as backdrop to an eclectic mix of up-and-coming bands. There are two alternating stages, so you don't have to make any tough decisions. The spring festival in May features a groovier vibe with dance, world, electro-funk, and groove artists. The fall in October gets rootsier, dipping into folk-adelic, raw rock and roll, space rock, newgrass, and rootsicana realms. Communal festival tent camping is included with the price of a ticket. Cozy vintage trailers and limited RV spaces are also available. The all-ages festival is family-friendly, with a designated Kidsville for entertainment and activities. Festival amenities include organic food and bevvy vendors, yoga classes, a saloon, an espresso bar, a world market, bathrooms, showers, and free drinking water.

The annual **Desert Stars Festival** (www.desertstarsfestival.com, March, $50-75) is an indie micro-fest held on the east block arts district of downtown Joshua Tree. The two-day (Fri.-Sat.) festival features two stages of music set against the stars in a new outdoor theater. They play both kinds of music here: rock and roll (from heavy, psychedelic rock to alternative shoegaze) and all the raw, polished, desert, space, pop, folk nuances in between. Tickets give you access to the litany of impressive sounds set against the desert sky.

Desert Daze (desertdaze.org, October, $199-249 plus add-on camping packages from $99) music festival features psychedelic desert rock in a widely interpreted genre with heavy-hitting international bands across multiple stages over a three-day event. Past

A Rock-and-Roll Pilgrimage

Joshua Tree's mystical piles of boulders; spiky, lonely Joshua trees; and vast sky have long been a mecca for musicians from LA and elsewhere seeking inspiration. Musicians grow up here, creating a distinct sound to try to fill the open spaces and spare landscape that can make humans take stock of their place in the cosmos. Any way you look at it, Joshua Tree has a serious rock-and-roll résumé.

Follow this pilgrimage through Joshua Tree by starting at Room 8 in the Joshua Tree Inn (61259 29 Palms Hwy.). On the night of September 18, 1973, country rocker **Gram Parsons** overdosed on alcohol and morphine at age 26. Parsons has since attained cult status for his timeless music, as well as the strange events following his death. His body was on its way to Louisiana for burial in the family plot when friends, acting on Parsons' predeath request to have his body set on fire in the desert, managed to follow through on a drunken plan that involved borrowing a hearse and stealing his body and coffin off the tarmac at the Los Angeles International Airport. Hightailing it to then Joshua Tree National Monument, they promptly doused his body with gasoline and lit it on fire near Cap Rock. There is a small shrine at the Joshua Tree Inn and at the site of the "cremation."

Dublin-based **U2**'s cinematic, chart-topping album *Joshua Tree* evoked the open spaces of the American West with its iconic cover. The Joshua tree on display was actually closer to Death Valley, but you can still follow in their footsteps with a visit to the funky, low-key **Harmony Motel** (71161 29 Palms Hwy., Twentynine Palms) where they stayed during their desert sojourn.

U2's 1987 album, distinctive as it was, fit squarely into a long line of musicians trying to connect with the quintessential American West experience. **The Eagles** shot their 1972 debut album cover in what was then Joshua Tree National Monument, tripping out around a campfire in a band-bonding visit to the desert. In the 1970s, **John Lennon** recorded the rare *Joshua Tree Tapes*, including "Imagine" and "Come Together." In a faded 1960s video, Doors front man **Jim Morrison** drove his Shelby GT500 Mustang, dubbed "The Blue Lady," through Joshua Tree as the desert highway flashed by.

The stoner rock scene was born in the 1990s pioneered by the band **Kyuss,** a crew of kids (Josh Homme, Brant Bjork, John Garcia, and Nick Oliveri) who grew up in Palm Desert. It was the low desert as opposed to the high desert elevation near Joshua Tree, and their grittier sound was created at live shows out in the washes and canyons. These now-infamous "generator parties"

performers have included heavy psych-rockers Black Angels, Niger-based desert blues musician Bombino, and cult rockers My Bloody Valentine. Desert Daze has moved desert locations several times but settled an hour and a half west of Joshua Tree at Moreno Beach, Lake Perris State Recreation Area. Even though it is technically out of the desert, it maintains a desert spirit with an organic vibe that synchs landscape, music, and art.

Art Galleries and Events

Joshua Tree's reputation as a haven for creative types means that it has a robust visual arts scene. For three weekends every October, the arts community across the Morongo Basin is galvanized by the **Route 62 Open Studio Art Tours** (www.hwy62arttours.org, Oct.), sponsored by the Morongo Basin Cultural Arts Council. Artists (literally) open their studio doors to an art-thirsty public, showcasing the vibrant pieces available in the desert communities adjacent to Joshua Tree National Park. As diverse and compelling as its desert backdrop, works feature painting, sculpture, metal work, ceramics, assemblage, photography, textiles, illustration, conceptual art, jewelry, and more. Visitors and locals get the chance to view the art and meet the artists in their studios, where all the magic happens.

With over 100 participating artists and artist studios scattered up and down the Morongo Basin, you'll want to plan your art tour according to what speaks most to you.

Harmony Motel, where U2 stayed while shooting photos for their *Joshua Tree* album

were fueled by beer, psychedelics, and a single hardworking generator. Members of the band went on to notable projects, including Queens of the Stone Age, Fu Manchu, Dwarves, Eagles of Death Metal, and Mondo Generator.

The music scene is still alive and well. A smattering of recording studios, like the notable **Rancho de la Luna** (www.ranchodelaluna.com, closed to the public) in Joshua Tree, draw artists from all over the world, including Kurt Vile, Arctic Monkeys, The Duke Spirit, Mark Lanegan, Foo Fighters, and The Melvins. Drive through the national park and surrounding desert on any given day and you're likely to see a chicly clad poncho wearer posing photogenically against the iconic boulders, looking like they're shooting a music video. Pay attention—they probably are.

Highway 62 Open Studio Art Tours pamphlets and maps are available for free in local businesses. If you can't make the October exhibition, you can take in work by artists in the Morongo Basin at a few galleries open year-round or most of the year.

JOSHUA TREE

Downtown Joshua Tree is home to several galleries open year-round. The town hosts an art walk the second Saturday of each month, when local galleries have their monthly openings. For participating galleries and other events check out the Joshua Tree Visitors Guide (joshuatree.guide). In addition, larger installations can be found on studio space or private land dedicated to art across the desert.

Gallery 62 (61607 29 Palms Hwy. Suite H, http://gallery62.org, 12pm-3pm Fri., 9am-3pm Sat., 12pm-3pm Sun.) is the Morongo Basin Cultural Art Council (sponsor of the Hwy 62 Open Studio Art Tours) members cooperative gallery. The gallery is located in downtown Joshua Tree and offers a rotating series of gallery exhibits of different media, as well as openings and participation in the second Saturday art crawl each month.

Joshua Tree Art Gallery (JTAG, 61607 29 Palms Hwy., 760/366-3636, www.joshuatreeartgallery.com, 10am-3pm Sat., noon-3pm Sun. June-Sept.), a cooperative fine art gallery, features the work of painters, photographers, and sculptors. JTAG has opening receptions the second Saturday (6pm-8pm) of each month.

Artist Shari Elf displays her quirky, life-affirming original artworks at **The Art Queen** and **World Famous Crochet Museum** (61855 Highway 62, www.sharielf.com). **The Art Queen** has a gallery front just east of the Joshua Tree Saloon. **The World Famous Crochet Museum** is housed in a tiny green trailer in the back.

High Desert Test Sights (www.highdeserttestsites.com/) is a nonprofit organization based in Joshua Tree that supports experimental artwork in the high desert. HDTS offers programs including workshops and guided tours of experimental artwork sites. The most popular program is a two-hour tour of A-Z West, a sustainable permaculture living compound set on over 70 acres in the Mojave Desert. The compound was created by Andrea Zittel, the administrator of HDTS and one of the group's founders. Tours are offered monthly by reservation only ($45).

Simi Dabah Desert Sculpture Garden (5255 Sunfair Road, joshuatree.guide) is the creation of artist and welder Simi Dabah. He has been creating steel sculptures from scrap materials for more than 40 years. On the property of his Joshua Tree studio, more than 600 sculptures, some more than 20 feet high, are scattered across eight acres, where they rust to a warm patina in the elements. Visiting the studio is by appointment only, but you can see the sculptures from the road.

TWENTYNINE PALMS

Not to be overshadowed by Joshua Tree to the west, the town of Twentynine Palms has its own arts scene ranging from outsider installations to snowbird workshops. The first Saturday of every month opens up galleries in the area for ArtCruise29 (www.visit29.org), which occupies a vaster nonwalkable space.

Since 1963, the **29 Palms Art Gallery and Artist Guild** (74055 Cottonwood Dr., 760/367-7819, www.29palmsartgallery.com, 11am-3pm Thurs.-Sun., summer hours noon-3pm Fri.-Sun.) has been a nexus for high desert art. The well-established historic adobe gallery at the Oasis of Mara features ongoing exhibits as well as opening receptions and events, art classes, and social painting events. Just a few blocks west of National Park Drive and the Oasis Visitor Center, **Twentynine Palms Visitors Center** (73484 29 Palms Hwy., 760/367-6197, http://visit29.org, 10am-4pm daily; summer hours 9am-3pm Mon.-Fri., 9am-2pm Sat.-Sun.) offers local books, maps, local information, souvenirs, and an art gallery featuring local artists. Themed group exhibitions are on public display, highlighting the area's natural beauty and history.

The gallery offerings for the **29 Palms Creative Center and Gallery** (6847 Adobe Rd., Twentynine Palms, 760/361-1805, www.29palmsart.com, 10am-6pm Mon.-Sat., 10am-3pm Sun.) range widely and include painting, pottery, jewelry, furniture, and collage. Many of the sales benefit the Mojave Desert Land Trust. The center also offers a variety of art classes and activities for all ages on subjects such as pottery, stained glass, oil painting, drawing, tile mosaics, and bookmaking.

WONDER VALLEY

Locals from Joshua Tree and other communities farther west joke that the wonder of Wonder Valley is that anyone would live there at all. But don't tell that to the artists, desert dreamers, and others who call this austere desert valley home. The region took hold with passage of the Small Tract Act in 1938; would-be homesteaders flocked here in the 1940s to build tiny "jackrabbit" homesteads and eke out a living. Today you can still see the old homesteads scattered across the desert scrub—tiny wooden dwellings, some inhabited, some in disrepair. Artists seeking both refuge and inspiration have made a small arts community in this neck of the desert. Wonder Valley is about 13 miles east of Twentynine Palms, along Highway 62.

The **Glass Outhouse Gallery** (77575 Hwy. 62, Twentynine Palms, 760/367-3807, 1pm-5pm Tues.-Sun.) is one display of the visual arts scene in Wonder Valley featuring gallery exhibits and opening receptions for local valley artists in a range of media.

Casino

Tortoise Rock Casino (73829 Baseline Rd., Twentynine Palms, 760/367-9759, www.tortoiserockcasino.com, 24 hours) is located north of Joshua Tree National Park in the town of Twentynine Palms. The large casino offers slots and table games plus a lounge, live entertainment, and a casual eatery.

Shopping

The two main hubs for shopping in the area are in the gateway towns of Yucca Valley and Joshua Tree. Yucca Valley is best for vintage and boutique browsing. The town also has big-box stores for supplies. Joshua Tree offers limited boutique shopping and several outdoors outfitters. Outlier communities like Morongo Valley and Landers are feeling the influence of Joshua Tree as a destination, and shops are springing up in these areas.

MORONGO VALLEY

Located on Highway 62, 11 miles west of Yucca Valley, Morongo Valley is a tiny outpost with a café, gas station, saloon, and dig your own ★ **Cactus Mart** (49889 29 Palms Hwy., 760/363-6076, cactusmart.com, 8am-5pm Mon.-Sat., 9am-5pm Sun.). Known for its array of irresistible cacti and succulents, their **boutique** and gift shop also offers original artwork, hiking and landscape books, candles, jewelry, Joshua Tree Coffee Co. coffee, pottery, crystals, gems, and minerals.

YUCCA VALLEY

Most of the shops are clustered at the intersection of 29 Palms Highway and Pioneertown Road in Old Town Yucca Valley; a historic curved stucco building (a former pharmacy) marks the distinct junction. There's enough unique boutique clothing, vintage, antique, and lifestyle shops to easily fill an afternoon of browsing. Local tastemakers Adam and Jen preside over the impossibly hip (but not impossibly priced) retail shop ★ **Hoof and the Horn** (55840 29 Palms Hwy., Yucca Valley, www.hoofandthehorn.com, 10:30am-6pm Mon.-Sat., 11am-6pm Sun.), stocking it with a carefully curated selection of women's and men's new clothing, graphic tees, hats, jewelry, gifts, and housewares (plus some select vintage clothing and vinyl). The perfect leather boots for kicking around in the desert? Check. Flannel shirts to keep you warm and cool at the same time? Check. Tapping into Joshua Tree's reputation as a haven for rock and roll, art, and a bohemian lifestyle, Hoof and the Horn provides your desert chic trappings.

Pioneer Crossing Antiques (55854 29 Palms Hwy., Yucca Valley, 760/228-0603, www.pioneercrossingantiques.com, 10am-5pm daily) is a charming old-school antiques mall with multiple vendors featuring antiques, collectibles, furniture, knickknacks, and art. The highlight may be their ceramics and pottery offerings: sleek and festively colored Bauer pottery made in Los Angeles and original, collector vintage designs by Joshua Tree artist Howard Pierce (1912-1994).

Acme 5 Lifestyle (55870 Twentynine Palms Hwy., Yucca Valley, 760/853-0031, 10am-5pm Thurs.-Mon.) is a hip new boutique addition to Yucca Valley, offering bohemian modern home decor, plants, and furniture for you to take back to your humble abode and make it look as stylish as the Airbnb you just stayed in.

The vintage designer clothing and accessories at **The End** (55872 29 Palms Hwy., 760/418-5536, theendyuccavalley.com/, 11am-5pm daily) are the stylish beginning for savvy shoppers who dig a vibrant retro clothing score. It's a colorful stop chock-full of funky patterns and statement jewelry.

Whether the store's name of **Hoodoo!** (55866 29 Palms Hwy., 760/365-9505, www.shophoodoo.com, 10am-6pm daily) refers to the system of folk magic or the spires of rock that protrude from desert soil, it is into the mystical things in life. Specializing in rock and roll, comics, and tiki, this curiosity shop for the desert wanderer features graphic tees, tiki wares, and gifts—where it really shines is in its unique collection of vinyl records, comics, and graphic novels.

A trove of antique wares, **Route 62 Vintage Marketplace** (55635 29 Palms Hwy., 760/365-4330, 10am-5pm Mon.-Sat., 10am-4pm Sun.) features several vendors who provide a revolving supply of upcycled housewares and furniture ranging from vintage Coleman lanterns and suitcases to dressers, lamps, and art.

Located at the old Sky Drive-in Theater, the weekly **Sky Village Swap Meet** (7028 Theatre Rd., 760/365-2104, www.skyvillageswapmeet.com, 6am-2pm Sat., 7am-2pm Sun.) is a Yucca Valley institution with junk, gems, and everything in between. Permanent vendors and a variety of day sellers offer art, new and vintage jewelry, gifts, recycled housewares, Western wear boots, hats, belts, buckles, and random sundries set amid seven acres of recycled junk turned art. Highlights include: Dakota Bob's Western Wear (www.dakotabobs.com) and Bob Carr's Crystal Cave. Not a shop, duck into the crystal cave to be surrounded by a miniature world of crystals that feels strangely removed. The swap meet is also home to High Desert Test Sites headquarters. Stop in to check out their calendar of events, shop their gear, or pick up a driving map to desert art installations (9am-1pm Sat., 9am-noon Sun.)

LANDERS

Desert lifestyle boutique **Moon Wind Trading Co** (1141B Old Woman Springs Rd., 801/896-4352, moonwindtradingco.com, 11am-6pm Thurs.-Sun.) offers a pitch-perfect selection of new and vintage clothing, beauty and wellness products, and jewelry that may make you want to trade in your entire look for their dreamy desert style. The shop would be in the middle of nowhere except that it's across the street from **La Copine** restaurant.

JOSHUA TREE

The main hub of Joshua Tree is at the intersection of Highway 62 and Park Boulevard, leading to the main (west) park entrance. Anchored by the Joshua Tree Saloon and three outdoors outfitters offering rock climbing, camping, and other outdoor gear, Joshua Tree's downtown also has an increasing selection of shopping for new and vintage clothing and gifts.

Stop into **Ricochet Vintage Wears** (61731 29 Palms Hwy., 760/366-1898, 11am-4pm Mon., 11am-4pm Wed.-Sun.) for their selection of groovy American threads for men and women. They also offer boots, handbags, belts, jewelry, and more.

Coyote Corner (6535 Park Blvd., 760/366-9683, www.jtcoyotecorner.com/, 9am-6pm Mon.-Thurs., 9am-7pm Fri.-Sun.) is the place to go if you're looking for a souvenir, gift, or novelty item for yourself or the unlucky person who didn't get to come out to Joshua Tree. The store's eclectic inventory ranges from T-shirts, jewelry, and vintage clothing to novelty items, books, and gifts. The store also stocks camping and rock climbing gear.

BKB Ceramics (61705 29 Palms Hwy., 760/821-3765, www.bkbceramics.com, 10am-2pm Fri., 9am-3pm Sat.-Sun.) features rustic modern ceramics handcrafted by potter Brian Bosworth. His simple textured geometric patterns are available in several West Coast boutique retail outlets, his Joshua Tree shop, in limited quantities from his online store, and at the new location in Palm Springs.

Moss and Ginger (61865 29 Palms Hwy., 323/207-5151, www.mossandginger.com, 11am-5pm Fri.-Sun.) offers men's and women's vintage clothing and accessories as well as home and garden treasures. Their unique collection includes '60s and '70s vintage deadstock from India and Pakistan, Native American jewelry, and other boho goods.

Bohemian beach is the vibe at **Jen's Pirate Booty** (61729 29 Palms Hwy., 760/974.9800, www.jenspiratebooty.com, 10am-6pm Thurs.-Mon.), a boutique specializing in women's clothing designed and curated by Jen Rossi.

Gauzy dresses, kaftans, tops, and tunics are relaxed and stylish.

Find books, clothing, art, and other treasures at the **Sun Alley Shops** (61871 29 Palms Hwy., 11am-5pm Fri.-Sun.), a collection of shops including Dusty Deserette and Space Cowboy books and curio.

Housed in an old gas station, **The Station** (61943 29 Palms Hwy., 760.974.9050, www.thestationjoshuatree.com, 10am-5pm Thurs., 10am-6pm Fri.-Sat., 10am-5pm Sun.-Mon.), offers an eclectic blend of gifts including T-shirts and the locally made Wonder Valley olive oil. You can also pick up vintage and new housewares, including pottery and objets d'art.

FOOD

Yucca Valley

The location of the sushi restaurant **Kimi Grill** (54850 29 Palms Hwy., 760/369-1122, lunch 11:30pm-2:30pm Mon.-Fri., 12pm-3pm Sat., dinner 5pm-9:30 Mon.-Sat., closed Sun., $11-20) inside the Travelodge Inn and Suites in the desert town of Yucca Valley does not inspire confidence. However, I'm here to tell you that their sushi is pretty good. They serve all the standards plus some creative rolls, tempura, teriyaki, bento, and poke bowls as well as beer and sake.

Locals' favorite **C&S Coffee Shop** (55795 29 Palms Hwy., 760/365-9946, 5:30am-7:30pm Mon.-Sat., 6am-7:30pm Sun., $6-11) offers hearty breakfast and brunch in an old-school diner setting. The heaping plates and early open time set you up for a power breakfast before your morning hike in Joshua Tree. Lunch and dinner add classic diner sandwiches and hearty home-cooked daily specials like meatloaf and fish and chips.

Gourmet coffee shop **Frontier Café** (55844 29 Palms Hwy., 760/820-1360, www.cafefrontier.com, 7am-7pm daily, until 10pm on Thursdays, $3-11) offers breakfast sandwiches, oatmeal, and yogurt alongside coffee, espresso, and tea. Lunch adds specialty sandwiches and salads, including vegan options as well as a small but selective beer and wine list in an eclectic, artsy space with a small patio. Pick up a spot of Wi-Fi here or some local live music at their location in Old Town Yucca Valley near shopping.

Pioneertown

People drive many desert miles to the food, drink, and culture oasis that is ★ **Pappy & Harriet's Pioneertown Palace** (53688 Pioneertown Rd., 760/365-5956, www.pappyandharriets.com, 11am-2am Thurs.-Sun., 5pm-2am Mon., lunch and dinner served until 9:30pm, $7-30). Originally built in the 1940s as part of the Pioneertown Wild West film set, the barbecue restaurant and saloon, which also triples as a music venue, packs in die-hard fans and first-timers every night, managing to stay on the fun side of controlled chaos. The food (burgers, sandwiches, salads, Tex-Mex, steaks, chili, and veggie options) is legitimately good, far surpassing run-of-the-mill bar food. Reservations for dinner are highly recommended two weeks in advance (two seatings: 5pm-5:30pm and 7pm). Wait times without a reservation can be staggering (two-three hours). Pappy & Harriet's lineup is impressive, snagging groups you might only expect to see in a big city, and gives the whole place a honky-tonk vibe. Lunches are more mellow, and the back patio is a great place for a weekend brunch.

Landers

★ **La Copine** (848 Old Woman Springs Rd., Flamingo Heights, 760/289-8537, www.lacopinekitchen.com, 2pm-7pm, Thurs.-Sun., no reservations, $15-24) is not just good by desert standards, it is great by any standard. The nouveau-American restaurant is situated in an unlikely remote location near Landers, 10 miles north of Yucca Valley. The perfectly executed cuisine shines against the chic, spare black-and-white décor of the small restaurant with indoor seating and outdoor patio. Their seasonal menu includes small and large plates with complex dishes like the soccarat: wild-caught rock shrimp, crispy rice, piquillo peppers, and fennel, or the crispy blackened chicken with cheesy grits. They also offer a giant pork belly Banh mi sandwich that can be made veggie or gluten free. Desserts are on par with everything else, including delights like cinnamon beignets and coconut rice pudding. The wine and beer list are just as carefully selected as the fresh, vibrant ingredients.

Giant Rock Meeting Room and Coffee House (1141 Old Woman Springs Rd. Unit A, 442/272-1472, giantrockcoffee.com/, 7am-2pm Mon., Wed.-Fri., 9am-4pm Sat.-Sun., $4-10) offers muffins, granola bowls, and fancy variations on toast, a few lunch items, and a coffee and tea menu in a warm, modern-industrial space. Weekends add breakfast tacos.

Joshua Tree

The burgers are hot and the beers are cold at the ★ **Joshua Tree Saloon** (61835 29 Palms Hwy., 760/366-2250, www.thejoshuatreesaloon.com, 7am-midnight Sun.-Thurs., 7am-2am Fri.-Sat., $8-22). As the go-to place in a small town with limited options, the Joshua Tree Saloon does a surprisingly good job of obliging a steady stream of hungry tourists and locals with consistently good food and service amid weathered Wild West decor. The bar and grill is open daily, dishing out well-executed burgers, salads, sandwiches, and solid veggie options as well as a full bar. The Yard, their outdoor patio, is open on weekends (weather permitting) for barbecue, cocktails, and live music. Pets are allowed, and it's a good spot for kids. The inside saloon and outdoor patio are all ages.

Crossroads Café (61715 29 Palms Hwy., 760/366-5414, www.crossroadscafejtree.com, 7am-9pm daily $8-12) is a Joshua Tree institution, offering reimagined diner fare with a Southwest hippie bent and lots of vegetarian options. Knotty pine walls and reclaimed wood touches bring warmth to the small contemporary diner space, which bustles with hungry hikers as well as locals. Breakfast and lunch are the most popular times, but they have a simple dinner menu as well. Beer and wine are served.

The tiny **Natural Sisters Café** (61695 29 Palms Hwy., 760/366-3600, www.thenaturalsisterscafe.com, 7am-7pm daily, $6-14) serves organic, vegan, and vegetarian breakfast and lunch, coffee, smoothies, and made-to-order fresh juices in a casual spot. They also offer tempting pies and pastries. Hey, they're vegan, so they must be good for you! Lines can get long on busy weekends in the park.

If it was good enough for Anthony Bourdain, it's good enough for me. **JT Country Kitchen** (61768 29 Palms Hwy., 760/366-8988, 6am-3:30pm daily, $8-10 cash only) is a down-home café serving tasty American diner-style breakfast and lunch. New owners took over from fixture chef/owner Mareine Yu, who ran the diner from 1989 to 2016 and amped up the American greasy spoon menu with a flavorful hot salsa, her own secret recipe. New owners got rid of some of the interior bric-a-brac, but the space and menu remain true to form down to the salsa. Try the sausage breakfast burrito or pancakes.

The **Joshua Tree Coffee Company** (61738 29 Palms Hwy., 760/974-9272, www.jtcoffeeco.com, 7am-6pm daily) may be exaggerating slightly when they claim to serve the most delicious coffee on the planet, but it is pretty good. This is organic locally roasted coffee made by people who are super into coffee in a hip space tucked behind the yoga studio and Pie for the People. They are usually out of breakfast pastries. Grab some from Natural Sisters Café across the road and enjoy your coffee on their outdoor patio.

Pie for the People (61740 29 Palms Hwy., 760/366-0400, www.pieforthepeople.net, 11am-9pm Sun.-Thurs., 11am-10pm Fri.-Sat., $10-26 full pizza) tosses up very respectable thin-crust New York-style pizzas with a myriad of toppings as well as specialty pizzas. Dine in their casual contemporary space or call for delivery, something almost unheard of in this area.

While **Sam's Indian Restaurant** (61380 29 Palms Hwy., 760/366-9511, www.samsindianfood.com, 3pm-8pm Sun.,

11am-9pm Mon.-Fri., $10-15) primarily serves heaping plates of authentic Indian classics, they ingeniously appropriate some of their fluffy naan into pizza and subs, making for a diverse menu that totally makes sense once you think about it. Situated in a strip mall, the casual cozy space serves satisfying food and beer that hits the spot after a day in the park. Their menu is also available for takeout.

If you can tough it out through the often erratic service, the **Royal Siam Restaurant** (61599 29 Palms Hwy., 760/366-2923, 11:30am-9pm Wed.-Mon., $10-16) has tasty Thai food, even by Los Angeles standards. Crunchy vegetables, sticky noodles, and savory soups can make it worth your while. Tucked in a strip mall, the casual atmosphere tends toward the brightly lit. You may want to opt for carryout.

Twentynine Palms

The ★ **29 Palms Inn** (73950 Inn Ave., 760/367-3505, www.29palmsinn.com, lunch 11am-2pm Mon.-Sat., 9am-2pm Sun., $7-16; dinner 5pm-9pm Sun.-Thurs., 5pm-9:30pm Fri.-Sat., $15-32) is the charming center of the desert inn's 70-acre universe, offering dining room and poolside dining for lunch and dinner daily. The eclectic menu pulls off classic steaks, seafood, and pastas with a fresh touch. They bake their own sourdough bread and source fresh veggies and herbs from the inn's garden when they can. Acoustic music accompanies dinner nightly. If you're staying here, it's a no-brainer. If not, it's worth the drive.

ACCOMMODATIONS

There's great lodging with character as well as more basic choices (read: chain motels) in the gateway towns of Joshua Tree, Twentynine Palms, and Yucca Valley. In addition to inns, motels, and hotels, there are also many unique rental lodgings in the area in those gateway towns and in more far-flung outposts like Landers and Wonder Valley. Rising up to meet Joshua Tree's popularity as a destination, there is a proliferation of rentals through booking platforms like Airbnb or Vrbo (rehabbed homestead cabins, stucco ranch-style homes, sleek modern dwellings, reminted house trailers, etc.). Select private rentals in the Yucca Valley neighborhoods of Pipes Canyon, Pioneertown, and Rimrock are collected online at **Destination Pipes Canyon** (www.destinationpipescanyon.com).

Pioneertown

The artfully furnished, solar-powered **Rattler Ranch Cabins** (Joshua Tree, 909/224-8626, www.rattlerjoshuatree.com, $140-160) are homestead bungalows near the west park entrance. Two one-bedroom cabins are available with wood-burning stoves, kitchen or kitchenettes, outdoor patios, and desert views. Built in the 1940s as part of a permanent Wild West town film set, the ★ **Pioneertown Motel** (5240 Curtis Rd., Pioneertown, 760/365-7001, www.pioneertown-motel.com, from $200) offers 19 desert lodge-style rooms. The motel recently experienced a welcome overhaul, and behind the rustic log cabin facade you'll find sparely styled rooms (queen, king, and twin beds) with exposed concrete floors, reclaimed wood, and a Wild West chic aesthetic (no televisions or coffeemakers). The motel is situated between the rustic main street of the Pioneertown tourist attraction and the wildly popular **Pappy & Harriet's** restaurant and saloon. Rooms book quickly with guests coming to see live music at Pappy & Harriet's, and it can be a bit of a party spot depending on what's happening that weekend. Rooms on the back of the property are quieter. Pro tip: On busy weekends, put your name on the Pappy & Harriet's dinner wait list then kick back in your room.

Tucked away in Rimrock Canyon near Pioneertown, the **Rimrock Ranch Cabins** (50857 Burns Canyon Rd., 760/369-3012, www.rimrockranchcabins.com, $120-220) offer pitch-perfect 1940s-style accommodations on 10 acres of grounds with hiking trails, a firepit, and a summer plunge pool. Choose from a refurbished Airstream, one of four cabins, or the four-bedroom lodge. The showstopper is the Hatch House, a stylish

ANTIQUES
ANTIQUES
PIONEER CROSSING ANTIQUES
PIONEER CROSSING ANTIQUES
10501
1

29 PALMS INN
2

3

BAR-B-QUE STEAKS
HAMBURGERS
BAR&GRILL
SALOON
THURS BLUES NITE
ORGANIC GREEN TEA
BACKYARD OPEN
HIRING COOKS
WELCOM ETO J
FAMOUS SMOKED
BABY BACK RIBS
14 BEERS ON TA
4

corrugated metal and glass architectural gem named for its collection of Hatch show prints.

Landers

The brightly restored Airstreams of **Kate's Lazy Desert** (58380 Botkin Rd., 845/688-7200, www.lazymeadow.com, $200) offer a kitschy retreat in the open desert of Landers near the Integratron. The six vintage Airstreams have been artistically restored and have full beds, bathrooms, kitchenettes, air-conditioning, and space heaters for winter. The grounds feature a seasonal cold plunge pool in the summer (May-Oct.). This is a fun place for a weekend getaway or as a base camp for exploring Joshua Tree, a 20-minute drive away. Children are not permitted.

Joshua Tree

The 1950s hacienda-style ★ **Joshua Tree Inn** (61259 29 Palms Hwy., 760/366-1188, www.joshuatreeinn.com, office open 3pm-8pm daily, from $115) offers funky courtyard rooms and rock-and-roll history. With eclectic furniture, Spanish tile floors, and outdoor patios in its 11 rooms, as well as a huge seasonal pool, landscaped courtyard, and firepit, they've tapped into a formula that keeps a dedicated following coming back. Speaking of dedicated followings, room number 8 is where country rocker Gram Parsons spent his last days, going from rock star to cult status rock legend. Pay your respects at a small shrine in the landscaped desert courtyard.

For the price, the **Safari Motor Inn** (61959 29 Palms Hwy., 760/366-1113, www.joshuatreemotel.com, $74-88) is a good base camp for exploring Joshua Tree. This basic budget motel has drive-up motel rooms with single king, single queen, or two queen beds, coffeemakers, mini fridges, and a swimming pool on the property. It's the closest motel to the west park entrance and walking distance to food and drinks.

There's no way to tell from the unassuming outside of this 1950s desert hideaway that the ★ **Mojave Sands** (62121 29 Palms Hwy., 760/550-8063, www.mojavesandsatjoshuatree.com, $135-300) is an impeccably renovated, industrial-chic desert modern retreat with an emphasis on the *treat*. Its five rooms and suites faced with glass and steel beams look over common grounds brought to life with a reflecting pool, reclaimed wood, and metal. The rooms feature polished concrete floors, open showers, locally made bath products, vintage turntables, and mini record collections. The two suites add kitchens and living areas. Suite 5 has an outdoor clawfoot tub and shower. They're tapped into some deep feng shui here. Do yourself a favor.

The romantic **Sacred Sands B&B** (63155 Quail Springs Rd., 760/424-6407, www.sacredsands.com, $330-360) is a luxury retreat poised on a hill with sweeping desert views just 1.3 miles from the park's West Entrance. Each of the two serene guest rooms offers an indoor shower with river-rock floors. An outdoor shower, a private terrace with hot tub, and a meditation platform round out the amenities. Stays require a two-night minimum and include a complimentary gourmet breakfast.

Both secluded and colorful, **Spin and Margie's Desert Hide-a-Way** (64491 29 Palms Hwy., www.deserthideaway.com, $150-195) is a Southwestern-themed inn with Americana road trip-inspired grounds tucked away on the outskirts of Joshua Tree. Four suites and a cabin feature tile floors, fully equipped kitchens or kitchenettes, dining areas, outdoor courtyard and lounge areas, and flat-screen TVs.

The Desert Lily Bed and Breakfast (8523 Star Ln., 310/849-7290, http://thedesertlily.com, $175-$248) are a rustic-romantic collection of cabins and lodge near the West Entrance of Joshua Tree National Park. The property offers four self-catering cabins (available year-round) plus a bed-and-breakfast (closed July and August) in a main house with gourmet breakfast. Western-style

1: antique shops in downtown Yucca Valley
2: the entrance to the funky, historic 29 Palms Inn
3: rustic-chic lodging at the Pioneertown Motel
4: the Joshua Tree Saloon

adobes and haciendas plus a bunkhouse make it good for individuals and couples or whole ranch rentals for larger groups.

Twentynine Palms

The ★ **29 Palms Inn** (73950 Inn Ave., 760/367-3505, www.29palmsinn.com, $140-230) is so great that I once stayed there for a weekend and never left the premises, not even to visit Joshua Tree National Park just a few minutes away. Drive onto the grounds and you'll be greeted by a glass-lined, art-filled lobby and funky wooden signs that direct you over the inn's 70 palm-dotted acres. The eclectic lodging includes nine 1930s adobe bungalows with tile floors, fireplaces, and private sun patios, eight wood-frame cabins with private decks, and seven two-bedroom guesthouses. Stroll the grounds past the Oasis of Mara, a 9,000-year-old palm oasis used as a settlement by the Serrano and Chemehuevi Indians into the 1900s. The on-site **29 Palms Inn Restaurant** serves up lunch, dinner, and daily specials and draws inn guests as well as other visitors and locals to its dining room and bar. A charming swimming pool allows for poolside dining and great lounging.

The **Harmony Motel**'s (71161 29 Palms Hwy., 760/367-3351, www.harmonymotel.com, $75-95) claim to fame is that U2 stayed here when making their iconic album *Joshua Tree*. The colorful 1950s motel is set on a hilltop above Twentynine Palms, six miles from the north park entrance. The grounds have a pool, hot tub, and nice views of the Little San Bernardino Mountains. The hotel offers seven cheerful homey rooms and one cabin. Some rooms have kitchenettes, and a common dining room with coffee is available to guests. This place is a great value.

TRANSPORTATION AND SERVICES

Car

For getting around and between the gateway communities of Yucca Valley, Joshua Tree, and Twentynine Palms, having a car is preferable since distances are far between businesses and towns. Gas up in Yucca Valley before heading south into the park or farther east along Highway 62, where services become sparse and the stretches between them greater.

The town of **Yucca Valley** is located at the junction of Highways 63 and 247, approximately 28 miles north of Palm Springs. From I-10, take Highway 62 north for 20 miles. Access to the Black Rock Canyon area of Joshua Tree National Park is via Joshua Lane south (about five miles).

The town of **Joshua Tree** lies seven miles east of Yucca Valley along Highway 62. To enter the park through the West Entrance, follow Quail Springs Road as it heads south, becoming Park Boulevard at the park boundary. The sights of Hidden Valley can be reached in 14 miles.

The town of **Twentynine Palms** sits 15 miles east of Joshua Tree along Highway 62 in a remote section of the valley. The Oasis Visitor Centers and the North Entrance to the park are accessed by heading south on Utah Trail, which becomes Park Boulevard in about four miles.

Shuttle

In 2018, the national park began piloting a free shuttle service in the park to reduce traffic and pollution and make it easy for visitors to see the main sights. The **Roadrunner Shuttle** (www.nps.gov, 8am-5pm daily, free) leaves from the town of Twentynine Palms in two locations 1) Twentynine Palms Transit Center (Adobe & Cactus), and 2) Oasis Visitor Centers beginning at 8am daily. Routes are west along Park Boulevard, the park's main sightseeing thoroughfare. The shuttle stops at popular sights, hikes, and rock-climbing destinations, including Ryan Mountain, Barker Dam, and the Quail Springs Picnic Area. Campground stops include Jumbo Rocks and Hidden Valley. Parking can be a drama on busy weekends in fall and spring. This is a great way to get around for day trips or if you are camping in the park.

Public Transit

Limited public transportation is available in Morongo Basin (which includes the communities of Joshua Tree, Twentynine Palms, Yucca Valley, Morongo Valley, and Landers) in the form of the **Morongo Basin Transit Authority** (760/366-2395, www.mbtabus.com, $1.25-2.50 exact fare only). With the addition of the Roadrunner Shuttle into the park, it is possible to get around entirely via public transportation. Schedules are available online.

Taxi

There is one taxi company in the Yucca Valley region. **Lucky 777 Cab** (760/660-9115 or 760/366-1064, www.lucky777cab.com) is based in Yucca Valley and serves the communities of Yucca Valley, Pioneertown, Joshua Tree, 29 Palms, and Morongo Valley. They accept reservations. Cell service is limited, and wait times for a taxi can be long, so plan to book ahead. Lucky 777 offers special rates from any hotel in Yucca Valley to Pappy and Harriet's ($20 per way) or the Joshua Tree Saloon ($25 per way). There are no ride-sharing services available in the area.

Sand to Snow National Monument

The dramatic topography of California means that the sand, cacti, and palm trees of the Mojave and Sonoran Desert floors are in range of the pine forests and snow-capped peaks of the lofty San Bernardino Mountains. The Sand to Snow National Monument (www.fs.fed.us), established in 2016, knits together desert preserves, national forest, and mountain wilderness to create a 154,000-acre monument that extends from Sonoran low-desert to the soaring, forested mountains of the San Gorgonio Wilderness and the San Bernardino National Forest, which continues north and west beyond the monument boundaries.

The heart of the monument is located in the San Bernardino Mountains, home to snow-capped San Gorgonio Peak at 11,503 feet. Parcels of protected desert land include Whitewater Preserve, Mission Creek Preserve, and Big Morongo Canyon Preserve. The monument also protects sacred Native American archaeological and cultural sites, including petroglyphs and village sites. Some of these are located in the Black Lava Butte and Flat Top Mesa desert areas north of Yucca Valley and Pioneertown. These locations have not been developed for hiking or visitation.

Visiting the Sand to Snow National Monument can be done as a day trip or overnight add-on from either Palm Springs or Joshua Tree. From Palm Springs, a good destination is the Barton Flats Visitors Center, about an hour and a half from Palm Springs via Highway 111, I-10, and Highway 38. The drive is highly scenic, and you will have opportunities to hike. From Joshua Tree, the same destination (Barton Flats Visitors Center) will take about an hour and 45 minutes via Highway 62, I-10, and Highway 38. From Joshua Tree it is also possible to do a scenic loop by continuing north toward Big Bear Lake and then returning to Joshua Tree via Highway 247/Old Woman Springs Road. Be prepared for a long day in the car if you choose to do this, or stay in one of Big Bear's many lodgings. Staying overnight in the Sand to Snow will give you the chance for a longer hike or to kick back under the trees and cooler temperatures. If you choose to make a night of it, you will want to make reservations.

VISITORS CENTERS AND RANGER STATIONS

A combined visitors center and ranger station, **Whitewater Preserve Visitors Center** (9160 Whitewater Canyon Rd., Whitewater, 760/325-7222, www.wildlandsconservancy.org, 8am-5pm daily) is located in the

Sand to Snow National Monument

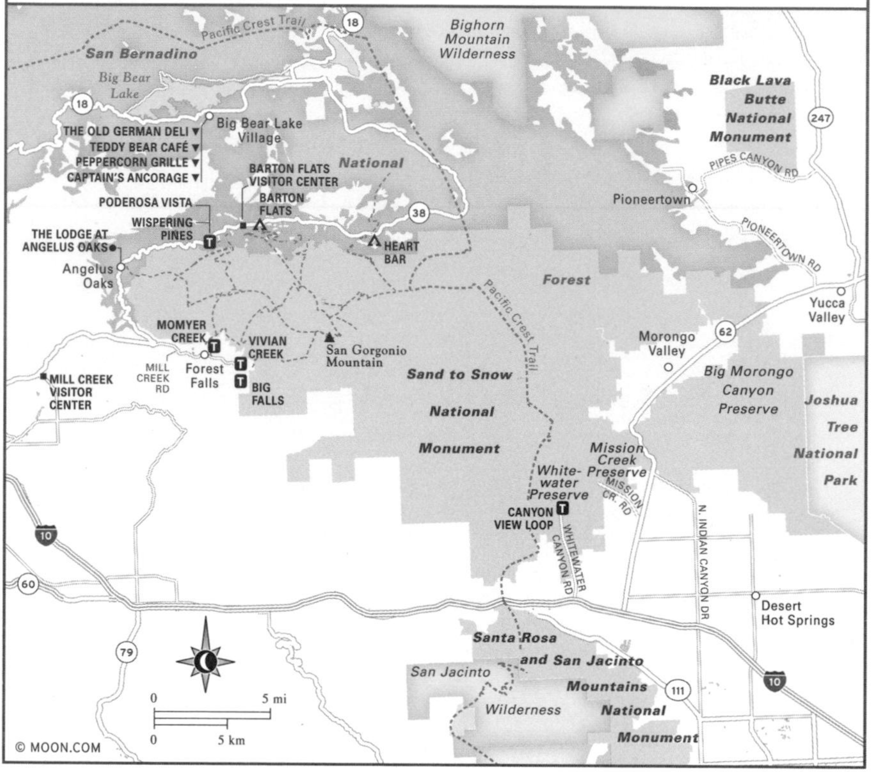

Whitewater Trout Farm's historic building, graced by a picturesque trout pond and wading pool. The visitors center has exhibits and hiking maps of the region. Permits are available for camping at the preserve. Permits are also available for backcountry trip parking or after hours hiking both in person and by phone. It is located off of Interstate 10, 16 miles northwest of Palm Springs and 35 miles southwest of the Joshua Tree National Park West Entrance visitors center.

Mill Creek Visitors Center (34701 Mill Creek Rd., Mentone, 909/382-2882, www.fs.usda.gov, 8am-4:30pm Mon. summer only, closed Mon. in winter, closed on select federal holidays, 8am-4:30pm Thurs.-Fri., 7am-3:30pm Sat.-Sun., may be closed for lunch noon-1pm) is a combined visitors center and ranger station offering a range of passes and permits, including San Gorgonio Wilderness permits, Forest Adventure Passes, and snowmobile permits. Call ahead for availability, especially for wilderness permits, which are subject to a quota. They also offer forest maps, gifts, and bear-resistant canisters for sale and rental. Mill Creek Ranger Station is located on the corner of Bryant and Highway 38 in Mentone, 45 miles northwest of Palm Springs and 65 miles west of the Joshua Tree National Park West Entrance visitor centers.

Barton Flats Visitors Center (State Highway 38, Angelus Oaks, 909/794-4861, www.fs.usda.gov, open seasonally Memorial Day-mid-Oct.) serves as the main hub for campgrounds in the area and visitors to the San Bernardino National Forest and San

Gorgonio Wilderness. The center is staffed and operated by the San Gorgonio Wilderness Association and provides San Gorgonio Wilderness permits. Other permits are available at the Mill Creek Visitors Center. The center also offers maps, books, and gifts. Staffers at the center are helpful and can provide trail conditions and sightseeing tips. The visitor centers also has picnic tables and very well-maintained bathrooms. A three-mile round-trip trail to Jenks Lake leaves from the visitors center parking area. The Barton Flats Visitors Center is located off of Highway 38, seven miles east of the hamlet of Angelus Oaks. It is 63 miles northwest of Palm Springs and 84 miles west of the Joshua Tree National Park West Entrance visitor center.

SIGHTS

Whitewater Preserve

The scenic riparian corridor at the **Whitewater Preserve** (9160 Whitewater Canyon Rd., Whitewater, 760/325-7222, www.wildlandsconservancy.org, 8am-5pm daily, free, donations encouraged) features 2,851 acres surrounded by the San Gorgonio Wilderness. Whitewater Preserve sits tucked behind the unlikely-looking arid hills north of I-10. The preserve is named for the Whitewater River, a wild year-round river winding through scenic Whitewater Canyon. Once used for cattle grazing, the river's crystal-clear waters have since been restored.

A combined visitors center and ranger station is located in the Whitewater Trout Farm's historic building, graced by a picturesque trout pond and wading pool. If you plan to hike, pick up a trail map at the ranger station or online. All day hikers are required to register at the ranger station or sign in at the trailhead. Other facilities include individual and group picnic areas, camping spots, and seasonal activities (free, but registration required). Check the preserve's online program calendar for bird walks, guided walks through Whitewater Canyon, and after-hours star parties guided by the San Bernardino Amateur Astronomers.

GETTING THERE

Whitewater Preserve is north of Palm Springs off I-10. From I-10, take Exit 114 and follow Tipton Road to Whitewater Canyon Road. Drive five miles north on Whitewater Canyon Road to the preserve entrance. The preserve gates are open for hiking 7am-6pm daily September 1-November 1; 7am-5pm November 2-March 9; 7am-6pm March 10-May 31. Visitors must park and then walk in outside of visitors center hours. June through August the gates are closed.

Winter storms severely damaged Whitewater Canyon Road and led to the temporary closure of the preserve. It is slated to re-open fall 2019. Check the website for current conditions.

Big Morongo Canyon Preserve

The Big Morongo Canyon Preserve (11055 East Dr., Morongo Valley, 760/363-7190, www.bigmorongo.org, 7:30am-sunset daily, free admission but donations welcome) is a desert oasis in the little San Bernardino Mountains, with interpretive trails, world-class bird-watching, and a chance to experience a desert riparian habitat. An interpretive kiosk has pamphlets describing the landscape. The diversity of native flora is what makes this space so special. Palm trees, aspen groves, mesquite, cottonwood, and willow blend together in this transition zone between the Mojave and Colorado Deserts, while views of snow-capped Mount San Jacinto are dramatic in the distance and bring home the sand to snow aspect of the monument. The preserve spans 31,000 acres, with elevations ranging from 600 feet on the canyon floor to 3,000 feet on ridgelines. Just over three miles of interpretive trails wind through the habitat, including wheelchair-accessible boardwalks across marsh and stream terrain. A longer 8.34-mile round-trip Canyon Trail leaves from the preserve and descends from the cooler Mojave Desert into the lower-elevation Colorado Desert then returns the same way. The preserve is open year-round, but the best times of the year to visit are fall, winter, and spring due to summer heat. It makes a good stop on your way into or out of Joshua Tree National Park.

GETTING THERE

The preserve is located in Morongo Valley one block south of State Highway 62. From I-10 take State Highway 62 /29 Palms Highway to Morongo Valley. Turn right into the signed preserve.

Valley of the Falls

The picturesque mountain hamlet of Forest Falls (www.forestfalls.com/) is nestled in Mill Creek Canyon at the base of the steep, mountainous San Gorgonio Wilderness. It is pitched in a pine forest at 5,700 feet elevation, making it a good place to escape the Southern California heat in summer or to play in the snow in winter. The scenic 4-mile stretch of road from the Highway 38 turnoff to the road's end gives access to the network of San Gorgonio Wilderness trails, including the Momyer Trail and trail camps. The road ends at a large parking and picnic area, where visitors can take the 0.7-mile round-trip stroll to Big Falls, hike some or part of the Vivian Creek trail (ultimately leading to San Gorgonio Peak), or picnic in the fresh mountain air.

GETTING THERE

From I-10 East take exit 80 for University Street in Redlands. Turn left onto North University Street and follow it for one mile. Turn right onto CA-38 East/E. Lugonia Avenue. Follow Highway 38 for 13 miles to a signed junction. Continue right, toward Forest Falls to reach the village in four miles.

HIKING

Hiking in the Sand to Snow National Monument is spectacular and the reason for many visitors to trek to the region. Hundreds of miles of trail network allow for plentiful day hikes as well as backpacking opportunities to established trail camps. Hikes range from interpretive low desert strolls to demanding sky-scratching summits reaching over 10,000 feet. The most impressive of these is the hike-able 11,502-foot San Gorgonio Mountain, which rises steeply from the Sonoran Desert floor. It keeps company with ten other peaks over 10,000 feet in elevation in the southeast San Bernardino Mountains.

Pacific Crest Trail

The famous **Pacific Crest Trail**, the continuous trail system that runs 2,650 miles from Mexico to Canada, crosses 30 scenic

aspen groves in Big Morongo Canyon Preserve

miles of the Sand to Snow. Starting at the southernmost end of the monument near the **Whitewater Preserve** and **Mission Creek Preserve**, the trail climbs up to the Mission Creek drainage south of Big Bear in a section known as the nine peaks challenge, featuring more than 8,300 feet of elevation change. The PCT hike here offers a striking cross-section of the Sand to Snow's diverse landscape. It passes through the exposed fanglomerate cliffs of the desert Whitewater Canyon cut by the snaking Whitewater River to end in the high pines. For an in-depth description of the Sand to Snow section of the PCT, check out *Hiking the Pacific Crest Trail, Southern California* by hiking expert Shawnté Salabert.

From the Whitewater Preserve parking, the PCT is accessed via the Canyon Loop Trail in 0.5 miles. From the Mission Creek Preserve, access to the PCT is 4 miles beyond the locked gate near the parking area. To get to the preserve from Palm Springs, take I-10 West to Highway 62 toward Joshua Tree. Continue 5.5 miles to Mission Creek Road on your left (signed with a small, green sign). Turn left onto Mission Creek Road and park at a parking area and locked gate. By prior arrangement, you can also request access to a second parking area located 1.5 miles beyond the access gate using an alone request form. From here, access to PCT is 2.5 miles along preserve trails.

WHITEWATER PRESERVE

To experience a tiny section of the PCT, check out the moderate and family-friendly **Canyon View Loop Trail** (3.5 miles round-trip), a rewarding trail that gives you great canyon and mountain views as well as passage along the Whitewater River. It leaves the Whitewater Ranger Station to follow a section of the PCT heading south across the riverbed. A small wooden footbridge leads across the river. In addition to the PCT section, a series of hikes ranging in length and difficulty start from the Whitewater Preserve visitor center. They offer great views of the surrounding mountains and canyon, and passage along the Whitewater River basin.

The hike to the colorful red rock outcropping known as **Red Dome** (4 miles round-trip) begins near the ranger station to cross the canyon's river basin. The family-friendly trail continues on the west bank of the canyon, connecting with the PCT to reach the destination to the left of the trail—a large colorful rock outcropping.

San Gorgonio Wilderness

The San Gorgonio Wilderness forms the largest and most dramatic segment of the national monument. Spanning nearly 95,000 acres, the topography shifts from low foothills to rugged canyons to lofty mountains, wildly vacillating from 2,300 to 11,500 feet. A vast network of hiking trails crisscrosses the wilderness region, making it a rich zone for day hiking and backpacking. Forest fires in 2015 and 2018 closed sections of the San Gorgonio Wilderness. Check for current conditions at the Barton Flats Visitors Center or online with the San Gorgonio Wilderness Association (http://sgwa.org) or U.S. Forest Service (www.fs.usda.gov). There are hiking access points along the Valley of the Falls Drive/Forest Falls, Angelus Oaks, and Barton Flats Visitor Center/Jenks Lake. For any overnight hikes in the San Gorgonio Wilderness, you must obtain a free wilderness permit. These are available at the Mill Creek Visitors Center or Barton Flats Visitors Center (summer only).

The crown jewel of the Sand to Snow National Monument is the lofty **San Gorgonio Mountain**. At 11,502 feet, it is the highest peak in Southern California. There are several routes to the summit; however, the classic is the **Vivian Creek Trail,** clocking in at 17 miles round-trip. The trail was built in1893 with the creation of the San Bernardino Forest Reserve. Today there are many other routes up the mountain, but this is the shortest, steepest, and the preferred route for some hikers. It is possible to do as a strenuous day hike or two-day backpacking trip. Trail camps at 1.5 miles (Vivian Creek

Trail Camp), 3.2 miles (Halfway Camp), and 5.2 miles (High Creek Trail Camp) offer possibilities to break up the hike. They also make shorter day-hiking turnaround points. None of them have a huge payoff, but they set a manageable goal as you delve into the wilderness. The Vivian Creek Trail begins at the parking area for Big Falls. It crosses Mill Creek before switchbacking up the flank of the mountain, offering views of the canyon. You will cross into the San Gorgonio Wilderness after approximately one mile. Vivian Creek is a shaded scenic glade for a pleasant stop. Other routes to the summit include the San Gorgonio via Dollar Lake Saddle (20 miles round-trip) and Mine Shaft Saddle (22 miles round-trip). Both begin from Jenks Lake Road at the South Fork Trailhead.

At 0.7-mile round-trip, popular **Big Falls** barely qualifies as a hike, but it does qualify as a destination. Big Fall Creek plunges into Mill Creek Canyon over a series of narrow cascades. The sight is best seen from a viewing platform 200 yards below the falls during spring, when snowmelt feeds the cascading waters. People also lounge and splash in the creek along the trail below the falls. The trail, falls, and picnic area are popular day use spots.

Big Falls is accessed at the end of Valley of the Falls Drive. From its junction with Highway 38, turn right toward the village of Forest Falls. Continue 4.3 miles through the village until the roads end at a parking and picnic area and the signed trailhead to Big Falls.

The **Momyer Creek Trail** (7.2 or 11.5 miles round-trip) offers views of Mill Creek Canyon and Yucaipa, scenic creeks, and two shaded trail camps. It is one of the more underused trails in the San Gorgonio Wilderness section of the Sand to Snow and makes good day hiking or backpacking overnight. From the trailhead, cross the wide wash of Mill Creek. Do not attempt if water is rushing in the creek which can happen during the spring snow melt. Check the San Gorgonio Wilderness Association website for trail conditions (http://sgwa.org). On the other side, the trail switchbacks through chaparral and oak and eventually Jeffrey pines as it navigates the divide between Momyer Creek and Alger Creek. The cedar-shaded Alger Creek Camp (7,100 feet) is located above Alger Creek, 3.7 miles from the Mill Creek wash. Continue for another two miles to Dobbs Camp, with the log foundation remains of John W. Dobbs's cabin, who built a section of the trail in 1898.

The trailhead is accessed on Valley of the Falls Drive. From its junction with Highway 38, turn right toward the village of Forest Falls. Continue toward Forest Falls for three miles to a large parking area on your left, 100 yards before the fire station.

San Bernardino National Forest

In the area around the Barton Flats Visitors Center and Jenks Lake, there are several easy, family-friendly hikes that make for nice outings in a day of mountain sightseeing.

The **Ponderosa Vista Nature Trail** offers a 0.7-mile loop walk around a hillside through varied forest flora marked by interpretive signs. You can hear cars on the rural highway below, so this is not a secluded spot, but it does prompt visitors to stop and take in the mountain air. Across the road, another interpretive trial, the 0.7-mile **Whispering Pines Nature Trail,** climbs to a vista point with far-reaching mountain views. Both trails can be reached from Highway 38 0.1-mile south from the turnoff to Jenks Lake (Jenks Lake Rd. West). They are 1.5 miles southwest of the Barton Flats Visitor Center.

A longer hike to **South Fork Meadows** (9 miles round-trip) follows a well-marked graded trail through stands of Jeffrey pine and white fir to a shaded glen where several streams converge. At 2.2 miles into the hike, there is a short side trails up Poopout Hill offering outstanding views of San Gorgonio. From Redlands, follow Highway 38 east to the Jenks Lake Road. Turn right and follow Jenks Lake Road 2.5 miles to the signed South Fork Trailhead.

CAMPING AND CABINS

Rustic cabins, developed campgrounds, and hike-in trail camps make up the overnight lodging in the Sand to Snow region. Limited supplies are available at the general store in Forest Falls. Big Bear to the north and Yucaipa to the south are full-service towns with gas, groceries, and other supplies. For an overnight visit, pack in everything you will need. Most campgrounds offer potable water.

★ **The Lodge at Angelus Oaks** (37825 Highway 38, Angelus Oaks, 909/794-9523, www.lodgeatangelusoaks.com, $130-180) was once a stagecoach stop on the route from Redlands to Big Bear. Now the lodge is under special permit from the San Bernardino National Forest, with eight rustic cabins dating from the 1930s for rent. Cabins accommodate from two to six people and have bathrooms, fully equipped kitchens, and front porches. Owners Sunny and Charlie are welcoming and hospitable, brightening an already lovely spot. The primary activities here are nearby hiking and biking trails, or you may opt for my favorite: porch sitting. There are no TVs, cell phones don't work, and the simplicity here becomes the best feature under the trees and stars. Sitting on said porch you can hear the occasional car go by on Highway 38, just enough reminder of civilization to make you glad you're sitting it out for a moment.

Campgrounds

Barton Flats Campground (www.recreation.gov, Apr.-early Nov., $31-64) is a popular, family campground offering single and double campsites for tent, trailer, and RV camping. Located at 6,360 feet, the level campsites are tucked into pine and oak forest. The campground has 51 reserve-able sites with picnic tables, fire rings, flush toilets, and drinking water. The campground is located on Highway 38, 0.8 mile east of the Barton Flats Visitor Center. The campground is very popular and can fully book on weekends throughout the season. Reservations are recommended and can be made up to six months in advance through www.recreation.gov.

★ **Heart Bar Campground** (www.recreation.gov, May-Oct., $25-52) features 89 spacious sites planted widely under pine forest at an elevation of 6,880. Of the sites, 63 are reserve-able and 26 available on a first-come, first-served basis, with single, double, tent and RV sites (no hook-ups; dump station with potable water nearby). Reservations are recommended and can be made up to six months in advance through www.recreation.gov. July and August see the heaviest use. Amenities include campfire rings, picnic tables, bear boxes, potable water, vault toilets, and firewood sales. A camp host is on-site. The turnoff to the campground is located 6.3 miles east of the Barton Flats Visitor Center, and the campground is another 0.3 mile on the right. If you are prepared for dispersed camping, continue down this road to find other forest service sites.

Big Bear

Big Bear to the north offers every type of accommodation from rustic lodges to hotels to cabin rentals. Hundreds of cabins are available through third party booking platforms like Airbnb and Vrbo as well as local property management companies like www.bigbearcoolcabins.com and bigbearcabins.com. Cabins range from small rustic getaways to luxury lodging for groups with hot tubs and game rooms.

GATEWAY COMMUNITIES

Forest Falls

The charming little town of Forest Falls serves as a jumping-off point for hikes in the San Gorgonio Wilderness or as a destination for its scenery and picnic opportunities around Big Falls. It offers a restaurant, gift shop, and general store. **El Mexicano Restaurant** (40977 Valley of the Falls Dr., 909/794-3186, 9am-7:30pm Sun., 11am-8pm Mon.-Thurs., 11am-9pm Fri., 9am-8pm Sat., $7-18) is a rustic café with a cozy interior and open-air patio

1

2
NATIONAL FOREST

Welcome
The Village
3

4
ANGELUS
OAKS
LODGE

for Mexican standards and cold drinks. **The Elkhorn General Store** (40987 Valley of the Falls Dr., 909/794-1212, 7am-8pm Mon.-Fri., 8am-8pm Sat.-Sun.) stocks basic groceries, beer, and wine as well as other sundries and supplies. **Jessica's Treasures** (40987 Valley of the Falls Dr., 909/794-4359, 11am-5pm Tues.-Sun.) offers mountain decor, gifts, and novelty items.

Angelus Oaks

The tiny community of Angelus Oaks offers rustic cabins and two small restaurants. It began as a stagecoach stop on the way from Redlands to Big Bear Lake in the 1800s and 1900s. The drive from Redlands in the valley below to Big Bear Lake used to take two days along a rugged mining road. Stagecoach service stopped in Angelus Oaks and continued via burro train. The trip today is much quicker, one hour along a paved road. Now, the tiny community serves as a gateway to hiking and exploration of the surrounding San Gorgonio wilderness. The village is made up of the rustic Angelus Oaks Lodge cabins, The Oaks Restaurant and the Seven Oaks Mountain Resort. **The Oaks Restaurant** (37676 Hwy. 38, 909/794-2777, 8am-2pm Mon.-Fri., 7:30am-7pm Sat., 7:30pm-6pm Sun., $7-17) is a family restaurant serving American diner standards, including breakfast, burgers, sandwiches, pasta, and entrees. Food and hours can be hit or miss; they have been known to close early.

Located just seven miles south of the Barton Flats Visitors Center and nearby to popular trailheads in the San Gorgonio Wilderness, **The Lodge at Angelus Oaks** (37825 Hwy. 39, Angelus Oaks, $130-180) is a good place to set up your base cabin for a weekend of exploring. Five miles to the north, **Seven Oaks Mountain Resort** (39950 Seven Oaks Rd., 909/794-2917, restaurant $8-13) is home to a historic lodge still in operation that serves basic bar food and sandwiches and offers campsites along the banks of the Santa Ana River. Seven Oaks began as a sheep ranch but grew into a large cabin resort by the 1890s as the wagon road from Redlands ended here and travelers continued to Big Bear Lake via burro train. William H. Glass bought and expanded the resort in 1902, and the Glass family continued to run it until the 1960s. Another small group of cabins one mile to the east was constructed in the 1920s to provide additional resort lodging. These still stand but are privately owned and separate from the resort. Today, the resort has seen better days. The original cabins are intriguing and picturesque but now mostly privately owned, and the resort area is pushed into over-used campsites on the banks of the Santa Ana River. However, if you are nosy about history, it is a worth a stop.

1: Whitewater Preserve **2:** the Barton Flats Visitors Center **3:** the scenic mountain town of Big Bear Village **4:** rustic cabins at Angelus Oaks, a historic stagecoach stop

Big Bear Lake Village

Big Bear Lake Village is a charming mountain resort town in the San Bernardino Mountains. In winter, skiers and snowboarders flock to the slopes. In summer, visitors come to enjoy Big Bear Lake, rent a cabin, hike, camp, and explore the village's shops, restaurants, and bars. The adjacent Big Bear City has grocery stores, gas stations, chain stores, a hospital, and all the trappings of civilization. Big Bear is surrounded by the San Bernardino National Forest. It is located near the confluence of mountain Highways 18 and 38 on the northern edge of the Sand to Snow National Monument and San Gorgonio Wilderness. It makes an excellent day or weekend visit and is also handy if you forget something major on your weekend camping trip to the Sand to Snow. It is approximately 45 minutes from the Barton Flats Visitors Center and surrounding campgrounds, and one hour from Angelus Oaks.

Being a tourist town, Big Bear Lake Village has an array of restaurants that give the people what they want on vacation: stick-to-your-ribs breakfast, good Mexican, upscale American with a patio, and sandwiches great for taking on a picnic.

La Azteca (40199 Big Bear Blvd., 909/866-2350, 9am-9pm Sun., 10am-9pm Mon.-Thurs., 10am-10pm Fri-Sat., $8-15) serves up satisfying Mexican standards, better than average salsa, and a full drink menu, including good skinny margaritas in a casual space. The vibe is unfussy, and they have a large patio, which means that it is good for groups and kids. The game might be on in the bar. It is conveniently located near the cabin resorts on the west side of town before entering Big Bear Village.

★ **The Old German Deli** (40645 Village Dr., Big Bear Lake, 909/878-0515, 10am-4:30pm Tues.-Sat. 10am-4pm Sun., $10-13) is operated by Karl Winkelmann, who trained in Germany as a chef, and his wife, Carol. They opened the spare German deli and butcher shop in 2016. Their meat case showcases an arsenal of German sausages served as a lunch specialty with homemade sauerkraut and potato salad. Their menu also includes heaping cold-cut sandwiches served on crusty bread with pickles and German potato salad. Other offerings include pastries and German beers. It's a great spot to pick up a picnic lunch, or they have a tiny patio for dining on-site.

The popular ★ **Teddy Bear Café** (583 Pine Knot Ave., teddybearrestaurant.com, 909/866-5415, $8-15 cash only) has been serving giant portions of homespun American classics since 1944. The bracing mountain air up here can make you hungry for their gut-buster of a menu, including biscuits and gravy, omelets, pastrami, burgers, sandwiches, and signature pies. For a Mexican angle, try the machaca breakfast burrito or tacos. The casual spot offers breakfast served all day, lunch, dinner, and take-out.

★ **Peppercorn Grille** (553 Pine Knot Ave., 11am-9pm Sun.-Thurs., 11am-10pm Fri.-Sat., lunch $13-33, dinner $14-44) offers upscale new American cuisine in the heart of the village. Their extensive menu includes excellently executed salads, wood-fired pizza, pastas, sandwiches, seafood, chicken, and steak. Dinner specialties include lobster ravioli and a peppercorn-mushroom New York strip steak. The restaurant is bustling; make a reservation. A small patio allows for good people watching and dogs. It may be a good spot if you have kids also.

The atmosphere is the shining star at the 1946 landmark ★ **Captain's Anchorage** (42148 Moonridge Way, 909/866-3997, captainsanchorage.com, 4:30pm-9:30pm Sun.-Thurs., 4:30pm-10pm Fri.-Sat., $24-46). This time capsule of a restaurant features lodge-style wood paneling, cozy booths, dim lighting, and a cocktail lounge, making this a perfect date night or special occasion spot. Oh, and staff will tell you that the restaurant is haunted by a ghost named George. The food ranges from adequate to good with a menu that features seafood and steakhouse classics, including Alaskan King crab legs, scallops, chicken, prime rib, and steaks. Dinners come with a soup and salad and soup bar featuring a tasty clam chowder.

PERMITS AND PASSES

All visitors to the San Bernardino National Forest parking in developed parking areas (bathrooms, picnic tables, trailheads) must display an Adventure Pass ($5 per day or $30 annually, second car pass $5). This means that all mountain visitors to the Sand to Snow (excluding Whitewater Preserve and Big Morongo Canyon Preserve) will need a pass for any stops. They are available at visitors centers, ranger stations, and some local businesses, including convenience stores and outdoors outfitters. Information about specific outlets where you can buy a pass and when they are required is available on the forest service website (www.fs.usda.gov). Passes are also good for the Angeles National Forest and Los Padres National Forest.

Free permits are required for all overnight hikes in the San Gorgonio Wilderness. They are available in-person at the Mill Creek Visitor Center, Barton Flats Visitors Center (summer only) or by mail. Permit requests can be submitted via fax, email or USPS.

GETTING THERE

The Sand to Snow National Monument can be reached from the south via I-10 and Highway 38 at Redlands. From the north, the area is accessed by Highways 18 and 38 from Big Bear. From Palm Springs, count on an hour to an hour and a half drive via I-10 and Highway 38 coming from the south. From the town of Joshua Tree, the monument can be accessed from the north via Highway 247/ Old Woman Springs Road, Highway 18, and Highway 38, or from the south. Either way, count on approximately an hour-and-a-half of driving.

Background

The Landscape

GEOGRAPHY

Mojave and Sonoran Deserts

Joshua Tree National Park straddles the Mojave and Sonoran Desert ecosystems. The Mojave Desert covers an area of 35,0000 square miles and extends into Nevada and southern Utah. It encompasses the northwest section of Joshua Tree National Park, the most popular and heavily visited, for good reason. A drive through Joshua Tree's Mojave Desert reveals a surreal landscape of shattered boulder piles, fields of spiky Joshua trees, and broken mountains ringing broad valleys. The Mojave

is characterized by higher elevations (3,000-5,000 feet) and temperatures which can be 15-25 degrees cooler than its neighboring Sonoran Desert ecosystem, which spans elevations below 3,000 feet. The Mojave Desert is marked by distinct vegetation, including large swatches of Joshua trees. Above 4,000 feet, juniper and piñon pine woodlands take over, lending a more forested feel. Desert gardens that blend yucca plants, Joshua trees, junipers, and piñons are not unusual. On the lower end of the elevation range, cacti such as barrel cactus dot the rocky hillsides.

The Coachella Valley lies south of Joshua Tree National Park and encompasses Palm Springs. The valley extends northwest-southeast for approximately 45 miles, outlined in the west by the San Jacinto Mountains and then the Santa Rosa Mountains continuing south. On the north and east, the Little San Bernardino Mountains frame the valley. The San Andreas fault follows the foothills of the Little San Bernardino Mountains, spouting up at major fissures in a series of hot springs. The Coachella Valley lies within the Sonoran Desert system, which covers southeastern California, much of Arizona, and northwestern Mexico. This "low desert" encompasses the eastern section of Joshua Tree National Park as well as Palm Springs. It is lower and hotter than the neighboring Mojave, with elevations below 1,000 feet and more stark landscape. The plants that grow here are hearty, able to withstand searing heat and a lack of water. Spindly ocotillos resemble fingered sticks until they bloom with flame-like flowers in wet springs, while fuzzy cholla cacti spread out into strange armies of plants. Bushy creosote, an indicator of the Sonoran Desert, does well here, too.

The section of the Sonoran Desert that blankets eastern Joshua Tree National Park and the Coachella Valley is also referred to as the Colorado Desert. A subregion of the Sonoran Desert, the Colorado falls south of the Mojave Desert, extending east to the Colorado River, which marks the boundary between California and Arizona. The Colorado Desert covers more than seven million acres, spanning the Coachella Valley and the heavily irrigated agricultural Imperial Valley (location of the Salton Sea) to the south.

Joshua Tree Geology

The strange, jumbled rock formations that make up the labyrinthine Wonderland of Rocks and other striking formations in the northwest of Joshua Tree National Park are captivating. The cracked granite is strangely contorted: giant piles of melted rock are somehow thrown together in otherworldly piles. They rise up in seemingly random clusters, massive sculptures with rocks that resemble skulls or hollowed-out space stations.

The forces that sculpted the monzogranite boulders, peaks, and domes date back two billion years, about half the present age of Earth. Eroded sediment washed off of ancient continents into the ocean, forming thick layers that fused into sedimentary rock. Around one billion years ago, fragments of ancient continents collided to form a massive supercontinent, Rodinia. As mountain chains rose from the collision, some of the offshore sedimentary rock was buckled by heat and pressure, causing it to metamorphose into granitic gneiss. Joshua Tree has gneiss similar to types found in Australia and Antarctica, suggesting that a mountain chain once connected the three continents. When Rodinia broke apart, the North American continent drifted toward the equator. Likely part of a continental shelf, Joshua Tree lay underwater for 250 million years.

Another supercontinent formation (Pangaea) and breakup 210 million years ago finally forced Joshua Tree above water as North America drifted west and collided with the massive Pacific tectonic plate. The shifting plates caused an intense friction, and rising

Previous: the snow-capped San Jacintos

magma bubbled up, reaching the gneiss layer (Pinto gneiss) before cooling into granite.

The rock formations you see in the park are this bubbling magma turned into granite after millions of years of erosion of the overlying rock—sediment, volcanic ash, and metamorphic rock. Their cracked and sculpted shapes are the result of upheaval as rocks were squeezed to the surface and expanded as top layers eroded. When Joshua Tree was much wetter, trickling groundwater also eroded the granite along the crisscrossed fissures that had been formed during the tectonic plate shifts. As the climate in Southern California became drier, this type of erosion slowed, and surface erosion increased, revealing the surreal formations we see today.

San Andreas Fault and Transverse Mountain Ranges

The famous San Andreas fault extends 800 miles from the Salton Sea (south of Palm Springs in Imperial County) to Cape Mendocino in Northern California's Humboldt County. The fault marks the zone where two massive tectonic plates—the North American Plate and the Pacific Plate—come into contact. These plates, mostly rigid slabs of rock that make up the earth's mantle, are generally stable, but when they shift, they cause earthquakes. (The North American Plate is slowly drifting south, and the Pacific Plate is creeping north). The most famous shift was the 1906 San Francisco earthquake.

The San Andreas fault is also responsible for the unique transverse mountain system that dominates the Joshua Tree and Coachella Valley regions. The east-west trending mountain ranges are a geologic anomaly in North America, where most ranges are oriented north-south. This is because the San Andreas fault is not completely straight; north of the Coachella Valley (near the coastal town of Santa Barbara), the fault line makes a clear-cut east-west bend. This bend concentrated geologic pressure and forced up the transverse ranges in Southern California. These east-west trending ranges form the boundaries of the Coachella Valley—the San Jacinto Mountains and Santa Rosa Mountains on the west and Little San Bernardino Mountains to the north. In Joshua Tree National Park, the transverse formations are reflected in the Little San Bernardino Mountains that run along the park's southern border as well as the remote Eagle Mountains in the eastern wilderness of the park.

The San Andreas fault is also responsible

Sonoran Desert landscape

for some of the natural beauty of Coachella Valley as well as its profusion of natural hot springs. The fault runs 10 miles deep, connecting the surface with geothermal activity and underground water. You can see the fault as a dark green line of native California fan palm trees running along the foot of the Little San Bernardino Mountains. At times, these fan palms are clustered around surface pools and oases, such as the shaded pools in the Thousand Palms Oasis of the Coachella Valley Preserve.

Hot springs are largely responsible for making Palm Springs the destination it is. In particular, hot springs abound in Desert Hot Springs, feeding the mineral pools of the area's many resorts. Palm Springs' history as a resort town began around these natural mineral springs that bubbled up to the surface.

CLIMATE

When distinguishing between Joshua Tree National Park (and surrounding towns) and Palm Springs (and the Coachella Valley), locals refer to the "high desert" and the "low desert." These designations actually refer to their respective elevations and the two different desert zones that encompass them. The elevation is the largest factor on the two region's very different climates.

Joshua Tree mostly lies within the Mojave Desert, a transition desert between the hot Sonoran Desert to the south, and the cold Great Basin Desert to the north. The Joshua Tree section of the Mojave has elevations generally between 3,000 and 5,000 feet. The highest point in Joshua Tree National Park is Quail Mountain at 5,816 feet. At these elevation levels, the Mojave is considered a high desert, cooler than the neighboring low desert. Joshua Tree's climate is characterized by wild temperature swings, and the region experiences cold winters and blazing hot summers. Rainfall in the area is generally only about 3-5 inches per year, but Joshua Tree can receive late summer storms that produce flash floods. Occasionally, Joshua Tree receives a very light blanketing of snow in winter.

Below 3,000 feet, the Sonoran Desert encompasses the eastern part of the park as well as the Coachella Valley and Palm Springs to the south. With its lower elevation, it is significantly hotter than the Mojave (depending on where you are, this can be up to 10-15 degrees hotter). Palm Springs is only 479 feet above sea level. This low elevation means that temperatures are fairly mild in the winter. Summers, however, can be brutally hot, with temperatures holding fast in the triple digits for much of June, July, August, and September. October through April are the most temperate months, with temperatures ranging from the high 60s to the low 90s during the day.

In the desert, there is also the wind to contend with; the San Gorgonio Pass on the northern end of the valley is one of the windiest places on Earth. (The vast wind farms there give testament to this claim.) Temperatures in the Coachella Valley drop at night due to the dry air and lack of cloud cover, which allows temperatures to plummet with the sunset. However, plummeting from 115 degrees during the day in summer to 90 degrees at night is still pretty warm. In contrast, the towering peaks of the San Jacinto Mountains to the south and San Bernardino Mountains to the west (Sand to Snow National Monument) are often snowcapped through late spring, offering a dazzling contrast to the sometimes hairdryer-like heat below. This snowmelt feeds the streams in the Indian Canyons and percolates into ravines, natural rock tanks, and springs.

ENVIRONMENTAL ISSUES

Air Quality

In 2015, Joshua Tree National Park earned the dubious distinction of being one of four national parks to receive a failing grade on its air quality report card. The ranking, conducted by the National Parks Conservation Association, surveyed 48 national parks. Joshua Tree was the fourth worst, in company with the popular Sequoia and Kings Canyon National Park in the southern Sierra Nevada and iconic Yosemite. Population growth in the Coachella Valley, as well as pollution coming from the Los Angeles Basin, has created reduced air quality, affecting views and quality of life. In addition to being unhealthy, smoggy and hazy air can diminish the park experience. People come for the area's beauty and sweeping views, which can stretch for 200 miles on a clear day. That natural visibility has been seriously impacted with poor air quality that has limited views to about 90 miles on average.

Adding to the problem are dust particulates from the Salton Sea at the southern end of the Coachella Valley. The 350-square-mile Salton Sea is shrinking due to rapid evaporation in the region's high summer temperatures and a decrease in the agricultural runoff that supplied the water. The agricultural water source contains pesticides, which makes the dust blowing in from the Salton Sea even more polluted. Without an environmental intervention, the Salton Sea has the potential to become a huge dust bowl as the playa becomes more and more exposed.

Overuse and Vandalism

Though the desert may seem impervious to visitors, it is a delicate and fragile ecosystem relying on tiny amounts of rainfall to sustain life in extreme conditions. Joshua Tree welcomed nearly 3 million visitors in 2018, a heavy concentration of visitors for the park's size. The park spans just under 800,000 acres (approximately 1,200 square miles), and while it is twice as big as the median size for U.S. national parks, most of its traffic is concentrated in the popular western section. This is partially because this is where the striking rock formations and Joshua trees for which the park is known are concentrated, and partially because the only developed roads run through this section. This is not by accident—most of the remote eastern (Pinto Basin) section of the park is being preserved as wilderness.

At its most benign, the park's heavy visitation numbers can translate into crowded park entrances, a lack of solitude on trails and at picnic areas, and a dearth of camping spots during the busy fall and spring seasons. At its most hostile, a higher incidence of visitors can mean a higher likelihood of vandalism, graffiti, and general abuse of the land and cultural resources. Vandalism and graffiti have become an increasing problem in Joshua Tree and other national parks. We like to think of our national parks as a place to be wild and free, but a lack of oversight in some areas may leave space for vandalism and graffiti. In 2016, the park service had to shut down two sensitive cultural sites, both linked to Joshua Tree's mining history, due to looting and vandalism. Social media can also play a role in the increase in graffiti; people want graffiti to be seen and often post graffiti pics on Instagram and other online venues. On the flip side, posting vandalism and graffiti on social media sometimes offers a way to identify the location and/or report it. The NPS asks visitors to report any vandalism and graffiti by emailing jotr_graffiti@nps.gov with a detailed description. Photos and GPS coordinates are also helpful to clear up the issue.

Water and Drought

The Coachella Valley is one of the fastest-growing regions in the state of California, and it is also one of the driest places in North America, receiving only 3-4 inches of rain annually. This tension surrounding competition for resources is growing in a region that is known for luxury resorts, golf courses, and swimming pools. In 2015, the state ordered the region to cut water use by 36 percent, and resort cities like Palm Springs and Rancho Mirage have adopted strict conservation measures. For now, the region continues to take full advantage of its water rights, receiving billions of gallons annually from the Colorado River and other sources to replenish its underwater aquifer and feed the growing number of housing developments as well as the recreation industry. The valley's population continues to grow even as resources shrink into a hotter and drier future, representing the challenges that California faces as a whole.

Fan Palm Oases

As the San Andreas fault runs through the Coachella Valley, native California fan palms cluster around surface pools, forming shaded oases worth seeking out for their natural beauty—and their relief from the desert heat.

- **Lower Palm Canyon:** The world's largest fan palm oasis lies at the bottom of a rocky gorge in Palm Springs' Indian Canyons (page 56).
- **Thousand Palms Oasis Preserve:** Across the preserve, clusters of native California fan palms flash in the glaring sun, protecting hidden pools (page 88).
- **Oasis of Mara:** A short interpretive trail leads from the Oasis Visitors Center to this lush palm grove (page 114).
- **49 Palms Oasis:** Hike to this miragelike fan palm oasis (page 138).
- **Lost Palms Oasis:** From lush Cottonwood Spring, this trail crosses desert ridges to the largest collection of fan palms in the park (page 140).

Palm Canyon fan palms

Plants and Animals

Joshua Tree and the Coachella Valley are home to a wide range of desert plants and animals, including 700 plant species, more than 50 mammal species, and 40 reptile species, a thriving ecosystem existing within the seemingly stark landscape.

MOJAVE DESERT FLORA

Referred to as piñon-juniper woodland or piñon-juniper forest, a mix of low, bushy evergreens occurs at higher desert elevations above 4,000 feet. The woodlands span regions of the Southwest, including northern Arizona and New Mexico, the Canyonlands region of Utah, and the Sierra Nevada. A good place to find this piñon-juniper forest mix in Joshua Tree is along the Pine City Trail in the Queen Valley.

Joshua Trees

The signature plant of the Mojave Desert and Joshua Tree National Park, the spiky Joshua tree (*Yucca brevifolia*) favors the higher elevations. You can find them in large stands on the western side of Joshua Tree National Park. With their sharp demeanor, these specimens resemble cacti but are actually members of the agave family. They were named by Mormon explorers who thought their jaunty shapes resembled the upstretched arms of the prophet Joshua pointing them toward the promised land. Joshua trees can reach more than 40 feet and, although dating is difficult due to their fleshy interior (no tree rings), several hundred years old.

Mojave Yucca

The bayonet-like Mojave yucca (*Yucca schidigera*) thrives at elevations from 1,000 to 4,000 feet and is often found mixed in with Joshua trees in transition zones leading to the higher elevation piñon-juniper forests, creating a desert garden feel. The fibers of the yucca were a staple Native Americans used to weave rope, sandals, baskets, and other items.

SONORAN DESERT FLORA

There are clear contrasts between the Mojave and Sonoran Deserts as vegetation shifts at the lower elevations on the desert valleys and floors.

Smoke Trees

Ephemeral in appearance, smoke trees inhabit low washes, their gray-green leaves puffing from spindly branches. These natives of the eastern Mojave Desert and Colorado subsection of the Sonoran Desert are most prevalent in Joshua Tree National Park. The best place to find them is along the Pinto Basin Road north of Cottonwood Spring.

Mesquite

If you're wandering in the low desert and see a plant that you want to identify, mesquite is a good guess. Mesquite is the most common shrub of the Southwest, not to take away its power. This drought-tolerant plant survives in harsh environs via its long taproot, which it can use to suck water out of a very low water table. It was an integral resource for Native Americans, who ground the mesquite pods and seeds into flours that were turned into cakes. Hard-up settlers ate the beans roasted or boiled.

Ocotillo

The whiplike funnel shapes of the ocotillo dot the low-desert landscape, its spindly branches bare for most of the year but flaming out in red bloom each spring. It favors the Sonoran Desert of southeastern California, extending to Texas and Mexico.

Creosote

The creosote bush can be found in ranges from California to West Texas and Mexico, dominating the Mojave, Sonoran, and Chihuahuan Deserts. The creosote is hardy, surviving in regions with temperatures more than 120 degrees Fahrenheit and surviving through periods of intense drought with waxy leaves that maintain moisture and roots that choke off the water supply of surrounding plants by releasing toxins. The creosote was valued by Native Americans for its medicinal properties; indeed, it emits a medicinal smell when slightly wet. Maybe the strangest thing about the creosote is its propensity for longevity. To reproduce, new plants grow from a single progenitor. The creosote ring dubbed King Clone in the Mojave Desert is thought to be 11,700 years old, making it one of the oldest living organisms on earth.

Cholla

The cholla cactus, also known as the jumping cholla, may look fuzzy and cuddly, but it is known for its spiny stems, which easily detach when brushed, clinging to unsuspecting visitors who have gotten too close. If you see one cholla cactus, you will likely see them all since new plants grow from stems that have fallen from an adult. Their bristly ranks extend across the desert in mini cactus gardens.

WILDFLOWERS

Spring wildflowers begin to color the lower elevations of the Pinto Basin in February, climbing to higher elevations in March and April. Above 5,000 feet, desert regions may see blooms as late as June. The colorful display varies each year depending on winter precipitation and spring temperatures. Optimal conditions include a good soaking of rain and warm spring temperatures.

The staunchly shaped barrel cactus offers beautiful blooms in spring; pink and yellow crowns form at the top of the cactus. Barrel cacti are highly ornamental, cultivated by nurseries for their symmetric and easy-growing properties. But they are also dangerous, easily puncturing skin. The beavertail has broad, flat stems growing in clusters and can be identified by its vivid magenta flowers.

Brittlebush is ubiquitously cheerful across

Contra Costa County Library
El Cerrito
3/7/2024 12:52:46 PM

- Patron Receipt -
- Charges -

ID 21901028513829

Item 31901095402382
Title Moon Joshua Tree & Palm Springs /
Call Number 917.9497 MOON 2019

Due Date: 3/28/2024

Account information, library hours,
and upcoming closures can be found
at https://ccclib.org/contact-us/

the lower elevations. Vibrant yellow flowers bloom on the silvery gray bushes that dot washes and hillsides. The tiny purple flowers of the sand verbena have been known to quilt large areas, favoring dunes, washes, and sandy areas.

MAMMALS

Bighorn Sheep

The most dramatic sight in Joshua Tree may be bighorn sheep. Three herds (about 250 animals total) of bighorns live in the park. The largest herd (about 120 animals) ranges through the remote Eagle Mountains in the southeastern section of the park. The second largest (about 100 animals) lives in the Little San Bernardino Mountains along the park's western boundary. The smallest herd (only about 30 animals) lives in the Wonderland of Rocks. Bighorn sheep prefer steep, rocky terrain in order to elude predators, as they are able to navigate canyons and cliffs, bounding as far as 20 feet from ledge to ledge. Their distinctive concave hoofs have a hard outer shell and a softer interior sole perfect for gripping the steep canyon walls. Scan the hillsides to make a sighting; male sheep in particular have impressive curved horns and can weigh more than 220 pounds.

Mountain Lions

Mountain lions, also known as cougars or pumas, are the second-largest wildcats in the Western Hemisphere (jaguars are the largest). Mountain lions historically ranged across all of the contiguous 48 states but were hunted almost into extinction. Conservation efforts have brought their populations back in the West. Mountain lions are lethal hunters; they often stalk animals before they pounce, which can span more than 30 feet in one leap. Solitary hunters, mountain lions range far over a home territory and generally go out of their way to avoid humans. If you do happen to encounter a mountain lion, maintain eye contact, back away slowly, make yourself appear larger; make loud noises, and speak slowly, firmly, and loudly.

Coyotes

Coyotes roam all across Joshua Tree and are common wildlife sightings. Even if you don't see one, you may hear their howling at night—a diabolical-sounding series of yips and yaps when they are in a pack. Coyotes mainly eat small mammals and rodents, but they are scavengers that have been known to get into trash receptacles looking for food.

Jackrabbits

Another commonly spotted animal in Joshua Tree is the jackrabbit, originally called the "jackass rabbit." It is distinguished by its long ears, which give it exceptional hearing to help protect it from predators.

REPTILES

Joshua Tree abounds with reptiles, which are well suited to the dry climates of the desert.

Desert Tortoise

The largest reptile in the Mojave and Sonoran Deserts is the desert tortoise, which can weigh up to 50 pounds. Desert tortoises were plentiful until the 1950s; since then, populations have drastically declined due to several factors, including development causing habitat loss, and speeding and off-road vehicles. Studies estimate that up until the 1950s, the desert tortoise population maintained at least 200 adults per square mile; these numbers have dropped to only 5-60 adults per square mile. The desert tortoise is on both the California and the federal Endangered Species List. Desert tortoises survive the heat by staying cool in burrows and rehydrating after a rainstorm. If you come across a desert tortoise, do not disturb it—even getting close can stress a tortoise, causing it to void vital water stored in its bladder.

Chuckwalla

The chuckwalla is an iguana distinctive for its potbelly. After the Gila monster, it is the second-largest lizard in North America. The chuckwalla inflates when frightened, puffing up its lungs to three times their normal capacity. Desert Indians hunted them for food, and there is at least one account of a later settler serving up chuckwalla. "Chuckwalla Bill," a would-be miner who lived in a canyon south of Desert Hot Springs in the 1930s, earned his nickname by serving chuckwalla to a priest and trying to pass it off as fish. The priest was not fooled, and the nickname stuck.

INSECTS AND ARACHNIDS

Hairy tarantulas are the largest spiders in the world, and while they may look creepy, the reality is that their venomous bites, which paralyze insects, lizards, and small mammals, are harmless to humans. Also misunderstood is the giant hairy scorpion, with its famous stinger. Although stings are painful, they are generally harmless to humans (approximate to a bee sting). The giant hairy scorpion is the largest in the United States and common in the Joshua Tree region. However, because it is nocturnal, it is rarely seen.

Rattlesnakes

The Mojave and Sonoran Deserts have their share of venomous creatures, although only the rattlesnake poses a real health threat. Of the 11 rattlesnake species in North America, six reside in the region around Joshua Tree National Park, including the Mojave rattlesnake—one of the most toxic of all rattlesnakes. Fortunately, it is highly unlikely you will encounter a rattlesnake as they prefer open rocky habitat with crevices to hide in and plentiful rodents. Still, if you do hear the rattle of a snake, consider it a warning and back away, giving it a wide berth.

BIRDS

Joshua Tree and the Coachella Valley are in the direct path of the Pacific Flyway, a major north-south flight path for migratory birds extending from Alaska to Patagonia in South America. The Salton Sea, at the south end of Coachella Valley, is a notable stop on the migratory path. Joshua Tree National Park and the surrounding desert are also home to many nesting bird species, including the golden eagle. This predatory bird has an eight-foot wingspan, which makes it the largest bird of prey in North America. You may also see the long-legged roadrunner dashing across roads (seriously!) and the desert floor in Joshua Tree National Park and Coachella Valley neighborhoods. What they lack in flying abilities, they make up for with ground speed and maneuverability.

Chuckwalla lizards can inflate to ward off predators.

History

PALM SPRINGS

Agua Caliente Band of Cahuilla Indians

The first inhabitants came to Palm Springs 2,000 years ago, establishing complex communities in the well-watered canyons at the base of the San Jacinto Mountains. These people fished, trapped, and gathered as well as developed agricultural systems by diverting streams to irrigate crops. Named after the natural hot springs in the canyons, the Agua Caliente (hot water) Band of Cahuilla Indians still owns these canyons. You can see evidence of the ancient habitation in Tahquitz Canyon, Chino Canyon, and the Indian Canyons. Indian artifacts, including baskets and pottery, can be viewed at the Palm Springs Art Museum.

In 1876, the federal government deeded land to both the Southern Pacific Railroad and the Cahuilla Indians in a checkerboard of alternating tracts. The Indians' land turned out to be highly valuable real estate. The next year the Southern Pacific Railroad built a line linking Yuma, Arizona, with Los Angeles and running through the Cahuilla reservation.

The Birth of Tourism

The presence of water is what set Palm Springs' course. In the mid-19th century, there was a plan to irrigate the area around Palm Springs to create an agricultural valley, but grander things were in store. A railroad engineer "discovered" mineral springs in 1853, calling them "Agua Caliente." With the railroad in place, tourists began to visit the hot climate for their health, hiking the canyons, and learning about Native culture. The first structures were canvas-and-wood huts clustered together.

In 1884, pioneer settler "Judge" John Guthrie McCallum built the first permanent structure. McCallum had come seeking a climate to aid his young son's tuberculosis. His adobe homestead is still standing, now home to the Palm Springs Historical Society. Right next door is the Cornelia White House, built entirely of railroad ties. The White House was part of the first hotel, the Palm Springs Hotel, built in 1893 by Welwood Murray. He drummed up business by having a local Indian dress in Arabic clothing and ride a camel to the railroad station to greet passengers as they stopped at the railroad watering stop. The timing of the hotel was a rough one, coinciding with a drought that lasted until 1905.

Palm Springs as a destination didn't take off until 1915 when "Mother" Nellie Coffman built the Desert Inn across the street. Stars of the silent screen, including Fatty Arbuckle and Rudolph Valentino, spent winter months at her hotel for their health, triggering Palm Springs as a destination for desert and Wild West-themed movies.

Another game changer, the Oasis Hotel, was built in 1928 and had the first swimming pool in Palm Springs. The building of the luxurious, Spanish-Moorish-style El Mirador, as well as the opening of the ranch-style accommodations at Smoke Tree Ranch, ushered in the Palm Springs era as a glitterati destination, hosting stars like Marlene Dietrich, Clark Gable, Bette Davis, and Errol Flynn, and Hollywood moguls such as Samuel Goldwyn and Walt Disney.

Palm Springs' Heyday

Following World War II, tastes moved from the traditional adobe and stucco construction into a more futuristic style. Palm Springs has an astonishing concentration of first tier modernist architecture, one of the highest concentrations in the world. The sleek lines and use of glass, concrete, and metal distinguish hotels, public buildings, and private homes throughout the chic resort town. Beginning in the 1930s, Hollywood began decamping to the desert; the 1950s and 1960s were the zenith of the legendary Hollywood party scene as well as architectural style.

Noted architects Albert Frey, E. Stewart Williams, William Cody, Donald Wexler, John Lautner, Richard Neutra, John Porter Clark, and others literally shaped the town, commissioned to build celebrity homes, businesses, civic buildings, and stylish and affordable tract homes.

Many of these houses were second homes, thus architects did not have to adhere so much to the daily functionality required of a main residence. The architectural lines, like the lifestyle out in Los Angeles' desert backyard, were freer. The optimism of the 1950s also inspired creative risk-taking, and architectural designers began playing with the modern form. Modernism was an international trend, but it was a brilliant match with the austere landscape and sun-soaked climate of the California desert. Architects were able to erase barriers between indoors and outdoors, opting for open spaces that integrated with the landscape. Palm Springs' magnificent scenery, such as the striking escarpment of the San Jacinto Mountains, inspired clean lines and low designs that deferred to the views, creating a harmony of nature and culture.

Soon iconic celebrities like Frank Sinatra, Marilyn Monroe, Sammy Davis Jr., Bing Crosby, and Bob Hope were regulars in Palm Springs. Frank Sinatra and Bob Hope even built houses here.

The 1970s and 1980s were a low point for Palm Springs, as modernist designs (and as a result, the town) fell out of fashion, and celebrities and vacationers gravitated toward luxurious resorts in Rancho Mirage and farther south. Palm Springs limped along as a seedy spring break destination, much of its downtown shuttered. As a resort town, Palm Springs stagnated, and developers did not care enough to even raze and rebuild it to conform with newer ideas of luxury (ahem, Las Vegas). It was this apathy that saved Palm Springs. When members of the fashion world started to buy properties in the late 1990s, it turned out that the town was a trove of architectural treasure waiting to be rediscovered and rehabbed.

JOSHUA TREE

Ancient Culture

The first known culture to inhabit Joshua Tree was the Pinto culture, dating as far back as 8,000 years. The Pinto occupied today's Pinto Basin, the stark rolling landscape in the southern part of the park. At the end of the Ice Age, roughly 10,000 years ago, California's deserts had been lush and filled with rivers, lakes, and large mammals such as mastodons, camels, and mammoths wandering the grassy landscape. A river flowed through Pinto Basin, but by the time the Pinto culture arrived, many of the Ice Age mammals had gone extinct and the river was dry. Still, the Pinto culture persisted for as long as 4,000 years. Though very little is known about them, what we do understand is based on archaeological finds from the 1930s, which include stone tools and spear points. These artifacts suggest that the Pinto culture was mobile, mostly dependent on large game for survival.

Serrano and Cahuilla Indians

The Serrano and Cahuilla Indians moved into the region several thousand years after the Pinto culture had left. They used the park seasonally, moving to where food sources were plentiful. The largest village was at the Oasis of Mara (near the Oasis Visitors Center), the winter home of the Serrano Indians. In summer, the Serrano moved west to the pine forests of the San Bernardino Mountains. The Cahuilla Indians occupied the southern reaches of the park (their northernmost boundary) and regions farther south into Palm Springs and the Indian Canyons.

The harsh landscape and climate dictated the daily activities of the desert Indians. They were primarily hunters and gatherers living in seasonal small villages of 25-100 individuals. The most important food sources were pine nuts, acorns, and mesquite beans as well as small animals like jackrabbits and rodents. Villages consisted of communal structures for storage, a sweat house, and a ceremonial room; family houses were circular thatched huts made of palm fronds. Serrano and Cahuilla women were expert weavers, crafting baskets, netting, rope hats, sandals, and other items from palm trees and yuccas. Pottery made by desert Indians included earthenware vessels called ollas for food and water storage.

The Mission Era

The 1771 construction of the Spanish Mission San Gabriel Archangel in present-day Los Angeles marked the start of a land and power shift away from the native tribes in the California desert to European control, although it would be another 100 years before the full impact was felt. The mission was just one of the 21 that Spanish officials had ordered to be constructed along the California coast. The Spanish largely avoided the deserts, seeing them as remote and dangerous. With the dominance of Spanish missions on the coast, Native Americans fled inland, sharing the land with groups who were already living in the Joshua Tree region. The Spanish built a second chain of missions inland. The closest to Joshua Tree National Park was erected in 1819 in Redlands, less than 40 miles away, impacting Serrano and Cahuilla Indians within its reach. More far-flung villages like the one at Oasis of Mara evaded the mission's control.

Miners, Ranchers, and Homesteaders

The year 1848 was eventful for California. It became a U.S. state, handed over from Mexico, and the gold rush had started in Northern California. As goldfields tapped out, prospectors chased the precious metal farther afield into California's deserts, which until this point had been mostly untouched. Gold was discovered near the Oasis of Mara in 1863. This discovery plus a smallpox epidemic that swept east from Los Angeles, decimating whole villages of the Indian population, marked the breakdown of traditional Indian life, including political and social structure, and shifted the culture of the desert. Indians at the Oasis of Mara hung on for several decades, sharing their precious water resources with the Chemehuevi who had been driven from their traditional lands to the east as well as gold prospectors, all the while locked in a land dispute with the Southern Pacific Railroad. By 1912 the last holdouts were gone, and there were no Indians remaining at the oasis.

Prospectors had been poking around Joshua Tree for decades, but 1883 marked the defining moment for mining when one discovered rich deposits in the Pinto Mountains east of the Oasis of Mara. Prospectors flocked to the boomtown named Dale that at its peak claimed over 1,000 citizens. Over time, the town moved, following the gold. Other mines sprang up. Today the region, called the Old Dale Mining District, is located just north of the Joshua Tree National Park boundary. It is littered with old mining camps and crisscrossed by a series of rugged roads.

It may be easy to think of Joshua Tree National Park as a pristine land, preserved in its natural state, but the reality is that ranching, mining, and homesteading were deeply entrenched in the region in the 1900s. The area was a stretch used for ranching; the sparse landscape required 17 acres per animal for grazing. The presence of concrete dams at places like Barker Dam and Twin Tanks are reminders of Joshua Tree's halcyon ranching days.

The most notable settler was resourceful homesteader, rancher, and miner Bill Keys who arrived in 1910 and thrived for decades on his property within the Joshua Tree National Park boundary. He got his start as supervisor of the Desert Queen Mine. When the mining company he worked for went bankrupt, Keys gladly accepted their offer of a deed to the mine. From there he settled a 160-acre homestead and built a ranch. On a trip to Los Angeles he met his future wife, and they raised a family on the ranch. Keys was a legendary scavenger, collecting machinery and spare parts from abandoned mines and other desert sites. His resourcefulness served him well in this hardscrabble desert environment. The couple lived at the ranch until well into the 1960s, when Joshua Tree had already become a national monument. It is possible to tour the still-standing Desert Queen Ranch via tours offered by the park service.

Joshua Tree National Monument

The 1930s brought the seemingly conflicting goals of settlement and preservation to Joshua Tree. In many of the Western states, including Arizona, California, Nevada, New Mexico, and Utah, the federal government was promoting development of "useless" lands unsuitable for ranching or farming; the 1938 Small Tract Act offered dirt-cheap land to individuals for settlement. To earn a right to purchase at the government's rates, applicants had to build a simple dwelling within three years. This homestead act tapped into a deep American desire to claim a piece of territory, even if the land was deemed unprofitable. Some of these "jackrabbit homesteads" are evident north of the park, particularly in the area of Wonder Valley, east of Twentynine Palms. In this scrubby desert, the tiny shacks stand in various degrees of preservation and decay, some housing a burgeoning artist community. The homestead program was not disbanded until 1976.

While the federal government was encouraging settlement, activists were calling for the preservation of Joshua Tree's unique geography. Beginning in the 1920s, Minerva Hoyt, a rich Pasadena widow, led the conservation effort to protect Joshua Tree. Following the untimely death of her husband and infant son, she made frequent trips to the California desert, taking solace there. While Joshua Tree had caught on as a tourist destination, the prevailing mentality was that the desert was indestructible. Landscapers catering to a desert garden craze in Los Angeles looted the area, uprooting plants by the acre and doing lasting damage to the ecosystem. Travelers setting up camp routinely set fire to Joshua trees at night to guide motorists coming in after dark. Hoyt, an active gardener, designed desert conservation exhibits that were showcased in New York and London to address the ecological damage she had witnessed on her trips. This got her elected as president of the newly created Desert Conservation League through which she campaigned for protected lands to encompass the Southern California deserts. In 1936 President Roosevelt signed a proclamation that established Joshua Tree National Monument. It spanned privately owned land, including massive swatches owned by the Southern Pacific Railroad and more than 8,000 existing mining claims, some operating and profitable, within its boundaries.

Joshua Tree National Park

Over the next decades, the park service negotiated and maneuvered, obtaining deeds and purchasing real estate. In 1964, Congress authorized the Wilderness Act, protecting federally managed lands from mechanized vehicles and equipment. In 1994, President Bill Clinton signed the Desert Protection Act, upgrading Joshua Tree to national park status and transferring three million acres for protection in Joshua Tree, Death Valley National Park, and the Mojave National Preserve. Joshua Tree National Park is wildly popular and receives more than one million visitors a year.

Local Culture

PALM SPRINGS AND THE COACHELLA VALLEY

Palm Springs began its current incarnation as a seasonal resort town in the 1920s. The 1930s to the 1970s mark the halcyon years for Palm Springs as Hollywood celebrities and others flocked to the stylish resorts springing up. In the 1970s, the city of Palm Springs began its fall from favor as visitors gravitated to increasingly grandiose resorts in Rancho Mirage and farther south in the Coachella Valley. As Palm Springs languished, the Coachella Valley became known as a golfing and retirement destination. Palm Springs itself veered into a seedy spring break destination and many of its downtown businesses were boarded shut. In the 1990s, some of the fashionable set began buying up the area's mid-century architectural gems, breathing new life into Palm Springs as a resort destination.

Today, the town of Palm Springs is a connected community of entrepreneurs with a forward-looking vision and passionate interest in the town's history. Palm Springs has a vested interest in preserving its mid-century architectural heritage while refreshing its hotels and businesses to be current and chic. New retail shops and restaurants continue to pop up in the town's stylish Uptown Design District. It's hard to keep up with the burgeoning business scene. Old hotels and residences are continually being shined and styled. Once a seasonal destination, the town is on the upswing as a year-round resort destination that attracts a wide variety of visitors. You may still see caftan-wearing golden-agers dining on shrimp cocktail and martinis or golfers whiling away the mornings on the greens, but there's also been an infusion of newer generations visiting Palm Springs. Hip hotels like the ARRIVE hotel draw a stylish millennial set (as well as the young at heart) to deejay and craft cocktail-fueled pool parties. Palm Springs is again a celebrity destination, with the Hollywood set buying homes (Leonardo DiCaprio purchased entertainer Dinah Shore's old mansion) or hiding out at desert retreats like the Korakia Pensione.

The gay community is hugely represented in Palm Springs' year-round residents, with many gay-owned hotels and retail shops. Palm Springs is also an international LGBT destination. Visitors come here for resorts that cater specifically to men or women, as well as destination parties like the all-male White Party and the all-female The Dinah, the largest gay and lesbian music festival parties in the world.

Native American groups in Palm Springs and the Coachella Valley have the corner on some of the region's stunning natural beauty as well as resort casinos. The Agua Caliente Band of Cahuilla Indians owns their land and allows visitors access (for a fee) to the gorgeous palm-tree and stream-filled Indian Canyons, as well as Tahquitz Canyon's creek and waterfall. The tribe also owns and manages several casinos in the Coachella Valley. The Morongo Band of Cahuilla Mission Indians operates a casino at the foot of the San Gorgonio and San Jacinto Mountains west of Palm Springs.

JOSHUA TREE AND THE HI-DESERT

Like many desert regions, the land around Joshua Tree National Park has grappled with competing visions for its use. In the 1930s when the park was made a national monument, the monument status blanketed a patchwork of homesteads and mining claims. It took the better part of the 20th century to fold these tracts into what was eventually Joshua Tree National Park. If you look at a map even now, you will see the strategically excluded district east of Twentynine Palms where the Dale Mining District once thrived.

Native American groups were not considered in the national monument status effort, having been driven out of the region in the early part of the 20th century amid pressure from the Southern Pacific Railroad and other hardships.

The region's identity as an outdoors destination was emphasized in 2016 by conservation efforts resulting in three newly established national monuments to protect desert lands. The 154,000-acre Sand to Snow National Monument (www.fs.fed.us) links Joshua Tree National Park to the east and the Santa Rosa and San Jacinto Mountain National Monument to the south with several preserves by folding in previously unprotected land.

The gateway towns of Yucca Valley, Joshua Tree, and Twentynine Palms draw a wide cast of characters, each town with its own distinct vibe. Joshua Tree is funky, artsy, and outdoorsy, luring park visitors, locals, and seasonal rock climbers. It's a tiny town with a saloon, outdoor outfitters, and a few small hotels to anchor its small main street. It functions as the main gateway to Joshua Tree National Park (the popular West Entrance is accessed via Joshua Tree) but feels like an authentic town instead of a tourist trap. Yucca Valley is more suburban, home to big-box stores and chain restaurants. It does not have a direct entrance to the park, but it does give access to the Black Rock Canyon Campground as well as the Covington Flats area of the park, making it a strange mix of suburban and natural beauty. Yucca Valley also supports a burgeoning boutique and vintage shopping market. For a visitor to the area, Yucca Valley is not without its charms. Twentynine Palms operates as the eastern gateway to the park with its Oasis Visitors Center and North Entrance. There are a few excellent hotels, but the town is not the gateway tourist destination that Joshua Tree, or even Yucca Valley, is. The town of Twentynine Palms is home to a Marine base, which forms the backbone of the community here.

The region around Joshua Tree National Park has long been a haven for musicians and artists. Musicians from Los Angeles and other locations come out here to record albums, shoot music videos, and soak up the silence and stunning landscape. The music scene is alive and well with small music festivals drawing some big names throughout the year. Many visual artists are also based here, showcasing their work in galleries across the Morongo Basin and in yearly open studio art tours every October.

The communities in the region of Joshua Tree are slowly growing as escapees from urban centers like Los Angeles find their way here. There is even a growing homestead movement in which people are attempting to rehab old homesteads, sometimes even creating permaculture systems.

Essentials

Transportation

GETTING THERE

Air

The **Palm Springs International Airport** (PSP, 3400 E. Tahquitz Canyon Way, Palm Springs, 760/318-3800, www.palmspringsca.gov) is in metro Palm Springs less than three miles from downtown. The airport provides service via 10 major airline carriers. It is also convenient to the Joshua Tree area, 40 miles (less than a one-hour drive) from Palm Springs. Several Palm Springs hotels offer airport shuttle service. The

Previous: San Gorgonio wind farm.

major car rental carriers are located here, including Enterprise, Hertz, Dollar, and Alamo.

Ontario International Airport (ONT, 2500 Terminal Way, Ontario, 909/937-2700, www.flyontario.com) is another good option. It is located off I-10 in the city of Ontario, about 90 miles southwest (a 1.75-hour drive) from Joshua Tree and 70 miles west of Palm Springs (a one-hour drive via I-10). Ontario Airport has all the major rental car companies on-site.

The two closest major cities to Palm Springs are Los Angeles to the west and San Diego to the southwest. Both airports provide options, though a car rental will be required to reach the Palm Springs area.

Los Angeles International Airport (LAX, 1 World Way, Los Angeles, 424/646-5252, www.flylax.com) is a major international airport with many carriers and flight options, as well as car rentals. Airport shuttles, hotel shuttles, long-distance vans, ride-share vans, and taxis can all be accessed at the lower Arrivals Level outside of the baggage claim area; median waiting platforms are marked by overhead signs. A **FlyAway Bus** service (no reservations, 24 hours daily) offers the best public transportation from LAX to destinations around the city, including Union Station (downtown), Van Nuys, Westwood, Santa Monica, and Hollywood. The drive from LAX to Palm Springs takes 2-4 hours, as traffic congestion can increase travel time significantly.

The **San Diego International Airport** (SAN, 3225 N. Harbor Dr., San Diego, 619/400-2404, www.san.org) is the farthest option, located 140 miles (about a 2.5-hour drive) southwest in the city of San Diego. Major airline carriers include Southwest, American, United, Alaska, and Delta, and there is a consolidated rental car center on-site.

Car

A car is necessary to visit Joshua Tree National Park and any towns in the Coachella or Yucca Valleys. Within the town of Palm Springs, it is easy to get around without a car, ride shares are prevalent, and there is a free shuttle bus connecting the main metro area.

FROM LOS ANGELES

If you're lucky and time your trip outside of rush hour, the drive from Los Angeles can take less than two hours via I-10. (Getting out of LA can be a slog, though, so you may need to factor in extra time, up to 2-3 hours more during rush hour or on Friday afternoons.) From Los Angeles, take I-10 east for approximately 100 miles to the town of Palm Springs. From I-10 take Highway 111 south toward Palm Springs. Highway 111B continues south to reach the Palm Springs city limit in just over 10 miles, turning into North Palm Canyon Drive, the main road through Palm Springs.

The I-210 and Highway 60 freeways can sometimes provide good eastbound alternatives if I-10 is jammed. Both I-210 and Highway 60 join up with I-10 west of Palm Springs.

To reach the West Entrance to Joshua Tree National Park, take Exit 117 north from I-10 for 56 miles. In the town of Joshua Tree, follow Highway 62 southeast into the park.

FROM SAN DIEGO

From San Diego, take I-15 north for about 50 miles. When I-15 splits off with I-215, follow I-215N and signs for Riverside/San Bernardino. Continue north on I-215N for 30 miles until it intersects with Highway 60. Take the exit for Highway 60, heading east for 18 miles. Merge onto I-10 E and continue east for another 18 miles until reaching the Highway 111 exit toward Palm Springs. Highway 111B continues south to reach the Palm Springs city limit in just over 10 miles, turning into North Palm Canyon Drive, the main road through Palm Springs.

Previous: San Gorgonio wind farm.

To reach the West Entrance to Joshua Tree National Park, take Exit 117 north from I-10 for 56 miles. In the town of Joshua Tree, follow Highway 62 southeast into the park

CAR RENTAL

Car rentals are available from all area airports. Approximately 40 car rental companies operate at Los Angeles International Airport; all vehicle rental companies are located off-site. Several companies offer courtesy shuttles that pick up customers at the lower Arrivals Level of all terminals.

To reach other car rental agencies, take the LAX Bus C to reach the **Off-Airport Rental Car Terminal** to meet the rental car courtesy shuttle. Many of these rental car companies provide phone links inside or near the baggage claim areas on the lower Arrivals Level of the terminals so travelers can request a free shuttle pickup to reach the rental car sites. Check with your car rental agency when making a reservation to make sure you know how to get there.

In addition to Palm Springs and LAX, **Enterprise Rent-A-Car** (57250 29 Palms Hwy., 760/369-0515, www.enterprise.com, 8am-noon and 1pm-6pm Mon.-Fri., 9am-noon Sat.) is located in the gateway town of Yucca Valley.

RV RENTAL

A few RV and camper van rental agencies have offices in Los Angeles convenient to LAX, including **Cruise America** (Carson or Downey locations, 800/671-8042, www.cruiseamerica.com). Camper van rentals are available through **Escape Campervans** (4858 W. Century Blvd., Inglewood, 877/270-8267 or 310/672-9909, www.escapecampervans.com), **Lost Campers** (8820 Aviation Blvd., Inglewood, 415/386-2693 or 888/567-8826, www.lostcampersusa.com), and **Jucy Rentals** (15318 Hawthorne Blvd., Lawndale, 800/650-4180, www.jucyrentals.com).

Train and Bus

For point to point travel, **FlixBus** (www.flixbus.com) is the best new option for public transportation between Los Angeles and Palm Springs. The company was founded as a German start-up in 2013 and has recently begun offering routes in the United States. It relies on technology and regional partners to offer direct routes between popular destinations. FlixBus offers three routes a day between downtown Los Angeles (Union Station or UCLA) and downtown Palm Springs ($10-$20 each way), with daytime and evening booking times that make sense for hotel check-in. Book tickets online or via an app. There is no station; pickup is curbside.

It's possible to take **Amtrak** (800/872-7245, www.amtrak.com) from Los Angeles to Palm Springs to arrive at one of three stations in Palm Springs: North Palm Springs Train Station (PSN), Airport Bus Station (PSP), and Downtown Palm Springs Bus Station (PSS).

The Amtrak routes have travel times ranging between 2.5 and 3.5 hours; however, their timing makes them not a viable option for most travelers. The Texas Eagle departs downtown LA's **Union Station** (800 N. Alameda St.) on Fridays and Saturdays at 10pm to arrive in Palm Springs **Airport Bus Station** (PSP, 3400 E. Tahquitz Canyon Way) or **Downtown Bus Station** at the Palm Springs Spa Resort Casino (PSS, 190 N. Indian Canyon Dr.) at 12:36 am. Returns (Palm Springs to LA) via the Sunset Limited are Monday, Wednesday, Friday, leaving Palm Springs at 2:02am to arrive in downtown Los Angeles at 5:35am.

GETTING AROUND

Palm Springs is immensely walkable; however, there is a free and convenient shuttle for getting around. The **Buzz Bus** (www.sunline.org/buzzisback, noon-10pm Thurs.-Sun.) runs every 20 minutes with stops along Palm Canyon Drive and Indian Canyon Drive.

In and around Joshua Tree National Park, the towns of Yucca Valley, Joshua Tree, and Twentynine Palms are all accessed from Highway 62. Public transit in this area is limited. Travel in this region requires that you have your own vehicle; however, a pilot shuttle, the Roadrunner (www.nps.gov, daily 8am-5pm), began in 2018, offering transportation within Joshua Tree National Park. It leaves from the north park entrance in Twentynine Palms and travels along Park Boulevard with stops at the main sights, hikes and campgrounds.

Travel Hub: Los Angeles

Los Angeles has a lot to offer as a gateway hub to Palm Springs and Joshua Tree, including a thriving downtown, beaches, a wealth of foodie neighborhoods, shopping, and cultural sightseeing. However, LA's reputation as a difficult driving destination precedes it. The number of freeways crossing the city, a rush hour that never ends, and the sheer sprawl of the metro region mean that it's best to come to Los Angeles with a plan. If you only have a day or two, set up your base camp in one of three major areas.

The official visitor website for **Los Angeles** (www.discoverlosangeles.com) is an excellent resource.

DOWNTOWN LOS ANGELES

Los Angeles' newly restored historic downtown has turned it into a vibrant destination for food, culture, and events. Located on the northeast side of Los Angeles, downtown is an excellent jumping-off point for exploring and continuing east to Palm Springs and Joshua Tree.

Sights and Activities

Los Angeles has a wealth of outstanding architecture. Downtown is home to notable landmarks such as the **Walt Disney Concert Hall** (111 S. Grand Ave.) designed by Frank Gehry. This distinct building, home to the Los Angeles Philharmonic, draws focus with the striking stainless steel curves of its exterior. The **Bradbury Building** (304 S. Broadway) is an architectural landmark built in 1893, commissioned by gold mining millionaire Lewis L. Bradbury. The Broadway Theater District stretches for six blocks from 3rd Street to 9th Street along South Broadway and includes 12 movie theaters built between 1910 and 1931, many of them in the process of being restored. Walking tours are available through the **Los Angeles Conservancy** (www.laconservancy.org).

A Mexican marketplace that is part of the El Pueblo de Los Angeles Historic Monument, **Olvera Street** (www.olvera-street.com, hours vary) features historic structures, restaurants, and shopping along the oldest street in Los Angeles. The Museum of Contemporary Art (MOCA) has three distinct locations in the Greater Los Angeles area. **MOCA Grand** (250 S. Grand Ave., 213/626-6222, 11am-6pm Mon., Wed., and Fri., 11am-8pm Thurs., 11am-5pm Sat.-Sun., $15, students $8, and seniors $10, children under 12 free) is the main branch in downtown Los Angeles on Grand Avenue near the Walt Disney Concert Hall. It features a prominent collection of post-1940s works.

The **Broad Museum** (221 S. Grand Ave., 213/232-6200, www.thebroad.org, 11am-5pm Tues.-Wed., 11am-8pm Thurs.-Fri., 10am-8pm Sat., 10am-6pm Sun., free) was financed by philanthropists Eli and Edyth Broad to house their prominent and world-renowned collection of postwar and contemporary art in a newly designed, stunning $140 million building.

Griffith Park spans 4,310 acres of surprisingly rugged landscape in the hills of northeast Los Angeles, nine miles north of downtown. Its 53 miles of trails are popular as well as its acres of picnic and recreation areas. Hiking trail maps are available from the **Griffith Park Ranger Station** (4730 Crystal Springs Dr.) as well as online (www.

modernhiker.com). Griffith Park also features the **Los Angeles Zoo and Botanical Gardens** (5333 Zoo Dr., 323/644-4200, www.lazoo.org, 10am-5pm daily, $21 adults, $16 children 2-15, children under 2 free), a 133-acre zoo that's home to 1,100 animals and a botanical collection that features more than 800 different plant species. The **Griffith Observatory** (2800 E. Observatory Rd., 213/473-0800, www.griffithobservatory.org, noon-10pm Tues.-Fri., 10am-10pm Sat.-Sun.) is an art deco landmark with a planetarium and grounds that feature stunning views of the city. The instantly recognizable Hollywood Sign became part of Griffith Park to protect the area from development. Hikes lead to the views of the city from above the sign.

The **Autry Museum of the American West** (4700 Western Heritage Way, www.theautry.org, 323/667-2000, 10am-4pm Tues.-Fri., 10am-5pm Sat.-Sun., adults $14, students and seniors $10, children 3-12 $6, children under 3 free) features exhibits that tell the stories of the peoples and cultures of the American West. **Travel Town Museum** (5200 Zoo Dr., 323/662-5874, www.traveltown.org, 10am-4pm Mon.-Fri., 10am-5pm Sat.-Sun., free) highlights railroad history in the western United States from 1880s to the 1930s. A miniature train once owned by Gene Autry takes passengers on a loop around the museum grounds.

The only horse ranch in Los Angeles, **Sunset Ranch Hollywood** (3400 N. Beachwood Dr., 323/469-5450, www.sunsetranchhollywood.com, day tours 9am-3pm daily, evening tours 4pm, 4:30pm, 5pm Sun.-Fri. and 7pm Friday, $50-145) offers a unique Griffith Park outing in the form of one- and two-hour trail rides featuring spectacular views of the Hollywood Sign, Griffith Observatory, and downtown Los Angeles.

Food

A landmark food and retail emporium established in 1917, **Grand Central Market** (317 S. Broadway, 213/624-2378, www.grandcentralmarket.com, 8am-10pm daily) is an incredible mix of old classics and exciting new chef-driven fare, with casual counter seating, on-site dining, take-out, and market groceries. Eateries include the rustic Italian menu at **Knead & Co Pasta Bar & Marketplace** (213/223-7592, 11am-3pm Sun.-Wed., 11am-9pm Thurs.-Sat.), the traditional Jewish **Wexler's Deli** (213/620-0633, www.wexlersdeli.com, 8am-4pm Mon.-Fri., 8am-6pm Sat.-Sun.), breakfast-centric **Eggslut** (www.eggslut.com, 8am-4pm daily), and seasonal Thai street fare at **Sticky Rice II** (213/621-2865, 11am-10pm daily). Several stalls pour a range of craft beers and fine wines in addition to tasty eats: **Olio GCM Wood Fired Pizzeria** (www.oliowfp.com, 9am-6pm Mon.-Wed., 9am-9pm Thurs.-Sat., 9am-4pm Sun.), Texas-inspired **Horse Thief BBQ** (213/625-0341, 11am-10pm daily), **Oyster Gourmet** (theoystergourmet.com, 11:30am-6pm Mon.-Wed., 11:30am-7:30pm Thurs., 11:30am-10pm Fri.-Sat., 11:30am-8pm Sun.) and local favorite **Golden Road Brewing Company** (http://goldenroad.la, 8am-10pm daily).

Phillipe the Original (1001 N. Alameda St., 213/628-3781, www.philippes.com, 6am-10pm daily, $7-9) serves up signature French dips and deli sides in this historic space (established in 1908) with sawdust-covered floors and communal tables. An old-school diner that has been operating since 1924, **The Original Pantry** (877 S. Figueroa St., 213/972-9279, www.pantrycafe.com, 24 hours daily, breakfast $6-17, lunch and dinner $12-30, cash only) serves American classics and all-day breakfast.

Marble floors and high ceilings are the backdrop for the bustling **Bottega Louie** restaurant (700 S. Grand Ave., 213/802-1470, www.bottegalouie.com, 8am-10pm Mon.-Thurs., 8am-11pm Fri., 9am-11pm Sat., 9am-10pm Sun., 9am-3pm weekend brunch $16-30), serving up pizzas, pastas, and small plates as well as weekend brunch and a café and patisserie (7am-10pm Mon.-Thurs., 7am-11pm Fri., 8am-11pm Sat., 8am-10pm Sun.).

A destination restaurant that feels like your favorite neighborhood hang, **Baco Mercat** (408 S. Main St., 213/687-8808, www.bacomercat.com, 11:30am-2:30pm and 5:30pm-11pm Mon.-Thurs., 11:30am-3pm and 5:30pm-midnight Fri.-Sat., 11:30am-3pm and 5pm-10pm Sun., $14-30) pulls in Western and Eastern influences for its tasty dishes, including the signature bäco flatbread sandwich.

Yxta Cocina Mexicana (601 S. Central Ave., 213/596-5579, www.cocinasycalaveras.com, 11:30am-9pm Mon.-Tues., 11:30am-10pm Wed.-Fri., 4pm-10pm Sat., $12-20) serves updated Mexican classics in a vibrant, airy space plus delivers a great daily happy hour.

Local favorite **Guisados** (541 S. Spring St. #101, 213/627-7656, www.guisados.co, 9am-11pm Mon.-Thurs., 9am-1:30am Fri.-Sat., 9am-9pm Sun., $3) has a number of locations on the east side of LA, including downtown, serving up homestyle braised tacos on handmade tortillas with meat and veggie options and agua frescas to wash them down.

Little Sister (523 W. 7th St., 213/628-3146, www.littlesisterla.com, 10am-10pm daily, $8-28) has a sleekly warm bistro setting and features contemporary Vietnamese small plates, craft beer, and wine.

The Little Jewel of New Orleans (207 Ord St., 213/620-0461, http://littlejewel.la, 10:30am-9pm Sun., Mon., Wed., Thurs., 10:30am-4pm Tues., 10:30am-10pm Fri.-Sat., $7-16) serves giant New Orleans-inspired po'boys and specials in a casual café setting in historic Chinatown, just north of downtown.

Family-run **Yang Chow** (819 N. Broadway, 213/625-0811, www.yangchow.com, 11:30am-9:30pm Sun.-Thurs., 11:30am-10:30pm Fri.-Sat., $12-18) is a Chinatown fixture, serving authentic Mandarin and Szechwan cuisine in a stripped-down space. Try the signature slippery shrimp.

Accommodations

The boutique **Ace Hotel** (929 S. Broadway, 213/623-3233, www.acehotel.com/losangeles, $250-320) has been stylishly renovated in the onetime location of the 1927 United Artists Theater and Tower. Amenities include a gym and rooftop bar and pool. The home of old Hollywood glamour, the historic 1923 **Millennium Biltmore Hotel** (506 S. Grand Ave., 213/624-1011, www.millenniumhotels.com, from $300) is a cultural landmark with 683 guest rooms and amenities including a Roman-style pool.

The historic **Hotel Figueroa** (939 S. Figueroa St., 213/627-8971, www.hotelfigueroa.com, $215-300) was renovated in 2016 to restore it to its original Spanish Colonial beauty. The hotel offers 285 guest rooms, lobby bar, and a veranda pool. Located in the Little Tokyo Historic District, **Miyako Hotel** (328 E. 1st St., 213/617-2000, www.miyakoinn.com, $175-200) is a contemporary hotel offering 173 Asian-inspired guest rooms and amenities including an on-site fitness room and a cocktail and karaoke lounge.

The Intercontinental (900 Wilshire Blvd., 800/424-6835, https://dtla.intercontinental.com, from $265) is the newest and tallest skyscraper in downtown Los Angeles, located in the Wilshire Grand Center and near L.A. Live and the Staples Center. Check in on the 70th floor Sky Lobby with 360-degree views of the city.

HOLLYWOOD AND MID-CITY

Centrally located between the beaches and downtown, mid-city gives the easiest access to famous Hollywood and Museum Row.

Sights and Activities

Museum Row, a walkable stretch of Wilshire Boulevard between Fairfax Avenue and La Brea Avenue, is home to four main Los Angeles museums. Visit the **Los Angeles County Museum of Art** (LACMA, 5905 Wilshire Blvd., 323/857-6000, www.lacma.org, 11am-5pm Mon.-Tues., Thurs., 11am-8pm Fri., 10am-7pm Sat.-Sun., $25 adults, $21 seniors, $11 children 4-17 and under 4 free) for the largest collection of art spanning ancient to contemporary in the western

United States. The **Petersen Auto Museum** (6060 Wilshire Blvd., 323/930-2277, www.petersen.org, 10am-6pm daily, $16 adults, $14 seniors, $11 children 4-17, children 4 and under free) celebrates the automobile with over 25 exhibitions, including automobiles in the movies, hot rods, and more than cars for the road. Kids and adults alike will love the **LaBrea Tar Pits** (5801 Wilshire Blvd., 323/857-6300, www.tarpits.org, 9:30am-5pm daily, $13 adults, $10 seniors and students 13-17 or college, $5 child 3-12, under 3 free), a museum and archaeological excavation where extinct animals were captured and preserved in tar. With a focus on the edge of craft and design, **Craft and Folk Art Museum** (5814 Wilshire Blvd., 323/937-4230, www.cafam.org, 11am-5pm Tues.-Fri., 11am-6pm Sat.-Sun., $9 adults, $7 students and seniors, children under 10 free) cycles exhibitions in a range of media, including glass, metal, paper, ceramics, photography, and textiles.

Originally established in 1934, the **Original Farmers Market** (6333 W. 3rd St., 323/933-9211, www.farmersmarketla.com, 9am-9pm Mon.-Fri., 9am-8pm Sat., 10am-7pm Sun.) is a destination gourmet market with more than 100 grocers and restaurants. It is adjacent to **The Grove** (189 The Grove Dr., 323/900-8080, www.thegrovela.com, 10am-9pm Mon.-Thurs., 10am-10pm Fri.-Sat., 10am-8pm Sun.), an upscale shopping, entertainment, and dining complex.

The highlight of Hollywood is the star-studded sidewalks of the **Hollywood Walk of Fame.** Beginning at La Brea Avenue (to the west), the famous pavement runs for 18 blocks to Gower Street on the east. You can also find the sidewalk stars along three blocks of Vine Street (running north and south of Hollywood Boulevard). Two historic cinema palaces, TCL Chinese Theatre, originally **Grauman's Chinese Theatre** (6925 Hollywood Blvd., www.tclchinesetheatres.com), and **Grauman's Egyptian Theatre** (6706 Hollywood Blvd., www. egyptiantheatre.org) are cultural landmarks worth a stop on your walking tour. The intricately designed Grauman's Chinese Theatre opened to celebrity fanfare in 1927 and is still sought after for movie premieres and events. Its renovated theater has a regular movie schedule. The iconic 1922 Grauman's Egyptian Theatre is operated by American Cinematheque and screens indie, classic, and rare movies. The newer **ArcLight Hollywood** (6360 W. Sunset Blvd., 323/464-1478, www.arclightcinemas.com) is a 14-screen multiplex located along Sunset Boulevard offering online tickets, reserved seats, a café, and concessions. The world's largest independent record store, **Amoeba Records** (6400 Sunset Blvd., 323/245-6400, www.amoeba.com, 10:30am-11pm Mon.-Sat., 11am-10pm Sun.), is a bustling outlet with a massive collection of vinyl records as well as CDs, videos, and live shows. The Hollywood fixture is slated to move locations in 2019 within blocks of its Sunset and Ivar location. If you're in town on a Sunday, the **Hollywood Farmers' Market** (Selma Ave. and Ivar Ave. between Hollywood Blvd. and Sunset Blvd., www.hollywoodfarmersmarket.net, 8am-1pm Sun.) is an outdoor street market offering impressively stacked blocks of fresh produce and goods from local farmers, ranchers, and vendors.

Food

At Hollywood's oldest eatery, **Musso and Frank** (6667 Hollywood Blvd., 323/467-7788, www.mussoandfrank.com, 11am-11pm Tues.-Sat., 4pm-9pm Sun., $15-51), tuxedoed waiters serve steaks, pastas, and American specialties in a classic setting.

Canter's Deli (419 N. Fairfax Ave., 323/651-2030, www.cantersdeli.com, 24 hours daily, $11-16) is an iconic Jewish deli serving up a vast menu of sandwiches and deli fare. The adjacent **Kibbitz Room** (323/651-2030, 10:30am-1:40am daily) offers an old-school cocktail lounge with a full bar and small stage.

The lines at **Pink's Hot Dogs** (709 N. La Brea Ave., 323/931-4223, www.pinkshollywood.com, 9:30am-2am Sun.-Thurs., 9:30am-3am Fri.-Sat., $4-10) attest that it is worth the wait at this landmark 1939 roadside stand.

Celebrity-owned **Trejo's Tacos** (1048 S. La Brea Ave., 323/938-8226, www.trejostacos.com, 8am-10pm Sun.-Thurs., 8am-11pm Fri.-Sat.) is a casual taqueria offering meat and vegan specialty tacos with kombucha, *aguas frescas*, and beer and wine in a bright, industrial-sleek setting.

Jon & Vinny's (412 N. Fairfax Ave., 323/334-3369, www.jonandvinnys.com, 8am-10pm daily, $10-24) features Italian-inspired fare, including creatively topped pizzas and pastas in a relaxed contemporary setting.

Accommodations

Hotel Wilshire (6317 Wilshire Blvd., 323/852-6000, www.hotelwilshire.com, $225-350), a Kimpton property, is a sleekly contemporary, glass and steel boutique hotel with a rooftop pool, restaurant, and bar near Museum Row.

California-country chic **Farmer's Daughter** (115 S. Fairfax Ave., 323/937-3930, www.farmersdaughterhotel.com, $250-270) is a boutique hotel offering retro rooms, an outdoor pool, and on-site restaurant and bar. It's convenient to The Original Farmers Market and The Grove complex.

The glamorous **Roosevelt Hotel** (7000 Hollywood Blvd., 323/856-1970, www.thehollywoodroosevelt.com, $300-350), established in 1927, is located along the Walk of Fame, offering a stunning pool and on-site restaurants and bars.

The family-friendly **Magic Castle Hotel** (7025 Franklin Ave., 323/851-0800, www.magiccastlehotel.com, $220-400) offers rooms and suites and a ton of amenities, including a 24-hour heated pool, complimentary continental breakfast, snacks, and robes. Rooms book fast.

SANTA MONICA AND VENICE

Los Angeles' beaches are a destination in and of themselves, and they're a great place to visit if you only have a day or two. The beach cities are also conveniently located near the Los Angeles International Airport.

Sights and Activities

Along the coastal towns of Venice and Santa Monica, **Venice Beach** and **Santa Monica Beach** (www.venicebeach.com) offer a gorgeous, recreational three-mile stretch of coastline along the Pacific Ocean with the Santa Monica Mountains creating a dramatic backdrop. Soaking up the sea, sand, and sun should be your major activity here. In the immediate vicinity, the funky **Venice Beach Boardwalk** is good for a stroll and people watching. An oceanfront skate park, the **Venice Skate Park** (www.veniceskatepark.com) has a fun vibe and is a great place to watch the talented kids. The **Santa Monica Pier** (www.santamonicapier.org) has an amusement park and offers good strolling on its weathered timbers. Rent bikes at one of several beach bike rental shops along the boardwalk connecting Venice and Santa Monica. A paved bike path connecting the two communities makes for an easy ride with gorgeous oceanfront views. Downtown Santa Monica offers retail shopping and dining on its **3rd Street Promenade** (www.santamonica.com/shopping/), a few blocks from the beach.

For exploring Venice, check out the cool **Abbott Kinney** (www.abbotkinneyblvd.com) neighborhood. This walkable one-mile stretch between Westminster and Venice Boulevard is a hub of fashionable retail shopping, restaurants, art galleries, and nightlife. If you're in town on Sunday, don't miss the weekly **Santa Monica Farmers Market** (2640 Main St., 9:30am-1pm Sun.), where local chefs regularly shop. It's a great place to grab coffee and breakfast and be dazzled by the array of seasonal produce, meats and dairy, artisanal goods, and flowers.

Food

The laid-back **Venice Ale House** (2 Rose Ave., Venice, 310/314-8253, www.venicealehouse.com, 11am-9pm Mon.-Fri.,

10am-9pm Sat.-Sun., $7-19) offers American gastropub fare on the Venice Boardwalk. **The Waterfront** (205 Ocean Front Walk, Venice, 424/309-5331, www.waterfrontcafe.com, 10am-10pm Sun. -Thurs., 10am-11pm Fri.-Sat. $10-22) revamped a casual tourist and local boardwalk spot to add tacos, burgers, salads, and a seafood raw bar. The ocean views and great people watching remain the same.

Opened in 1934, **The Galley** (2442 Main St., Santa Monica, 310/452-1934, www.thegalleyrestaurant.net, 5pm-midnight Mon.-Thurs., 5pm-2am Fri.-Sat., 1pm-midnight Sun., $13-44) is Santa Monica's oldest restaurant, serving seafood and steaks amid nautical decor.

At **Gjusta** (320 Sunset Ave., Venice, 310/314-0320, www.gjusta.com, 7am-10pm daily, $8-20), choose from the mouthwatering sandwiches, breakfasts, and cases of freshly made salads and sides at this artisanal gourmet bakery housed in a hip, industrial space.

The Albright (258 Santa Monica Pier, 310/394-9683, thealbright.com, noon-9pm Mon.-Fri., 11am-10pm Sat.-Sun., $11-23) reinvented a seafood joint on the Santa Monica Pier as a casual, rustic-chic eatery with a raw bar, burgers, sandwiches, and seafood specials.

Milo and Olive (2723 Wilshire Blvd., Santa Monica, 310/453-6776, www.miloandolive.com, 7am-11pm daily, $14-20) elevates everyday food with small plates, pastas, salads, wood-fired pizzas, and fresh baked goods served in a communal space.

The Tasting Kitchen (1633 Abbot Kinney Rd., Venice, 310/392-6644, www.thetastingkitchen.com, dinner 5:30pm-midnight daily, brunch 10:30am-2:30pm Sat.-Sun., $14-40) is a hip and charming setting for creative Mediterranean comfort fare and cocktails.

Accommodations

A hip boutique hotel near Venice Beach, **The Kinney** (737 Washington Blvd., Venice, 310/821-4455, www.thekinneyvenicebeach.com, $275-320) offers 68 guest rooms and suites as well as a relaxed social experience on the grounds including a heated pool and spa, ping-pong tables, and fire pit.

Inn at Venice Beach (327 W. Washington Blvd., Venice, 310/821-2557, $240-280) has a bohemian vibe with chic digs (43 guest rooms) set in a residential neighborhood on the border of Venice Beach and Marina Del Rey.

Hotel Erwin (1697 Pacific Ave., 310/452-1111, hotelerwin.com, $275-235) looks down on the Venice scene from its boardwalk front location, offering a low-key restaurant and rooftop cocktail lounge.

Venice on the Beach Hotel (2819 Ocean Front Walk, Venice, 310/429-0234, www.veniceonthebeachhotel.com, $245-375) provides a low-key stay in a 1950s style beachfront hotel.

Contemporary, eco-conscious **The Shore Hotel** (1515 Ocean Ave., Santa Monica, 310/458-1515, www.shorehotel.com, $369-529) overlooks the beach opposite the Santa Monica Pier, with a heated outdoor pool and hot tub.

The upscale beachfront **Loews Santa Monica** (1700 Ocean Ave., Santa Monica, 310/458-6700, www.santamonicaloewshotel.com, $425-700) is centrally located and offers an outdoor heated pool and two-tier pool deck with beach views.

Travel Tips

WHAT TO PACK

It's possible to pack lightly for the resort town of Palm Springs. Temperatures are usually mild year-round, if cooler at night and subject to cooler weather and temperature fluctuations in winter. Pack for poolside and dress up for dinners or brunch. Most hotels provide pool towels, and some provide sunscreen, water, snacks, or other amenities.

Temperatures are cooler in Joshua Tree, with cold winters (it's been known to snow) and hot summers (over 100 degrees). Always carry layers and be prepared for temperature fluctuations throughout the day. Nighttime temperatures can drop as much as 40 degrees. For hiking and touring around the desert, wear sturdy shoes, a brimmed hat, and sunglasses. The gateway towns around Joshua Tree are very casual; no formal attire required.

INTERNATIONAL TRAVELERS

The closest gateway city for international travelers to fly into is **Los Angeles (LAX).** The drive from Los Angeles to Palm Springs takes 2-4 hours depending upon traffic. There are no stops, checkpoints, or special concerns along this route, which sticks to I-10.

Palm Springs International Airport (PSP) has updated from a regional to an international airport with limited international flights. PSP is located in downtown Palm Springs with taxis and ride shares available from the airport.

Visas and Passports

Visitors from most other countries must have a valid passport and a visa to enter the United States. You may qualify for the Visa Waiver Program if you hold a passport from one of the following countries: Andorra, Australia, Austria, Belgium, Brunei, Chile, Czech Republic, Denmark, Estonia, Finland, France, Germany, Greece, Hungary, Iceland, Ireland, Italy, Japan, Korea Republic of, Latvia, Liechtenstein, Lithuania, Luxembourg, Malta, Monaco, the Netherlands, New Zealand, Norway, Portugal, San Marino, Singapore, Slovakia, Slovenia, Spain, Sweden, Switzerland, Taiwan, and the United Kingdom. To qualify, apply online with the **Electronic System for Travel Authorization** (http://esta.cbp.dhs.gov/esta) no later than 72 hours before departing for the United States, and make sure you have a return plane ticket to your country of origin dated less than 90 days from your date of entry. Holders of Canadian passports do not need visas or visa waivers. Arriving at the airport without a previously approved ESTA will likely result in being denied boarding. In addition, as of April 1, 2016, you must have an e-passport to use the VWP. An e-passport has an embedded electronic chip for enhanced security. You can tell if you have an e-passport by a unique international symbol on the cover. To learn more about visa and passport requirements, visit http://travel.state.gov.

In most countries, the local U.S. embassy or consulate should be able to provide a **tourist visa.** The average fee for a visa is US$160. While a visa may be processed as quickly as 24 hours on request, plan at least a couple of weeks, as there can be unexpected delays, particularly during the busy summer season (June-Aug.).

Los Angeles is home to **consulates** from many countries around the globe. If you should lose your passport or find yourself in some other trouble while visiting California, contact your country's offices for assistance. To find a consulate or embassy, check online (www.state.gov) for a list of all foreign countries represented in the United States. A representative will be able to direct you to the nearest consulate.

Customs

Before entering the United States from another country by air, you'll be required to fill out a customs form. Check with the U.S. embassy in your country or the **U.S. Customs and Border Protection** (www.cbp.gov) for an updated list of items you must declare. If you require medication administered by injection, unused syringes are allowed when accompanied by injectable medication. Also, pack documentation describing your need for any narcotic medications you've brought with you. Failure to produce documentation for narcotics on request can result in severe penalties in the United States. For information about current regulations on domestic flights, visit the **Transportation Security Administration website** (www.tsa.gov).If you are driving into California along I-5 or another major highway, prepare to stop at **Agricultural Inspection Stations** a few miles inside the state line. You don't need to present a passport or a driver's license; instead, you must be prepared to present any fruits and vegetables you have in the vehicle. California's largest economic sector is agriculture, and a number of the major crops grown here are sensitive to pests and diseases. In an effort to prevent known pests from entering the state and endangering crops, travelers are asked to identify all the produce they're carrying in from other states or from Mexico. If you are carrying produce, it may be confiscated on the spot. You'll also be asked about fruits and veggies on the U.S. Customs form that you fill out on the plane before reaching the United States.

Money

California and Nevada businesses use the **U.S. dollar** ($). Most businesses also accept the major credit cards Visa, MasterCard, Discover, and American Express. ATM and debit cards work at many stores and restaurants, and ATMs are available at banks and in some local businesses like convenience or grocery stores. Within the Joshua Tree area and Yucca Valley, ATMs are limited. Currency exchange offices are available at any international airport.

TOURIST INFORMATION

Entering the city of Palm Springs from the north via I-10, you will be greeted by the **Palm Springs Visitors Center** (2901 N. Palm Canyon Dr., 760/778-8418, www.visitpalmsprings.com, 9am-5pm daily), a good stop for books and information.

When visiting the Joshua Tree area, make sure to stop at one of the park's four visitors centers for maps and information. Three of these correspond to the park entrances: The **Joshua Tree Visitors Center** (6554 Park Blvd., Joshua Tree, 760/366-1855, 8am-5pm daily) is located in the town of Joshua Tree near the West Entrance to the park. The **Oasis Visitors Center** (74485 National Park Dr., Twentynine Palms, 760/367-5500, 8:30am-5pm daily) is en route to the park's North Entrance in the gateway town of Twentynine Palms. The **Cottonwood Visitors Center** (Cottonwood Spring Rd., 8:30am-4pm daily) is at the remote South Entrance to the park. In addition, the **Black Rock Nature Center** (9800 Black Rock Canyon Rd., Yucca Valley, 760/367-3001, 8am-4pm Sat.-Thurs., 8am-8pm Fri. Oct.-May) is a small visitors center used primarily as a check-in for campers to the Black Rock Canyon Campground. Other area visitors centers include the **Twentynine Palms Visitors Center and Gallery** (6847 Adobe Rd., Twentynine Palms, 760/361-1805, 8:30am-5:30pm daily) en route to the North Entrance in the gateway town of Twentynine Palms.

ACCESS FOR TRAVELERS WITH DISABILITIES

Palm Springs

The Palm Springs Aerial Tramway is fully ADA compliant, including the rotating tram cars and both tram stations. At the Valley Station on the desert floor, an outdoor lift takes visitors from the parking area to the ground floor station. There is an accessible viewing area outside the back of the station giving a look at tram cars as they ascend and descend Chino Canyon. At Mountain Station, there is an accessible outdoor patio and viewing area. From the back of Mountain Station, a paved path leads down to forest level; however, this path is steep and not necessarily appropriate for all wheelchairs.

The Living Desert Zoo and Gardens, in the Coachella Valley, has paved paths meandering through the main exhibits of the park.

While none of the trails in the Indian Canyons are accessible, there is a beautiful picnic area in the parking area at the head of Andreas Canyon set next to a stream and palm groves.

Joshua Tree

An **Access Pass** (www.nps.gov, free) permits free entrance to Joshua Tree National Park for U.S. citizens and permanent residents with permanent disabilities. Passes can be obtained online or in person at the park.

All Joshua Tree National Park **visitors centers** are ADA complaint, and all have accessible ranger desks. The Joshua Tree Visitors Center and the Oasis Visitors Center have low displays in their natural history areas. At the Oasis Visitors Center, there is an accessible sidewalk and garden area.

There are also several **accessible nature trails.** The Bajada Trail (near the South Entrance) is a 0.3-mile loop with a packed dirt and gravel surface that leads through exposed Colorado Desert featuring interpretive panels. The trail is 5.6 miles south of the Cottonwood Spring Ranger Station and 0.5 mile north of the south park entrance. The Cap Rock Nature Trail leads 0.4 mile along packed dirt and gravel through eroded boulder formations. Parking is available at the junction of Park Boulevard and Keys View Road. At the end of Keys View Road, Keys View Nature Trail is a paved 0.2-mile wheelchair-accessible trail offering sweeping views of Palm Springs, Coachella Valley, and the San Jacinto Mountains. At the historic Oasis of Mara, a 0.5-mile boardwalk trail winds through native vegetation and fan palms in an area that was used extensively by Native American groups.

A bounty of paved **pullouts** along Park Boulevard also offer close-up views of boulder piles, rock formations, and other spectacular scenery. A few sites worth admiring include Skull Rock (located on Park Boulevard near the Jumbo Rocks Campground entrance) and the Cholla Cactus Garden along the Pinto Basin Road. At the Intersection Rock parking area and the Hidden Valley picnic areas, sidewalks give access to wayside exhibits and vault toilets. Intersection Rock parking area also has an accessible sidewalk for access to wayside exhibits and pit toilets.

ADA-compliant **campground** sites include Jumbo Rocks Campground (site 122) and Black Rock Campground (site 61).

TRAVELING WITH CHILDREN

While it is possible to have a great family vacation in Palm Springs, many hotels are adults-only and do not allow guests under age 21. Be sure to check the individual policy of any hotel when booking a room. The Parker Palm Springs and the Ace Hotel are two hotels that welcome children and offer separate swimming pools geared toward families.

Joshua Tree is a great family destination. Children will enjoy being able to clamber around on the rocks and boulders, and there are a number of easy short hikes that families can enjoy. The Junior Ranger Program allows young visitors (typically between ages 5 and 13) to earn a badge by completing a series of activities, including drawing, writing, attending a ranger program, and picking up trash in the park. Ranger programs such as the Discovery Walks are geared toward families and can help kids earn a Junior Ranger badge. Joshua Tree also participates in national Junior Ranger programs, including Junior Paleontologist, Junior Ranger Night Explorer, and Wilderness Explorer. Booklets are available at park visitors centers.

Desert Survival Tips

Vast spaces, remote roads, and weather extremes can create potentially risky situations, but traveling in a desert is not any more dangerous than in other national parks if you are prepared for the unique environment. Know what weather to expect and where you're going and be prepared for the unexpected.

TELL SOMEONE WHERE YOU ARE GOING

Whether you're hiking, driving, or a combination, make sure you tell someone where you are going and when to expect your return. The desert covers a huge area, and in the event that you are stranded, the search effort can be pinpointed. For hiking or backcountry camping, obtain a backcountry permit from one of 13 backcountry registration boards located throughout Joshua Tree National Park.

BRING SUPPLIES

Temperatures can fluctuate 40 degrees between day and night. Bring a sleeping bag or emergency blanket even if you do not plan to be out overnight. Pack appropriate clothing for a range of temperatures, and be prepared for cold temperatures at night. Always bring extra water and extra nonperishable food that does not have to be cooked. GPS navigation is notoriously unreliable in the park. Be prepared with a paper map or an electronic offline map and a charger. Cell phones do not work in the park. Be prepared to survive until help arrives if you are stranded.

VEHICLE BREAKDOWNS

Sharp rocks, long bumpy roads, and heat can cause your vehicle to break down on backcountry roads. Always drive with a full-size spare tire. A fix-a-flat tire kit may also be helpful. If you are stranded, stay with your car until help arrives. It is much easier to spot a big metal car that flashes in the sunlight than a person walking. Also, it is dangerous to overexert yourself in the heat of the desert, so hiking out to safety is not generally the best option. Be prepared with extra supplies, including food, water, and warm clothes.

WINDSTORMS

The wind can be a relentless companion in Joshua Tree, especially in spring, with nights generally windier than days. Wind can be a minor irritant, or it can seriously impact your visit and create potentially dangerous situations. At times, wind can descend in the form of a windstorm preceded by a cold front. There may be very little warning, and a dark cloud may be the only indication that a windstorm is approaching. Always stake tents and secure other camp belongings such as camp chairs. Windstorms can create whiteout conditions with serious visibility limitations. If you are driving, use headlights and be prepared to pull over if visibility becomes limited to the degree that driving is dangerous.

SENIOR TRAVELERS

A **Senior Pass** (https://store.usgs.gov, $80 lifetime pass, $20 annual pass) is available to U.S. citizens/permanent residents over age 62 who are visiting Joshua Tree National Park. The Senior Pass is available online or in person at park visitors centers. The lifetime pass is a one-time fee. The annual pass is good for one year; if an annual pass is purchased for three consecutive years, the fourth pass can be traded in for a lifetime pass.

GAY AND LESBIAN TRAVELERS

Palm Springs is an international gay-friendly resort destination and a mecca for gay and lesbian travelers. Several accommodations cater exclusively to gay male travelers; however, all lodging in Palm Springs are open to gay and lesbian visitors. In addition to a range of gay bars and clubs, the spring festival season draws thousands of visitors annually to the all-male music and dance party weekend (White Party, www.jeffreysanker.com) and the all-female music and party weekend (The Dinah, www.thedinah.com).

TRAVELING WITH PETS

Many hotels in Palm Springs accept well-behaved pets for a fee; check with each individual hotel when booking. However, it is best to leave your pet at home when visiting Joshua Tree National Park. Pets are allowed in Joshua Tree, but they are not allowed on any trails and cannot be left unattended in a car, since desert temperatures can soar. Pets must be on a leash at all times and cannot be more than 100 feet from a picnic area, road, or campground.

HEALTH AND SAFETY

As a desert park, Joshua Tree National Park is no more dangerous than any other national park. However, there are a few extra precautions you should take to stay safe.

Heat

Heat is the biggest health threat in the desert. The hottest conditions occur at the lower elevations during summer and can be dangerously hot **May-October.** Many visitors choose to visit the park in summer, and it is possible to do so safely if you take some precautions. *Avoid hiking or other outdoor exertion at low elevations during summer.* In summer, confine hiking to high elevations or go out early in the morning (plan to be off the trail by 10am) or late in the evening; stick to paved roads for touring at low elevations. When hiking or exploring outdoors, wear a wide-brimmed hat, sunglasses, and proper sun protection. Lightweight, light-colored breathable clothing can offer better protection than sunscreen—wear both.

Dehydration

Dehydration is the biggest threat to health in Joshua Tree. Daytime temperatures can soar. Always carry plenty of water—at least two gallons per person per day (and more than you think you will need)—especially when hiking or engaging in other physical activity. Signs of heat exhaustion include dizziness, nausea, and headaches. If these occur, get into the shade and drink plenty of water or sports drinks.

Getting Lost

With its wide network of popular trails, it is easy to underestimate potential dangers when hiking in Joshua Tree National Park. Attempt to keep track of distant landmarks when hiking; the landscape can be extremely disorienting with its sweeping boulder piles and Joshua trees. This is especially important since trails in Joshua Tree's sandy soil are easily erased with wind and water, making them hard to follow across open landscape. Watch for trail markers, such as a row of rocks or downed Joshua tree marking trail boundaries. Also, because of the sandy soil, trails and washes can look alike. It is easy to get off course and follow a wide sandy wash instead of a trail. This may account for the prevalence of social trails (informal trails established by use) in Joshua Tree. Often these trails are made by people who have gone off course or are attempting a shortcut. Avoid social trails if possible; they have the potential to get you lost, and they damage the landscape.

Resources

Suggested Reading

GUIDEBOOKS

MacKay, Pam. *Mojave Desert Wildflowers: A Field Guide to Wildflowers, Trees, and Shrubs of the Mojave Desert.* Guilford, CT: Morris Book Publishing, 2013. An excellent field guide to Mojave flora.

HIKING

Cunningham, Bill, and Polly Cunningham. *Hiking Joshua Tree National Park: 38 Day and Overnight Hikes.* 3rd ed., Guilford, CT: Falcon Guides, 2019. An update of this classic hiking guide provides detailed trail descriptions for a wide range of hikes for hikers of all abilities and interests in Joshua Tree National Park.

Cunningham, Bill and Polly Cunningham. Best Easy Day Hikes Joshua Tree National Park. 3rd ed., Falcon Guides, 2019. A short, lightweight version of a classic hiking guide that includes hiking highlights of Joshua Tree National Park for hikers of all abilities and interests.

Ferranti, Philip, and Hank Koenig. *140 Great Hikes in and near Palm Springs.* Golden, CO: Colorado Mountain Club, 2013. This hiking guide offers a thorough overview of hiking near Palm Springs, including trail descriptions of hikes in the Coachella Valley, San Jacinto Mountains, Santa Rosa Mountains, and Palm Springs and the Indian Canyons.

Harris, D. M., & Harris, J. M. Afoot & Afield Inland Empire: A Comprehensive Hiking Guide. Berkeley, CA: Wilderness Press. 2009.

Robinson, J. W and David Money Harris. San Bernardino Mountain Trails: 100 Hikes in Southern California. 7th ed. Berkeley, CA: Wilderness Press, 2016.

Salabert, Shawnté. Hiking the Pacific Crest Trail: Southern California: Section hiking from Campo to Tuolumne Meadows. Seattle, WA: Mountaineers Books, 2017.

ROCK CLIMBING

Gaines, Bob. *Best Climbs, Joshua Tree National Park: The Best Sport and Trad routes in the Park*, 2nd edition. Lanham, MD: An imprint of the Rowman & Littlefield Publishing Group, 2019. A selection of more than 280 of the best routes in this climbing destination.

Miramontes, Robert. *Joshua Tree Rock Climbs*, 3rd *ed.* Silt, CO: Wolverine, 2017. An in-depth guide to rock climbing the entire park, this guide features 3,000 of Joshua Tree's easy and moderate routes and recommended bouldering circuits.

Vogel, Randy. *Rock Climbing Joshua Tree West.* Guilford, CT: Falcon Guide, 2006. Focusing on the popular western part of the park, this guide covers climbs from Quail Springs to Hidden Valley Campground.

Winger, Charlie, and Diane Winger. *The Trad Guide to Joshua Tree: 60 Favorite Climbs from 5.5 to 5.9*. Golden, CO: Colorado Mountain Club Press, 2004. This classic rock climbing guide details climbs for a moderate, trad climber in Joshua Tree National Park.

CULTURE AND HISTORY

Shulman, Julius, Michael Stern, and Alan Hess. *Julius Shulman: Palm Springs*. New York: Rizzoli, 2008. This photography book captures more than 60 iconic Southern California modernist buildings by 15 notable mid-century architects through the lens of photographer Julius Shulman.

Stringfellow, Kim. *Greetings from the Salton Sea: Folly and Intervention in the Southern California Landscape, 1905-2005*. Santa Fe, NM: Center for American Places, 2005. An artistic mix of cultural geography, history, and photography, this book provides a fascinating glimpse into the dissolution of California's Salton Sea.

NONFICTION

Nyala, Hannah. *Point Last Seen: A Woman Tracker's Story*. New York: Simon & Schuster, 1997. A compelling story of a woman who fled personal danger to become a tracker in Joshua Tree National Park. The author describes her time spent as a tracker and its intersection with her personal narrative.

MAPS

Joshua Tree National Park. San Rafael, CA: Tom Harrison Maps, 2017. A shaded-relief topographic map of Joshua Tree National Park with detailed hiking trails including mileages, road networks, campgrounds, picnic areas, and ranger stations. This map can be the backbone for hiking and driving tours.

Joshua Tree National Park Trails Illustrated Topographic Map. Evergreen, CO: National Geographic, 2005. A topographic map that details hiking trails with mileages, paved and dirt roads, campgrounds, picnic areas, and ranger stations in Joshua Tree National Park.

A Map of Modern Palm Springs. Palm Springs Modern Committee. This foldout map to mid-century modern landmarks includes location, address, architect, and the year built. The map is available through the Palm Springs Historical Society.

San Gorgonio Wilderness Map. San Rafael, CA: Tom Harrison Maps, 2015. Trailheads, trail mileages, topographic details, campgrounds, towns, roads, and ranger stations make this map indispensable for casual or backcountry travel.

San Bernardino Mountains Recreation Map, 7th edition. Wilderness Press: 2016. Good overall area map to get the lay of the land with trailheads, roads, campgrounds, and towns.

Internet Resources

Coachella Valley Preserve
www.coachellavalleypreserve.org

The website includes preserve information, including hours, location, history, and flora and fauna as well as downloadable trail maps for the preserve's 25 miles of hiking trails.

Joshua Tree National Park
www.nps.gov/jotr

The main park website is a good resource for planning your visit, including up-to-date visitor center hours and event calendars, an overview of the park's main sights, campgrounds, and climate as well as information about permits, fees, and park rules.

Sand to Snow National Monument
www.fs.usda.gov

The monument is managed by multiple agencies, but the U.S. Forest Service website provides a good overall description of the monument as well as listings for visitor centers/ranger stations and special destinations within the region.

Visit Gay Palm Springs
www.visitgaypalmsprings.com

The official gay and lesbian guide to hotels, resorts, nightlife, clubs, bars, and events that cater to a gay and lesbian clientele, as well as attractions and activities that may be appealing for all visitors.

Visit Palm Springs
www.visitpalmsprings.com

The official visitor website provides recommendations for where to dine, stay, shop, and explore as well as event listings and basic visitor information on traveling to Palm Springs.

Whitewater Preserve
www.wildlandsconservancy.org

The website lists visitor information, including trail map and descriptions, hours, program information, and plant and animal checklists.

Big Morongo Canyon Preserve
www.bigmorongo.org

An overview for visiting the preserve as well as trail maps and detailed information about the preserve's ecosystem, including birds, plants, and wildlife.

Index

D

E

F

G

H

I

J

KL

M

N

O

P

QR

S

T

UV

WXYZ

List of Maps

Front Map

Palm Springs and the Coachella Valley

Joshua Tree and the Hi-Desert

Photo Credits

All interior photos © Jenna Blough except pages 6 © (top left) Greg Epperson | Dreamstime.com; © (bottom) Laina Babb; page 7 © (top) ©Bcbounders | Dreamstime.com; (bottom right) © Patrick Lienin | Dreamstime.com; page 8 © (top) Laina Babb; page 9 © (bottom left) Nyker1 | Dreamstime.com; © (bottom right) Chon Kit Leong | Dreamstime.com; page 10-11 © Tlmpgofl1 | Dreamstime.com; page 13 © (top) Matthew Bamberg | Dreamstime.com; page 14 © (top) Larry Gevert |Dreamstime.com; © (bottom) Pancaketom | Dreamstime.com; page 15 © Nickolay Stanev | Dreamstime.com; page 19 © (bottom) Scott Griessel | Dreamstime.com; page 20 © (bottom) Laina Babb; page 28 © Jane Chapman | Dreamstime.com; page 37 © (top) Spvvkr | Dreamstime.com; page 44 © (top) Steve Kepple Photography; © (left middle) Steve Kepple Photography; © (bottom) Laurie Joliet; page 51 © (bottom) Adamjames184 | Dreamstime.com; page 116 © (right middle) Ryan Jones; page 141 © Ryan Jones; page 164 © (top) Ryan Jones; page 178 © Jimkresge | Dreamstime.com; page 193 © Jimkresge | Dreamstime.com

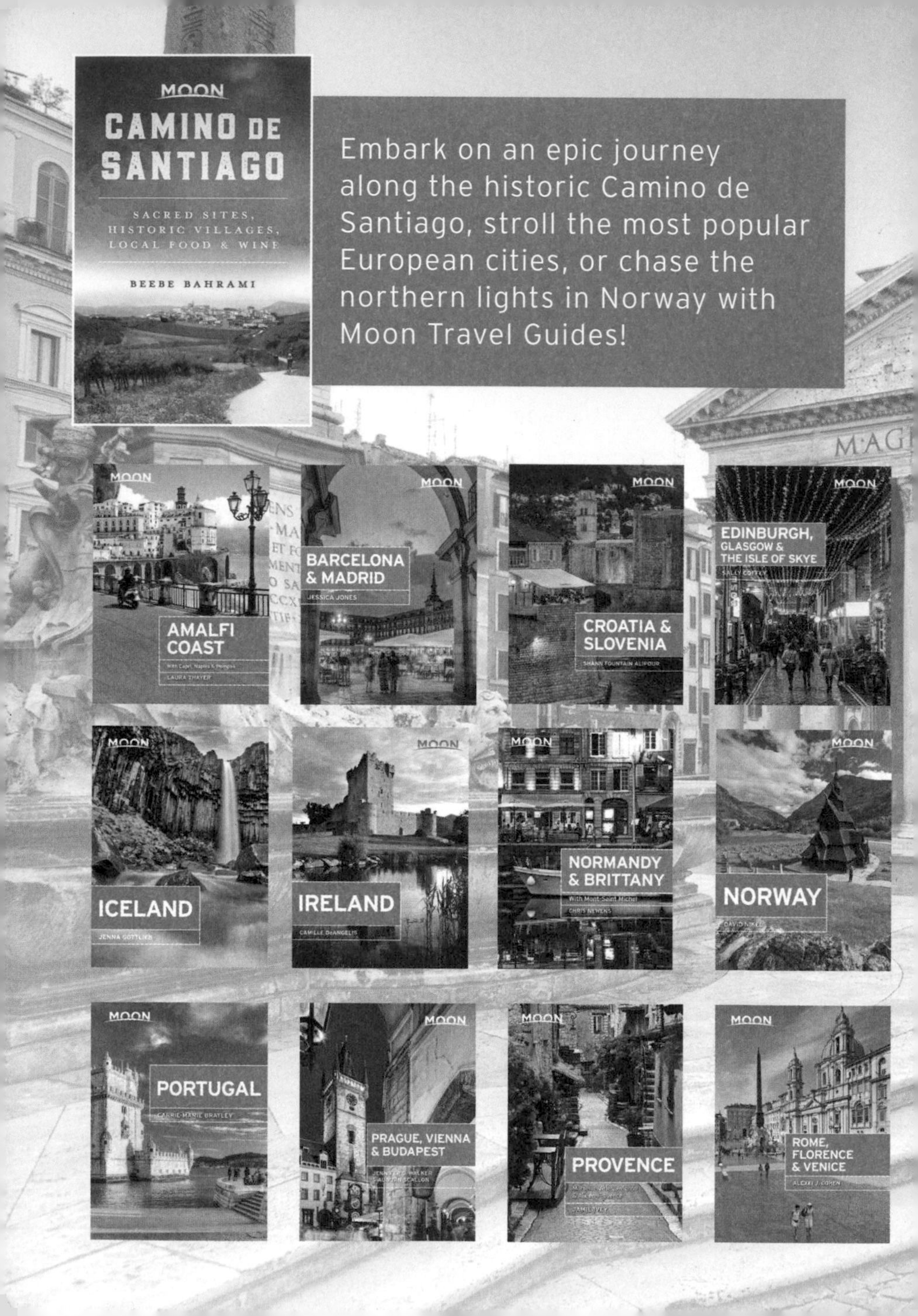
MOON
CAMINO DE SANTIAGO
SACRED SITES, HISTORIC VILLAGES, LOCAL FOOD & WINE
BEEBE BAHRAMI
Embark on an epic journey along the historic Camino de Santiago, stroll the most popular European cities, or chase the northern lights in Norway with Moon Travel Guides!
MOON
AMALFI COAST
LAURA THAYER
MOON
BARCELONA & MADRID
JESSICA JONES
MOON
CROATIA & SLOVENIA
MOON
EDINBURGH, GLASGOW & THE ISLE OF SKYE
MOON
ICELAND
JENNA GOTTLIEB
MOON
IRELAND
CAMILLE DEANGELIS
MOON
NORMANDY & BRITTANY
With Mont-Saint-Michel
CHRIS NEWENS
MOON
NORWAY
DAVID NIKEL
MOON
PORTUGAL
CARRIE-MARIE BRATLEY
MOON
PRAGUE, VIENNA & BUDAPEST
MOON
PROVENCE
MOON
ROME, FLORENCE & VENICE
ALEXEI J. COHEN

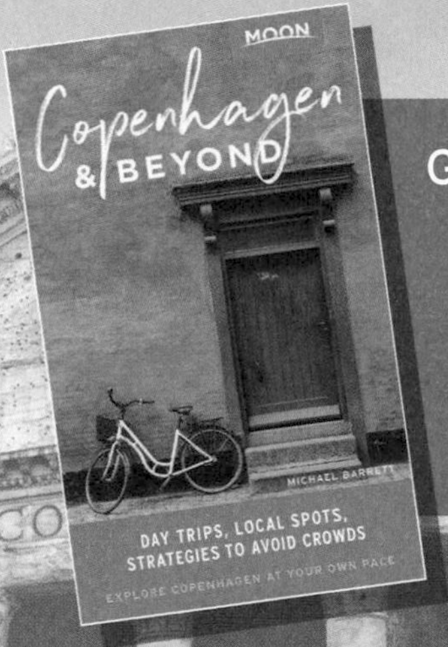

GO BIG AND GO BEYOND!

These savvy city guides include strategies to help you see the top sights and find adventure beyond the tourist crowds.

OR TAKE THINGS ONE STEP AT A TIME

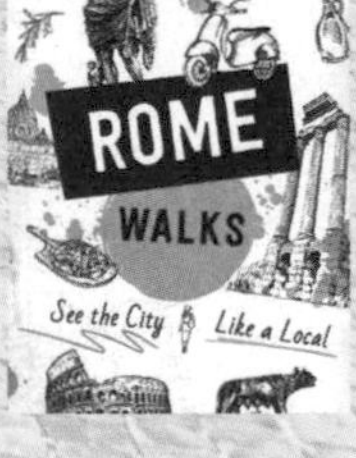

MOON
WANDERLUST
a traveler's guide to the globe

MOON
COASTAL CALIFORNIA
STUART THORNTON
MOON
DEATH VALLEY NATIONAL PARK
JENNA BLOUGH
MOON
LOS ANGELES
MOON
MONTEREY & CARMEL
STUART THORNTON
MOON
NAPA & SONOMA
MOON
NORTHERN CALIFORNIA
ELIZABETH LINHART VENEMAN
MOON
NORTHERN CALIFORNIA
Road Trip
STUART THORNTON & KAYLA ANDERSON
MOON
PALM SPRINGS & JOSHUA TREE
JENNA BLOUGH
MOON
SAN DIEGO
IAN ANDERSON
MOON
TAHOE
ANN MARIE BROWN
MOON
YOSEMITE SEQUOIA & KINGS CANYON
ANN MARIE BROWN
Getaways or the great outdoors: See more California with Moon
MOON
101 GREAT HIKES SAN FRANCISCO BAY AREA
MOON
CALIFORNIA CAMPING
TOM STIENSTRA
MOON
CALIFORNIA HIKING
MOON
NORTHERN CALIFORNIA CAMPING
TOM STIENSTRA
#TravelWithMoon

MAP SYMBOLS

Symbol	Name
	Expressway
	Primary Road
	Secondary Road
- - - - - - -	Unpaved Road
———	Feature Trail
- - - - - - -	Other Trail
···············	Ferry
	Pedestrian Walkway
	Stairs
○	City/Town
◉	State Capital
⊛	National Capital
★	Point of Interest
●	Accommodation
▼	Restaurant/Bar
■	Other Location
Λ	Campground
	Airport
	Airfield
▲	Mountain
✦	Unique Natural Feature
	Waterfall
	Park
T	Trailhead
	Skiing Area
	Golf Course
P	Parking Area
	Archaeological Site
	Church
	Gas Station
	Glacier
	Mangrove
	Reef
	Swamp

CONVERSION TABLES

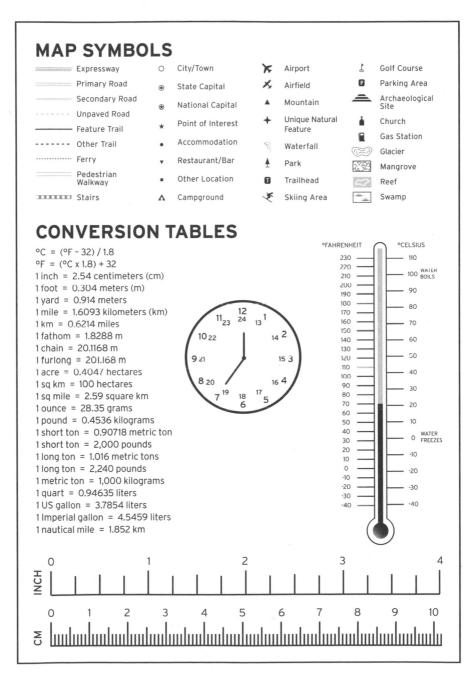

°C = (°F - 32) / 1.8
°F = (°C x 1.8) + 32
1 inch = 2.54 centimeters (cm)
1 foot = 0.304 meters (m)
1 yard = 0.914 meters
1 mile = 1.6093 kilometers (km)
1 km = 0.6214 miles
1 fathom = 1.8288 m
1 chain = 20.1168 m
1 furlong = 201.168 m
1 acre = 0.4047 hectares
1 sq km = 100 hectares
1 sq mile = 2.59 square km
1 ounce = 28.35 grams
1 pound = 0.4536 kilograms
1 short ton = 0.90718 metric ton
1 short ton = 2,000 pounds
1 long ton = 1.016 metric tons
1 long ton = 2,240 pounds
1 metric ton = 1,000 kilograms
1 quart = 0.94635 liters
1 US gallon = 3.7854 liters
1 Imperial gallon = 4.5459 liters
1 nautical mile = 1.852 km

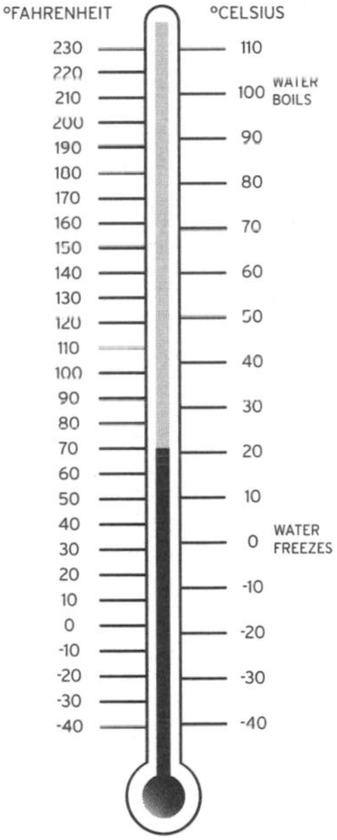

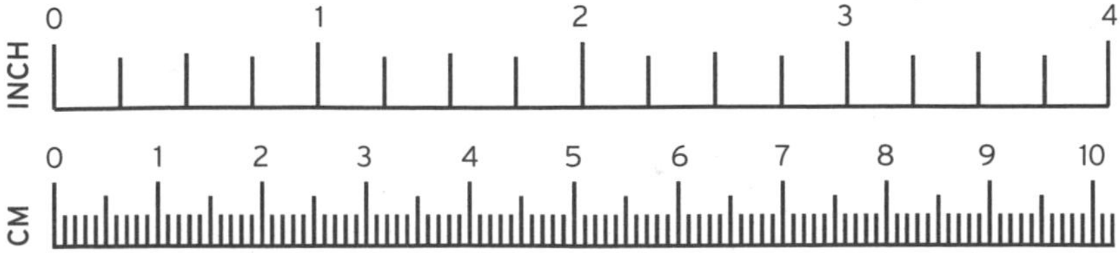

MOON JOSHUA TREE & PALM SPRINGS
Avalon Travel
Hachette Book Group
1700 Fourth Street
Berkeley, CA 94710, USA
www.moon.com

Editor: Rachael Sablik
Acquiring Editor: Nikki Ioakimedes
Series Manager: Kathryn Ettinger
Copy Editor: Ruth Strother
Production and Graphics Coordinator: Suzanne Albertson
Cover Design: Faceout Studios, Charles Brock
Interior Design: Domini Dragoone
Moon Logo: Tim McGrath
Map Editor: Kat Bennett
Cartographers: Lohnes + Wright, Karin Dahl
Proofreader: Kelly Lydick
Indexer: Rachel Kuhn

ISBN-13: 9781640490499

Printing History
1st Edition — 2016
2nd Edition — October 2019
5 4 3 2 1

Front cover photo: jumbo rocks in Joshua Tree National Park © America / Alamy Stock Photo
Back cover photo: palm trees and the San Jacinto Mountain range © Andrew Kazmierski / Dreamstime.com

Printed in Canada by Friesens

All recommendations, including those for sights, activities, hotels, restaurants, and shops, are based on each author's individual judgment. We do not accept payment for inclusion in our travel guides, and our authors don't accept free goods or services in exchange for positive coverage.

Although every effort was made to ensure that the information was correct at the time of going to press, the author and publisher do not assume and hereby disclaim any liability to any party for any loss or damage caused by errors, omissions, or any potential travel disruption due to labor or financial difficulty, whether such errors or omissions result from negligence, accident, or any other cause.

The publisher is not responsible for websites (or their content) that are not owned by the publisher.